Lectures
in
Old Testament Theology

Yahweh is God Alone

by Dennis F. Kinlaw
with John N. Oswalt

Editor – Dr. John N. Oswalt
Indexing – Dr. James E. Harriman
Designer – Vicki New

ISBN 978-0-915143-15-3

Library of Congress Cataloging-in-Publication Data

Kinlaw, Dennis F., 1922-
  Lectures in Old Testament theology : Yahweh is God alone / Dennis F. Kinlaw with John N. Oswalt.
    p. cm.
  Includes indexes.
  ISBN 978-0-915143-15-3
  1. Bible. O.T.--Theology. 2. God (Christianity)--Biblical teaching. I. Oswalt, John. II. Title.
  BS1192.5.A1.K56 2010
  230'.0411--dc22
                                        2010017538

For Information contact

Francis Asbury Society
P.O. Box 7
Wilmore, KY 40390
859-858-4222
E-mail: francisasb@aol.com
Web site: www.francisasburysociety.com

FOREWORD

Is there such a thing as *an* Old Testament theology? Or does the Old Testament simply reflect a number of competing theologies? In the first half of the twentieth century, the magisterial works of Walter Eichrodt and Gerhard von Rad argued for the former. But now as we begin the twenty-first century, the latter position seems once more to be gaining ground.

In these lectures, first delivered in 1993, Dennis F. Kinlaw shows that there is indeed a single theology that rings through the pages of the Old Testament. That theology is centered in the unchanging nature of the transcendent Yahweh. Kinlaw does not slight the diversities of the text, but uses those diversities to underline the amazing consistency to be found in the treatment of Yahweh and in the understanding of the world arising from that perspective.

Although it has been seventeen years since these lectures were first given, Kinlaw's penetrating grasp of, and love for, the text and its message makes the content as fresh as tomorrow. Anyone looking for a broad introduction to Old Testament theology will benefit from reading this book, but so will those who desire nothing more than to have their love for Yahweh rekindled.

—John Oswalt

EDITOR'S NOTE

Bringing these lectures from live classroom recordings to print presented a considerable editorial challenge. In order to preserve their unique oral quality we retained many of Dr. Kinlaw's personal illustrations, parenthetical comments, and southern colloquialisms. Those who have heard him speak will recognize his voice in these pages.

CONTENTS

ACKNOWLEDGEMENTS

The Francis Asbury Society owes special thanks to the following persons who contributed so much to the publishing of these lectures by Dennis F. Kinlaw.

- John Oswalt for using a sabbatical to edit the lectures
- Walter Boyd for preserving the recordings and arranging for a typescript
- Jim Harriman for doing the index
- Mark Royster, Harold Burgess, Vicki New and Peggy Allender for designing and copyediting the book and for publishing it
- Stan and Carolyn Lewis for their gift to underwrite the editorial development of this very important book

Paul Blair, President
The Francis Asbury Society

Lecture 1

. . . .

Knowing God

According to Edmond Jacob, "The theology of the Old Testament is a systematic account of the specific religious ideas which can be found throughout the Old Testament and which formed its profound unity." [1] This is not a complete definition, but it is comprehensive enough that it will give us a good starting point. There are a number of things in that statement to which we need to pay attention. The first point is that it defines what we are after: the religious ideas, the specific religious ideas that are to be found in the Old Testament. Then the statement raises the question of how we can go about systematizing the multiplicity of ideas that are to be found in the Old Testament, from its monotheism and its presentation of the high ethical nature of God to things like its concept of history, its concept of law, and its understanding of salvation, among many others. How can we bring these into some kind of systematic

---

[1] Edmond Jacob, *Theology of the Old Testament*, tr. A. W. Heathcote and P. A. Allcock (New York: Harper, 1958).

account? Furthermore, the statement assumes that underneath all of this diversity there is a profound unity. So while this statement does not include all we might need to say about the nature of the enterprise before us, at least it gets us started.

Apart from the Old Testament itself there are two books I would recommend for further study. The first is a two-volume set by Walter Eichrodt titled *Theology of the Old Testament*.[2] This is an older work (1933–39), but it has become something of a classic in the field. The evidence for this is that all of the other Old Testament theologians react to him and discuss him. Eichrodt sees a central concept running through the Old Testament from end to end—the concept of covenant, which he believes is the unifying theme that binds all of it together. God wants to be in a covenant relationship with you and with me. This includes such ideas as election, that God has chosen a group of people to be in covenant relationship with Him, through whom He can reach a world that needs to know Him. Nor is the concept of covenant limited to the Old Testament; it is of special importance because of the way it is picked up in the New Testament. When we come to the sacrament of the Lord's Supper, we speak about this being a new covenant in His blood. Furthermore, if you turn to the book of Hebrews or to Paul's writings, you will find that covenant is either explicit or implicit there. So, there are good grounds for Eichrodt to make it the theme for Old Testament thought; it certainly does not exhaust that thought, but it gives you a core around which to work.

A second important book is by Brevard Childs, a long-time professor of Old Testament at Yale University. He is probably the most highly regarded Old Testament scholar in the last four decades of the twentieth century. His work is titled *Old Testament Theology in a Canonical Context*.[3] It is of particular value in that it attempts to save the Old Testament for us as a practical, working document within the church. Much of modern scholarship has tended to divide the Old Testament into hypothetical sources and to interpret it according to these different sources. The result has been to atomize the Old Testament text and to

---

[2] Walther Eichrodt, *Theology of the Old Testament*, 2 vols., tr. J. A. Baker (Philadelphia: Westminster, 1961).

[3] Brevard S. Childs, *Old Testament Theology in a Canonical Context* (Philadelphia: Fortress Press, 1986).

make it useless as a working document for the faith and practice of the church. Childs has attempted to address this issue, dealing not so much with how the supposed original documents developed or what their provenance was as with the final result on which the Christian church has been built.

But even more important than texts such as Eichrodt and Childs, we need to have a direct, firsthand knowledge of the Old Testament itself. You need to know what it says so that you are not trusting somebody else's judgment of what is there. The basis of the ministry of the church of Christ is in the Scripture. And let me remind you that the Christian church was built, founded in the first century A.D., without the New Testament. The first-century church was founded on the Old Testament. And so, you will need to know it, and it will need to be something that is very much a part of your life, your heart, your mind, your soul, your being, your thinking, your passion. So I say again that the primary document for our study is not Eichrodt nor is it Childs nor is it Kinlaw; the primary document here is the Old Testament itself. My prayer is that the Lord will save you from Eichrodt and Childs and Kinlaw and let you know something of what the Word itself actually says.

The place to begin reading the Old Testament theologically is with the book of Psalms. Let me explain why I say that. There are different ways that one can come at Old Testament theology, but my concern is that too often we separate theology from worship. If the goal of theology is the knowledge of the true God, the end result of that experience ought to be adoration and praise and prayer. I suspect I can find out more of what you really believe if I can listen to you pray awhile than in any other way. When I hear you witness, I hear you saying something you think the people around you expect you to say, but when you are alone before God and express yourself freely, then you begin to reveal what you really believe and who you really are.

The book of Psalms is, without question, one of the greatest pieces of human literature. Neither you nor I can imagine how cheated we would be if we did not have the Psalms. Of course there are passages in the Psalms that concern us, but that must not blind us to the profoundly theological nature of this massive piece of devotional thought. It is for that reason that I recommend the use of the Psalms as a window to begin to get a glimpse of what the theology of the Old Testament really is. We will go back later and pick up the story of Israel from creation to the return from exile. We also will examine the Wisdom Literature and the Prophets. But let us take Psalms for our starting point, because here is where we find what Israel really believed, and how it affected their daily lives.

As you read, look for certain things. See how much you can learn about the actual religious life of Israel through the book of Psalms. For instance, examine how the Psalms refer to sacrifice. As you know, a significant part of the Pentateuch is devoted to sacrifice, and one of the great issues in Old Testament theology concerns the role and importance of sacrifice. This is absolutely crucial to an understanding of the New Testament, because what took place on Calvary will be interpreted largely in terms of what the Old Testament teaches in regard to sacrifice. The Psalms tell us what the Israelites believed in practice, just as the biography or the autobiography of a Christian leader in our day would tell us, in part by the number of references, what that person thought of, say, the Lord's Supper and the other sacraments of the church. It also would be interesting to discover what that person believed about church attendance on the basis of his or her actual practice. So be alert in your reading for references to such things as sacrifice, offering, vows, and prayer.

Look also for references to sacred places. I read through the Psalms and jotted down in the margin of my Bible every time the word *Zion* occurred. I was amazed to discover how often it does occur. Why is that? It is because it was a special sacred place where God met his people, met Israel. You are certainly going to have to deal with the fact that the religion of Israel is closely associated with Jerusalem and what we know today as Israel.

Look to see what those people who wrote the Psalms knew about Genesis 1 and 2. Did they really know about that account? Did they have it? We know they did not have a Bible like we have. No one who wrote a psalm had a complete Old Testament. How much Scripture did they have? That can be a very significant question in your understanding of how God deals with people like you and me. How frequently are there references to the law? Is it given the kind of prominence we would expect on the basis of the large block of material found in Exodus through

Deuteronomy? Look for covenant. How often is it referred to and what is meant by it? See how much the writers of Psalms know about the history of Israel. Do they refer to Noah, to Adam and Eve, to Abraham, to Moses and the Exodus, to the conquest and the kingdom?

See how much the book of Psalms says about other gods, the idols, the gods of the other nations, and about Yahweh's relationship to them. What are the fates of the righteous and the wicked in the Psalms? Or what about eternal life? Without answering that question too fully in advance, let me say that these writers were clearly not familiar with either John 14 or 1 Corinthians 15! The same is true for such a foundational book as Genesis: There is almost no reference to life after death to be found in it. How would you call people to faith in God if this life was all there was to it? Nevertheless, the fact is that the basis of our faith was laid by people for whom life after death had very little significance. Look for things like that to see what is there.

One of the beautiful things you will see as you move through the book of Psalms is the growing understanding of God. You will see the development of the faith of the people of God and the enrichment of that faith as they lived. It is not all there in the beginning; perhaps it is there implicitly, but certainly not explicitly. Look for the treatment of sin, its definition, character, and consequences. In the same way look for the treatment of righteousness, its definition, character, and consequences.

However, the thing I want you to investigate most closely as you read the Psalms is the nature of the God of the Old Testament. Who is the God of the psalmist? This is why we begin with the Psalms. Although it is not popularly thought of as a book of theology, but as the hymn book of Israel, it is, as I have said, the truest record of Israel's faith. The Psalms portray Israel at prayer. And it is when we pray that we find out what we really believe, what our theology actually is. Furthermore, true theology ought to end in prayer. If theology is the study of God, the knowledge of God, and if God is God, then the end of the study ought to be worship. If it is not, if it has been only a study about a subject and our thoughts on that subject, that is idolatry; I have made God a thing. It does not matter how accurate my thought is; if it does not bring me to Him as a living Person, I have only found a substitute for Him, a knowledge of something other than God. When one comes to know the true God, the only response is, in the language of the Old Testament, fearful worship. I do not mean fearful in the sense of craven terror, but rather a deep-seated awe that you have come into the presence of the Holy One of Israel, the Creator and Lord of all. In every one of those passages in the Scripture where we find a person meeting God, that response of fearful worship is always there. Whether it is Isaiah or Moses, or whether it is Paul on the road to Damascus or John on the island of Patmos, there it is. So in your study, whatever else you look for, look for God. You will know you have found him if you find yourself on your face before him.

You will not find Him in a bit of superficial reading. You must immerse yourself in the text. This is not because God is hiding Himself or "playing hard to get." He wants to be found far more that we want to find Him. It is just that we are so superficial that God cannot break through to us very easily. So you live in the text. You must get to the place where God's Word is a part of you. But if you do, you will go back and give thanks for this study the rest of your days, not because of the teacher or the textbook, but because of the exposure to the Word of God.

I think the most significant hour of all of the hours I have had in all of the years I went to school was in a New Testament theology course at Princeton University. It was under an old German professor by the name of Otto Piper. It was a course for which I was woefully unprepared. As a result about sixty percent of the material floated right past me, for I had no categories in which to place it. The professor had been injured in the World War, and his face was half-paralyzed. It looked like a piece of stone; he had no facial expression at all. This was accompanied by a monotonous tone of voice. I would go to sleep and wake up and realize that I was hearing the richest stuff I had ever heard. But one day in that class something happened that I will never get over. It must have been in late April or early May. On a Thursday, Dr. Piper would sit on the edge of the desk and answer anyone's questions. One of the students in the class had been a chaplain in the Army and had come back to Princeton for graduate work. He later became a leader in the Presbyterian denomination and president of Grove City College. On this day, this fellow looked up and said, "Dr. Piper, many of us are going to be graduating in a few weeks. We will be going out into the ministry. Is there a list of 'must' books for every pastor? Is there a list of books that every pastor should have read?" Well, I became rather interested at that point and looked up. Dr. Piper looked away and then looked back with that unmoving face of his and said, "I know of only one 'must' book." I caught my breath. Otto Piper was, in my estimation, the greatest scholar I ever sat under. He was a brilliant man. But not only was he a brilliant man, he was also a humble man and incredibly broadly educated. And he looked at a bunch of us and said, "I know of only one 'must' book." And then he waited a moment and said, "You know, we make a mistake. Somehow in our Reformed tradition we think that Luther and Calvin produced the Reformation. It wasn't Luther or Calvin who produced the Reformation. What produced the Reformation was that Luther studied the Word of God. And as he studied, it began to explode inside him. And when it began to explode inside him, he didn't know any better than to turn it loose on Germany. And it was the Word of God that transformed Germany. Now," he said, "the same thing was true of Calvin. You knew what Calvin was going to preach on next Sunday. He would start with the verse after the one where he had stopped on the last Sunday, and he preached his way right through the Bible. Now, the tragedy of the Reformation was that when Luther and Calvin died, Melancthon and Beza edited their work. And so all the Lutherans began to read the Bible to find Luther and all the Calvinists began to read the Bible to find Calvin. And," he said, "the great corruption was on its way." He said, "Do you know there is enough undiscovered truth in the Scripture to produce a Reformation and an evangelical awakening in every generation if we would simply expose ourselves to it until it explodes within us and then we turn it loose?"

I have wished many times that I had a recording of those moments, because you would be awed by how monotonous that voice was. But you know, even though I was thirty years of age and working toward a degree in Philosophy of Religion for which Hebrew was not required, I went three weeks later, changed to Old Testament and signed up for beginning Hebrew. I've never had any regrets about that. We need our philosophers—I have no interest in doing away with them; we could not make it without them. But what our world needs is the Word of God. And the heart of it, or the base of it, is found in the Old Testament. One of the reasons the New Testament does not live for us is because we do not really know the Old Testament the way we should.

So the purpose of this study is directly related to the concept of knowing God. Thus, I would like for you to think more in terms of the change it will make in you than of knowledge gained or information gathered as you read these lectures. There are two sides to this concept of knowledge, and I would like to keep both of them before you. As I have said, the Old Testament is not a book of theology, but it has a great deal of theology in it. It is history, it is story, it is law, it is wisdom, it is preaching. Thus, when we study the Old Testament we have to look at the History, the Law, the Wisdom Literature, the Poetry, the Prophecy, and as we study it we have to abstract from that material the theology contained in those different literary genres. What binds this study all together and gives it a center is the fact that what we are after is the God who is revealed in those different literary genres. And our purpose is so that we can know Him. Our purpose is knowledge of God, but we need here to understand what the Scripture means when it talks about know-ing God. The Old Testament concept of knowledge in this sense is very different from most of ours. There is something in an academic setting that makes it more difficult for us to come to understand and come to grips with that biblical concept.

Let me quote for you three passages from the book of Jeremiah.[4] The first is from the fourth chapter of Jeremiah, verse 22, where God is quoted as saying,

> My people are fools. They do not know me. They are
> senseless children; they have no understanding. They are
> skilled in doing evil; they know not how to do good.

What is God saying? He is saying that they may be very intelligent, but they are fools because they do not know Him, the living God. Another passage is found in Jeremiah 2:8:

> The priests do not ask, "Where is the Lord?" Those
> who deal with the law do not know me; the leaders re-
> belled against me. The prophets prophesied by Baal,
> following worthless idols.

---

[4] Biblical quotations are from the *New International Version* unless otherwise stated. At times, the author paraphrases Scripture. These paraphrases are contained within quote marks.

Now, the priests are the experts on God and they do not say, "Where is the Lord?" "These who deal with the law, they do not know me," says God. When I read that I tend to think of the second chapter of the Gospel of John. When the One for whom Israel had been waiting for two thousand years came to them, the people who were authenticated to recognize Him said, "Who do you think you are?" and threw Him out. They could lecture by the hour on the Messiah; it was their business. But when He came they missed Him because they did not know Him.

The third passage is that magnificent one in the thirty-first chapter of Jeremiah where he speaks of the new covenant. At that point Jeremiah was looking beyond the tragedy of his own day, including the destruction of the City of Jerusalem and the carrying off of the people of God into the Babylonian exile. He was looking beyond his own day, a day in which God's covenant had been not merely broken, but forgotten. He saw a day in the future, and it was a good day. It was a day when God would establish a new covenant with His people. In that day the law would not be on tablets of stone in the Ark or on scrolls of leather in boxes somewhere or within the covers of a book. Rather, the law of God would be written in human minds and hearts and souls. And so Jeremiah says in 31:34:

> "No longer will a man teach his neighbor, or a man his brother, saying, 'Know the LORD,' because they will all know me, from the least of them to the greatest," declares the LORD. "For I will forgive their wickedness and will remember their sins no more."

Now, Jeremiah is saying the day is coming when the people of God will know God. That will be a remarkable day, won't it? But we need to understand that when Jeremiah uses *know* in those passages he is using it in a very different way from the way the modern English typically uses *know* or *knowledge*. He is using it in a typically biblical way, which is not primarily "knowledge about" (the common modern English sense) but "knowledge of," that is, "personal experience of." What he is talking about is knowing a person, and that is very different from knowing things. It is even different from knowing things about a person. You can know about a person by detached observation. You can obtain that knowledge without its ever affecting you in any way except to add a little more data to your mental computer. There is little of what I call dialogical character in the knowing of things. But when you know a person it implies a very different relationship. It is no longer detached observation but response, involvement.

The Dutch Old Testament theologian, Theodore Vriesen, has a passage that I want to share with you.

> Knowledge, as a general conception in the Old Testament, is quite unlike that in our occidental world which has been influenced so much by great philosophy. For us, knowledge implies grasping things by reason, seeing things and their connection of cause and effect and the understanding of the component factors of something. The Westerner says that he knows a thing when he has analyzed a thing fully and when he can explain all the factors from which it evolved or from which it arose. That is, when he can give it a place in the whole of his range of ideas. In the Old Testament, knowledge is living in a close relationship with something or somebody, such a relationship as to cause what may be called communion.[5]

I would like to get this concept clear from the outset. If this study does what it ought to do, it will make a difference in your communion with God as well as with others. The goal is not just information, but communion. Thus, in the Old Testament, sexual intercourse is called "knowing." And that is more than observation. The Hebrew term *da'at 'elohim* ("the knowledge of God") and the greatest Old Testament word for grace, *hesed*, can be used almost as synonyms. This is the case in Hosea (4:1). Likewise, when Peter denies Christ and says, "I do not know the man" (Matt. 26:72), he is denying that there has been any relationship between himself and that person. So, biblically, the knowledge of God is different from having a conception of God by which one defines His nature. It is not a theory about Him. It is not ontological reflection upon

---

[5] Theodore Vriezen, *An Outline of Old Testament Theology*, 2nd ed., tr. S. Neuijen (Oxford: Blackwell, 1970).

His being, but it is existential, and if it is a true knowing of Him it will affect you and it will affect Him. It is life in a true relationship with God. So the Old Testament does not try to bring us to a theology that defines the being of God.

I remember a university student in my younger days. He was a friend of mine and he was not a Christian, and we were talking. He said, "If you will show me one page in the Bible like what I read in Aristotle, I will pay attention to it." And I can remember how I shuddered and felt insecure and threatened because I knew I could not find a page in the Bible, particularly the Old Testament, like Aristotle. But that is because it is not ontology, but something very different. The Bible's purpose is that we might have communion with God. We know Him as well as know about Him. But that does not mean that we despise the acquisition of theological information, data for our mental computer. It does not mean that we despise the kind of thing that Aristotle would have been very interested in. That is the other side of the coin in our concept of knowledge, and it is vital to link it with the personal element. For it is easy to get interested in the data and keep the Living God on the margin. True knowledge is only obtained when you put those two things together.

Recently I came across a magnificent statement by William Temple. I will not quote him exactly, but let me share the gist of what he said. He said that if the image of God in your mind is wrong, the more religion you get the more dangerous you are. Now, after Waco, Texas, we ought to have a little understanding of that.[6] What Temple is saying is that the more passionately devoted we are to a God who is in fact a monster, a completely wrong understanding, the more deadly we are. So, there needs to be a fine-tuning of these two kinds of knowledge as we work our way through this kind of a study where we gain more information to get a clearer picture of what He is. This is true because most of us have been idolaters for much of our lives; the God that we worshipped was one that we thought was there and it was more of what we have thought than the One who actually is. But we are not the first people who have had that kind of problem. You see, when Jesus turned and began to wash the disciples' feet, Peter looked at Him and said, "Jesus, you've got

---

[6] This is a reference to the religious sect calling themselves the "Branch-Davidians," who walled themselves into a compound in Waco, Texas, and apparently destroyed themselves when government officers attempted to enter by force.

it all wrong. We believe you are the Christ. That is not the role for you."
They did not know what to do with Jesus as he actually was. Many of us
are like Peter and the other disciples. We need the cleansing, the clarifica-
tion, of our concept of God, but it ought to be more than intellectual. It
ought to be something that comes and touches the depths of our person.
That is why the Old Testament is so very important to us. Here is the
place where the basic truths about the nature of God, the one true God,
the Author of all, the Finisher of all, where the basic truth is given upon
which the New Testament depends. That is so that we can know about
Him and so that we can know Him personally. The understanding affects
the knowing, and it is the understanding that keeps us from thinking we
know Him when we really probably have only met ourselves and our
own ideas instead of meeting the One whom to know is to know eternal
life.

There is one final introductory point that I need to make. In the
first verse of Psalm 8 there is an interesting phenomenon. We find two
occurrences of the word *Lord* spelled differently in that verse. What is
the difference? One has only the first letter capitalized while the other
has all four letters capitalized. What is the reason for this? It is because
the first one is an honorific title whereas the second one is standing for
God's personal name. As you read through the Psalms, notice how many
times that capitalized LORD appears. Every time it is standing for the personal name of God. Why does the Hebrew Bible do this? Why not just
spell out his personal name?

The answer to these questions is found in a Jewish idea called
"fencing the Law." That is, after the Babylonian exile the returned Judeans
were very concerned that they never break God's law again and suffer
such a terrible fate. In order not to break the laws they put more laws
around them. It is as though, if the speed limit were sixty-five miles per
hour, you would put a governor on your car so you could not go over
forty-five miles per hour. That would guarantee you would not break the
speed law. So, how can you be sure that you never break the Old Testament law that forbids boiling a kid in its mother's milk? Well, if you never
eat a hamburger and drink milk at the same time, you will not break that
law. So to this day an orthodox Jew will not eat meat and milk together.
Now, the Jews spread that concept rather extensively so that when they
came to the commandment, "Thou shalt not take the name of the Lord

thy God in vain," they said, "You know, if we never pronounce His name, we won't break that commandment." Whenever they came to the name of God, they said the word that means "lord" instead. They did this so thoroughly that eventually they, the people of God, lost the pronunciation of the name that was given to Moses at the burning bush. They lost their greatest treasure.

Sometimes I think that the real effect of the work of those of us who are professional religious people has been to put distance between people and God. So the book of Psalms and indeed, the entire Old Testament in our English translations, can only speak of God in one of His roles, "the Lord," and never in the richness of His person, as conveyed in His name. My wife's name is Elsie Blake Kinlaw. I knew a preacher once who always referred to his wife in public as, "the wife." I heard him do it in the pulpit. If I had ever done that to my wife, when I got home my bags would be packed sitting on the front porch. Elsie is not a role, she is a person. When I was president of Asbury College many people would call me "Mr. President." It was not about me but about my business role. What you do with names determines relationship, doesn't it? I want you to notice how prominent the personal name of God is in Psalms. In fact, the book of Psalms is about Yahweh*, yet He never appears by name in our translation.

Before reading the next chapter, read Psalms 121 and 146. Notice how many times God's personal name occurs, how common it is. I think that is one of the reasons for the Incarnation. God was wanting to overcome the distance that had crept in between Him and His people in the loss of His name. There is something about the name "Jesus" that has a closeness and an openness that the term "God" does not have.

---

* [Editor's note] We know that the consonants of God's personal name were y-h-w-h, but we do not know what the vowels were. This is so because when the Jewish scholars were adding vowel markings to the text, which had originally contained only consonants, the vowels they inserted in the divine name were the vowels of the word for "lord" –a-o-a-. Using evidence from personal names that include parts of the divine name (like "Abijah," "my father is Yah") scholars have conjectured that the name was pronounced "Yahweh," which would mean "He Causes to Be." Because this is not certain, most English translations continue to use "Lord.

Lecture 2

· · · · · · · · · ·

The Theology of Personal Encounter Psalm 146

Praise the LORD.
Praise the LORD, oh my soul.
    I will praise the LORD all my life;
    I will sing praise to my God as long as I live.
Do not put your trust in princes,
    in mortal men, who cannot save.
When their spirit departs, they return to the ground;
    on that very day their plans come to nothing.
Blessed is he whose help is the God of Jacob,
    whose hope is in the LORD his God,
the Maker of heaven and earth,
    the sea, and everything in them—

the LORD, who remains faithful forever.
He upholds the cause of the oppressed
and gives food to the hungry.
The LORD sets prisoners free,
The LORD gives sight to the blind,
the LORD lifts up those who are bowed down,
The LORD loves the righteous.
The LORD watches over the alien
and sustains the fatherless and the widow,
but he frustrates the ways of the wicked.
The LORD reigns forever,
your God, O Zion, for all generations.
Praise the LORD.

This is Psalm 146, the first of the last five in the book of Psalms. In Jewish tradition these five psalms are grouped together. They are called "The Great Hallel." Perhaps you know that the Hebrew word *hallel* means praise. So we find it in English in "hallelujah," meaning "Praise the Lord." These five psalms all begin with that injunction, "Praise the Lord." Furthermore, all five end with it as well. The *hallelu* is a plural imperative, commanding a group of people, "Give praise!" while *yah* is the short form for the name "Yahweh" in the Old Testament. This is the name that God gave to Moses at the burning bush when Moses wanted to know with whom he was talking. God gave Moses His personal name, and that name was probably pronounced, as best we know, Yahweh.

This group of psalms is called a "hallel" because they begin and end with that call to praise. There is another "hallel" in the book of Psalms as well. It is made up of Psalms 113–18. That group is known as the "Passover Hallel." It is of special significance to us because on Thursday evening of Holy Week, the week of our Lord's crucifixion, when Jesus met together with His disciples they, along with Jews everywhere, sang those six psalms, 113–18, together. So, I never find myself reading those psalms but that I think back to what that must have meant to those disciples that night before the Cross and how the rest of their lives they must have looked upon those six psalms as very special and very precious to them.

I believe the reason we have the Great Hallel at the end of the Psalms is because it was a Hebrew conviction that when you come to

God, no matter why you come, you ought to leave Him with gratitude, with thanksgiving, with praise, with adoration in your heart. No matter what it is you bring when you come, when you are in His presence, His greatness ought to be such that when you finish your time with Him your problems have been reduced in size in relation to Him and you can walk out, no matter what you face, with praise. So these final psalms begin, "Praise Yah. Praise Yah." And they end the same way.

When you look at Psalm 146, it is a rather simple one in many ways. You will not find anything especially new in it, but I think that if you live with it a little while, it will become more exciting to you. The title of this lecture is "The Theology of Personal Encounter" because I believe that is what is behind this psalm. It is not that the psalmist said to himself, "I ought to sit down and write a prayer," but that he met God and could not do anything else. So the poetic expression that you find here is not something that was written in praise of God in order to get to God. Rather, it is something that was written because the writer had met God. And when we really meet Him, unless it is an encounter of complete judgment, if we meet Him in grace, always the end of that meeting with the gracious God will be an experience of joy and of praise.

Now let me say why I particularly believe that this is an expression of the theology of personal encounter. As you read the Psalms and the Old Testament you should take notice of the great words that are there, the vocabulary that we have. You possess many treasures, but you have no greater treasure than the vocabulary that exists for certain purposes. It would be a horrible thing to have no words to express the deepest feelings inside you. We have those words and they are great words and there is a sanctity about them. That is the reason why there is in Christianity an instinctively negative reaction toward profanity. And you will notice that profanity is not cursing; profanity is just taking something sacred and making it profane. So we as Christians have an inherent instinct within us that reminds us that words are very important. Perhaps you are remembering what John says in the first chapter of his gospel, "In the beginning was the Word . . ." because that is who He was when he came to us, a Word coming from the Father to us about Himself and about the triune Godhead.

The most important word in this psalm is the word that is covered up in English translations by the word LORD. As we said in the first lecture, it is printed in this way because it is standing for the personal name of God. The four Hebrew consonants of that name are YHWH. It is probable that it is a third person masculine singular verb from the root meaning "to be." There is discussion as to whether it means "He is (the One who is)," or whether it is a causative form, "He is the One who causes (everything) to be." Most scholars believe it is the latter, but there are some who take is as the simple stem, the *Qal,* yielding the former meaning, "He is." In any case, this is a personal name, not a title, not a sobriquet, not an epithet. Of course there are wonderful titles for God in the Psalms. As you go through, mark them.[7] He is a Rock, a Shepherd, a Refuge, a Help, and on and on. Notice those titles. But when it comes to YHWH, you are not dealing with a title; you are dealing with a personal name. Some people call me Dr. Kinlaw; some people call me Mr. Kinlaw; some people call me Dennis, and I won't tell you what else they call me. But my grandchildren have their own name, and when I'm in any crowd, if one of my grandchildren were to call me, I would know instantly who it was, because there is a personal relationship.

This psalm, you will notice, is built around that personal name. Shall we go back through it again? After the opening call to praise, "Praise Yah," we find the full form of the divine name being used: "Praise Yahweh, O my soul. I will praise Yahweh all my life. I will sing praise to my God." "Yah" is to "Yahweh" as "Tim" is to Timothy or "Bill" to William. So what is the psalmist saying? He is saying God is the person Yahweh. And on the other hand, that's who Yahweh is, God.

> I will sing praise to my God as long as I live. Do not put
> your trust in princes, in mortal men, who cannot save.
> When their spirit departs, they return to the ground; on

---

[7] As you go through the Psalms I hope you will mark many things. For instance, I have gone through, and everywhere the word *Jacob* occurs in the Psalms I have put a "J" in the margin. Do you know that the name of Jacob occurs thirty-three times in the Psalms? And every time, it is "the God of Jacob." It is interesting that God wants to associate Himself with someone like Jacob, isn't it? Thief of thieves. But there is great theology in that. At least there is for me. There was a great Methodist preacher in Detroit a half-century ago who always had an Irish cop attending his Wednesday night prayer meeting, and every time they had a testimony meeting the Irish cop would give a witness. And his witness usually ran, "I'm glad that the Lord is the God of Jacob because if there is hope for Jacob, there is hope for people like me."

that very day their plans come to nothing. Blessed is he whose help is the God of Jacob, whose hope is [Yahweh] his God, the Maker of heaven and earth; the sea, and everything in them.

I do not know about you, but I think it would be nice to be able to call the One who created the heavens and the earth by His first name, would it not? But that is what we have in this psalm. He does not say, "Blessed is he whose help is Yahweh, whose hope is in the God who made the heavens and the earth." Rather, he turns it around and says,

Blessed is he whose help is the God of Jacob, whose hope is in [Yahweh], his God, the Maker of heaven and earth, the sea, and everything in them—[Yahweh], who remains faithful forever. He upholds the cause of the oppressed and gives food to the hungry. [Yahweh] sets prisoners free, [Yahweh] gives sight to the blind, [Yahweh] lifts up those who are bowed down, [Yahweh] loves the righteous. [Yahweh] watches over the alien and sustains the fatherless and the widow, but he frustrates the ways of the wicked. [Yahweh] reigns forever, your God, O Zion, for all generations. Praise [Yahweh].

Now, it is almost monotonous, is it not? But that is the purpose of the Psalms. The psalmist is expressing his adoration and praise, and it is centered around the personal name of God because he knows Him personally.

There is nothing in the Old Testament more important than that. There is a sense in which you can explain everything from Genesis 1:1 to the last verse of Malachi in terms of the character, nature, and personhood of Yahweh. Read the literature of Babylon, of Egypt, of Canaan, of Greece, or of Rome or India, and then read the Old Testament and you find a difference there. That difference is because of the nature, the character of Yahweh. And so the Old Testament is the story and the book of that God, that personal God. What difference does it make whether you say "God" or whether you say "Yahweh"? It is interesting to notice that Yahweh occurs in the Old Testament about 6,800 times, while Elohim, "God," only appears about 2,600 times. So, the preponderance of references to the Deity in the Old Testament use the personal name.

What difference does it make? Let me illustrate it. I was in a pastorate many years ago, and I had two ladies who were not members of my congregation come to me one day and say, "There was a lady in our community who was teaching a Bible class. But she got sick and can't teach us anymore." So, one of them who had a gravelly, bourbon voice said, "And a whole bunch of us are going to hell unless somebody does something for us. Would you help us start a Bible class?" So, we started a Bible class. About six years later, both of those ladies were Sunday school teachers in our Sunday school. One day the two of them came to see me again and said, "You know, you prohibitionist, if you had known how much hard liquor we had to drink to get up the courage to come ask you to start that Bible class, you never would have let us in the front door." But that is the kind of class it was, you never knew for certain who was in it.

One day, after the class had been going about five minutes, I noticed a new lady in the crowd, and her hand went up. I said, "Yes?" She said, "I don't believe a word of that." And I said, "Oh?" And that started fifty minutes of intense conversation back and forth. Some of the ladies came to me afterwards and said, "If it's going to be like that, we don't know if we want to come back or not." I said, "Wait a minute, she's never been in anything like this before. Give her a chance." So, the next week, as I lifted my head from offering the opening prayer, up went Betsy's hand. I thought, "Oh, no." And then I said, "Yes?" And she looked up at me and said, "You know, you remember our discussion last week? Well, I went home and I checked and I found out you were right and I was wrong." So I thought, "Well it's nice that a few things turn out right." And so, we went into the class. About five minutes later, up went Betsy's hand and around we went for another forty minutes.

Well, that started a fascinating friendship. She got her husband to come. He came every Sunday morning to correct my grammar. At the end of every Sunday morning, as he would walk out the door, he would hand me a slip of all my grammatical mistakes, which is not necessarily a bad thing, you know. One day, Betsy turned to me and said, "Now, Dennis, this love of Jesus bit nauseates me." And I said, "Oh?" She said, "Yeah, it nauseates me. Loving God . . . I think I could live with that comfortably, but this love of Jesus bit nauseates me." But then one Sunday afternoon at about 1:20 the telephone rang. It was Betsy. She said, "Dennis, could you come over?" I had had three services that morning and was sitting with my family at the table at home and was grateful for a chance to sit down, but there was something about her tone of voice that caused me to say, "Do you mean right now?" And she said, "Yes." And the way she spoke, I felt I had no option but to go immediately. I walked in the door of a palatial home. Her husband was a steel man. She was standing in the hallway leading into their living room, and there were tears streaming down her cheeks. I said, "Betsy, what's wrong? What happened?" She looked at me and said, "Dennis, I see it. For the first time in my life I see it." And the tears flowed. I said, "Betsy, what do you see?" She said, "It was this morning. It was in church. I was sitting in the choir; it was during the Communion service. 'And He took the bread and broke it and said, "This is my body which is broken for you." And He took the cup and He said, "This is my blood which is shed for you for the remission of your sins."'" And she said, "Dennis, for the first time in my life I saw it. He did it for me." And she wept. You know, she never had any problem with that "love of Jesus bit" after that.

Now, a world changes when you meet Him, when that personal encounter is there. He steps out of the textbooks, He steps out of the rational and the abstract and He steps into personal encounter and He becomes the other person in your life, the one from whom you cannot get away, who is always there. It is like getting married. When Elsie and I walked out of Broadway Methodist Church, we sat down in the front seat of the car I had borrowed to go start our honeymoon. I sat there behind the steering wheel and looked over at her and thought, "Am I hooked to her forever?" And I was. That is the way it is when you meet Him; it is never the same again. Now, what happens when you meet Him? Notice what you do. You praise Him. There's a lot of good New Testament theology in that, isn't there? And a lot of Christian evidence to that. I dare you to go through a hymnal and notice every line about the name of Jesus. Do you know this old one?

> How tedious and tasteless the hours
>   when Jesus no longer I see.
> Sweet prospects, sweet birds and sweet flowers
>   have all lost their sweetness to me.

The midsummer sun shines but dim,
    the fields strive in vain to look gay,
but when I am happy in Him,
    December is as pleasant as May.
His name, His name yields the richest perfume
    and sweeter than music His voice.
His presence disperses my gloom
    and makes all within me rejoice.
I should, were He always thus nigh,
    have nothing to wish or to fear.
No mortal as happy as I;
    my summer would last all the year.[8]

Working your way through the Psalms I want you to note every place where "the name" is referred to. Put an "N" in the margin and then go back and notice how often the name of God appears. The Hebrews were the people of the name. And the Bible, the Old Testament, is the book about the One whose name we know. The psalmist responds to this glorious truth by saying, "I want to praise Him." The opening call to praise, "Praise the Lord," begins with a plural imperative. The singer thinks the whole world should praise the Lord. But then he says, "Oh my soul, praise Him." That is Himself. So that is the scope of praise. Then he says, "I will praise [Yahweh] all my life. I will sing praise to my God [Yahweh] as long as I live." There is the duration of praise. He goes on to say, "Do not put your trust in princes, in mortal men, who cannot save. When their spirit departs, they return to the ground; on that very day their plans come to nothing." Here is the opposite. Is there any reason to praise mortal men? Hardly! Trust in them will always leave us disappointed.

It is vital that we notice this move. What is the cause of praise? It is the trustworthiness of God. It may be that next to the name Yahweh in the book of Psalms, the most important word is *trust*. As you read through the book of Psalms put "TR" in the margin every time you find the word *trust*. Let me mention something about Hebrew in this regard.

---

[8] "How Tedious and Tasteless the Hours," John Newton, *Olney Hymns* (London; W. Oliver, 1779).

There are five words in the Old Testament that can be translated into English with "trust."[9] I want to talk about the first two here. The first is frequently translated with "believe." It appears in Genesis 15:6, "Abraham *believed* the LORD, and he credited it to him as righteousness." That is the concept that the New Testament picks up and uses in connection with justification by faith. "The righteous will live by faith" (Gal. 3:11). But that verb in Genesis is from the Hebrew root *'-m-n,* which means "to be sure, to be certain." It is the source of the Hebrew word *Amen,* meaning "Certainly, surely," which has been borrowed into English through the New Testament. In a causative form the verb has the idea of making something certain and thus means "to believe in." Again, as with "know," to believe is not merely to perform a mental act. This is to put your weight down on something. This is to accept the word of someone. It was in this sense that Abraham "believed." He was, in effect, saying "Amen!" or "I will live in the certainty that what you say is true." Why was it credited to him as "righteousness"? It is because the only right thing a human can do is to put absolute confidence in the trustworthiness of God. Without that, everything else we do is filthy rags.

But there is a second word in Hebrew: *batah,* which means "to trust." Of the two words, this is the more common one in the Psalms. *'amen* is found in the psalms, but not a great many times. It is a bit like an obligato line in music, while *batah* is the main motif that the psalmist never gets through playing. It just keeps coming back, and coming back, and coming back.[10] Of the two, *batah* is the more graphic. It is "to lean upon." You are leaning against something or someone, and if he or it falls down, you're in trouble.

So the psalmist is saying, "In whom shall I trust?" And that is the basic biblical question, isn't it? Salvation by grace through faith. He says, "Do not put your trust in princes." The word there means "the noble ones," and I suggest it implies the very most reliable things in creation other than Yahweh. But the writer says, "Don't do it! The very best that creation has will fail you in the end." Don't put your trust in mortals because they cannot save. There is no salvation in you and me. Do you see how New Testament this is? There is no salvation except in

---

[9] They are *he'amin, batah, qawa, hasa,* and *yahal.*
[10] The ratio is about seven to one.

Christ. There is no salvation except in Yahweh. We cannot save. When our spirits depart we return to the ground. On that very day, our plans come to zero.

But those who find their help and hope in the God of Jacob are "blessed." Now, there is a great Old Testament word and a great word in the Psalms. How does the first psalm begin? "Blessed is the man . . ." and in that psalm you get a picture of the kind of person the psalmist wants us all to be. "Blessed" is the blessed person; he is the truly rich person. Who is he? "Blessed is he whose help is the God of Jacob, whose hope is in [Yahweh] his God."

Now, let me make a comment about "help." That is the same word used about Eve in relation to Adam in the Creation story. She is made to be a help to him. And do you know that that is one of the major titles for Yahweh in the Old Testament? When you see the word *help*, do not give it a connotation of inferiority, because the greatest being in the universe is glad to be called our Helper. You see it in *Ebenezer*, the Stone of Help (1 Sam. 7:12). *Eben* is "stone" and *ezer* is "help." The stone was to remind the Israelites, whenever they saw it, that God had helped them from the very beginning up to that point. We can think also of Psalm 10:14, which says of God, "You are the helper of the fatherless," and Psalm 118:7, "The Lord is with me; he is my helper." When you get hold of this truth, it is a lot more difficult to think that a helper is someone who is second-rate. So, blessed is the one who has Him for his Helper. That is a great thought: to have God as your Helper. It is not surprising that the psalmist should say such a person is "blessed." It is also important to notice who this Helper is; He is "the God of Jacob." The God who can save a man like Jacob and change the history of the world through him is a Person whose help is not to be sneezed at.

"Whose hope is in the Lord his God." He is our Helper now and our hope for the future. The word translated "hope" here does not occur very commonly in the Old Testament, but like the two more common words it has the underlying idea of "to wait." We remember Isaiah 40:31: "Those who wait for the Lord shall renew their strength" (*NRSV*). Isaiah uses a different word, but the same idea. Why do you wait? You wait because you have hope. And because you have hope, you refuse to run ahead of Him and put your trust in anything created, especially, yourself. To wait for God is the ultimate expression of trust and hope. And the good news is, Yahweh is the God of all hope (Rom. 15:13). He is the God of the future. So, the psalmist can say, "Blessed is he whose help is the God of Jacob." Yahweh is the One who has made heaven and earth, the sea and everything in them. Yahweh remains faithful forever.

There are two interlocking themes here in what I have just said. Both of them are major Old Testament themes, and both of them are major themes in the Psalms. The first is the one you get in Genesis 1 and 2: Creation; Yahweh is the Creator. If you see it, He made it. Do you realize that the Hebrews were the only people in the world who had that kind of faith? The rest of the world could not be certain where anything came from, because there were so many conflicting gods. How much simpler the Hebrew faith was. If you saw it, you knew who put it there. Of course, that idea could present you with a problem when you encountered something that was obviously destructive and wrong. But the Hebrews were willing to put up with that problem for the sake of the far greater truth: God alone is the maker of heaven and earth.

The second theme here is the theme of history. I hope, before we finish our study, you will understand how closely linked these two themes are. The fact is, the only reason secular universities in the world today have Philosophy of History courses is because of the biblical doctrine of Creation. Many of the professors of those courses would like to forget that fact, but the facts are on my side. Yahweh started everything, and He's going to end it. So time has a beginning and an end, and tomorrow is not yesterday. Believe that and you can write history. Deny it and the intellectual study of history cannot long survive. We will come back to that. But it was one of the intellectual revolutions of human history. It was infinitely more significant than Einstein, and here it is in the middle of a psalm, an expression of praise. Do you know what your future is? I don't know what your future is, but I know who is going to determine it. He is the Lord of history.

But along with the linked doctrines of creation and history you also find the doctrine of redemption, because the story of history shows something has gone badly wrong. God the Creator, the Lord of history, has to be a redeemer. It would not have been necessary if humanity had not gone wrong. But you will see these themes of creation and redemption pitted against each other, interacting with each other all through the

Old Testament. That interaction is reflected in the phrase "the God of Jacob."

But the psalmist moves on. He has told us that Yahweh is the Creator and that He is the Lord of history. But now he says, "Let me tell you what I really like about Yahweh. Did you know, He cares about the oppressed, He cares about the hungry, He cares about the prisoner, He cares about the blind, He cares about the broken, the bowed down?[11] He cares about those who are pushed down. He cares about the foreigner. He cares about the fatherless, the orphan, and He cares about the widow. He reigns forever. Praise Yahweh.

So in this psalm the writer starts out with the doctrine of history, then moves to that of Creation, and then moves to God's interest in the people other people don't care about. In the world in which the psalmist lived, who was going to care about the oppressed? In particular, the oppressors didn't care. Who is going to care about the hungry or the prisoner or the blind or the broken or the foreigner or the fatherless or the widow? As you study the Old Testament I hope you will note the continual linkage of three types of people: the widow, the orphan, and the stranger. You have different translations for "the stranger" in English, including "sojourner," "foreigner," and "alien." But it is a single category. Why is this the case? What do these three have in common, and what do they represent? These three go together because none of them had any legal status. You had no one to stand up for you in court. If you were an orphan and had no father, there was nobody to protect you. If you were a widow and had no husband, there was nobody to protect you unless you had a relative who was a man. And if you were foreign, you had no rights at all. You were like Abraham in Genesis 23 trying to buy a gravesite for his wife. He had no rights. They were people who were without rights. But God has taken the defender's place. If you touch a man's wife, you will have that man to deal with. If you touch a man's child you will have that man to deal with. But if you touch that widow or that orphan, you don't have her husband or a father to deal with—you have Yahweh to deal with.

I want you to now notice a fundamental point here. What is the basis for the Christian's social concern? Is it our legal right? Is it because

---

[11] The Hebrew word is *kapap*, "to be bent over."

we are equal? That is the point at which we usually pitch the battle. So we go back to the Constitution. Where does the psalmist go? He goes back to the absolute foundation of all things: the absolute nature of God. And what do we know about the nature of Yahweh on the basis of His name? Let's take the simple form first. He's the One who is. He is the One who was before you took advantage of somebody. He's the One who was there while you were doing it, and He is the One who will be there when you finish doing it. And there is no way to escape Him. Where does the psalmist's concern for the oppressed, the hungry, the prisoner, the blind, the broken, the foreigner, the orphan, the widow come from? All of that arose because he met Yahweh. I believe the proof that someone has met the living God is that he or she gets turned inside out and personal concerns shift from inward to outward. Do you know how badly we have corrupted that? What does "to be born again" mean to the typical American evangelical? Doesn't it mean how to get my soul saved? Get me safe for heaven? I think that is an absolute perversion of biblical truth.

The psalmist met God, and God said, "I would like to be in a personal relationship with you. I want to tell you my name. I want to be on that kind of basis with you, a first name basis." But when the psalmist gets to know who God is and what His nature is, he is astounded to discover that this Yahweh cares about the people nobody else cares about. This is one of the reasons we as Christians cannot afford to give up the fact that there is no salvation anywhere except through Jesus Christ. Jesus is the only source for the kind of compassion that is necessary to reach the needy of the world: the blind, the broken, the hungry, the prisoner.

When I say that, I always shake a bit because we have not lived up to all the implications of what we preach. There are a lot of hungry people we have not fed. There are a lot of blind people we have not taken care of, and a lot of broken people we have not helped. But the reality is that in the history of the world most of the help that has come to people in great need has come when somebody met God, the living God, the true God, and got turned inside out. Then the other person's welfare became more important than their own. The fact that we Christians have fallen short cannot obscure the fact that where the Christian gospel has not reached, care for the needy is largely unknown.

This truth can be illustrated in many ways. Some years ago I read a biography of William Wilberforce. When he was twenty-one he was elected to Parliament. He came from a well-to-do family in England and so, at twenty-one he had a seat in Parliament. He was sort of an odd young man, and so his family felt that Parliament would be a place where he could make his mark and become something. He was a member of the Anglican Church but was far from a Christian—he did not even believe in God. He was not even sure if he believed in much of anything. When he was twenty-five years old his mother said, "I want to take a vacation. I want to go to the Riviera." In those days there were no airplanes, so she had to go by coach. How would you like to ride in a stagecoach from here to New Orleans . . . with your mother? And you are a member of the House of Commons. But he was a dutiful son so he said, "Let's take two carriages"—and he looked for a friend to go with him. Finding such a friend, he said, "We ought to take something to read; it's going to be a long ride." So they checked the best-seller list. At that time, a book by Philip Doddridge, titled *The Rise and Progress of Religion in the Soul* was very popular. Now, being a good politician, he was interested in what folks were reading, so when that was suggested he agreed. So, to the Mediterranean and back, they read Philip Doddridge's *The Rise and Progress of Religion in the Soul*. By the time they got back to England, Wilberforce believed there must be a God. The next year his mother wanted to go back. So, William Wilberforce went to find his friend. This time they decided to read the Greek New Testament. There are very few seminary graduates today who can read a Greek New Testament. But one hundred fifty years ago a twenty-six-year-old member of Parliament in Britain could. So, they read the Greek New Testament all the way to the Mediterranean and back. When William Wilberforce got back to London, he believed in Christ. In the next session of Parliament he introduced the bill to free the slaves in the British Empire. For thirty-seven years he reintroduced the bill every year. And thirty-seven years later, on a Friday, they passed the bill to free the slaves. On the following Monday night, about 2 o'clock in the morning, William Wilberforce died.

I read Psalm 146 and I think I understand. You see, William Wilberforce met the same person the psalmist met.

Lecture 3

· · · · · · · · · ·

God the Creator/Redeemer Psalm 121

Dr. Thomas Oden is a systematic theologian at Drew University. His conversion is one of the most interesting stories of the twentieth century, and I suspect it may be as important as any conversion in the latter half of the twentieth century.

Here is how Thomas Oden told it to me. He decided to go into the Methodist ministry because he felt it would make a good platform for social reform. However, he was dismayed when he got to seminary and found out he had to use the Bible, which he did not believe. But he was introduced to the work of Rudolf Bultmann and found you could use the Bible without believing it. So, he began his ministry. Ultimately he ended up teaching at Yale. He had three objectives in his life. They were to master Freud, Nietzsche, and Marx. He thought that if he could thoroughly master those three, he would understand modern thought and would be on the crest of the wave of the future. As such, he thought he could very easily become one of the determinative intellects at the end of the twentieth century and the beginning of the twenty-first.

Oden got along well with his project until about 1970, when a Jewish philosopher named Will Herber began to invite himself to dinner at the Odens' every other Tuesday night. Mrs. Oden told me that at first she thought he was just a lonely bachelor but then, she said, "After several Tuesday nights, we discovered he had an agenda. Herber would look at Oden, this brilliant young theologian, about forty-five, and say, according to Tom, 'Tom, you will never be a wise man.' And Tom would say, 'What do you mean?' 'No,' Herber would answer, 'you will never be a wise man.' But Tom would persist, 'Well, Herb, what do you mean?' He would say, 'You will never be a wise man because you don't know how to read. A man who doesn't know how to read can never be wise.' Tom would say, 'What do you mean I don't know how to read? That's all I do!' Herber would reply, 'Yes, but you really don't know how to read, because when you read you can't hear, and a man who can't hear when he reads will never be wise.' Oden would cry, 'What do you mean, I can't hear?'"

Oden told me, "Dennis, he went on with that every other Tuesday night. Finally he would explain himself. 'Tom, when you pick up a manuscript, you've already decided what it can say and what it can't say, so you can't hear. And no man will ever be wise who can't hear.'" Oden said, "You know, as he kept beating me with it, slowly I began to realize he was right."

Tom Oden explained it like this:

> I began to realize that I had a whole set of assumptions. And that set of assumptions which I had never looked at, did not even realize I had committed myself to, determined what I heard when I read. When I began to examine the set of assumptions, I began to realize I didn't believe many of them myself, and they had not been rationally tested and proved. So I began to read, listening.

Within three years, in 1973, Thomas Oden had come to the place where he accepted the fact of the physical resurrection of Christ. And with that began the change in one of the more brilliant theological minds of our time. He said it all started when somebody told him he did not know how to read.

I am convinced that you and I have been in the same place. Furthermore, I am convinced that to really read you have to have more than a text in front of you. If you don't know anything about that text and about its context and about its origin, then you will not hear what is there. And so, I want to use Psalm 121 as an illustration of that today.

Psalm 121 is a beautiful little thing. I first began to memorize it as a child in vacation Bible school. I have always been glad for that, but I have to say that the interpretation given me there had little to do with what the psalm actually says.

> I lift up my eyes to the hills—
>> where does my help come from?
> My help comes from [Yahweh],
>> the Maker of heaven and earth.
> He will not let your foot slip—
>> he who watches over you will not slumber.
> Indeed, he who watches over Israel
>> will neither slumber nor sleep.
> [Yahweh] watches over you—
>> [Yahweh] is your shade at your right hand;
> The sun will not harm you by day,
>> nor the moon by night.
> [Yahweh] will keep you from all harm—
>> he will watch over your life;
> [Yahweh] will watch over your coming and going
>> both now and forevermore.

It is a beautiful little thing, isn't it? But the *King James Version* says, "I will lift up mine eyes unto the hills from whence comes my help." And that's the way it was presented to me in vacation Bible school when I was a child. It made a good deal of sense to me because I grew up in the swamps of North Carolina. So I remember well the first time I ever saw a mountain. It was very impressive and majestic. There was something exalting about looking at it. And there are many people who think that is what this psalm is about. But that is exactly the opposite of what the psalm is saying. The correct phrasing is: "I will lift up mine eyes into the hills. From whence comes my help?" The final statement is not an affirmation about the hills. Rather it is a recognition that the hills do not really provide any help and a question as to where real help can be found. As such, it is the key to the whole psalm. But more than that, it is the essential religious question. Why do people have gods and goddesses? And why are we interested in religion? It is because there is something in us that says, "I need a little help. I cannot handle the pressures and difficulties of life with my limited resources. I am worried about facing an uncertain fate. I could use some favors from whoever is in charge here. If there is anybody or anything out there that can help me, I would like to know about it." So the psalmist is asking the perennial religious question. That is not unusual. But the answer he gives is unusual in his world. He says, "My help comes from Yahweh who made the heavens and the earth." He does not look to the mountains for his inspiration. Rather, he looks behind them to the One who made the mountains.

But why might the psalmist be inclined to look to the lofty places of earth for his inspiration? Turn with me to Deuteronomy 12:1: "These are the decrees and laws you must be careful to follow in the land that the Lord, the God of your fathers, has given you to possess—as long as you live in the land." This word is being given by God to the elect people, to Israel. God is about to lead them into the chosen land, into the land of promise. He is telling them how to live if they are to be His people and He is to be their God in this new land. In particular He warns them not to live like their neighbors. They cannot do that because their neighbors' view of reality was so very wrong. Next, He says:

> "Destroy completely all the places on the high moun-
> tains and on the hills and under every spreading tree
> where the nations you are dispossessing worship their
> gods. Break down their altars, smash their sacred stones
> and burn their Asherah poles in the fire; cut down the
> idols of their gods and wipe out their names from those
> places. You must not worship [Yahweh] your God in

their way. But you are to seek the place [Yahweh] your God will choose from among all your tribes to put his Name there for his dwelling. To that place you must go; there, bring your burnt offerings and sacrifices, your tithes and special gifts what you have vowed to give and your freewill offerings, and the firstborn of your herds and flocks. There in the presence of [Yahweh], your God, you and your families shall eat and shall rejoice in everything you put your hand to, because [Yahweh] your God has blessed you."

You will notice God says that the first thing He wanted the Israelites to do when they entered the land was to clean off the hilltops because it was on the hilltops that the pagan deities were worshipped. So you find the psalmist saying, "I lift up mine eyes unto the hills. Where shall I go for help? My neighbor goes to the top of the hill, but I will go somewhere else."

Now turn with me to the third chapter of 1 Kings, and let me call your attention to some things there. There are dozens and dozens more examples like these in the Old Testament, but we will use these as representative. We are talking now about Solomon, the successor to David, David's son. Remember that David rode a donkey whereas Solomon rode horses, and that signals a very significant shift in the kingdom. It is a shift that is especially interesting here in Kentucky. I remember back in the late 1980s, when the Arab kingdoms were beginning to have a great deal of disposable oil money, that an Arab sheik bought a horse that had never run a race for $8.4 million. The next year one was bought for $10.2 million. And the year after that $12.5 million was paid for one—and none of these had ever run a step in a race. So at that time I asked what the going price on donkeys was in Lexington, and I found out you could get a good donkey for between forty and sixty-five dollars. Now when you read the Psalms and it says do not trust in horses, remember that the horse was the F-16 of that day. It was the military power. But David rode a donkey. G. Campbell Morgan said they had royal donkeys in that day. I don't believe that for a minute. No Egyptian pharaoh rode a donkey. No Roman emperor rode a donkey. No Roman general rode a donkey through Jerusalem. They rode horses, and under Solomon, Israel had become a horse kingdom.

How did that come about? According to 1 Kings 3:

> Solomon made an alliance with Pharaoh king of Egypt
> and married his daughter [so he could get some F-16 jets].
> He brought her to the City of David until he finished
> building his palace and the temple of the Lord, and the
> wall around Jerusalem. The people, however, were still
> sacrificing at the high places, because the temple had
> not yet been built for the Name of [Yahweh]. Solomon
> showed his love for the Lord by walking according to
> the statutes of his father David, except that he offered
> sacrifices and burned incense on the high places.

Now, turn with me to chapter 11 of 1 Kings. Again, we are
speaking about Solomon. "King Solomon, however, loved many foreign
women besides Pharaoh's daughter—Moabites, Ammonites, Edomites,
Sidonians and Hittites" (11:1). Any time Solomon wanted to be sure a
neighboring country would not make war on him he would bring one
of the daughters of the king of that country home as one of his wives,
and that was the way he made his political alignments. "They were from
nations about which the Lord had told the Israelites, 'You must not in-
termarry with them, because they will surely turn your heart after their
gods.' Nevertheless, Solomon held fast to them in love. He had seven
hundred wives of royal birth." You would almost think he would have
run out of kings to make contracts with.

> He had seven hundred wives of royal birth and three
> hundred concubines and his wives led him astray. As
> Solomon grew old, his wives turned his heart after oth-
> er gods, and his heart was not fully devoted to [Yahweh]
> his God, as the heart of David his father had been.
> He followed Ashtoreth, the goddess of the Sidonians,
> [who was worshipped on the high places. He followed]
> Molech the detestable god of the Ammonites. So Solo-
> mon did evil in the sight of the Lord; he did not follow
> [Yahweh] completely, as David his father had done. On

a hill, east of Jerusalem, Solomon built a high place [on a hilltop] for Chemosh the detestable god of Moab, and for Molech the detestable god of the Ammonites. He did the same for all his foreign wives, who burned incense and offered sacrifices to their gods (11:3-8).

Look down toward the end of that chapter at verses 29-33.

About that time Jeroboam [one of Solomon's officials] was going out of Jerusalem, and Ahijah the prophet of Shiloh met him on the way, wearing a new cloak. The two of them were alone out in the country, and Ahijah took hold of the new cloak he was wearing and tore it into twelve pieces. Then he said to Jeroboam, "Take ten pieces for yourself, for this is what [Yahweh], the God of Israel, says: 'See, I am going to tear the kingdom out of Solomon's hand and give you ten tribes. But for the sake of my servant David and the city of Jerusalem, which I have chosen out of all the tribes of Israel, he will have one tribe. I will do this because they have forsaken me and worshipped Ashtoreth the goddess of the Sidonians, Chemosh the god of the Moabites, and Molech the god of the Ammonites, and have not walked in my ways, nor done what is right in my eyes, nor kept my statutes and laws as David, Solomon's father, did. But I will not take the whole kingdom out of Solomon's hand.'"

Now, turn with me to the next chapter, chapter 12. Solomon has died and his son Rehoboam has succeeded him, and the prophecy to Jeroboam has been fulfilled. The ten northern tribes have revolted, and Jeroboam is trying to get his new kingdom established. Jeroboam has fortified Shechem in the hill country of Ephraim and is living there. He makes two golden calves and sets them up in Bethel and in Dan, so as to keep the people from going to Jerusalem and perhaps turning back to Rehoboam (12:26-27). Now, look at verse 31:

Jeroboam built shrines on high places and appointed priests from all sorts of people, even though they were not Levites. He instituted a festival on the fifteenth day of the eighth month, like the festival held in Judah [the fall festival] and offered sacrifices on the altar. This he did in Bethel, sacrificing to the calves he had made. And at Bethel he also installed priests at the high places he had made. On the fifteenth day of the eighth month, a month of his own choosing, he offered sacrifices on the altar he had built at Bethel. So he instituted the festival for the Israelites and went up to the altar to make offerings (12:31-33).

So at the very outset of the northern kingdom's existence there was paganism and syncretism. As a result, the worship of the true God was always in conflict throughout that kingdom's entire history. One of the flashpoints of the conflict is found in 1 Kings 18. This is, of course, the story of Elijah. I love the way the story of Elijah is told. His story begins at the end of chapter 16. "In Ahab's time, Hiel of Bethel rebuilt Jericho. He laid its foundations at the cost of his firstborn son Abiram. . . ." Now, what does that mean? He buried his son in the foundation of the city so he could have the blessing of his god. That was Canaanite religion. That is the kind of religion that was practiced on the hilltops. The son's name was Abiram, which means "my father is the exalted one—the high one." And undoubtedly, that name is talking about Hiel's god. He looked upon his god as the exalted father, and so he gives to his heavenly father his son, his own son, his fleshly son, in the foundation of the city. The verse continues: ". . . and he set up its gates at the cost of his youngest son Segub, in accordance with the word of the Lord spoken by Joshua son of Nun." That is a reference to Joshua 6:26, where Joshua predicted that anyone who rebuilt that pagan city would do so in a pagan way. But then comes 17:1: "Now Elijah the Tishbite, from Tishbe in Gilead, said to [the king], 'As [Yahweh], the God of Israel, lives, whom I serve, there will be neither dew nor rain for the next few years except at my word.'" There is not a word of explanation about Elijah's background, or who he is. I love it. We are given an example of the dreadful condition in which the country stood, but nothing about the prophet. He just showed up and said, "I have a word from Yahweh." Why? Because it does not matter about Elijah; just as it does not matter about you and me. That is a magnificent model for a preacher. The important thing is the word of God, which he or she carries. And if he or she does not have such a word, nothing else counts.

Now, in chapter 18 we get Elijah talking to the king. He obviously had access to Ahab because there hadn't been any rain. It is interesting who you will talk to if you think the other guy can finally help you, even your enemy, so Ahab is willing to talk to Elijah. Ahab had been looking for Elijah and finally had sent out Obadiah, one of his high officials. Obadiah found him, and verse 16 picks up the account:

> So Obadiah went to meet Ahab and told him, and Ahab
> went to meet Elijah. When he saw Elijah, he said to him,
> "Is that you, you troubler of Israel?" "I have not made
> trouble for Israel," Elijah replied. "But you and your
> father's family have. You have abandoned the Lord's
> commands and have followed the Baals. Now summon
> the people from all over Israel to meet me on Mount
> Carmel. And bring the four hundred and fifty prophets
> of Baal and the four hundred prophets of Asherah
> [goddess of love, fecundity], who eat at Jezebel's table."
> So Ahab sent word throughout all Israel and assembled
> the prophets on Mount Carmel. Elijah went before the
> people and said, "How long will you waver between two
> opinions? If the Lord is God, follow him; but if Baal is
> God, follow him" (18:16-21).

Now, do not miss the significance of what Elijah said. He put the choice in terms of either/or as opposed to both/and. The Baal prophets did not object to a little Yahweh worship going on the side; they would be in favor of that. But the one prophet of Yahweh left says, "You've got to go one way or the other, Ahab. You can't have both Yahweh and Baal because the Baals are not gods. There is only one God. So you must choose one or the other."

And here is where Israel is always in conflict with its context.

But the people said nothing. Then Elijah said to them, "I am the only one of the Lord's prophets left, but Baal has four hundred and fifty prophets. Get two bulls for us. Let them choose one for themselves, and let them cut it into pieces and put it on the wood but not set fire to it. I will prepare the other bull and put it on the wood but not set fire to it. Then you call on the name of your god, and I will call on the name of [Yahweh]. The god who answers by fire—he is God." Then all the people said, "What you say is good" (18:21b-24).

Why did the people think this was a good idea? It is because Baal was supposed to be the god of the thunderstorm. So he was the lightning god, the one who controlled the lightning. So Elijah was saying, "Let's play it on your court. We will do it according to your god's strength. The one that answers by fire—let him be God."

Elijah said to the prophets of Baal, "Choose one of the bulls and prepare it first, since there are so many of you. Call on the name of your god, but do not light the fire." So they took the bull given them and prepared it. Then they called on the name of Baal from morning till noon. "O Baal, answer us!" they shouted. But . . . no one answered. And they danced around the altar they had made. At noon Elijah began to taunt them. "Shout louder!" he said, "Surely he is a god! Perhaps he is deep in thought, or busy, or traveling. Maybe he is sleeping and must be awakened." So, they shouted louder and slashed themselves with swords and spears, as was their custom, until their blood flowed.[12] Midday passed, and they continued their frantic prophesying until the time

---

[12] [Editor's note] Mutilation is never a part of the worship of Yahweh, because the body as well as the spirit is made in the image of Yahweh. There is a sanctity to the physical body all through the Old Testament, because the body is the gift of God. But they felt that if they cut themselves, as if in mourning, that would let Baal know how precious he was to them. It is also probable that this reflects some of the harvest ritual when it was felt that god had died and might not return in the spring unless he felt the people were really grieved over his death.

for the evening sacrifice. But there was no response, no one answered, . . . no one paid attention.

Then Elijah said, . . . "Come here to me." They came to him, and he repaired the altar of the LORD, which was in ruins. He took twelve stones, one for each of the tribes descended from Jacob. . . .[13] With the stones he built an altar in the name of [Yahweh], and he dug a trench around it large enough to hold two seahs of seed. He arranged the wood, cut the bull into pieces and laid it on the wood. Then he said to them, "Fill four large jars with water and pour it on the offering and on the wood."

"Do it again," he said, and they did it again.

"Do it a third time," he ordered, and [a third time they doused the offering]. The water ran down around the altar and even filled the trench.

At the time of sacrifice, the prophet Elijah stepped forward and prayed: "O [Yahweh], God of Abraham, Isaac and Israel,[14] let it be known today that you are God in Israel and that I am your servant and have done all these things at your command. Answer me, O [Yahweh], answer me, so these people will know that you, [Yahweh], are God, and that you are turning their hearts back again."[15]

Then the fire of [Yahweh] fell and burned up the sacrifice, the wood, the stones and the soil, and also licked up the water in the trench.

When all the people saw this, they fell prostrate

---

[13] Notice the emphasis on Israel's identity. Elijah is not an individual here standing before God. He is a prophet representing the elect people. He is a prophet representing the body of Christ, as it were, the New Testament counterpart to Israel. And so, he took twelve stones to represent the twelve tribes of Israel.

[14] The worship of Yahweh is always in a historical context. The emphasis on tradition found in Eastern Orthodoxy has some of its basis here in the Bible. Yahweh is the God of human-historical time.

[15] Notice that he did not say, "Let it be known that you are Yahweh." The big question here is whether Yahweh is God or not. And he is saying, "Yes, he is, and there is no other God."

and cried, "[Yahweh]—he is God! [Yahweh]—he is God!" (18:25-39).

But did you notice the taunting that he did? When they did not get a response he said, "Maybe he's thinking. Maybe he's busy,[16] or on a journey, or maybe he's sleeping." Now, there we get back to Psalm 121.

I lift my eyes to the hills—where does my help come from? My help comes from [Yahweh], the Maker of heaven and earth. He will not let your foot slip—he who watches over you will not slumber nor sleep.

Do you suppose the person who wrote this was on Mt. Carmel that day? But whether he was or not, he understood what Elijah did, that there is a categorical distinction between Yahweh and all other gods. The gods of all the ancient pantheons were simply projections of you and me. We sleep, so they sleep. When the light of revelation goes out, there is nowhere to go but to nature. Now, I am using the word "nature" in the broadest sense to mean things of this world. If there is no revelation from beyond this world, then in our sinful darkness we are going to say that reality must look like this world. And that is what the worship of the Baals was; it was the worship of the forces of nature.

In my graduate work I had to read some Babylonian. The script in which both Babylonian and Assyrian are written is what is called "syllabic." That is, a written sign stands not for a single sound, but for a combination of sounds, a syllable. So there is a sign for "ba" and another one for "bu" and another one for "ab" and so forth. You can imagine that gets pretty complicated. There are more than 800 signs needed to write those languages. And over the course of history a given sign came to have several possible meanings. So to help out the reader a bit they used signs called determinatives to tell you what kind of a word it was that was coming up. For instance, maybe the word coming up was the name of a certain type of tree. So, at the beginning of the word is the sign,

---

[16] [Editor's note] The Hebrew of this phrase is *sig lo*, which is literally ". . . there is a moving back to him." It has been very plausibly suggested that this is actually a reference to moving the bowels. That would make the taunt all the more trenchant.

the determinative, for tree. If it is a human being and if it is a female, there would be a sign to let you know that a female thing is coming up. You learn to give thanks for determinatives. The determinative for god appears before all those natural forces that were considered divine. So, if you came across the Babylonian word for the sun, *shamash*, it would be preceded by the god determinative. The same is true for the word for earth, and so forth.

As I was reading Psalm 121 one day, it dawned on me that if this psalm were written in ancient Babylonian, there are four places where the god determinative would appear. "My help comes from [Yahweh]— the Maker of. . . ." And in front of "heaven" you would have a divine determinative because the heaven was a god, and in front of the earth you would have a divine determinative because the earth was a goddess, normally. A little later on where he says, "The sun will not harm you by day, nor the moon by night" there they would be another determinative because the sun was a personal deity and the moon was normally his female consort.

This puts what the psalmist is saying in an even clearer light, does it not? "I will lift up my eyes to the hills—where do I go for help? Do I go where my neighbors go as they worship the sun and the moon and the heavens and the earth? Or do I go to the One who made my neighbor's gods?" Like Elijah, that is not going to make you very popular in a syncretistic, or should I say, inclusive, society, is it? But that is exactly what you have in this beautiful little sentimental psalm about the hill.

The psalmist goes on to say, "He will not let your foot slip." That is a recurring Old Testament theme. Be on the lookout for it. Yahweh will give you a place to stand that will not change with the passing of time. Did you know that the original root of the word *truth* is the ancient Indo-European word for "tree"? Now, how do a tree and truth relate to each other? If it is true, it will be there tomorrow morning when you get up. If it is true, it is not going to collapse on you in the first wind of adversity. If you are a man of truth, you will stand. And if a movement is a movement of truth, it will stand. So, he is saying your foot will not slip. Yahweh is not merely a projection of this changing world onto the heavens. He stands outside of this world, and he will not let you slip; He will take care of you on that.

He who watches over you is not like Baal, who needs to sleep.

He neither slumbers nor sleeps. Yahweh will be your protection from the forces that your neighbors try to propitiate. "The sun will not harm you by day, nor the moon by night. [Yahweh] will keep you from all harm—he will watch over your life. He will watch over your coming and your going," when you go out and when you come in. He will be there to take care of you.

In the fifth chapter of Amos, the prophet describes a man having a really bad day. He is walking down the mountain path, and in front of him he sees a lion. So he turns around to run, and there stands a bear right behind him. But he sidesteps the bear and runs into his house. But when he slams the door behind him and leans against the wall in relief a snake sticks its head out of a crack in the wall and bites him. That was Amos' way of saying that you cannot escape God. It does not matter whether you are outside or in. It doesn't matter where you are. He is the omnipresent One and the omniscient One and you can't get away from Him. Now, if you are under God's judgment, as the Israelites of Amos' day were, that is a terribly frightening word. On the other hand, if you are living in His grace and doing His will, there is nothing in this world, either outside or in, that can harm you ultimately. He will take care of you, both now and forevermore.

That word translated "forevermore" is interesting. The Hebrew *wᵉad ʿolam* is literally translated "and unto an age." Are you aware that in the English language we do not have any words for eternity? Because, you see, the word *eternity* only means something that does not have an end. Is that all there is to eternity? Is it just endless time or is it a different dimension of time? In Greek, you know, the way you say eternity is you put an "s" on "age." But if you get "ages," is that eternity? Is there no qualitative distinction between eternity and time? Of course there is, because God lived in eternity before there was time. And do not tell me there was no qualitative difference between time when He created it and what it was for eternity. But we do not have language to express what that difference is because it is not a part of our experience, and our language limits our ability to talk about this. So in Hebrew, there is one expression where he says, instead of "forevermore," the Hebrew will be "for an age and unto" *mēʿolam wᵉad*, and there is no object to the preposition "unto." It is open-ended. How long is He going to take care of me? For an age and unto. It is really not until we get into the New Testament that we learn what the object of that "unto" is. We have to have 1 Corinthians 15, and John 14, and the book of Revelation before we begin to learn what the object of that preposition is, what it is that lies beyond death. But in the Old Testament the writers are beginning to say it. "I don't know about all that eternity stuff, but I know about Yahweh, and He will take care of my going out, and He will take care of my coming in. . . ." Then it takes the rest of the biblical story to begin to flesh out just how far that faith really reaches.

Let me go back for a minute to what sets the stage for the psalm. "I lift up mine eyes unto the hills—where does my help come from?" He's looking for help. Now, where will he go for help? We said he goes to the one who made the "helps" to whom other people turn. And we said that the pantheons of the Ancient Near East, like all the religions of the world except where biblical truth has come in, are natural forces. If someone says that a mythological religion is about supernatural beings, that is a contradiction in terms, because the one thing that is never found in a myth is a being that transcends the creation. Let me illustrate. The psalmist speaks of the heavens and the earth. Whether you go to Rome, Greece, the Hittite territory (Turkey), Canaan, Babylon, Assyria, or Egypt, the earth is a god and the sky is a god. But interestingly, in every one of those places—Greece or Rome or the Hittite world, or Babylon or Assyria or Canaan—the sky is masculine and the earth is feminine, whereas in Egypt the sky is feminine and the earth is masculine. I remember that intrigued me because one of the most beautiful and impressive pieces of ancient Egyptian art is a painting of the sky goddess Nut. She is arched over the earth with her fingertips at one horizon and her toes at the other. What separates her from the earth, from father Geb, is the god Shu, who is the god of the atmosphere, standing between us and the heavens.

Now why the gender reversal? The reason is very simple: It never rains in Egypt and it is the male that inseminates the female. What you have for moisture in Egypt is the Nile, and so the earth must be the masculine. You can take that principle and go through all of the pantheons of the ancient Near East and you will find that the gods are nothing more than a reflection of the regional particularities of the natural world that Yahweh created. Not one of them is *super*-natural. So in Greece you have these original ancient deities before Zeus. You have

Uranus, the heavens. You have Kronos, time. You have Gaia, the earth, Arabis, evening, Humeri, day, Eros, passion. Then you have Zeus, who is the sky, the atmosphere, the wind, the cloud, the rain, the thunder, the lightning, the Greek Baal. Now let me ask you, is Uranus supernatural? Is Kronos? There is not a deity in a single one of these pantheons that transcends the biblical creation.

So how much technical philosophy or theology did the writer of this little psalm know? I have no idea. But I do know this, there is an incredible philosophy and an incredible theology implicit in its fundamental conviction that there is a God who transcends the creation. What difference does that make? Let me illustrate it. When I think about Tom Oden and his conversion in our day, in my mind I go back to another remarkable conversion in the earlier half of the twentieth century. It happened between 1927 and 1930. Again, it was a Methodist theologian who was shut up with the Scripture because he was one of the commentators on the *Abingdon Bible*, a Bible commentary. For about three years, Edwin Lewis was locked up with the biblical text, and when he came out of that he was never the same again. I met Lewis when I was part of a group of young preachers the Methodist church pulled together to promote evangelism. There were about three hundred of us who met in Iowa, and he was one of the lecturers. It is one of those moments I will never forget. He stood up and said, "Now, I can divide you right down the middle on one question. Your answer to that question will tell me whether you have a gospel to preach or not, and that question is this: Was Jesus the son of Mary who became the Son of God? Or was He the eternal Son of God who became the son of Mary? And if you go with the first, you have no gospel because there is nothing saving that is in us. Salvation is in God and in God alone. So if Jesus emerged out of us, He can do nothing more for us than we can do for ourselves. But if He came to us out of the nature of the eternal Deity, then He can do for us what only God can do."

It may surprise you, but the Old Testament is the best means for getting that truth nailed down firmly in our hearts and minds. And where you come out on that will determine everything. Today we turn everywhere except to the Word of God. But the Word of God is the only thing that ever created anything. We live in a day when we turn to the social sciences. We live in a day where we turn to the political processes.

We live in a day where we turn to the best of the resources we have, and with every one of them we fall flat on our faces again and again.

A Christian psychiatrist who had been a missionary in Africa said to a friend of mine, "I want put on my tombstone, 'Nobody ever changes.'" There is no help from within us; there is no help from within the creation. This is not to denigrate this great creation. You will find no higher view of creation anywhere in the literature of the world than you will find in the Bible, but the solution to our problems is not from it or us.

"I lift up mine eyes unto the hills. . . ."

Lecture 4

. . . .

Intimacy with the Living God Psalm 16

I have recommended Walter Eichrodt's *Theology of the Old Testament* for your reading, and I want to give you some background on him to help you. In my opinion he is the greatest Old Testament theologian in the twentieth century. So it will repay you to immerse yourself in his work so that you begin to think the way he thinks. But one of the problems you will encounter is his higher critical presuppositions. This means that he will date certain passages according to that system, and that dating may be a surprise to you. But because the so-called "Documentary Hypothesis" dominated the understanding of the development of the Old Testament for so many years, you must be prepared for it. If you are going to be in the ministry, you are going to have to live with this situation for the rest of your life as it relates to most of the books and commentaries on the Old Testament that you will buy and put on your shelves. So, do not be surprised when you encounter some of this in Eichrodt. Fortunately, his theological insights normally triumph over his critical presuppositions. On the positive side, facing these matters here will prepare you to deal with them when you encounter them in other sources later in your life.

In a previous lecture we dealt with Psalm 146, and my purpose there was to take you behind the language of titles to the fact that the Old Testament is dealing with a personal encounter with the living God. Behind the term "Lord" there is a personal name, and this shows us that what you have in the Old Testament comes out of that personal encounter where the living God becomes a person, another, an inescapable reality in a person's life, changing that life forever.

We dealt also with Psalm 121. My purpose in that study was to let you get a glimpse of the contrast between the way the Old Testament looks at the world and the way Israel's neighbors looked at it. To be sure, there are similarities between Israel's religion and the religions of her neighbors. On the lowest level it is because both are religions, and there are some fundamental characteristics of religious behavior and thought that are the same everywhere. There are also some elements of the shared broader culture. But once we get beyond these and penetrate to the respective hearts of the two systems, we find radical differences. It is no accident that it is at the point of the differences that we find the redemptive element in the Israelite faith. Yahweh is the ultimate while all the rest of the world deals with relatives. That is the unique claim of the Old Testament about Yahweh.

Today I want to turn to Psalm 16, which is one that has become more and more precious to me as the years have passed. If I were to pick out any passage in the Old Testament as an indication of what is the best of Old Testament piety, I would take this psalm. It is written by a man who never read the New Testament, never heard the Sermon on the Mount, who knew nothing about Pentecost. Yet, if you read the psalm carefully, you will find that those of us who are on this side of Christ, on this side of Pentecost, on this side of the New Testament canon, will be able to add very little to its understanding of what the ideal relationship to the Lord ought to be.

Psalm 16 is a personal psalm. It is interesting that the writer begins with his conclusion: "Keep me safe, O God, for in you I take refuge." It is where he begins, but that is really the final word that he has to say. He is speaking to God, and he says, "I need you to keep me, for if you do not, I will not be what I am supposed to be. I will not be what you want me to be. I will not be what I know deep within my own spirit I ought to be, so keep me. My relationship to you is one of refuge; I hide in You." That is a foundational concept—that Yahweh is our Hiding Place, our Rock, our Fortress, our Strong Tower—and those titles for him recur throughout the Old Testament.

Now, having given us his conclusion, the psalmist begins to tell us about his experiences. He says, "I said to [Yahweh] . . ." Who is Yahweh? He is the God to whom he has just said, "I want you to keep me." Now he says, "I said to Yahweh, 'You are my Lord.'"[17, 18] In effect he says, "I am making a separation. I have decided that You (and not someone else) are to be my Lord." That is a perfectly good New Testament concept. We remember what the apostle Paul said was the key to salvation: "If you confess with your mouth, 'Jesus Christ is Lord'. . . you shall be saved" (Rom. 10:9). Furthermore, Paul said, no one can say that Jesus is Lord except by the power and aid of the Holy Spirit (1 Cor. 12:3). Here in the Old Testament the psalmist is making that affirmation about Yahweh, "You are my Lord."

The next line is very interesting. Literally, what he is saying is,

---

[17] The term *Lord* (the Hebrew word *adonai*) occurs 449 times in the Old Testament. It occurs 134 times as a separate term, as it does here. But 315 times it appears with the word *Yahweh* as a title (thus, "the Lord Yahweh"). In Genesis to 2 Kings, the combination occurs only twenty-one times, but it occurs 320 times in the prophets. Obviously, it is a particularly prophetic concept. It occurs 217 times in Ezekiel alone. It occurs about fifty-five times in the book of Psalms. But perhaps most amazing is the fact that in the five chapters of Lamentations, "the Lord Yahweh" occurs fourteen times. So, it occurs two-thirds as many times in that little book as it does from Genesis to the end of 2 Kings. Perhaps the reason for this frequency is that Lamentations was dealing with the destruction of the city of Jerusalem and everybody was saying, "Where is He? Is He still in control, or are the Babylonian gods the ones in control now?" So perhaps the writer is emphasizing the truth that Yahweh is still "the Lord."

[18] The present Hebrew text has "You said" (so *KJV*). But since the consonantal text could have been either "you" or "I," and since all the ancient versions are in agreement that it is "I," we should probably conclude that an error was made when the vowels were put in sometime after 500 A.D. and that the original was "I said" (so *NIV* and most others).

"Besides You, no good." That is a very significant theological statement in the Old Testament. He is saying, "Apart from You, O Yahweh, nothing is good." Fundamental to this statement is the understanding that Yahweh made everything that is made, and if it is there, he made it. Furthermore, everything he made is good. This point is emphasized in Genesis 1; when Yahweh had finished the creation of all things, He looked at all that He had made and said, "It is good, very good,"(*tob me'od*). So, if there should be anything apart from Yahweh and His purposes, it is not good.

But the psalmist is saying that it is possible there are some good things in this world that Yahweh created that are not good. That is, they are not good for me. Why is this so? Because it is possible to use something out of God's will. What the text is implying is that evil is simply good misused. So the psalmist says, "I have come to the place where I will let You decide what is good for me." Evil is simply good in the wrong place or at the wrong time. It is not an eternal entity independent of the good gods as it is in most of the religions of the Ancient Near East. Even the snake of Genesis 3, which many interpreters equate with Satan, the accuser, in Job is nothing more than a creature of God. Yahweh created everything that exists, so if you find something or someone acting contrary to God's will, it is not because there is an independent evil force over against the creator God and in eternal conflict with Him. In the Old Testament, if something exists, no matter whether it is good or evil, God made it. But the reality is that evil is something that was originally good.

You can apply this truth in many ways. It is an old adage in the study of anthropology that two people doing the same thing may not be doing the same thing. One may be carrying out the most sacred expression of love, while the other may be performing a brutal rape. So the psalmist is here saying, "I have learned that even if it is good in itself, if it is not part of Your will for me, then it isn't good for me. It was good when it came from Your hand, but if it is not a part of Your will for me, then it is not good for me. And I will let You make a decision on that."

In my opinion this is as fine a statement of the nature of entire sanctification, or perfect love, or Christian perfection, or holiness of heart, or whatever else you may call the fulfillment of Christian experience, as can be found anywhere in the Scripture. What I love is that it is found here in the Old Testament, in what is perhaps a very early psalm.

"I have come to the place where I know that good isn't good unless it is Your will for me."

Anyone who has been a Christian very long has faced a crisis in his or her life when having to decide between goods. It may have been whether to study law or go into the ministry, or whether it was the blond or the brunette, or which church to serve in, or which phase of Christian ministry, or whether it was to be in this country or overseas. Again and again, the key for you and me is whether we let Yahweh make the choice on good. If the difference between the unregenerate person's life and the Spirit-filled person's life is what they are going to do about sins, the question of a holy heart is what we are going to do about goods. So here in this psalm, written centuries ago, the author is pointing right at the heart of the most crucial problem in any of our lives: Will Yahweh be Lord, and will He decide what I choose to be good?

Then the psalmist says, "Having made that decision, I find there are two groups of people in the world, and there are only two." There is a line between those two and most of us try to straddle that line, but that is not the case for the psalmist. He says, in essence, I see now that there are two groups of people in the world. As for the saints, the holy ones who are in the earth, in the land, they are the glorious ones in whom is all my delight. But the sorrows of those who run after another will increase. I will not pour out their libations of blood nor take up their names on my lips.

Notice how he differentiates the two groups. The first group is the *q'doshim*, the holy ones. This is an unusual expression, and I will comment on it below. In the second group are those who "hasten after another," *'aher*. All of our translations say, "The sorrows will increase of those who run after other gods," but the term "gods" is not found in the Hebrew. The Hebrew simply says, "run after another." To be sure, the next part of the verse makes it very clear that the writer is ultimately addressing the question of idolatry. But I am grateful the text here does not specify other "gods." Your sorrows will increase if you run after *anything* that is out of the will of God. It does not matter whether it is a blond or a brunette, or whether it is a place of ministry in this country or overseas, or whether it is the type of ministry, or whatever it is. Sorrows will increase for those who run after anything other than the will of Yahweh and His sovereign purposes and His sovereign control.

He says, "I will not be a part of those that make their sacrifices to anything other than to Yahweh, that pour out their lives [their blood] for anything other than Yahweh, or that take up their names." As you know, a person's language reveals a great deal about that person. If you let me listen to you long enough, I can tell what is in your heart. So, the psalmist says, the very nouns I use, or don't use, will tell you what my commitments are. My language will reflect the fact that I have set Yahweh always before my face. He is the one whom I seek, and He is the one whom I want to serve.

So the second group of people in the world are those whose motivation is divided, whose motivation is not single. Sören Kierkegaard, the Danish philosopher-theologian, said that purity of heart is to will one thing. That describes the psalmist's heart when he says at the opening of this psalm, "I said to [Yahweh], You are my lord." But it is not so for this second group of people.

Now what about that first group? Our poet says, "As for the saints who are in the earth, they are the glorious ones in whom is all my delight." At this point, with the reference to "saints," or "holy ones," let me introduce the concept of "the holy" in the Old Testament. The way in which this concept is developed there is very fascinating. In the Semitic languages the basic meaning of any term is conveyed by its consonants. Typically, there are three consonants for a concept. Grammarians have called this cluster of consonants the "root" of words relating to that concept. In this case, the "root" is *q-d-sh*. Words based on this root only appear in two places in Genesis. The first is in 2:3 where we are told that God made the seventh day of Creation holy. But it is the other group of occurrences that I want to call attention to here. They all appear in chapter 38 in reference to Judah's daughter-in-law, Tamar. Three times she is referred to as a "holy woman," a *q'desha*.

The context in which these references occur is a very interesting one. Judah, one of Jacob's sons, head of the tribe from which Christ came, had found himself in a dilemma. He had married his eldest son, Ur, to a Canaanite woman named Tamar. But Ur died before Tamar had borne him any children. In that culture a woman had a duty to bear children to carry on the name of her husband, so it was required that her husband's brother marry her and allow her to bear children who would carry the dead brother's name. So Judah commanded that Ur's brother

Onan carry out this duty. Onan did not want to publicly disobey his father, but neither did he want to father a child for his dead brother. So, attempting to fulfill both desires, he took Tamar and had intercourse with her but withdrew himself from Tamar's body just prior to ejaculation. Unfortunately for Onan, while you may be able to deceive your father, you cannot deceive God, and the Bible says that God took Onan's life.

So Judah promised that he would give Tamar his third son in marriage when the boy, who was still a child, came of age. However, he was actually trying to buy time because he feared that he would lose yet a third son because of this woman. So that is the situation: The third son Shelah is grown, but Judah has reneged on his promise. What is to be done? Tamar learns that Judah is going to a certain place to shear sheep, and she reasons that he might like to take advantage of the services of a q'desha, a cult prostitute, a holy woman, to ensure that all would go well in the important activity of shearing. Her intuition was correct, for when she dressed in the typical garb of a cult prostitute and set up shop beside the road on which Judah was traveling, he did indeed stop and have sex with her. He promised to send her a kid from the flocks where he was going, but she asked for some security and he gave her his identification, his personal seal and his staff. At this point she changed clothes and the "holy woman" was nowhere to be found when Judah later sent a friend to pay his debt and reclaim his deposit.

Three months later Tamar was obviously pregnant and, since she was unmarried, was evidently guilty of prostitution. But when she was about to be stoned in front of Judah, the head of the clan, she produced the seal and staff and asked if he recognized them. Judah admitted what he had done and vindicated Tamar who finally had a child to rear in the name of her dead husband.

So Tamar was the first person who is called holy in the Scripture. That is a good clue as to what q-d-sh meant in Canaanite. It had to do with the temple, it had to do with the gods, it was a religious term and it had to do with the worship of the gods of Canaan and their ways of living. Cult prostitutes were a common part of that, and their titles reflected that fact—a male was called a qadesh and a female was called a q'desha. This was part of the temple practice, as it still is today in many parts of the world.

But now let us move to Isaiah chapter six. There Isaiah finds himself in the immediate presence of Yahweh. The awe and the mystery of that presence is conveyed by the smoke and the fire and the shaking of the doorposts—and he hears the heavenly creatures singing, "*qadosh, qadosh, qadosh* is the Lord of Hosts. The whole earth is full of his glory." Isaiah's reaction is immediate and devastating; he cries out, "Woe is me! for I am undone; because I am a man of unclean lips, and I dwell in the midst of a people of unclean lips: for mine eyes have seen the King, the LORD of hosts" (6:5 *KJV*). He had seen the Holy One, the only Person in the universe who could legitimately be called that.

It is a long journey, intellectually, between Genesis 38 and Isaiah 6. Something of the nature of that journey can be seen in the Greek translation of the Old Testament called the *Septuagint*. In 200 B.C. the Jews found themselves living in a world that was influenced heavily, if not actually controlled by, the Greek world. Every educated person spoke Greek, and if you were going to move through that world you had to become reasonably fluent in that language. Jews who were scattered across the Mediterranean world often found their children more familiar with Greek than they were with Hebrew. So the Jews began to say, "If we can't translate the Old Testament into Greek, we are going to lose our children." It was out of that concern that the work was begun in Alexandria, Egypt, one of the intellectual centers of the Mediterranean world.

The term *Septuagint* means "Seventy" and is derived from the legend that seventy translators worked on the project in isolation from one another and came up with translations that were word for word the same. We don't have to accept the truth of that legend to recognize that the *Septuagint* is a magnificent work. While it is valuable for the evidence it gives us on the history of the development of the text of the Old Testament, it is even more valuable as our first commentary on the Old Testament. This is so because, by their choices of Greek words, the translators are telling us what they understand the Hebrew to mean. Let me illustrate that with the way they translated words in the *q-d-sh* family.

When the translators came to choose Greek equivalents for words in the *q-d-sh* family, they had several possibilities. One of the terms they might have used was *hieros*. We get the English word *hieratic* from it, and that has to do with priestly functions, with temple activities with the cult; it is primarily a cultic term. Another possibility was *semnos*. It was a word that had to do with the gods and was used in connection with them. Besides these there were at least two other possibilities, including that which has to do with the pure.

But the translators did not choose any of these terms to translate the majority of words in the *q-d-sh* family. The term they did choose, *hagios*, is rather surprising, for it is almost unknown in classical Greek. There is a debate about whether it appears once in the writings of the dramatist Aeschylus; if it does not appear there then it never appears in the tragic poets of classical Greece. Neither Homer nor Virgil used it. But it does occur a few times in scattered places, so it was available for the translators of the *Septuagint* to use if they chose to. So, why did they choose to? I believe, and I am not alone in believing it, that they chose *hagios* because it had the fewest negative connotations that came with the pagan concept of the holy. In order to convey what they knew to be true of Yahweh, they very carefully chose a word that was almost unknown.

So when they talked about the temple and referred to the Holy of Holies, they never spoke the way a Greek would speak using the word *hieros* to describe the temple shrine, but they called it *ton hagion ton hagion*. They were creating new words that do not occur in classical Greek to describe Yahweh and that which pertains to Him. The New Testament word for "sanctify" does not occur in classical Greek. The first place you find it is in the *Septuagint*, and from there you find it in the Greek New Testament, and in the church fathers who wrote in Greek. In all, you will find six or seven different words that were created to explain a Yahweh who could not be expressed in ordinary Greek concepts. What were the translators doing? They were saying, "We are bound to use the language of our world, and we are bound to use the language that the other religions of the world use, but the God that we describe is radically different, and we have to stretch a point, we have to move a bit, to convey adequately how different He is."

Having said all that, let me point out that apart from the technical terms *qadesh/qadesha* there are only six places in the Old Testament where *q-d-sh* is used as a noun describing a human being, in the sense of saying, "That person is a holy one." The first occurrence is in Deuteronomy 33:3, and the second is here in Psalm 16. Another is found in Psalm 34:9. Two more appear in Psalm 89 (5 and 7). The final occurrence is in Daniel 8:24.

Now, why was the noun form so rarely applied to persons? I

believe it is because the writers of the Old Testament under the Spirit's leadership were building a concept that ultimately the only Holy One is Yahweh. All holiness comes from Him. So, if it is a holy place, it is because He is there. When God said to Moses, "The place you are standing on is holy ground," it was not because it was a religious site; it was not because it was a high place; it was not because other people had worshipped there before. It was holy because Yahweh was there. He alone is the source of holiness. And if there is anything holy, it gets its identification from its relationship to Him. So, the Old Testament declines to use the noun of humans except on six occasions, this being one of them. For human beings like you and me, this is Yahweh's word. But then, along comes the *Septuagint* and translates that with *ton hagion*, "the Holy One." Do you know what you and I are described in the New Testament as? We are called *hagioi*, "the holy ones," the plural form of the noun that is used almost exclusively for Yahweh in the Old Testament.

So the apostle Paul, writing to the Roman Christians says, "To all in Rome who are loved by God and called to be *hagioi*" (Rom. 1:7). The people in Rome were called to be what is almost exclusively used in the Old Testament for Yahweh Himself. The apostle begins his first letter to the Corinthians in the same way, "To the church of God in Corinth, to those sanctified in Christ Jesus and called to be *hagioi*." If you look at 2 Corinthians, Ephesians, Philippians and keep going—to be a believer in the New Testament is to share the identity of the God of the Old Testament, that identity that the Greek translators had such trouble finding adequate language to explain.

Data like this suggests that the central reality, the central thrust about Yahweh in the Old Testament, is that He is the Holy One. This is being spelled out in those dry portions of Leviticus where at the end of some of the strange restrictions it says *'ani yahweh*, "I am Yahweh." And who is Yahweh? He is the Holy One, and it is because He is holy that He is asking us to act in these ways.

To return to our psalm, we remember that the writer is saying there are two groups of people. There are those who are the holy ones, and there are those who seek what they want, and that is the difference between the two groups. Those in the one group let Yahweh be Lord and let Him decide what is good for them, while those in the other group have their own ideas, seeking and wanting what they want. At the most basic level that is the difference between the holy and the unholy.

Now, how does this distinction play itself out in life? Look at the way in which the psalmist continues. "[Yahweh], you have assigned me my portion and my cup; you have made my lot secure. The boundary lines have fallen for me in pleasant places; surely I have a delightful inheritance." Now, pay close attention to the nouns in this section of the psalm. Four of the five primary nouns here—"portion," "lot," "boundary lines," and "inheritance"—are language found in the book of Joshua. They are Promised Land terminology. What is the primary thrust of Joshua? God is repeatedly saying to Israel, "I am going to give you a *portion*. I am going to give you a *lot*. I am going to let the *boundary lines* be drawn for your advantage and you will have a delightful *inheritance*." So, this is Canaan land language, land of promise language. It is describing in concrete ways the kind of blessing for which God redeemed His people. When the psalmist uses this same language, he is not only testifying to God's goodness, he is also saying that the receiving of God's ultimate good purposes for us is dependent on our allowing the Lord to draw the lines. Most of us do not let Him draw the lines because we think if He draws them we will get cheated in some way, but the psalmist knows better: "I let Yahweh draw the lines, and it has been good and pleasant and beautiful."

The Hebrew of the first line in verse five is very cryptic. It is translated, "Lord, you have assigned me my portion and my cup." But a more literal translation would be, "Yahweh, you are the measure of my portion, my cup." This is really a New Testament concept, it seems to me, but it is there in the Old Testament very plainly. It occurs a number of times in the Old Testament where the psalmist or the writer will say, "Yahweh, you are my portion, my measure." It will occur again and again. Here are a few of the occurrences: Psalm 73:26; 119:57; and particularly, Jeremiah 10:16, where the word *portion* is capitalized and is a title for God. He is called the "Portion of Jacob." Let us think about this for a moment. Is the person who only has God actually poorer than the person who has God plus everything? I think the psalmist is saying that if you have God, you need nothing more. You cannot possibly be any richer.

Remember what we read about the Levites and their portion. When the Hebrews were coming out of Egypt, God said, "When we get into the land of promise, we will split the land, draw the lines, divide the portions, and give each tribe an inheritance. One of the tribes, the tribe of Joseph, is going to get two portions. But that doesn't mean there will be thirteen tribal territories in Canaan; there are only going to be twelve, because the Levites will have no portion." The Lord says of the Levites, "I will be their inheritance." When the tribal allotments were given out, God commanded the Israelites to set aside certain cities in which the Levites were to live, but the tribe of Levi received no land as an inheritance. The Levites were supposed to give themselves to serve God. He was their portion.

I believe this is the point of Matthew 6:33, "But seek ye first the kingdom of God. . . ." Lord, I will let you choose what is good for me. That is really what it means to let Him be Lord, is it not? Seek first the rule of God and His righteousness, and all of these other things will be added to you because He does not want you to be thinking about what you will eat, what you will wear, or what you will possess. He wants you to think about a world that is lost and needs to be reached. This ought to be especially true of those who are in what we speak of as full-time Christian service.

Let me illustrate what I mean. I am a United Methodist clergyman, and the Methodist connection, as you know, is a very hierarchical system. When you are ordained, you start at the bottom, and then you start moving up. When you meet your colleagues at annual conference each year, you ask, "Where are you going this time?" When the person tells you, you calculate whether he moved down, sideways, or up. I was talking recently with a United Methodist clergyman. He is forty-seven years old and believes that God has called him into evangelism. He is in a very desirable church according to the system, and he is a fine pastor. He said, "I've been talking with my colleagues, the men who are in my bracket. There is not a one of them who thinks I ought to do it, because once you step out of line, if you ever want to take a church again, you start at the bottom. It does not matter whether you are fifty years old or older. It does not matter what your record is." Now, it would be interesting if you could get a Methodist preacher to move down for the kingdom's sake. But do you know one of the reasons the world has not been fully reached? It is because we have a lot of portions other than Yahweh. But do you know what? If we go down the hierarchical order and God is there, the company is better than it is if you go up that order and He is not there.

Now this is Old Testament religion, and I wish that we in the New Testament era could become good Old Testament believers. The psalmist is saying, "Yahweh, You are my portion. If You will give Yourself to me, You can take me anywhere, You can do anything You want to with me. It does not matter as long as I have You."

Now notice what else the psalmist says: "I will praise [Yahweh] who counsels me; even at night my heart instructs me. I have set the LORD always before me." He is the object. Seek first His rule. There it is. There are moments when I think if I wanted to explain to anybody what Matthew 6:33 meant, I would turn and give that person this psalm where he says, "I have set [Yahweh] always before me. Because He is at my right hand, I will not be shaken. Therefore my heart is glad and my tongue rejoices;[19] my body also will rest secure, because you will not abandon me to the grave, nor will you let your Holy One see decay."

What is the source of the psalmist's joy? It is the security that arises from the assurance that God will not abandon him to the grave. Yahweh will not let one who is in covenant[20] with him see decay. He will reveal that path which, because it leads to Him, the Source of life, is the path of life. God will fill him with joy in God's presence, with eternal pleasures at His right hand.

The word translated "presence" is literally "face" in Hebrew. "You will fill me with joy with your face." We were speaking above about how intimate we can be with Yahweh, how personal we can be with Him, and how personal He wants to be with us. That is the point here. "You will fill me with joy with your face." What are those pleasures that are in God's right hand? It is the reality of intimacy with the One who made

---

[19] The Hebrew text of this clause presents an interesting problem. Where the English has "tongue," we find the word *kabod* in the Hebrew. This is the word normally translated "glory." The English "tongue" comes from the *Septuagint*, and that certainly makes more sense than "my glory rejoices." But "liver," *kebed*, shares the same consonants as *kabod*, and scholars have suggested that *kebed* might have been the original. Since the liver was understood by the Israelites to be the seat of the emotions, there might have been a progression from heart to liver to body. For the Hebrew the body and the person were inseparable because the person was whole and was not to be divided. This is what lies behind the Incarnation and the Resurrection.

[20] *Hasid*, a concept dealt with in a later lecture.

you. And pleasure is yours forever if you will just put Him first and let Him be the Lord and let Him choose the good and the evil.

Lecture 5

* * * * * * * * * *

Old Testament Theology against the Backdrop of the Pagan Worldview

Walter Eichrodt sees Old Testament theology as the climax of all your biblical studies, or at least of your Old Testament studies. He says everything else is *prolegomenon* to that, so this course should be the capstone on your Old Testament studies in seminary.

He says there are two connections that must be made if you are to see the Old Testament belief system clearly. One of them is: You must see the prolific varieties of pagan religions that affect Israel. You must have some control of comparative religion in that ancient world; i.e., what the other religious options were for Israel or for anyone else in that period of human history. The second connection that must be made if one is to understand the Old Testament and to see the full faith that is there is an understanding of the New Testament. He says this because he believes there is a forward thrust in the Old Testament, a movement that is not brought to completion in the Old Testament. The Old Testament is an incomplete volume, finding its fulfillment in Christ and in the gospel, which comes out of the Old Testament. So a person needs to know both testaments if he or she is to understand the first one properly. Before the completion of this course of lectures we will deal with that topic more thoroughly. There is a Christian way of understanding the Old Testament and a Jewish way, and you will have to make up your own mind as to whether the Christian way is the legitimate and valid understanding of the Old Testament.

While this involves mastering a great deal of material, it involves a greater mastery than that. The most significant thing about the Old Testament is that the people of Israel thought differently from all the people around them. The world inside their head was different. They could look at the same thing an Egyptian would look at, and they saw something the Egyptian could not think of, could not conceive. And we must learn to think the way they did.

In order for us to grasp this difference in thinking, we need to recognize how much of Christianity there is in our thinking that we do not attribute to Christianity, and how much of biblical insight there is in our thinking that we never knew had any connection with the Scripture. The reality is that any good atheist today is about sixty-five percent Christian. And if you listen to him, you will find that most of his arguments for his position had their origins in biblical revelation.

Let me try to illustrate this point by reference to a book that appeared many years ago. Archbishop Fulton J. Sheen, who was a great Roman Catholic preacher and scholar, wrote a book called *Communism and the Conscience of the West.*[21] I read it in the 1940s. For a brief time during World War II we had been allies of Russia. But then the Cold War started, and it was mortal conflict. So the world was divided, with communism on one side and the West on the other. But Archbishop Sheen was saying that communism was the conscience of the West. So I read the book with great interest. Do you know where Karl Marx spent most of his life? In the British Museum. He was a part of the Western world.

---

[21] Fulton J. Sheen, *Communism and the Conscience of the West* (Indianapolis: Bobbs-Merrill Co., 1948).

And do you know where his basic concepts came from? They came from German theological seminaries. What he was proposing was Christian messianism—the idea that there can be a kingdom of God—but with God thrown out. These ideas did not come out of paganism. For if you go back to the ancient world, you will find there is no messianism of any significance there. There is not even progress. Neither is there any eschatology as we think of it in terms of Christianity, that is, of a great golden age to come. All those ideas are biblical. So here were thinkers who took that basic biblical concept of God's great kingdom to come, and said, "We don't need these religious trappings to get there." So you had Christian eschatology stripped away from its Christian roots—a kingdom where everybody would be well-fed, where we would all be brothers. Everything would be just the way it was supposed to be, all without God or without Christ. But history is often full of wonderful ironies. Do you know on what day the Soviet flag last flew? It came down on the afternoon of Christmas Day! I think Somebody was saying, "Yes, He will reign, and when you try to build a kingdom without Him, that kingdom is not going to stand."

So I am saying that here in the West even people who deny God have their thinking infused with Hebrew concepts, and the Hebrews thought differently from the people around them. Because of that Eichrodt says there are two connections that are essential if you are to see Old Testament belief clearly. The first thing you have to see clearly is the wide variety of pagan religions that had an impact upon Israel. In my graduate work, when I was trying to understand the world in which Israel grew up, there was a time when rather impatiently I wished God had put them somewhere else. Because, you see, it is not enough to know Egyptian religion. The Israelites lived in Egypt for four hundred years, but they also lived for a thousand years in Canaan in close contact with the Phoenicians and with all the other peoples in Canaan. They were just south of the Hittite world, in steady contact with the Greek and the Roman world. They were unable to escape the influence of the Assyrian and the Babylonian worlds, both of which were affected by the Sumerian world, which may have had ties to India. I realized that if a person is to have any control of biblical religion in terms of where it started and the womb in which it grew up, he or she has to have some knowledge of almost all the religions of the ancient world. Do you expect to spend the rest of your life preaching the Gospel? If you are to know the uniqueness of the Gospel, you need to know the alternatives that people follow. So you will find all the way through Eichrodt continual reference to the religions around Israel. And often the reference will be made in such an offhand way that if you are not sensitive and have not done your homework, you will miss what he is saying. Because he just simply makes a reference and assumes that you know all of that. It is because of the impact of these other religions that Harnack changed Max Muller's quotation and said, "The man who knows the religion of the Old Testament knows many religions."[22] And if we really know the Old Testament, that will be true. That is one of the reasons that many times the study of comparative religion tends to take the place of Old Testament theology. But knowing the original influences on Old Testament religion is not enough. We have to push on through to where we see the uniqueness of biblical religion.

The second thing that we must know if we are to understand Old Testament theology correctly is the New Testament and its theology. Once again, it is not enough to know the books of the New Testament and the content of the New Testament. We also must understand its implications. One of the doctrines that is implicit within the New Testament is the doctrine of the Trinity. But how long was it before the doctrine of the Trinity emerged in the early church? It was not definitively declared until three hundred fifty years after Christ when the church had lived with the New Testament and with the Old Testament long enough until Christians began to say, "Wait a minute. This thing is saying more than we thought it was saying." And it took that long for the church to begin to hear what was implicit within the biblical text. Now that always makes me wonder, how much is implicit within the biblical text that has never impinged on my mind, my consciousness, at any point. I suspect when the truth is fully revealed to us, we will find that all we ever did was live on the margins of biblical truth.

So Eichrodt says that we must understand both the pagan religions around Israel and the New Testament. On the first point he says that to study Old Testament theology properly one has to know its relationship to the world of the Ancient Near East. In the rest of this

---

[22] Eichrodt, 25. Muller's original was, "The man who knows one religion knows none."

lecture I want to pursue that point. Much of what I want to say I found first and most clearly in a volume that appeared in 1960 by a Jewish scholar by the name of Yehezkel Kaufmann. The single volume that we have in English, *The Religion of Israel*,[23] is an abridgement of no less than eight volumes in modern Israeli on the religion of Israel. Although Kaufmann is little known, there is no question in my mind that he was one of the most brilliant minds of the twentieth century, and one of the great minds in human history in terms of religion.[24] He displays an encyclopedic knowledge of religion, all the religions of the world. I have never read another writer whose knowledge is as wide and who is as incisive in his analysis. What a marvelous thing it is when you find these two things put together. And because he was not a Christian he cannot be accused of a Christian bias on the points he makes. I have never thought about the ancient world in the same way since reading him. If you intend to do further studies in Old Testament, I would urge you to read this book carefully. You will not agree with everything he says, as I do not. But there is a great deal of absolutely magnificent scholarship in it.

Kaufmann's basic thrust is this: You can take all the religions of the world and, except for three, lump them all together. The three that cannot be combined with the others are Judaism, Christianity, and Islam. Now why are they different? They are different because they all come out of the Old Testament. It is because of the religion of the Old Testament. So he says that when he uses the term "pagan religions" he simply means all the religions of the world except Christianity, Islam, and Judaism. He says this means that Hebrew religion is unique, one of a kind. All the others, he says, have a great deal in common. There may be

---

[23] Yehezkel Kaufmann, *The Religion of Israel*, tr. and abridged by M. Greenberg (Chicago: University of Chicago, 1960).

[24] Kaufmann came to Israel as an exile from Poland. He had a Ph.D. and was a scholar, but when he applied for a job in the university they rejected him. So he taught high school for the rest of his life. And while he taught at the high school level, he did this unique work on the religion of Israel. Ultimately, he was recognized for his brilliance and his great scholarship, and over time he was awarded all three of the most prestigious academic prizes in Israel. For the first two he failed to show up to receive them. That was to let the academic hierarchy know his scorn, because they never would permit him to teach in a Hebrew university in Jerusalem. So when they awarded him the third one, they called him and asked him where he was. He was in Caesarea, and they said, "Well, we want to come to Caesarea and give you this prize." He replied, "When you get here I'll be in Jerusalem."

variations in the expressions, but when you get to the heart of them they are basically the same. Now what is the common essence of all of these nonbiblical religions in the world? Kaufmann argues that the distinguishing idea behind paganism is this—that there exists a realm of being prior to the gods, above them, beyond them. Now I had read those myths before. For instance, there is the *Enuma Elish,* the Babylonian story of the origins of the world. It is a marvelous piece of literature. But when I read it, I had been told that Genesis was based on the *Enuma Elish.* So, when Genesis says, "And darkness was upon the face of the deep," the Hebrew word for deep is *tehom,* which is etymologically related to *Tiamat,* the goddess of watery chaos in the *Enuma Elish.* So we were taught to read Genesis looking for all the similarities, recognizing that these Hebrews with their "second-rate minds" had borrowed from their Babylonian forebears. What we really needed to do to understand Genesis, we were told, was to read the Babylonian creation story *Enuma Elish.*

Then I read Kaufman, and when I read the *Enuma Elish* again I saw things I had never seen when I read it the first time. That is what I mean about being sensitive to the mindset that we bring with us. Why did I not see this reality behind the gods the first time? It was because I was reading *Enuma Elish* from a biblical point of view and reading into *Enuma Elish* concepts that came to me from Scripture by way of Sunday school and vacation Bible school. Any child in a good vacation Bible school is capable of thinking thoughts that Plato could not conceive of. That is not a credit to Sunday school and vacation Bible school, but it is just the fact that we are on the other side of the biblical divide. We have that advantage, and most of us have no idea where we have gotten it from.

For instance, there is no question in my mind that modern science owes its basic existence to the unique concepts of Genesis. We simply assume a universe and a unity in that universe and a cosmic order. Science could not exist if there was a basic conflict, disunity, at the heart of the universe, as the *Enuma Elish* presupposes. We read about global positioning systems that can tell us, by way of a satellite, exactly where we are to the inch on the planet. Would that be possible if the world were simply the result of arbitrary forces continually struggling against each other for power? Now there are things like this that in our day we assume, not realizing that they have come to us through this ancient biblical text. I did some graduate study at Princeton. Nobody ever told me this.

So we have Kaufmann's statement, "There exists a realm of being prior to the gods and above them, upon which the gods depend, and whose decrees they must obey."[25] What does that mean? It means that none of the pantheons of the ancient world contained any absolute or any unconditioned element. Zeus was not an absolute. Baal was not an absolute. Baal and Zeus, Re in Egypt, were all conditioned by a world they did not control. In other words the deity, the divine world, depended for its existence on a primordial realm, a realm behind the gods. Now that primordial realm was conceived in darkness, and Genesis tells us, "and darkness was upon the face of the deep." So people read Babylonian darkness into what is simply water in the biblical text. In the beginning in the *Enuma Elish* you have the primordial fresh waters and the primordial salt waters, and they mingle together and everything came out of their sexual intercourse. And so when we read about water in Genesis we try to read into that the Babylonian story of cosmic origins. But in the *Enuma Elish* and all the other pagan stories of the origins of the cosmos, there is always that primordial realm that was looked upon as a—do not miss this word—*a womb* in which the seeds of all being were contained. And everything that came to exist came out of that womb of primordial existence. So since that primordial existence was the source for the gods; the gods were derived from it and the gods were secondary to it.

What does that mean? It means the gods are as much concerned over magical power as humans are. In the Babylonian story of cosmic origins, the one who reigned had the tablets of destiny around his neck, and they had magical power. Did you notice any reference to magic in the book of Psalms? Did you notice any appeal to witchcraft or sorcery? Yet there is no god in any of the pantheons in the Ancient Near East who was not very skilled in magic, sorcery, witchcraft, and the occult. Why is that? If you are a god, why do you need a magical amulet and the skill to use it? One of the biggest businesses in Egypt was making amulets. And if you read the religious literature of Egypt, you will find that the major-ity of it is magical texts that are an embarrassment to the Egyptologists. The same is true, although perhaps not quite to the same extent, in all the

---

[25] Kaufmann, *Religion of Israel*, 21.

other pagan cultures. Why is that? It is because there is a power behind the gods to which we must turn if we are to gain power. Notice that in magic there is no appeal to a personal god. The realm for magic, sorcery, witchcraft, and the occult is what Kaufmann calls the "metadivine," the realm beyond the gods. So he says, behind everything in the pagan understanding of reality there are two worlds, not one. There is the divine world and behind the divine world, there is the metadivine one. And the gods are as dependent on that metadivine world, the world of raw, faceless power, as we humans are. This idea is at the heart of every mythology; if you will read Greek mythology, you will find it; if you read Norse mythology, you will find it, and on and on. In every one of them you will find that the nature, the activity, and the fate of every god is determined by a force outside of themselves.

So the gods are not the source of everything, nor do the gods transcend the universe. They are rooted in and come from this prior realm, and they are bound by that prior realm, by its nature. So where does the concept come from of one sovereign, divine will that is absolute and unconditioned, yet personal, which governs everything and which is the cause of all being? I would be interested in finding anybody who can find that concept anywhere in human history and in human literature where it was not derived from the book of Genesis. Do you understand the relationship between what I have just said and the global positioning system? The universe is predictable because it does not have multiple sources, and the One who put it together is consistent with Himself, and He is not at the same time capricious and fated like the gods of Egypt or Babylon or Greece.

The dichotomy between the two realms, the divine and the metadivine, produces the marks of paganism. What are they? Two things—mythology and magic, or the occult. Eichrodt does not express this very explicitly, but he assumes it throughout his work. You will notice his continuing references to "natural" and "nature," and his recurring statements to the effect that those religions rooted in "nature" could not produce history or even conceive of the idea of history. A similar understanding to Kaufmann's lies behind these kinds of statements.

Now what is mythology? Mythology is the tale, the story, of the life of the gods. "Mythology" is used very loosely in modern biblical and theological thought but, simply put, it is the literary expression of polytheism. That is its origin; that is its source; that is where it developed its significance. In myth the gods both act and are acted upon so that none of them is unconditioned. At the heart of mythology is the tension between the gods, and that tension is what makes it delightful literature. But beyond this, there is also a tension between the gods and the other forces that shape their destiny. There is a fate that conditions the destinies of the gods, just as the gods shape human destiny.

The gods tend to be personal embodiments of the seminal forces of the primordial realm or of nature. So you have Shamash, the sun, in one section of the world—in Egypt he was known as Re. You have Nut as the heavens in Egypt; and in the Semitic world, Anu; and in Greece, Uranus. You can go through all these, and they are all divine beings. You have the earth, Asherah; you have Baal, who is the storm; you have Chronos, time; Tiamat, primal water.

But the essence of polytheism is not in the "poly"; it is not in the plurality of the gods. It is the fact that in their multiplicity and diversity, there is no ultimate personal will. The reality is that the divine world is a reflection of the human world, not visa versa. This also means that since everything came out of the same womb, there is a certain continuity in everything. That word *continuity* should become part of your language because it is a very significant theological concept. There is a certain continuity of both the divine realm and the human/nature realm with each other and with the primordial realm, since everything came ultimately from that primordial womb.

Thus, both the human and the divine have a common source. In Babylonian myth, man is created from the blood of a slain god. There is an Indian story that is very similar. The Greeks also regarded their gods as genetically related to us. There was no clearly defined boundary between the gods and mortal. Thus, Zeus oftentimes lusted after and cohabited with mortals, and children were born of that divine/human union.

Have you noticed that you cannot cross a horse and a cow? There are lines between the species that cannot be crossed. But in all these mythologies, you can cross the divine and the human. There is a continuity between them. Gilgamesh, in the Babylonian epic called by his name, is courted by the goddess Ishtar. Gilgamesh, to everybody's horror and amazement, refused her advances and very scathingly reminded her of all the trouble that she had caused for her previous lovers, both human and divine. To have an affair with Ishtar always cost you. The same was true for the Greek Aphrodite and the Canaanite Anat. But the point is that although Gilgamesh was a mortal it was still possible for there to be that crossing of the divine and the human. The kings of Sumer and Akkad, in ancient Mesopotamia, were considered husbands of Ishtar and so had the divine right of kings. This was even more the case in Egypt. Speaking from a philosophical viewpoint, we may say that in this understanding there was a continuity between all things because all came from an original source by procession. The concept of *creatio ex nihilo* never crossed their minds. The thought that the divine realm was truly other than the realm of the human and nature was unthinkable to them.

In many of the circles I moved in when I was younger, if you had said you believed in *creatio ex nihilo*, creation out of nothing, you would have felt them dismiss you because of your ignorance. They were sure that concept was not to be found in the Bible. But please take careful note of the section on cosmology and creation in Eichrodt.[26] He makes it plain that although Moses might not have known what you were talking about if you had asked him if he believed in *creatio ex nihilo*, it is the logical implication of what is taught in the Pentateuch. In the same way, if you had asked the apostle Paul if he believed in the Holy Trinity, he might have been baffled, never having heard of the word *Trinity*. But it was out of his writings that the doctrine of Trinity developed. It seems likely to me that if Eichrodt had ever had the opportunity to read Kaufmann, he would have found himself in essential agreement with him.

My interest in this issue springs from the background in which I grew up. I was taught that the philosophical system most compatible with Christianity was philosophical idealism. This philosophy taught that behind everything else the ultimate reality is the mental, the intellectual, the idea. That is the realm where God is to be found, so there is a very comfortable continuity between Him and us. To my knowledge, Dr. Harold Kuhn only taught his course on Aristotelian metaphysics once at Asbury Theological Seminary. I was fortunate to be a student

---

[26] Eichrodt, *Theology*, vol. 2, ch. 15.

in that course because somewhere in the middle of it I got the line drawn between the Creator and the creation. That was a critical moment because up until then I had accepted that there was a continuity between us and God, with the consequence that there is a little divinity in us all. That is the world in which I grew up, and we all called ourselves biblical Christians. It may be that the most essential single biblical truth is that line between the Creator and the creation. If you do not recognize the difference, where are you going to go for help?

In that ancient world, the absence of a line between Creator and creation was at the heart of their thinking. So it is no accident that pagan religions express themselves in two directions: one in pantheism,[27] which is a supreme example of a philosophical idealism, and the other in polytheism.[28] Both of them come from the same intellectual womb.

This continuity system is the basis of the pagan concept known as apotheosis—the possibility of a human being attaining divinity—godhood. This concept was especially prominent in Egypt because the pharaoh was considered to be divine. He was called the beneficent god, the great god, the son of Re, the sun god. Therefore, the pharaoh was worshipped as a god. Knowing this makes a radical difference in how one reads the Moses story. Moses came into pharaoh's court and said, "God says for you to let his people go." Pharaoh responded, "You don't know to whom you're speaking, do you?" Pharaoh knew himself to be God and here was this upstart saying, "God says for you . . ." Moses did not say one of the gods or a god had spoken, he said, "God said . . ." That immediately deprived Pharaoh of his chief claim to fame. The reason he was supposed to be on that throne was because he was divine. He had nursed at the goddess' breast and so forth.

You will read Exodus incorrectly if you think that the conflict there is between Moses and Pharaoh; it is between Yahweh and a false understanding of who God is. Pharaoh was worshipped as a god. When a pharaoh died he became the god Osiris. Now in our understanding of reality, one that is common both to the Bible and to Greek philosophical thought, a thing cannot both be and not be at the same time. But in the thought world of continuity, that is not a problem because what

---

[27] "Pantheism" means "all is god."

[28] "Polytheism" means the world is inhabited by "many gods."

is is continuous with what is not. So, you would find in ancient Egypt the hill out of which the earth came in a dozen different places, each with a temple built on it. And if someone should say, "But I thought the hill where the earth came out was over yonder," the priest at this temple would say, "Oh, it is," because a thing could both be and not be at the same time. So, when the king died, he became Osiris, reigned with Horus, and rose and set with Re.

Little wonder then that the mystery religions in the ancient world promised their adherents that they would become divine after death. We would merge back into the one from whom we came, and we would be divine. This was the fundamental element in the mystery religion in that the purpose of their rite of purification, of their asceticism, of their sacrament, was either union with the godhead or else enthusiasm. Where did the word *enthusiasm* come from? It is derived from the Greek word *entheos* which is a combination of *en* "in" and *theos* "god." So in its origins the enthusiastic person was the person who is in God and has God in him. So, the mystery religions said that either a person becomes divine or will have god live inside them. Even in Plato, the ultimate goal was to rise above the world of matter and move into the realm of the divine idea.

Now, the fact that in nonbiblical religion there is a realm beyond the gods accounts for a universal characteristic of religion—apart from biblical religion.[29] And what is it you find wherever you find nonbiblical religion? You find divination, sorcery, witchcraft, magic, the occult, mediums, necromancy—and you can keep on going. It is an incredible list.

The religions of the Ancient Near East were permeated by magical belief. Egypt, as we said, had an enormous literature on the subject and had a very big business manufacturing magical objects. Magic was called on at almost every turn of life by good Egyptians. They were playing it safe. Magic was used to ward off the spirits of the dead so that one's ancestors could be kept from haunting and hurting one. Magic was used to ward off the demons, to ward off scorpions, serpents, fire, physical injury, sickness, to protect one from one's enemies.

Now, where does that magical power come from? It does not come from the realm of the gods, because the gods draw on it as well. It

---

[29] I am using "biblical religion" in the purist sense, because much of what we find in the Old Testament is not pure biblical religion.

comes from that primordial realm behind the gods. To be sure, the gods had an important role to play in all of this use of magic. Some of them were themselves magicians. Their names, uttered in spells or written in charms, were a chief means of conjuring. The gods themselves practiced magic, and that is the reason they wanted to know it. The power that supposedly inhered in their names was but a part of the universally pervasive power, which the gods on occasion needed to know how to use for their own protection, safety, and benefit.

Now listen to this account from Egyptian literature: Re the great god has a secret name that Isis, the goddess, wants to know. So she makes a snake from the mud where Re had spat on the ground. Re is bitten by the snake and is about to die. So Isis offers to cure him with sorcery if he will tell her his secret name. He tries to avoid that, but cannot, and finally tells her the name, after which she cures him.[30] We did not find anything like that in our study of the book of Psalms, did we? The magnificence of the book of Psalms! We today have hardly the vaguest concept of this world of magic because we have been freed from it through the Christian church's dependence on the Bible. But there was nobody in that ancient world who was free from it except the Hebrews who took Yahweh seriously. Re was bitten by a scorpion and so Isis brought "great magic and cured the god Re." Magic, you see, was an autonomous force operative beyond the divine world but also on the divine world, oftentimes for its benefit, but oftentimes for its harm.

That is the kind of world in which Moses grew up. It is the kind of world in which Abraham grew up, and it is the kind of world you and I would have grown up in if it had not been for the Old Testament.

---

[30] James B. Pritchard, *Ancient Near Eastern Texts Relating to the Old Testament,* tr. W. F. Albright, 2nd ed. (Princeton: Princeton University Press, 1955), 12-13.

Lecture 6

. . . .

Yahweh Alone Is God

In the previous lecture we noted that Eichrodt said two things must be taken into account if we are to understand Old Testament theology correctly: the pagan thought world that Israel emerged from and the New Testament faith to which it led.

He goes on to say that there are two ways to go about putting together an Old Testament theology. In one of them the emphasis is upon the historical development of the Old Testament faith. In this approach, which is known as the "diachronic" (through time) approach, there is an attempt to trace the development of the theology, from its supposed earliest forms to its supposed latest ones. The focus is on the genesis and the organic development of the faith on a chronological basis.

Eichrodt in fact prefers the second approach, which is known as the "synchronic" (across time) approach, and I will return to an explanation of that later. But in order to understand what he is doing you need to know that he was heavily affected by the historical, critical reconstruction of Israel's history that prevailed in the scholarly world when he was writing. So, you will find that when he deals with the cult, patterns of worship, he is using a chronology of his own that differs from that of the Old Testament. For him the anchor point of Old Testament faith is the man Moses and the experience of Israel in the Exodus from Egypt and in the covenant that was established at Sinai. You will search vainly in the two volumes for any detailed treatment of the patriarchal period.

He will refer to the patriarchal period many times, but there is no specific treatment of it. The reason for that is that when Eichrodt was writing there was considerable doubt about our ability to get behind Moses in any authentic way. It was believed that the literature from the patriarchal period was written much later, with the result that the faith we find in that literature is, in fact, a retrojection of later faith. However, he does affirm that there were undoubtedly certain basic elements in that patriarchal tradition that formed a commonality with the later faith, giving some validity to the retrojection. At the time when he was writing, even to say that was a distinct step forward from most of the historical criticism of the day.[31]

From his beginning with Moses and the Sinai covenant, Eichrodt moves on to three documents. They are two "J" documents and then an "E" document—two Yahwist documents and an Elohist document.[32] He says that these three are old enough that they are useful as the second step in understanding the chronological development of Old Testament theology. He grants that there may be some retrojection from later stages of the faith in them, but he also argues that we must grant the possibility that what they are telling us may be older than the century in which a given document was finally edited and set.

The third unit that he believes we can use as a chronological anchor point is the literature of the eighth-century classical prophets, that

---

[31] One of the certainties of historical criticism is that the final result of historical criticism today will not be the final result tomorrow. A study of it across the twentieth century will show a great deal of vacillation. After Eichrodt there was a period when it was felt that the patriarchal accounts were quite reliable. But today there are many historical critics who would not even allow any historical credibility to the Exodus accounts, let alone the patriarchal.

[32] These hypothetical documents were supposedly composed in the ninth and eighth centuries B.C. Among them they contained the narrative parts of the Pentateuch and could supposedly be distinguished from each other in Genesis by their use of two different divine names: Yahweh and Elohim. Elsewhere, they could supposedly be distinguished by somewhat different theological emphases, local preferences, etc.

is, Amos, Hosea, Isaiah, and Micah.[33]

Eichrodt's fourth anchor point is the book of Deuteronomy. From his point of view Deuteronomy was the basic manuscript that was found in the temple in Josiah's day when the chief priests came to the king and said, "We have found the Book of the Covenant." (Remember Eichrodt's central emphasis on covenant.) Out of that discovery came one of the most remarkable revivals in Israel's history and perhaps in human history—it was radical. Although it did not last, it was a radical transformation under the leadership of Josiah. And it was all because of the manuscript they read together, which they called the Book of the Covenant.

The fifth unit of the text in Eichrodt's understanding is the priestly documents, which supposedly began before the Exile and con- tinued through it and after. In it are to be found the Creation story of Genesis 1, and much of Leviticus and Numbers. Many believe that the writer or writers of these documents were those of the "P" school who supposedly gave the Pentateuch its distinctive theological outlook.

The sixth unit is the prophets from the end of the seventh cen- tury, from the late 600s into the 500s. These are Zephaniah, Habakkuk, Jeremiah, Ezekiel and, for him, Deutero-Isaiah.

The seventh period is the postexilic period—after they came back from Babylon. That is the remainder of the canonical literature that was written after the return from captivity. That will include the remain- der of the minor prophets as well as many of the psalms and the books of Chronicles.

He also includes the intertestamental period as the eighth period of literature. Although this is not a period we Christians tend to pay much attention to, it will be very helpful to see what happens to the theology as that period progresses. In that light it will be easier to understand some of the reasons why Judaism is different from Christianity.

In summary, Eichrodt's approach to Old Testament theology assumes that it developed according to this reconstruction of the history of the development of the Canon. However, this assumption is rather significantly affected by his view of the wholeness of the theology. For

---

[33] He of course only considers Isaiah chapters 1–39 in this body of literature, relegating chapters 40–66 to a hypothetical sixth-century prophet conventionally called "Deutero-Isaiah."

this reason, he does not follow a thoroughly diachronic approach.

He recognizes that both approaches have problems. The problem with the first is historicism, in which the theology is buried under historical questions and methodology. On the other hand there is the danger of taking a dogmatic system and imposing it on the Old Testament. He says that is what orthodox scholarship did in the seventeenth and eighteenth century A.D. They took the final result of biblical revelation in the New Testament and then went back into the Old Testament looking for anything that would seem to lend support to their system with little or no concern for the way it was used in the Old Testament context. He argues that rather than imposing a system on the material, you should find a system from within the material that will emerge as you immerse yourself in it.

That is, of course, much easier to talk about than to do. Take, for instance, the book of Psalms. It would not be easy to write a systematic theology on the book of Psalms, would it? That is so because you are not dealing with systematic literature or systematic thinking. You are reading the works of people who are expressing their faith in God out of a whole range of experiences in their lives. They are worshipping God and not at all concerned about stating their ideas in some sort of rational order for a presentation in a theological seminary classroom or in a theological society. They are letting their hearts explode to God for what God has done for them and what they want from God and about their relationship to Him. But in all that variety, there is in that material, both implicit and explicit, a coherent set of ideas about God, humanity, and the world, and for that reason it is possible to organize those ideas in a systematic way.

This is an important clue to understanding Eichrodt's approach, for he says that the purpose of Old Testament theology is to develop a complete picture of the Old Testament structure of belief. That is, it is the final understanding that is important, not so much what was believed at any stage along the way. As I have already said, that is difficult to do without imposing something from outside the text, something alien to it. When we complete our study of the Psalms, I want to move to the patriarchal narratives, and it is not going to be easy to isolate the theology there either because they appear to be simple stories. When you read them you find almost no theological editing anywhere in them. They just seem to be straightforward stories. Nevertheless, as any good course in literary criticism will demonstrate, it is possible to take a simple story and to discover within it basic principles and basic beliefs. That is what Eichrodt sought to do and what we will seek to do as well.

It was once fashionable to say that if you want to grasp New Testament theology, you would certainly not go to the gospel of Mark because it is just a collection of simple stories. But as the years have passed, I have become convinced that the gospel of Mark is one of the most magnificent theological treatments in human history. Now, Mark's method of teaching theology is very different, but he does have a system. I do not always see all of it, but I see enough to know that the work is put together as carefully as a Beethoven symphony. There is an intentional plan and structure in it. To be sure, it is easier to recognize that theological structure in Mark, because we have a systematic presentation of New Testament theology given to us in the book of Romans. We do not have anything comparable to Romans in the Old Testament. Nevertheless, the point is still true that an author's belief system can be discovered in any type of writing.

I want to illustrate this point in the next several lectures as we synthesize the theology to be found in the Psalms. In our previous study of the Psalms, I have insisted that the central figure is not David, nor any of the other psalmists. Neither is it Israel. Rather, the central figure is Yahweh, and we can distill from the Psalms a rather extensive theological understanding of Him.

What is it that we have been learning about Yahweh as we lived with these prayers, these expressions of praise and petition? One of the things is that He is the center of everything. As we said earlier, the name Yahweh occurs 6,800 times in the Old Testament. The main word for God, *Elohim*, occurs only 2,500 times. So we have two and a half times as many usages, occurrences, of the personal name. He is the center of it all. Now, what is He like according to the Psalms?

One of the things you can say as a kind of bottom line statement is that He is God alone. I have said that before, but let me emphasize it. He is God alone—without rival or competitor. Now, that needs to be clarified because it is crucial to an understanding of what is taking place in the book of Psalms.

Take, for instance, Psalm 115:

Not to us, O Lord, not to us
>   but to your name be the glory,
>   because of your love and faithfulness.
Why do the nations say,
>   "Where is their God?"
Our God is in heaven;
>   he does whatever pleases him.
But their idols are silver and gold,
>   made by the hands of men.
They have mouths, but cannot speak,
>   eyes, but they cannot see;
they have ears, but cannot hear,
>   noses, but they cannot smell;
they have hands, but cannot feel,
>   feet, but they cannot walk;
>   nor can they utter a sound with their throats.
Those who make them will be like them,
>   and so will all who trust in them.
O house of Israel, trust in [Yahweh]—
>   he is their help and shield.
O house of Aaron, trust in [Yahweh]—
>   he is their help and shield.
You who fear him, trust in [Yahweh]—
>   he is their help and shield.
[Yahweh] remembers us and will bless us:
>   He will bless the house of Israel,
>   he will bless the house of Aaron,
he will bless those who fear [Yahweh]—
>   small and great alike.
May [Yahweh] make you increase,
>   both you and your children.
May you be blessed by [Yahweh],
>   the Maker of heaven and earth.
The highest heavens belong to [Yahweh],
>   but the earth he has given to man.
It is not the dead who praise [Yahweh],
>   those who go down to silence;

it is we who extol [Yahweh],
    both now and forevermore.
    Praise [Yahweh].

Now, the psalmist is speaking about Yahweh in relation to the deities of his friends and neighbors around him. And you will notice there is no sense of any tension here; those deities are no threat to Yahweh; they are neither rivals nor competitors.

Let me show you a passage in Isaiah that makes this thought even more specific, Isaiah 43, verses 10-13. This is one of those magnificent passages from Isaiah.

"You are my witnesses,"
    declares the Lord.
"and my servant whom I have chosen,
    so that you may know and believe me
    and understand that I am he.
Before me no god was born,
    nor will there be one after me.
I, even I, am [Yahweh],
    and apart from me there is no savior.
I have revealed and saved and proclaimed—
    I, and not some foreign god among you.
You are my witnesses," declares [Yahweh],
    "that I am God.
Yes, and from ancient days I am he.
    No one can deliver out of my hand.
When I act, who can reverse it?"

So, you begin to get very clearly the picture that Yahweh stands alone without rival. If you look at chapter 44, verse 6, it is stated even a little more sharply.

"This is what Yahweh says—
Israel's King and Redeemer, [Yahweh] Almighty:
    I am the first, I am the last;
    apart from me there is no God."

So you see, Yahweh is the only one when it comes to the realm of the Deity. Now, the Old Testament uses different terms for Him. It will use the term we have mentioned, "Elohim." It will use the strong Old Testament word for God, *God* with a capital "G," which is "*El.*" This is the name for the high god in the Canaanite pantheon as well. It will use an ancient word, *Elyon*, which is like *El*, but somewhat less particular. But in every case where *Elohim*, *El* or *Elyon* is used, Yahweh is the one who is intended in the Old Testament. The word for God (*Elohim*, *El* or *Elyon*) does not define Yahweh. Rather, the movement is in the opposite direction. It is Yahweh who defines what a Hebrew meant when he used the word *God*. That should be significant for you and me in terms of religious dialogue today. It is significant because when you get into a religious dialogue today, one of the first questions you need to ask when the other person uses the word *god* is, "What do you mean?" Without that vital definition you may be sailing right past each other, never connecting at any point. What the other person means by *god* may be something very different from what you mean. Remember what William Temple said, "If your concept of God is wrong, the more religion you get, the more dangerous you are." How crucial it is that there be consonance between the words we use and the reality behind them.

So we have been able to derive one crucial theme from the Psalms: Yahweh is God alone, and He is without rival or competitor. The second theme we can discover is this: God is incomparable. There is nothing and no one to be compared with Him. Look with me at Psalm 89:

> I will sing of [Yahweh's] great love forever;
>> with my mouth I will make your
>> faithfulness known through all generations.
> I will declare that your love stands firm forever,
>> that you have established your faithfulness
>> in heaven itself.
> You said, "I have made a covenant with my chosen one,
>> I have sworn to David, my servant,
> I will establish your line forever
>> and make your throne firm through all
>> generations."
> The heavens praise your wonders, O LORD,

your faithfulness too,
in the assembly of the holy ones,
For who in the skies above can compare with
[Yahweh]?
Who is like [Yahweh] among the heavenly
beings?
In the council of the holy ones God is greatly feared;
he is more awesome than all who surround
him.
O [Yahweh], God Almighty, who is like you?
You are mighty, O [Yahweh]
and your faithfulness surrounds you.

The psalmist continues by telling about Yahweh's mastery over nature, about his moral character, and about his commitment to righteousness and justice. For the same theme read Psalm 104. It is rich in the variety of its themes, but once again its central focus is on the incomparability of Yahweh. Another treatment of this theme is found in a hymn with which I am sure you are quite familiar, Isaiah 40. Isaiah was struck with this concept. Let me read from verse 10 and following:

See the Sovereign [Yahweh] comes with power,
and his arm rules for him.[34]
See, his reward is with him,

---

[34] In his commentary on Isaiah 40–66 John Oswalt argues that the "arm" is Christ. Remember that Isaiah 53 begins, "Who has believed our report and to whom has the arm of the Lord been revealed." Oswalt is suggesting "arm" is a technical term for the Christ. So, Isaiah says here: "See, the sovereign Lord comes with power and his arm rules for him. See, his reward is with him." The story of Christ is definitive for the interpretation of Isaiah 53. Earlier in this lecture we talked about the two-way movement between the testaments. Many years ago I was sitting in a class at Princeton Seminary on Good Friday and the subject that day was a lecture on Isaiah 53. The professor presented sixteen options as to who Isaiah 53 was talking about, and Jesus was not one of them. So, when we got to the end of the hour I looked up and said, "Doctor, could I ask a question? What Scripture do you read on Good Friday in public worship?" He put his head down, and when he looked up, he roared in his deep, bass voice, "Isaiah 53, what do you think, Kinlaw?" But he had not referred to Jesus until that point. But how are you going to interpret Isaiah 53? I don't know what to do with it if I do not have insights that come to me from the New Testament. I hate to think how little equipment I would have to understand Isaiah 53 if it were not for Good Friday.

and his recompense accompanies him.
He tends his flock like a shepherd:
    He gathers the lambs in his arms
and carries them close to his heart;
    he gently leads those that have young.
Who has measured the waters in the hollow of his
    hand, or with the breadth of his hand marked
    off the heavens?
Who has held the dust of the earth in a basket,
    or weighed the mountains on the scales and the
    hills in a balance?
Who has understood the mind of [Yahweh],
    or instructed him as his counselor?
Whom did [Yahweh] consult to enlighten him,
    and who taught him the right way?
Who was it that taught him knowledge
    or showed him the path of understanding?
Surely the nations are like a drop in a bucket;
    they are regarded as dust on the scales;
    he weighs the islands as though they were fine
    dust.
Lebanon is not sufficient for altar fires
    nor its animals enough for burnt offerings.
Before him all the nations are as nothing;
    They are regarded by him as worthless
    and less than nothing.
To whom, then, will you compare God?
    What image will you compare him to?
As for an idol, a craftsman casts it,
    and a goldsmith overlays it with gold and
    fashions silver chains for it.
A man too poor to present such an offering
    selects wood that will not rot.
    He looks for a skilled craftsman to set up an
    idol that will not topple.
Do you not know?
    Have you not heard?

Has it not been told you from the beginning?
Have you not understood since the earth was
founded?
He sits enthroned above the circle of the earth
and its people are like grasshoppers.
He stretches out the heavens like a canopy,
and spreads them out like a tent to live in.
He brings princes to naught
and reduces the rulers of this world to
nothing.
No sooner are they planted,
no sooner are they sown . . .
than he blows on them and they wither,
and a whirlwind sweeps them away.
"To whom will you compare me?
Or who is my equal?" says the Holy One.

That is both magnificent literature and magnificent theology. What is being said is that there is nobody like Him. He has no equal or challenger. He is incomparable.

Now let us explore a third theme. He is the Creator who makes all things, but He transcends His own creation. He is not involved in the flux and flow of the universe. There is an infinite qualitative distinction between Him and what He has created, an infinite ontological distinction between them. He is one order of being and the creation is another. There is a discontinuity between them.

That is the reason revelation is so crucial; there is a gulf between us and Him that we cannot cross. If we are ever to know Him, He must come down to us. That chasm is uncrossable apart from revelation. He must reveal Himself, and that is what we are getting in the Scripture. If you will look at Isaiah 45, you will get an example of this. We begin to read at 45:5:

"I am [Yahweh], and there is no other;
apart from me there is no God.
I will strengthen you,
though you have not acknowledged me,

> so that from the rising of the sun
>
> > to the place of its setting
>
> men may know there is none besides me.
>
> > I am [Yahweh] and there is no other.
>
> I formed the light and I create darkness.
>
> > I bring prosperity and I create disaster."

The translation "disaster" for the last word may be a bit weak, because the Hebrew word is *ra'*, which is often translated "evil," as in Genesis 6:5, "Every inclination of the thoughts of his heart was only *evil* all the time." So it would be entirely correct to translate that phrase, "I create evil."

This brings us to the heart of the most difficult problem in Old Testament theology and perhaps the most difficult problem in human existence, that is, the problem of evil. The other religions solved the problem with a dualistic understanding of reality. Dualism supposes that there are two eternal entities, which might be thought of as gods or not, as the case might be. The good entity is responsible for good things, and the bad entity for bad things, and there is never a resolution between them, only constant conflict. But the Old Testament reaches a radical resolution, and I suggest that in this issue we come to the very heart of what this course is about.

Now look at the parallel statement, "I formed the light; I create the darkness." You could not say that of the gospel of John because that gospel makes light and darkness the metaphorical representatives for good and evil and makes them polar opposites. But in the Old Testament we find a special word for deep darkness: *'araphel,* and that is where Yahweh dwells (1 Kings 8:12; 2 Chron. 6:1; see also Deut. 4:11; 5:22; Ps. 139:12). He dwells in deep darkness, He is the Lord of the night as well as the day.

Obviously, these simple statements will require a great deal of amplification. This is why you will find that at the end of chapter after chapter in Eichrodt there is a long final paragraph of synthesis. Here he is taking what appeared to be contradictory elements and trying to find a resolution to them. And that is what has to be done. You and I distinguish between primary causes and secondary causes. Why did the car go into the ditch? Well, it was because the driver swerved to miss a rabbit.

Ah, but who made it possible for a car to swerve? The auto-maker! If he had not made the front wheels steerable, that accident would never have happened! So it is here: God does not cause people to make evil choices, but it *is* God (and no other) who is responsible for the possibility of the evil choice. The Old Testament is so concerned to make its point that there is one God and one alone that it insists in the most simplistic terms that everything that is: light and dark, good and evil, goes back to one source alone. But do you see what that means? It means that God can be with you in the dark as well as the light and that theoretically, at least, the One who created the possibility of evil can indeed find a resolution for that problem. That is a great deal more than any other approach to the problem can offer. The Old Testament says that He is the God who created darkness as much as He created light.

But if God really did create the possibility of evil, is He good? Once again, the Old Testament points beyond itself. We cannot fully understand the biblical answer to that question until we have gone to Calvary where God Himself takes our evil upon Himself and finds an atonement for it. The end of the question is the Cross. But the Cross is only a possibility because there is no independent evil entity outside of the Creator.

There is one more theme (the fourth) that we need to introduce. Because God transcends His own creation, there is no theogony. Again, this word is derived from the Greek. As we know, *theos* refers to deity, while *genea* refers to birth. In paganism, with its understanding of the continuity of all things, it was a given that creation was given birth to by the gods. That is not true in the Old Testament. The universe is not born out of God; there is a radical discontinuity. There is no theogony, but the creation, instead of coming out of God's being, is spoken into existence. He speaks and it is. That is one of the most significant philosophical and theological concepts to be found in the Old Testament, and it is absolutely basic to any reasonable treatment of the New Testament. Look at Psalm 33, verses 1-9, but especially 6 and 9:

> By the word of [Yahweh] the heavens were made,
>   their starry hosts by the breath of his mouth. . . .
> For he spoke, and it came to be;
>   he commanded, and it stood firm.

Even here in the Psalms, we find that the doctrine of Creation found in Genesis 1 is fairly well spelled out. God speaks and things exist.

What is being said by this assertion? It is that the creation did not emerge from the Creator, being of the same stuff as He is. It is affirming that infinite, qualitative distinction between the Creator and the creation and the uncrossable chasm between us and Him that we mentioned earlier. It is a chasm that can only be crossed from Him to us. We are not a part of God. He spoke it all into existence. He did not even take another god and form creation out of that god's body. Neither did he take something he had created and form the universe out of that.

The Hebrew term translated "create" is *bara'*. It appears primarily in Genesis and in Isaiah, but it is also found several times in the Psalms, as in Psalm 148:1–5 where it says God commanded and the heavens, the heavenly hosts, the sun and the moon, the shining stars, the highest heavens and the waters above the heavens were created. The various contexts make it clear that what is created has never existed before. But it is also important to note that there is no place where it is said something is created *out of something else*. In other words this term is used to express creation out of nothing. To be sure, this is an argument from silence. However, with fifty-three total occurrences, that is a remarkable silence.[35]

So in the end even the grammar and the vocabulary of the Old Testament support the doctrine that Yahweh is God alone, without rival or competitor, incomparable in all the universe, not a part of the creation He created, but the One who brought it into existence through the simple act of purposeful speech.

---

[35] [Editor's note] It should be pointed out that *creation ex nihilo* is an implication drawn from the usages of *bara'*. The word alone connotes bringing into being that which had not existed previously. Clearly in the case of Psalm 51:10, "Create in me a pure heart, O God," the point is not to affirm *creatio ex nihilo*, but rather the radical newness of what is created.

Lecture 7

· · · · · · · · · ·

The Nature of Yahweh

In this lecture I want to continue the introduction to the nature of Yahweh that we were presenting in the previous one. Eichrodt says that the purpose of Old Testament theology is to enable us to develop and see the system of belief that is found in the Old Testament. We said that at the center of all of that is Yahweh. If I wanted to deal with the most radical intellectual revolution in the history of mankind, it would be in Israel's development of the concept of Yahweh. There is nothing comparable to that anywhere else in the literature of the world, so it is fair for us to concentrate there.

We said in the previous lecture that He is the God who is alone, in radical contradiction to all the other religious systems of human history that go either to pantheism where everything is God, everything is divine; or go to polytheism where you may have hundreds and thousands of gods and you deal with all sorts of forces that are personified. But this God is alone. The "pantheon" has only one being in it, and that is Yahweh.[36] As we saw, the obvious implication of that fact is that since He created everything else and was alone in the beginning, He is without rival and competitor.

There is an implication here that I want to tease you with now, and develop further later on. If God was alone before the act of Creation, then the concept of sovereignty is not the ultimate concept of God, the ultimate word to be said about Him. In the beginning when there was nothing but Yahweh alone, there was nothing for Him to be sovereign over! So, there must be something about Him that is greater than His sovereignty. His sovereignty is an expression of who He is in relation to everything that He created. But who was He and what was He like before there was anybody or anything else to whom he could relate?

We said earlier that in the Old Testament, in every case where the word *God*, meaning the supreme Deity, is used, Yahweh is understood. Let me underline that point. The word *God* in the Old Testament does not define the character of Yahweh. Yahweh defines, by His nature, what a Hebrew was supposed to mean when he used the words `elohim` or `el` or `elyon` (all words for "God") when he spoke of the Deity.

Originally, I read it the other way around. When I would read "Yahweh" I would assume that meant "God." But the reality is that in the Old Testament it is the distinctive character of Yahweh that determines what meaning you give to the general term *God*. So when a Phoenician used the term *God* it did not mean the same as when a Hebrew used it.

We said that Yahweh is incomparable, and we referred to those passages in the Old Testament where it says, "Who is like unto Him?" There is no one with whom you can compare Him. Of course, the reason He is incomparable is because He is the one who created everything else and He originally was alone—there's only one in His category. We also said that He creates and in creating transcends His own creation. He is not caught in the flux and flow of life that you and I are caught in as a part of Nature.[37]

---

[36] The New Testament will present a slightly more complex, though not contradictory, picture of the heavenly realm.

[37] Notice that the translator of Eichrodt has capitalized *Nature*. This is so because it is a consistent frame of reference for Eichrodt. The term reflects the

Now, because God is not a part of the creation and is not caught in the flux and flow of nature, the cosmos, the universe, whatever language you want to use to describe whatever is there besides God, there is no theogony (god-birth) or cosmogony (nature-birth)—being born from God. In that regard notice how Eichrodt belabors the fact that Yahweh transcends human sexuality. Yahweh is not a part of that flux and flow.

We went on to say that this is illustrated by the doctrine of *creatio ex nihilo*. It is not a case of Him taking a part of Himself or taking a part of something else and then creating what is, the creation. Rather, He speaks and it is there. I believe that this device of speaking creation into existence was used to show the discontinuity between the Creator and the creation, a discontinuity that was never crossed, really, until the Incarnation. You will notice how all of these concepts bear upon New Testament truth.

All this is to say that Yahweh is the unconditioned One, the Absolute, which puts Yahwism, the worship of Yahweh, in tension with all the other religions of that ancient world. So, when Moses said to Pharaoh, "Yahweh said to let his people go . . ." Yahweh is pitted against the entire divine world that Pharaoh represented. The same is true when you come to Elijah and the prophets of Baal. Elijah stands alone against them and the controversy exists because it is God with a capital "G" against gods with a small "g", and the Hebrew would say it is an illegitimate use of the word *god* to apply it to the Baals.

This means that there is what some people have called an imperialistic note in Old Testament religion. It is the fact that the Old Testament is saying, "Since this is the only God who exists, this is the only way to find a norm for religion and to find a way for salvation." I do not think there is any question but that what we speak of today as the exclusiveness of Christianity is rooted in the Old Testament concept of Yahweh. So when Jesus comes and says, "I am the Way, the Truth and the Life," He is not trying to shut anyone out, He is just simply trying to point us to where the door is, because He says there is no other door. In other words, the Bible is simply saying this is the way it is: There is one God and one alone. When Jesus says, "No one comes to the Father

concept of the cosmos over against Yahweh, and it is important to understand this in order to understand what he is saying about Yahweh.

but by me," the purpose is not to exclude. He is speaking so that all may enter in. "Whosoever will, the Spirit and the bride say come. Whosoever is athirst, let him come." This is to let us know where the entryway into salvation is.

This is the reason for a theme that oftentimes bothers us in the Old Testament, and that is the jealousy of Yahweh. If we are to understand this concept correctly, we need to look very carefully at the contexts in which it first appears. The first significant one is in Exodus 20:5. You remember that Exodus 20 is where the Decalogue, the Ten Commandments, is given. It follows chapter 19, which tells about Mt. Sinai, the burning mountain onto which Moses walked to meet Yahweh and where Yahweh gave to him the commandments, which Jews call "the ten words," the basic moral words of existence.

The Ten Commandments open in this way:

God spoke all these words. "I am Yahweh, your God. I am the one who brought you out of Egypt, out of the land of slavery. You shall have no other gods before me. You shall not make for yourself an idol in the form of anything in heaven above or on the earth beneath or in the waters below. You shall not bow down to them or worship them; for I, [Yahweh], your God, am a jealous God, punishing the children for the sin of the fathers to the third and fourth generation of those who hate me, but showing love to a thousand generations of those who love me and keep my commandments."

Here Yahweh speaks and lets us know about His relationship to us. The words are spoken in the context of the Sinai Covenant, where Yahweh is, as it were, putting His arms of embrace around Israel and asking for them to return that embrace. He says to them, "You are to be my people; but you need to know that I am jealous." Now, many of us have found that a bit offensive at times, but I think if you will explore it with me, you will realize there is something incredibly magnificent here.

How does Yahweh view Israel? In Exodus 19:5 we read, and I am paraphrasing:

"Now therefore, if you will indeed obey my voice and
keep my covenant, then you will be a special treasure to
me above all people, for all the earth is mine."

The word that is translated here "special treasure" is an important one. It only occurs eight times in the Old Testament, and most of
the occurrences are used by Yahweh to speak of Israel. The Hebrew
word is *segulla*, and it speaks of a special possession, such as a bride's
special jewelry.[38] It is not special in the sense of something that can be
owned and used, but in the sense of something that is a prized possession, something in which the owner finds great personal pleasure. So
just as a bride takes special care that these jewels should not be lost or
misused, so does God say that He is going to be very possessive of His
people.[39] They are very special to Him. So it is in the context of telling
the people who He is, which is the purpose of the Ten Commandments,
that He says, "You need to know I am jealous for you."
The second place where the concept appears is in chapter 34 of
Exodus. You will remember that after the giving of the covenant, Moses
had returned to the mountain to receive the plans for the tabernacle.
But while he was there, the people prevailed on Aaron to make them a
golden idol, which they worshipped with all that pagan worship involved.
In other words, within five weeks of entering into the covenant, they had
already broken it in its two most significant points: recognizing other
gods and making idols. It is as though a bride of five weeks has become
a prostitute on the side. The latter part of chapter 32 and all of chapter
33 deal with the ramifications of that tragic failure. In the end, Yahweh
unilaterally reinstated the covenant and that is what you have in chapter
34. We begin to read at verse 10:

Then [Yahweh] said, "I am making a covenant with you.
Before all your people I will do wonders never before

---

[38] See Deut. 7:6; 14:2; 26:18; 1 Chron. 29:3; Ps. 135:4; Ecl. 2:8; Mal. 3:17.
[39] Scholars have noted that when the word is used in a covenant context
outside of the Old Testament it can refer to the close vassal of a suzerain. (See e.g.,
Jeffrey H. Tigay, *Deuteronomy*, The JPS Torah Commentary, ed. Nahum M. Sarna
[Philadelphia: The Jewish Publication Society, 1996], 87).

done in any nation in all the world. The people you live among will see how awesome is the work that I, [Yahweh], will do for you. Obey what I command you today. I will drive out before you the Amorites, the Canaanites, the Hittites, the Perezzites, the Hivites and Jebusites. Be careful not to make a treaty with those who live in the land where you are going, or they will be a snare to you. Break down their altars, smash their sacred stones, cut down their Asherah poles. Do not worship any other god, for [Yahweh], whose name is Jealous [Yahweh is his personal name, but one of the sobriquets for him is Jealous] is a jealous God."

So, you see, God's jealousy is expressed again in the context of the covenant.

The third place where divine jealousy is presented is in Deuteronomy, chapter 4. Once again, the setting is covenant, although not the actual making of the covenant. Look at verse 21. Moses is speaking. This is at the end of his life, just before God took him up on Mt. Nebo where he looked at the Promised Land and then was taken to be with the Lord:

"[Yahweh] was angry with me because of you, and he solemnly swore that I would not cross the Jordan and enter the good land [Yahweh], your God is giving you as your inheritance. I will die in this land; I will not cross the Jordan; but you are about to cross over and take possession of that good land. Be careful not to forget the covenant of the LORD your God that he made with you. Do not make for yourselves an idol in the form of anything the LORD your God has forbidden, for [Yahweh] your God is a consuming fire, a jealous God."

So here again divine jealousy appears in the context of loyalty to Yahweh alone as expressed in keeping the terms of the covenant.

A fourth example is found at the end of Joshua. Look at verse 14 of chapter 24 of Joshua. This is a very dramatic moment. This whole chapter is the renewing of the covenant at Shechem at the end of Joshua's life. We have seen it at Sinai; we have seen it at Moab; now we see it at Shechem:

> "Fear [Yahweh] and serve him with all faithfulness. Throw away the gods your forefathers worshipped beyond the river and in Egypt, and serve [Yahweh]. But if serving [Yahweh] seems undesirable to you, then choose for yourselves this day whom you will serve, whether the gods your forefathers served beyond the River or the gods of the Amorites, in whose land you are living. But as for me and my household, we will serve [Yahweh]."
>
> Then the people answered, "Far be it from us to forsake [Yahweh] to serve other gods! It was [Yahweh], our God himself who brought us and our fathers out of Egypt, from that land of slavery, and performed those great signs before our eyes. He protected us on our entire journey and among all the nations through which we traveled. [Yahweh] drove out before us all the nations, including the Amorites, who lived in the land. We too will serve the LORD because he is our God."
>
> Joshua said to the people: "You are not able to serve [Yahweh]. He is a holy God; he is a jealous God. He will not forgive your rebellion and your sins. If you forsake [Yahweh] and serve foreign gods, he will turn and he will bring disaster on you and make an end of you, after he has been good to you."
>
> But the people said to Joshua, "No! we will serve the LORD."
>
> Then Joshua said, "You are witnesses against yourselves that you have chosen to serve the LORD."
>
> "Yes, we are witnesses," they replied.
>
> "Now then," said Joshua, "throw away the foreign gods that are among you and yield your hearts to the LORD, the God of Israel."

Now, make note of the fact that at the end of Joshua's life, he is saying to the people of Israel, "Throw away your false gods," which lets you know there never was a time when Israel was pure. It was always a battle, and at many times greater than at others, but in the midst of Israel there were these who were the spokesmen, the voices for the Lord God, for Yahweh.

But it is in the heart of that context of renewal of the covenant, that you see this expression, "Yahweh is jealous." Once again the context is covenant; so that the jealousy of Yahweh is one manifestation of the covenant relationship, one of the ways the covenant God relates Himself to His people. Do not ever let your thinking about God's jealousy get separated from the concept of covenant.

Now what theological implications should we draw out from this study? The first is that to say that God is jealous is simply to say in a strong, personal, even a psychologized way that He is the only God there is and He loves His people and does not want them to head down a dead-end street. He is the only God there is, He loves His people and He is angry when they turn to a false alternative. The first commandment is given, not to take the people away from other realities, but from delusions. God does not want to take them away from other gods, but from false, human conceptions of reality that humans have called gods. So He says, "My purpose is to take you away from delusion because I am the God of truth."

In this regard it is important to remember that the Hebrew concept being translated here is much larger than our English word *jealous*.[40] It is "to be passionately concerned for." So sometimes the term had to be translated with the now archaic "zealous." A good example can be found in Jesus' so-called "cleansing of the Temple" (John 2:13-22). After it was over, the disciples remembered the line from the Psalms: "Zeal for your house consumes me" (Ps. 69:9). That is the same word we are thinking of here. So in one sense, Jesus was jealous for His Temple. He was furious to see it being misused and abused; He was passionately concerned for its well-being. But He was not "jealous" in the way we commonly use the word today. For us jealousy is a petty emotion expressing a desire to possess the beloved at all costs merely because the lover wants

---

[40] The Hebrew term is *qana*.

the other person for himself or herself. And the lover wants to take the other person away from somebody else so that he or she can have the joys related to that person. What Yahweh is saying is, "There isn't any other and I don't like you living in a world of delusion."

A second theological aspect of this study is one that will develop as we move along in our study of the Old Testament, and it has to do with love—Yahweh's love. If you read the Old Testament with any care at all, you will find that Yahweh is a passionate lover, and He has fallen in love with Israel, and He wants Israel for His own. We will develop this point much more thoroughly later, but we cannot get past this point without referring to it. If you will read Hosea, you will find that the basic paradigm of the relationship of Yahweh to Israel is the paradigm of marriage and, significantly, it is monogamous marriage that is modeled there. In a world that knew plenty about polygamy, it is monogamous love that is exemplified when Hosea speaks about the relationship of Yahweh and Israel.

Or read the sixteenth chapter of Ezekiel. It is at the same time one of the most tender and one of the most painful stories in the Old Testament. It describes both the depth of Yahweh's love for the creature whom He made and whom He has chosen and the fury He feels at her rejection of Him. She is His bride and yet is copulating in the streets with whomever she can find. Have you ever wondered about the first miracle Jesus performed? He changed the water into wine—that's not the way I would have begun his ministry, but that is what He did. And where did He do it? He did it at a wedding. Why a wedding to begin the ministry of salvation? Genesis 1 says human history began with a wedding, a wedding between Adam and Eve. The book of Revelation says human history ends with one, the wedding of the Bride and the Lamb. So there is a sense in which you can say that biblical theology is a nuptial theology. What is God looking for? He is looking for children for the Father and a bride for His Son. It is in that kind of context that we must face that Yahweh is a jealous God. But it is the love that cares more about the well-being of the beloved than of the lover. The jealous Yahweh, let me remind you, is the One who speaks in Jesus and says, "The good shepherd lays down his life for his sheep." His primary concern is for His sheep's well-being, even at the sacrifice of Himself. And the One who says, "I am a jealous God," is the One who orchestrated what happened on Good Friday on Golgotha. So, be very careful not to read into these biblical concepts our use of these kinds of language.

This kind of passionate exclusivism was in striking contrast to paganism, to the polytheism and the pantheism expressive of it. This is so because the one thing characteristic of paganism is its normal tolerance. Why is that? It is so because of the very nature of the continuity upon which paganism rests. Everything is equally divine and equally profane. One god is no better and no worse than another. So, you can put all the different gods on the same shelf if you want to and pay a little tribute to all of them, and none of the gods has a right to object. But things are very different when you come to the Old Testament. Here Yahweh is the only ultimate and the only absolute and He is completely other than His creation. So, your relationship to everything else is to be determined by Him. That is an astounding, intellectual change in the mind of man.

This brings me to the fifth comment I want to make about Yahweh. Yahweh is a person. He is not a universal force that has been personified, but He is an individual person of ultimate power and authority. We will give this fuller attention later, but it is important for us to fix it in our thinking now.

In an earlier lecture I reported what a shock it was when I found that the word *person* only came into Western language (Latin, Greek) in the third and fourth century through the discussion of who Jesus was in relation to the other members of the Trinity. So this magnificent term that we have to express the nature of that creature we are living with or sitting next to or rooming with, a person and not a thing, comes out of biblical religion.

In paganism the gods have no unique personal characteristics. They are clearly forces that have been given generalized human characteristics. But they have none of the complexity or variety of emotions and responses that characterize Yahweh and all real personality. Yahweh's passionate involvement with His people may present us with some problems as we attempt to make that consistent with His deity, but those are good problems to have as opposed to the alternative.

Furthermore, it is this understanding of God's personhood that enables us to come to the next thing I want to say. And that is, that Yahweh is the Holy One. Why is that related to personhood? It is because the moral, the ethical, is a personal dimension. To be holy is to be different, set apart. But Yahweh's set-apartness, at the heart of it, is ethical and moral. That is the reason for all those moral and ethical commandments in the Old Testament that many of us find so boring.

Why do I say that the moral and the ethical is a personal dimension? It is because wherever you find personal beings, you have a tension between the "ought," what should be, and the "is." Now it is interesting that each of us tends not to feel very strongly about the "ought" when it applies to us, but we feel very strongly about it as it applies to the ways others treat us. We do not like it when someone overcharges us. Neither do we like it when someone lies to us. Notice what lying does to relationships. The minute deception comes in and candor is gone, trust disappears. And when trust is gone, you can do everything you want to keep the relationship intact, but at the center of it will be a vacuum. Real relationship is gone because something within us freezes when we are deceived.

So this conflict between the "ought" and the "is" is a fundamental part of personal existence. But where does this sense of the "ought" come from? There are some people who say that this is just a part of social life; society develops its own norms. So when a professor on the campus of UCLA was asked by a group of students in the 1960s what was wrong with their behavior, she thundered, "You just don't do that here!"[41] Every group of people on the face of the earth has its sets of "you just don't do that here." Perhaps it is the family, where the father says to the children, "A [family name] doesn't do that."

Without social norms we have chaos and anarchy rules. In Israel's world, there were social norms related to land ownership. The inheritance you received from your fathers was a sacred responsibility and nobody else had a right to touch it. You were supposed to take care of it. There was also the principle of blood revenge. If you killed my brother it was my business to kill you because there was no local police force, no FBI, to enforce order. Since it is not right for one person to kill another, if you kill my brother it is my moral responsibility to kill you in order to maintain social order. "An eye for an eye and a tooth for a tooth," is not the rule of the jungle, but the rule of society. If you don't think so, just

---

[41] As reported by Professor Edward McKinley, Asbury College faculty member, who was one of the students involved.

let someone take advantage of you legally and then examine how you feel about it.

We depend on the incorruptibility of a judge, so that if you take someone before a judge with a complaint and you find that your opponent has bought off the judge, you are furious. Have you read the account of Socrates' condemnation in which his friend came to him and said, "I have fixed it with the judge so that all you have to do is escape." But Socrates replied, "But what happens to me? I have two people inside of me and I must live with that other person the rest of my life, and if there is an afterlife, there too. Having spent my life teaching that a good person will obey the law, shall I then break it in my last moments?"

Not only are we offended at a corrupt judge, we expect people to keep their promises to us. We see a broken promise as a personal breach of faith. When a person was asked why he left a certain Christian organization, he responded that the person who was in authority over him would say one thing to his face, but then when the pressure was on he would do something else.

We are offended when someone returns evil for good. Everyone instinctively recoils against the manifest unfairness of such behavior. That is why there is honor among thieves and murderers. On the other hand we admire the person who returns goodness and charity to someone who has sinned against him or her. In almost any human society such a one will be said to be a good person. There is a concept of goodness.

So we can say that societies require and produce these moral and ethical norms. But why? What is their basis? Why does every society have them? Many people would suggest that it is because there exists an abstract concept of justice. Somewhere out there, there is a reality that we can call justice, which ought to be capitalized with a capital "J." You sense that in Socrates' speech about law. It is there; it is an abstract reality. And there are many who would say that that reality is the general basis of our moral principles.

So what are some of those behaviors that abstract justice demands? In Abraham's day, it demanded hospitality to a foreigner. There is a vivid example of this at the end of the book of Judges. A couple of incidents are evidently picked out to illustrate the moral collapse of the Israelite society at that time. In the second of these, found in the nineteenth chapter, a Levite and his concubine came to the town of Gibeah to spend the night. But no one would take them in. Finally, one person rather reluctantly took them. But during the night the men of the town demanded that the visitor be sent out so they could have sex with him. The host was so horrified by this that he offered his virgin daughter in the place of his guest. Better that than offend the law of hospitality. Still today, the Arabs are famous for this sort of thing; once they accept the obligation of host, nothing is too good for the guest.

Other examples are modesty—we remember the lengths to which Noah's sons, Shem and Japheth, went to avoid looking at their father's nakedness—respect for piety, and disapproval of unnecessary cruelty. Of course, there are different levels of all of these in different societies. In one society you cannot chop off people's hands and arms and feet and in another you can, but in both of them there is some sense of recoil from whatever they consider to be unnecessary cruelty. Still other examples are sympathy for the weak, disapproval of abuse of confidence, and disapproval of gross ingratitude.

Now, where do all these originate and what is the basis for them? One explanation, as we have seen, is that they are merely social norms that were codified into legal codes that became binding. Others would go further and say that "justice" is written into the nature of the universe, like gravity, and that if you violate it you must suffer the consequences. But what does Israel say? They argue that this inner sense of "ought" that resides in every human breast has its basis in the nature of Yahweh. Because He is the ultimate and the absolute and is the sole Creator, He is the one being in the universe who has the right to be called the Holy One. His character, His holy character, is the determining factor for the behavior of all of His creation.

This understanding is spelled out in the most remarkable way in the legal literature of the Old Testament. I remember a Sunday school teacher saying,

> What a pity it is that when the Old Testament gave us the Ten Commandments, it gave them negatively. "Thou shalt not. . . ." Because anybody knows that once you've stated it negatively, you've challenged the person to break it. So, how much better it would have been if the Scripture had

said, "Now, this is the way you should do it," and stated
it positively.

I remember that made sense to me then. I knew
when my mother said, "Dennis, don't," there was something inside me that instantly said, "Why not? I'd sort of
like to." The prohibition sort of challenged my autonomy.
Of course, you need the doctrine of original sin to explain
that response, but in my childhood, optimistic humanism
had long since disposed of that archaic doctrine.

But then I remember getting into a course with Samuel Noah
Cramer from the University of Pennsylvania and Cyrus Gordon from
Brandeis University. These two great scholars began talking about the
difference between Hammurabi's Code and the Sinaitic Law in Exodus.
Do you know what they said was the unique thing in Exodus? It was
that "Thou shalt not." In Hammurabi's Code and indeed in every other
law code we have from the ancient world the laws are all stated as actual
cases; if such and such happens then this is what shall be done about it.
There are many of those kinds of laws in Exodus chapters 21–23, but
the entire section is headed by those absolute prohibitions that we know
as the Ten Commandments, and they set the stage for all the rest. In the
law codes the only basis for the king's saying what should be done and
not done was in his own authority. Change kings and you get changed
laws. So there is nothing that is absolutely wrong. Everything is relative
to the preferences of this king or that one. But that is not the case in
the Old Testament. Why must the person who steals something be punished? It is because stealing is absolutely wrong in the light of the character of the sole Creator of the universe. There is nothing that can be
done humanly speaking to undo it. It is not merely a matter of the wishes
of some king and what he will accept. Thou shalt not steal. . . . When
you've done it, you may pay the guy back, but that does not undo it because Yahweh does not like thieves. The moral law in the Old Testament
is rooted totally in the moral character of Yahweh so that everything has
to be decided as to whether it is right or wrong on the basis of His likes
and dislikes.

What does that do to our contemporary discussion about morality? You see, the problem with the misuse of sex is not just that you may

damage another person, but that you have alienated yourself from the eternal God. And these two positions come in conflict. If you look at the book of Leviticus, chapter 18, to see how sexual behavior is addressed in Israelite society, you will find at both the beginning and the end of the chapter the simple expression, "I am Yahweh, your God." What is the point of this? It is providing one simple explanation for the commandments regarding sexual behavior: because I am Yahweh. Why don't you do this or that? One simple answer is given: "I am Yahweh." The basis for moral differentiation and for ethical discrimination lies ultimately and solely in the very nature of the God of Israel.

In chapter 19 of Leviticus this point is made even more forcefully. This chapter is dealing with the general norms for behavior, and here you will find the motivation clause, "I am Yahweh" occurring no less than sixteen times. Why do God's covenant partners behave in certain ways? It is because of the distinctive—holy—character of their covenant Lord. I am convinced that this is the reason why moral reform has normally been a part of biblical religion wherever that religion has taken root. This is so because as people get to know Yahweh, they get to know Yahweh's likes and dislikes, and they begin to adopt those likes and dislikes for themselves. So, you will find throughout the Old Testament, God's people are to take good care of the orphan, the widow, and the foreigner. There is one simple reason for this distinctive behavior: "I am Yahweh and you belong to Me and you are supposed to be like I am."

This is why misbehavior with regard to God is not crime but sin, and the reason why "sin" in one sense only applies to one's personal relationship with God. I may do wrong to another person, but it is really only wrong because it is ultimately a sin against Him, because it is offensive to the One who created the universe and He created it to be a universe of goodness and beauty and righteousness. So, you will find in that prayer in Psalm 51, "Against you, you only, have I sinned and done what is evil in your sight." Had David not sinned against Bathsheba, or against Uriah, or against an unborn child, or against his own family, or against his nation? Yes, he had. But ultimately what he had done was wrong precisely because "against you, you only, have I sinned." The world is filled with people who have justified the most horrible behavior because they themselves were the standard for their behavior. One need look no further than the Nazis and their treatment of the Jews. Many a king has justified

worse things than David ever did because he recognized no ethical standard outside of himself. But precisely because there was a single standard
for behavior outside of David and outside of Israel and indeed outside
of this world, David's treatment of those people was tragically, terribly,
wrong.

Lecture 8

· · · · · · · · · ·

Why God Called Abraham Out of Ur of the Chaldees

We have now completed our introduction to Old Testament the-ology based on the Psalms, and we turn to the book of Genesis and to the patriarchs. It is not hard, biblically, to make a case for the importance of the patriarchs, and especially Abraham. Let me take you to Psalms again. As I have gotten to know the Scripture better, one of the things that convinces me of the inspiration and the unity of Scripture, is the way that in different sections, in passages written centuries and centuries apart, you have the basic themes all coming together and tying into each other. So we find in Psalm 105:

> Give thanks to [Yahweh], call on his name;
>> make known among the nations what he has done.

Sing to him, sing praise to him;
    tell of all his wonderful acts.[42]
Glory in his holy name;
    let the hearts of those who seek [Yahweh] rejoice.
Look to [Yahweh] and his strength;
    seek his face always.
Remember the wonders he has done, his miracles,
    the judgments he pronounced,
O descendants of Abraham his servant,
    O sons of Jacob, his chosen ones.
He is [Yahweh] our God;
    his judgments are in all the earth.
He remembers his covenant forever,
    the word he commanded, for a thousand generations,
the covenant he made with Abraham,
    the oath he swore to Isaac.
He confirmed it to Jacob as a decree,
    to Israel as an everlasting covenant . . .
And he sent a man before them—
    Joseph, sold as a slave . . . then Israel entered Egypt.

What follows is a history lesson, one that is remarkably like what Stephen gave when he was on trial for his life.

I remember when I first became a Christian and began reading the New Testament. I was interested in the exciting passage in Acts 6 where a man is on trial for his life. This business of being a Christian can get pretty serious. Somebody could get hurt because he believed in Jesus. But then we come to chapter seven, and I always wanted to skip it because it sounded like Sunday school . . . just a history lesson. But Stephen was saying that what was happening there was simply the next step in that process that started when God called Abraham out of Ur of the Chaldees.

Now look at Isaiah 41:8 and you will find this eighth-century prophet saying,

---

[42] Note that what Yahweh has done, His acts, has been done in history, not in some invisible, mythical realm.

"But you, O Israel, my servant,
>   Jacob, whom I have chosen,
>   you descendants of Abraham, my friend,
> I took you from the ends of the earth,
>   from its farthest corners I called you.
> I said, 'You are my servant';
>   I have chosen you and have not rejected you.
> So do not fear. I am with you;
>   do not be dismayed, for I am your God."

Now, this is Yahweh. He has married Himself to Abraham and to his descendants.

Or look at the passage in Deuteronomy 26. You remember that Moses was telling them what to tell their children, when the children say, "Why do we do these things?" The parents were to say, "Our father was a wandering Aramean." So, many generations after Abraham, when a Hebrew child looked at his or her parents and said, "Why are we different?" the answer was, "Our father Abraham . . ." and a history lesson.

This truth carries on into the New Testament. Notice that when Matthew begins his gospel, he begins it with Abraham. As I have gotten older I have come to love the genealogies more and not to find them as boring as I once did. This is because every one of them is a theological statement. When God called Abraham, He had Jesus in mind. And when Jesus was born it was a consequence of what had been started with Abraham. So all of this is to say that the call of Abraham is of great historic significance. That significance continues into the present as the attention of the world continues to be focused, after four thousand years, on Abraham's descendants and the struggle over the land that was promised to him.[43]

---

[43] [Editor's note] At the time the lectures were given the historic meeting of Yitzhak Rabin and Yasser Arafat had just taken place. Dr. Kinlaw saw this event as an example of the ways God makes His truth inescapable. He likened it to the incident of Malchus' ear in John 18: *As the arrest of Jesus was taking place, Peter felt the need to "to do something." Always beware when someone feels the need "to do something." So Peter pulled a sword and started swinging. The amount of detail given is interesting; not only do we know whom Peter hit but we know where he hit him. He hit his ear; and we even know which ear it was. It was his right ear. That raises questions about Peter's ability or about the nature of the fight. But we*

The central question here is the one of election: a chosen people and the promise that God gave to Abraham. Brevard Childs makes an interesting point in this regard in his section on election. He says that there is a certain polarity, a tension, in the Old Testament doctrine of election.[44] By this he means, is this election conditional or unconditional? Is there a doctrine in the Old Testament that says, "I have chosen you and you are going to be saved whether you want to be or not?" Or is there also in the Old Testament a doctrine of rejection alongside the doctrine of election? The two concepts certainly exist side by side in the Hebrew

---

are not finished. Not only do we know who lost his ear, we know also know who Malchus' employer was. He was Caiaphas, the chief priest. Might this not mean that Malchus was the leader of the temple delegation? At the least he was part of that delegation. And where did that delegation take Jesus after the arrest? They took him to Caiaphas. Imagine the conversation:

Caiaphas: "Well, Malchus, how did it go?"

Malchus: "Well, we got him."

And Caiaphas said, "Did you have any problems?"

"Well, not too much."

"What do you mean? Did you have some problems?"

"Well, we had a little problem."

"What happened?"

"You know that big fisherman? He pulled his sword and swung . . ."

"Well, did he hit anybody?"

"Yeah, he hit me."

"You look alright to me."

"Well, it was this ear. He clipped it off."

Caiaphas said, "Well, it's on there now."

And I can hear Malchus saying, "Yes, sir, that's the problem. Do you think we got the wrong man?"

My question is: Was Malchus' ear Jesus' last love note to Caiaphas, saying, "Caiaphas, do you really want to go through with this?"

What do you think it was like the next day? I'm sure every time Malchus walked in, Caiaphas was looking at one thing. And I'm sure that after three or four days Caiaphas transferred him to somewhere else so he wouldn't have to look at that ear. And that's what you and I do with God. That's what human society, culture, does with God. God has written Himself into our culture in a thousand ways, and we do our best to ignore them all.

For instance, the New York Times is one of the most hostile publications to historic Christianity in the United States and the world. But every morning there is a "Malchus' Ear" on the second line of the front page, [the date] ano domini. Now, these evidences are in our life because God made His world and does not want anybody to be lost, and they are here to bear witness.

[44] Brevard S. Childs, *Biblical Theology of the Old and New Testaments* (Minneapolis: Fortress Press, 1993), 427.

language. Alongside the Hebrew word *bahar*, "to choose," you also have the Hebrew word *'azab*, "to reject." And so, there are two themes that you could develop.

Look with me at Deuteronomy 28. This is at the end of Moses' life. Moses is standing, speaking to the people of God, the chosen people. He begins by speaking of the blessings that will come upon them if they will hear God's voice, walk in His ways, and do what He says. These blessings will be on every aspect of their lives: their health, their family, their cattle, their fields, everything. That takes us through the first fifteen verses.

But then come the curses if they refuse to live according to their covenant with God. This begins at verse 16 and continues all the way to verse 68! The chapter closes in this way, beginning at verse 64:

> "Then the Lord will scatter you among all the nations, from one end of the earth to the other. There you will worship other gods—gods of wood and stone, which neither you nor your fathers have known. Among those nations you will find no repose, no resting place for the sole of your foot. There [Yahweh] will give you an anxious mind, eyes weary with longing, and a despairing heart. You will live in constant suspense, filled with dread both night and day, never sure of your life. In the morning you will say, 'If only it were evening!' and in the evening, 'If only it were morning!' because of the terror that will fill your hearts and the sights that your eyes will see.[45] [Yahweh] will send you back in ships to Egypt, on a journey that I said you would never make again. [Isn't that interesting? God says, "I'm going to have to do what I told you I would never do." Don't forget that.] There, you will offer yourselves for sale to your enemies as male and female slaves, but no one will buy you."

---

[45] What a picture this is of modern humanity. Here are the reasons for alcoholism, drug abuse, and all the rest.

So Moses is clearly talking about what Childs called "the polarity of election." If the Israelites kept the covenant, their election meant blessing; but if they did not keep it, that election meant a worse condition than what they started with. Childs' final comment on this topic is this:

> There remained the dark shadow of life apart from God, which threat was never rendered harmless.[46] Yet, finally, Israel testified that God's faithfulness transcends all human frailty. As unthinkable as it was that the creative power of God to establish the world could end, likewise was the thought that Israel would ever cease being a nation before God.[47, 48]

Now, Abraham is different from all the other figures in Scripture in this sense: He is picked out more than any other person in the Scripture as the model for you and for me. It is not hard to make a case for that. If you turn to the book of Romans and read the fourth chapter, you will find that the crux of Paul's argument is that salvation is by grace through faith; that we are justified by faith and by faith alone. Then he looks around for an example, and instead of taking one of the apostles or John the Baptist or one of the prophets or David or Moses, he leaps over every one of those and goes back to Genesis 12 and picks the father of the people of God, Abraham.

But as true as that is, it is also evident that Abraham is far from being a perfect model. He was a man who could lie. He would even endanger his wife's life in order to protect his own. He was willing to put her in a spot where she ended up in somebody else's harem. Nevertheless, the New Testament picks him out as the model for you and me.

---

[46] That is his way of saying that the possibility of lostness was always there, and there was no way to nullify it.

[47] Childs, *Biblical Theology,* 427.

[48] [Editor's note] This issue involves the biblical idea of "the one and the many." On the one hand, there was the community, and in this sense God's promises to Israel are unconditional. But, unlike other ancient cultures, Israel did not merely submerge the many (in this case, individuals) into the one (the community). God's promises to individual Israelites were not unconditional. They were conditional upon keeping of the covenant.

In the book of Galatians, Paul belabors the point. He was speaking to first-century Christians and explaining what the Christian faith actually is, what its essence is. He felt the need to do this because he was dealing with a group of people who had received the gospel but had then succumbed to a dilution of it so that they had departed from the basic Christian faith. So Paul reminded them that they had not been saved by any work of theirs. Rather, it was the work of God. Then as he reached for an illustration, where did he turn? He jumped back across the centuries to Abraham. That is very interesting. He was talking to Gentile Galatians about a Jew. He says that when we Gentiles believe the gospel about Christ, we become the children of Abraham. He says in effect that when God told Abraham that all nations of the earth would be blessed through him, he was thinking about the Galatians. He is saying that we need exactly what Abraham had, and that if we will trust in Christ, we will get exactly what Abraham got. That is a remarkable argument.

It is fortunate for us that Paul did not choose Moses as his example. If he had, we would have a difficult time extricating faith from all the requirements of the law. But as far as we can tell, there was none of that in existence for Abraham. I believe that the choice of Abraham as the model for us is one of those exquisite evidences of the love of God and of His desire for us to understand clearly what is at the heart of relationship with Him. He said, "If you believe, you will receive the Spirit and you will get what Abraham got." Grace is a promise, not a payoff, just as it was to Abraham. It was promised to him; he did not earn it. You find this point being made in Galatians, in Romans, and in Hebrews 11. In fact, in that roll call of faith in Hebrews 11, the longest section deals with Abraham (11:8-10; 17-19).

But then turn to the book of James. James also uses Abraham's life as a model to illustrate another aspect of Christian faith. As you remember, James was concerned about that aberration of the faith in which it was thought that a believer only had to exercise faith, apart from any evidence of that faith in his or her behavior. James shows that Abraham's faith was proved by his willingness to sacrifice his son Isaac (2:21-24). So in this one man, who was, as far as we know, the first man to follow Yahweh consciously, we have the very core of all that would characterize life with Yahweh for all the successive generations. I find that truly amazing, but more than that, a profound confirmation of the truth of the Word.

Now think with me about what Abraham did not have. He never had a page of the Bible, and he had never heard of those seven characteristics of Yahweh that we just finished talking about. How could he know them? There was nobody to tell him. When the darkness in which he walked is compared to the light in which we walk, the difference is incredible. Yet, he is the model for you and for me. Beyond this there was no church; Israel did not exist. That says something about where salvation is to be found. If there is no salvation outside of the church, Abraham would never have gotten in. There was no cult, or to use the Old Testament theologians' terms, no liturgy, no ritual. In fact, as you read the story of Abraham, you discover that he did very few "religious" things. He did build a few altars and made a few sacrifices, but there is no description of how he did those things or what their significance was. He expresses religion, but there is no "how to" involved in it. There were no sacraments. Circumcision is not found until later in the life of Abraham. That should put baptismal regeneration in its place once and for all, because Abraham's circumcision, which is the counterpart of New Testament baptism, came as an evidence of his salvation, not as a means of his salvation.[49]

Furthermore, there was no creed. You get some statements later in the Old Testament that are somewhat creedal. Gerhard von Rad, in his *Old Testament Theology*, argues that the core of Israelite faith is to be found in the book of Deuteronomy, in the basic creed found in chapter 26:5b-10a.[50] But that was more than four hundred years after Abraham, and that is a long time. So it is not right belief, theologically, intellectually, that saves a person. Those of us in intellectual circles need to remember that.

But beyond all of these there is another absence that is really surprising to me. There is no evidence in Genesis of any belief in life after death. Let me ask you: What would happen to some of our evangelistic

---

[49] As a follower of Wesley, I am interested that the male children were circumcised when they were eight days old. This means the children were in the covenant when they were born into a covenant family. Does that mean they were saved? Remember Deuteronomy 28; it is possible to be a member of the chosen people, the elect people of God, and be under a curse.

[50] Gerhard von Rad, *Old Testament Theology*, tr. D. Stalker, vol. 1 (New York: Harper & Row, 1962), 121ff.

efforts if we could not talk about heaven and hell? In Genesis there is no discussion of life after death. But Abraham is the model for us all. He believed God, and we are supposed to see something in Abraham that will cause us to believe even before we know about the New Testament teaching on life after death.

There was no law. Abraham never heard the Decalogue, the Ten Commandments. That helps explain some of the things he did. I am a little more lenient with him as a result. But it obviously means that a person can be saved without knowing the details of the moral law.

The most astounding thing about all of this is that Abraham is an example of justification by faith. What is justification? Justification by faith is a legal concept for most of us, is it not? How can you make someone understand "justification by faith" if you do not have a law code, if you do not have a court, and if you do not have a judge? Yet Abraham is the supreme example of being justified by faith. He believed God and it was accounted unto him for righteousness. Clearly that is not according to some legal system of accounting. So what is the righteousness that God is seeking and which accrued to Abraham? The essence of it is a personal relationship with the living God. Notice Genesis 17:1. God says that if Abraham is to be all he is meant to be as a human being ("perfect" in the language of the *King James Version*), he has only to "walk" before God. That is not surprising when we remember that in Genesis the most characteristic way of describing what we mean by the term *salvation* is to say that a person "walked with God."

Think about how little Abraham knew about the One whom he was following. The gods of his neighbors and of his personal friends were really personifications of natural forces, like the sun and the moon, or like human sexuality or reproductive capacity, fertility. His world knew nothing of the kind of God Yahweh is, that we described in those seven characteristics, a God who transcends time and space. He is beyond it all, yet sovereign over all of the creation, and Sovereign Lord of history.

Now, the greatness of Abraham's faith is that in a vacuum like that, in an intellectual and religious wilderness like that, he came to believe that behind everything he could see there was Someone, and that that Someone wanted to talk to him. In fact, he felt that that One wanted to know him and wanted him to know the One who was there, whose name he did not know. And somehow or other he felt that that One wanted to bless him, that His motivation toward him was good. Think of how much of the religion of the world is based on the assumption that if there is anyone out there, He is against us and we must find ways to appease Him. To a significant degree that attitude either is, or has been, in every one of us. If it is not in you, the probability is that the deliverance is simply a product of God's presence and grace as you have come to know Him. So it was against all the odds that Abraham felt that this unnamed One out there was benevolent toward him and wanted to bless him.

This conviction of the benevolence of this One who had spoken to him inclined Abraham to follow Him, and to believe that it was safe for him to do so. Now, that is a marvelous, miraculous, amazing thing. He felt it was safe, not only to follow but, more importantly, to risk absolutely everything that he was and owned on the Person that he believed had spoken to him. In other words, he apparently thought that it was safe to believe that this Person who wanted to communicate with Him was God. He did not have the content for that word that you and I have, but despite that he was willing to risk everything on God, whereas you and I who do have the content are not ready to risk everything and let Him be God. He obviously believed the truth of something I said earlier, that if you have everything in the world plus God, you are not a bit richer than if you had nothing but God. On the other hand, if you have God and not one other thing in the world, you are not a bit poorer. When you have God, you have enough. It is so because God is the Lord, Sovereign, Master of it all. We used to say it this way: If you are a guest of the Rockefellers, it does not matter that you forgot your wallet. Apparently Abraham came to believe that about this One whom he had never seen and, as far as we know, had never heard about from anybody else.

Here we come to the essence of what it means for Abraham to be the model of faith for us. It is not intellectual, it is not moral and ethical, it is not institutional, all the terms we tend to think of. No, the essence of it all is that absolute reliance on, that personal relationship with, the God whom he says has spoken to him. Without the externals that you and I have, Abraham staked everything on this One.

Lecture 9

· · · · · · · · · ·

Implications of Abraham's Call

We said in the previous lecture that the faith that Abraham models for all of us is his absolute dependence on his personal relationship with God. Now, I would like to share with you a couple of the implications of all of this that move me and affect all my thinking. If Yahweh is the One whom the Scripture says He is, the eternal One, the ultimate, the absolute, then he does not change. Time has neither improved Him nor diminished Him. If he could make that much difference in Abraham's life, so that the next four thousand years tell a story as they do, one that makes it plain that what happened to Abraham was the key to the most significant intellectual advances in human history, what would happen if one of us did that? God has not changed.

Furthermore, there is no indication that Abraham was expecting God to do something in the other world. Abraham was expecting Him to do it in the here and now. What are you expecting Him to do while you live? If God does not change, and if He could do this in a person like Abraham, then what we ought to pray for is that He would do something like that in some of us, so that the world would be a different place and so that time would be different. So many times there is this subtle feeling in Christianity that we need to get out of time, and that if we can escape time, things will be better. But the only salvation heaven will know anything about will have taken place in time. The only salvation eternity will know anything about will have taken place in time. How many years do you have ahead of you? Forty, fifty, sixty? You ought to think, "What does God want to do with those?" Because He is the Savior, not just of souls, He is the Savior of time, and it was in time that God promised to do some things for and with Abraham. I hope God will put some promises inside you about time and what He wants to do there.

If God has never changed and if we can count on that, then what He wants from me is the same thing He wanted from Abraham. Likewise, what He was able to do in Abraham, He can do in the likes of me. The form that obedience or following will take will be different. Whether it is a Quaker meeting or high Anglican worship in Westminster Abbey; or a Pentecostal meeting or a group of Christians under a tree somewhere; or a house church in China today, the trappings may be very different but the essence ought to be the same. It ought to be a personal experience, a personal relationship with the living God, in which a person says, "I believe it is safe to trust Him. I believe His will toward me is good, that His heart toward me is benevolent and it is safe for me to stake everything on Him."

If that happened in the ancient world, could it happen in your world or mine? I want to share with you an account that I came across a few years ago that in my mind illustrates exactly what I am talking about.[51] The central figure is a woman who, in the 1930s, had graduated from Hunter College in New York City. She came out of a Jewish family. While her mother was rather devout, going to synagogue, her father seldom attended, only going for an occasional high holy day. So, religion was not a vital part of her life. There was a lot of rebellion in those days and, in the midst of the Depression, a lot of heartache. So,

---

[51] Joy Davidman, "The Longest Way Round," in *These Found the Way*, ed. D. W. Soper (Philadelphia; Westminster, 1951), 10-26. The following quotations from that account may be found on pp. 23-25.

finding nothing she thought to be authentic in her parents' religion, she abandoned it and adopted the Marxism of some of her friends. She was a very brilliant young woman, and so she ended up as an editor on the staff of *New Masses*, which was the communist publication in New York City in the 1930s. All of her personal friends were drawn from that circle of communists. Of course, a part of all that was atheism as a practicing way of life. She was very brilliant, very arrogant, very abrasive, and very clever, and she won her way by her brilliance.

But, she was a normal human being. She met a fellow who was a great storyteller and a writer and later she married him. And after she married him she began to change a bit because it was not too long until she had a child. And when the child came she found herself studying some Marxist literature where she learned about Marxists who sacrificed their children for the communist party. And she looked at her baby and said, "I don't know whether I could do that or not." She said, "Helping mankind in the abstract is one thing, but when I've got a child here, that is another matter." [I take that as one of God's love notes in the world, like Malchus' ear.] Soon, a second child came. Then her husband began to come apart. He had fought in the Spanish Civil War, one of the great left-wing causes of the day, and was a capable novelist and Hollywood film writer. But he succumbed to alcohol and other women. As a result she found herself under considerable strain. They had moved to Westchester, north of New York, where living expenses were high. Not only did she have to cope with the strain of two babies, her husband's drinking and unfaithfulness, and constant worry about money, but also with the fact that her husband was rapidly approaching a mental collapse.

So, she wrote, "One day he telephoned me from his New York office—I was at home in Westchester with the children—to tell me that he was having a nervous breakdown. He felt his mind going; he couldn't stay where he was and he couldn't bring himself to come home. . . . Then he rang off." She spent the rest of the day frantically making phone calls trying to locate him through friends and acquaintances. She said about it, "By nightfall there was nothing to do but wait and see if he turned up, alive or dead. I put the babies to sleep and waited. For the first time in my life I felt helpless." Now, as she looked back on that night, telling about it later, she said, "C.S. Lewis once remarked that every story of conversion was the story of blessed defeat." And if anyone was defeated, it was this young lady. Her babies were quiet and in bed, nobody else was in the apartment, there was no one left to call. She was alone with herself, her fears and the stillness. She confessed, "For the first time my pride was forced to admit that I was not, after all, 'the master of my fate' and 'the captain of my soul.' All of my defenses—the walls of arrogance and cock-sureness and self-love behind which I had hid from God—went down momentarily. And God came in." Now, I expected a paragraph on that. She put it in four words and the four words is a better way to say it. You never introduce the president of the United States. You simply say, "Mr. President." Why should there be any description when God comes in?

She described her perception of the experience in this way:

> It is infinite, unique. There are no words, there are no comparisons. Can one scoop up the sea in a tea cup? Those who have known God will understand me; the others, I find, can neither listen nor understand. There was a Person there with me in the room, directly present to my consciousness—a Person so real that all my previous life was, by comparison, mere shadow play. And I myself was more alive than I had ever been; it was like waking from sleep. So intense a life cannot be endured long by flesh and blood; we must ordinarily take our life watered down, diluted as it were, by time and space and matter. My perception of God lasted perhaps half a minute.

All this was stunning to a Jewish communist Marxist atheist. She found herself on her knees. She said, "I think I must have been the world's most astonished atheist." To her astonishment, the formerly ardent materialist not only knew that God was there, but that He had always been there and that He loved her. It was safe to trust Him; He was benevolent toward her; He wanted to bless her. That sounds like Abraham, does it not?

This was Joy Davidman's conversion experience. She said, "I saw myself as I really was, with dismay and repentance; and seeing, I changed. I have been turning into a different person since that half minute, everyone tells me." Now, she said, "My awareness of God was not a comforting illusion, conjured up to reassure me about my husband's safety. I was just as worried afterward as before. No, terror and ecstasy, repentance and rebirth." Some of you may know this story because later, after her husband divorced her, Joy Davidman was to become C.S. Lewis' wife. Now this happened in our century, in the state of New York, just outside of New York City, but what fascinates me is how much it is like what I think happened back in Ur of the Chaldees four thousand years ago when in some way or another, "God came in," and just like Joy Davidman, that ancient Semite knew. I do not know whether it was a half-minute, or perhaps two minutes, but he knew. And he knew with a knowledge that was to change his life and that of the world.

Joy Davidman said that after that minute, the question was to find out who He was, what His name was. She acknowledged that she was by no means a Christian at first. "All my atheist life I had regarded 'the apostate' [a Jew-become-Christian] with traditional Jewish horror." To clarify her vision, she consciously tried to revive her commitment to Marxism, at least to Marxist economics. She thought, in this way, she could help others. In her quest she read Marxist theory in depth for the first time. "It was a difficult and painful study. Inch by inch I retreated from my revolutionary position; fallacy after fallacy, contradiction upon contradiction, absurdity upon absurdity turned up in Lenin's *Materialism and Emperio-Criticism*, one of the basic textbooks of Marxist philosophers." Marxism, she found, was a blind alley. So if that was not the way, perhaps she should do what her family would suggest. She would try Judaism as the next logical step. So she decided "to become a good Jew, of the comfortable 'Reformed' persuasion." But as she studied Judaism and other religions she discovered that all religions are not the same. While each of the religions, including Judaism, had partial understandings, "only one of them had complete understanding of the grace and repentance and charity that had come to me from God. And the Redeemer who had made Himself known, whose personality I would have recognized among ten thousand—well, when I read the New Testament, I recognized Him. He was Jesus."

I have given this account at such length because I believe it is too easy for us merely to analyze the Abraham narrative in a scholarly way and thus dismiss it as a real human experience. But I want to say, that if we knew where to find them, I think we could point to many other stories like this, where God came and the person began to follow even though they were not quite sure who it was they were following. And the same thing that happened in an individual life has happened in human culture where Israel, a people, set out to follow a God they only knew very imperfectly, and in the process came to know who the true and living God is.

At the end of the previous lecture I pointed out that the book of Genesis describes this relationship with God as a walk. It does not describe it in terms of a relationship to a religion; it does not describe it in relationship to a moral and ethical code; and it does not describe it in relationship to any religious institution. But it does describe it in terms of a person and an ongoing relationship to a person, and the language used is incredibly simple. It begins to be spelled out in Genesis 13:14. This is after the call in chapter 12; Abraham has followed to Canaan and is moving about the land following the instructions of this One whom he is coming to know. The Lord says,

> "Lift up your eyes from where you are and look north and south, east and west. All the land you see I will give to you and your offspring forever. I will make your offspring like the dust of the earth, so that if someone could count the dust, then your offspring could be counted. Go, walk through the length and breadth of the land, for I am giving it to you."

Now, that gets a little more specific when you get to chapter 17. Look at the introduction. "When Abraham was ninety-nine years old, the Lord appeared to him and said, 'I am God Almighty [El Shaddai]; walk before me and be blameless. I will confirm my covenant between me and you and will greatly increase your numbers."

Here you get that word *walk* which is used so significantly in the book of Genesis. Let me call your attention to some passages where it occurs. The first of them is in the Garden in the third chapter. You will remember that God came down and "was walking in the cool of the day. . . ." and the implication is that when He came in the cool of the day

He came for companionship and fellowship with His creatures whom He had created and put in that Garden. This time they have sinned and are running from Him. But the implication of that story, I think, is that there were other evenings before they had sinned when they had walked with Him in unbroken fellowship. As you proceed along through the fourth chapter, you encounter a lot of sin and sinners. But then you come to Enoch in the fifth chapter. It is amazing how cryptically his story is told. You will recall that it occurs in the middle of a genealogy where each entry had followed the same pattern up to this point. Enoch's entry starts out in the same way, but ends up differently.

> When Enoch had lived 65 years, he became the father of Methuselah. And after he became the father of Methuselah, Enoch walked with God 300 years and had other sons and daughters. Altogether Enoch lived 365 years. Enoch *walked* [emphasis mine] with God; then he was no more, because God took him away.

After that things deteriorated still further, and the world became more and more evil. In Genesis 6:5 we are told, "The thoughts of his [mankind's] heart was only evil all the time." Clearly something had to be done. So, he looked around and found Noah. In verses 7-8 Yahweh said,

> "I will wipe mankind, whom I have created, from the face of the earth—men and animals, and creatures that move along the ground, the birds of the air—for I am grieved that I have made them." But Noah found favor in the eyes of [Yahweh]. This is the account of Noah, Noah was a righteous man, blameless among the people of his time, and he *walked* [emphasis mine] with God.

When Eleazar, Abraham's servant, was in Laban's house telling him how Abraham had sent him to find a wife for his son, he said (Gen. 24:39-41):

> I asked my master, "What if the woman will not come
> back with me?" He replied, "[Yahweh], before whom
> I have *walked* [emphasis mine], will send his angel with
> you and make your journey a success so that you can
> get a wife for my son from my own clan and from my
> father's family. Then, you will go to my clan, you will
> be released from my oath even if they refuse to give
> her to you."

The important point is that Abraham believed God would prosper the servant's mission because Abraham had been walking with God.

Now move to the end of the Joseph story in Genesis 48. Jacob
had come down to Egypt and is there with his son and he is blessing
Joseph's sons before his death.

> Then he blessed Joseph and said, "May the God before
> whom my fathers Abraham and Isaac *walked* [emphasis
> mine], the God who has been my shepherd all my life
> to this day, the Angel who has delivered me from all
> harm—may he bless these boys. May they be called by
> my name and the names of my fathers Abraham and
> Isaac, and may they increase greatly upon the earth"
> (48:15-16).

It is interesting that in that speech of Jacob you get two great
Old Testament concepts for the first time. One of them is Yahweh as
"my shepherd," and the other is Yahweh as "my redeemer," my *go'el*, the
Redeemer. They are both in that passage. But notice especially how Jacob
understood that his religion and the religion of his fathers was a matter
of walking with God.

You will find this same understanding of the relationship
with God throughout the Old Testament. In his valedictory address in
Deuteronomy, Moses called upon Israel to "walk in all his ways" (Deut.
10:12). In 1 Kings 3:14, Yahweh urges the newly inaugurated Solomon to
"walk in my ways." When Hezekiah begs for longer life, as reported in 2
Kings 20:3, he calls on Yahweh to remember "how I have walked before
you faithfully and with wholehearted devotion." And you will find many

more examples in the Old Testament, not the least of which is Micah's well-known, "What does the Lord require of you? To act justly and to love mercy (Heb. *hesed*) and to walk humbly with your God" (6:8).

But beyond that, the same concept can be found in the New Testament. Look at Luke, chapter 1, verses 5-6: "There was in the days of Herod, the king of Judea, a certain priest named Zecharias, of the division of Abijah. His wife was of the daughters of Aaron, and her name was Elizabeth. And they were both righteous before God, *walking* [emphasis mine] in all the commandments and ordinances of the Lord blameless" (*NKJV*). There at the outset of the gospel that understanding of what true religion consists of is introduced into the New Testament. And you remember how frequently Paul says that our business is to walk in the Spirit (Rom. 8:4; Gal. 5:16, 25). In Ephesians he says we are to walk in love (Eph. 5:2) and in Colossians we are to walk worthy of the name of the one who has called us (Col. 1:10). And John spells it out very clearly: "If we walk in the light as He is in the light, we have fellowship one with another, and the blood of Jesus Christ His Son, cleanses us from all sin" (1 John 1:7).

In the light of this discussion, think about this: Jesus seldom ever told anybody to believe in Him. Take a look at the Gospels. But what He did say was: follow Me. It is very easy for us to intellectualize that, to theologize it. And of course there is a connection between what we believe and how we live. If you believe, you will follow. Abraham believed God and so he followed. But I think sometimes that our language takes away the sharp edge of what is here, that what God wants above all is for me to walk in unbroken fellowship with Him.

It will be a fruitful study for you to work through the Abraham narrative noting down each occurrence of promise, what is promised, and any response to the promise that is called for. Another question to ask yourself as you are reading is why some incidents are told in considerable detail, while in other cases glaring gaps are left. Years pass with no mention at all, whereas what may seem to us a trivial incident is given detailed discussion. Why is that? While most of the critical texts will tell you why the church or the body of believers put them there, I urge you to go one step behind that and ask the question, Why do you think God had those things included in Scripture? For while God certainly did use human writers and the human body of believers to see that we got the Scripture, the ultimate cause of the text that we have is that the Spirit of God in his sovereignty was giving us data for our benefit. So, as far as I am concerned, every single unit in that narrative has something to say to you and me if we have the wisdom and the spiritual sensitivity and the knowledge necessary to understand. So let's start at the beginning of the narrative, at Genesis 11, and look at the first of the promises. As the years have passed I have come to love the way the Scripture does not use long, wordy buildups to introduce things. It just lands you right in the middle of life. So here:

> Terah took his son Abram, his grandson Lot son of Haran, his daughter-in-law, Sarai the wife of his son Abram, and together they set out from Ur of the Chaldeans to go to Canaan. But when they came to Haran, they settled there. Terah lived 205 years, and he died in Haran (Gen. 11:31-32).

And then the most remarkable story in human history begins. It begins very simply, "Yahweh said to Abram. . . ." Remember how creation began: "And God said. . . ." When Yahweh speaks there is eternal potential, always, in that moment. And that is recorded for us:

> [Yahweh] said to Abram, "Leave your country, your people and your father's household and go to the land I will show you. I will make you a great nation and I will bless you; I will make your name great, and you will be a blessing. I will bless those who bless you, and whoever curses you I will curse; and all peoples on earth will be blessed through you" (Gen. 12:1-3).

There is no discussion of Abram's reaction, no discussion of what he thought. This is very similar to what is in my mind one of the most impressive passages in the Bible: Genesis 22 where God says to Abraham, "I want you to take your son, Isaac, and sacrifice him on Mount Moriah." The next sentence begins, in Hebrew, *wayyashkem*. That means, simply, "and he arose early in the morning. . . ." And a curtain is drawn across what must have been a night of anguish, because that is not the important thing. The important thing is that by the next morning it was settled. Abraham arose and was on his way to sacrifice his son. So here, what matters is that Abraham decided in the end to risk all.

Notice what it is that God asked of Abram in the beginning. Three things: I want you to leave your country; I want you to leave your people; and I want you to leave your father's household. Now, what do you think those three things represented? The simple response is: everything. Now, he carried some of his people with him and some of his possessions. But his country, his people, and his father's household were his identity. We live in such a very different world with its rootless individualism. In Abram's world a rootless individual was a cipher. Without the identity to be found in country, people, and clan, a few possessions and an immediate family were worth next to nothing. We can thank God for the concept of individual worth that has come to us as a by-product of biblical truth, but that was something utterly foreign to Abram.

So what God was asking Abram was not what it would be for God to say to you, "I want you to spend the rest of your life as a missionary on a foreign field." You could almost say there is no similarity between those two. God was asking him to give up his security, but more than that, He was asking him to give up his identity. He was asking him, for all practical purposes, to give up his future, as far as that world was concerned. And, here is the astounding thing, he did it! He gave up his country, he gave up his people, and he gave up his family. But why did God ask him to do that? It is not as though any of those things is a sin. Not one of those things is an evil. He didn't ask him to give up adultery. He didn't ask him to give up stealing or lying. He asked him to give up good things.

I came across a collection of essays written in tribute to Aleksandr Solzhenitsyn some years ago. There was one article in it reflecting on the fact that the book of Revelation speaks about every tongue, every tribe, every nation. And the thrust of the article was this: that there will be nations in heaven. That thought had never crossed my mind. I always thought that when we got there everybody would be the same. But the book of Revelation says, there will be Nigerians in heaven, and they won't hang their heads because they are Nigerians. And there will be Italians in heaven. The author was saying there would be Russians in heaven. So what am I saying? I am saying that having a national identity is a good thing, a God-given thing. But that is just the point: the test of whether you are a believer is not in what you do with the third through the tenth commandments; but it is what you let the God of the first two commandments do with the good, the goods, in your life. The greatest enemies to God in our lives are the gifts and the goods He has given us. There is where the competition is. And God said to Abram, "I want you to lay your good in my hands and let me relate you to them as I will and separate you from them as I will." Yahweh was asking Abram from that day forward to find his identity in his relationship with Him. And Abram said, "You are Lord." What a story.

Lecture 10

. . . .

God's Covenant
with Abraham

In this lecture I want to continue our examination of the Abraham narrative, seeking to point out some items in it that may not be familiar to you and that may be helpful. The big thing I would like to do here is for you to begin to get a sense of the covenant that was established with Abraham and the relationship he had with Yahweh and how different it was from the Mosaic covenant. And yet despite the differences, the essence of the two covenants is basically the same. It is important to remember this when we read Paul in Galatians and see the ways he talks about the fact that the covenant was given to Abraham before the Law was given. The danger is that we will get our eyes on the differences rather than on the basic, essential similarity.

Let me walk through the narrative with you, highlighting some of the key points. At the end of Genesis 11 we get the story of Terah leaving Ur of the Chaldees with his family and moving to Haran. Then, when we get to Haran, Terah dies and Abram receives the promise. So Abram leaves Haran and comes to Canaan. When he gets into Canaan, you will remember that Yahweh appears to him. In Haran, when God appeared to him, He said, "I will give you progeny, I will make of you a great nation, and I will let you be a means of blessing to the world." Now, in the end of chapter 12, God speaks more specifically and identifies the land that He is to give to him. He was now in Canaan and God said, "This land I will give to you."

Famine comes and drives him to Egypt, and there is where we get the first case of the deception on the part of Abram about his wife, Sarai, in relation to Pharaoh. In chapter 13, we get the conflict between Lot's herdsmen and Abraham's herdsmen. The text tells us that they agreed the hill country where they were living was "not sufficient to care for" them. So Abram graciously permitted Lot to choose the more favorable land. This is one of the good moments in Abram's life. Then Yahweh appears to him again and as He does He is more specific now about the extent of the promise to him. He says, "Lift up your eyes from where you are and look north and south, east and west. All the land that you see I will give to you and your offspring forever" (13:13). So, because you refused to grasp for the best, all the land will be yours. When you get to chapter 14 you find the story of Abram saving Lot from captivity and you get that unusual entry about Melchizedek, which is picked up in the book of Hebrews and used there.

Now we come to chapter 15. Up to this point, Abram has been told that he is to have progeny, his descendants will be a great nation and they are to have land, and out of him blessing will come to the world. Now Yahweh comes to Abram and speaks more specifically about what He wants to do with him. He says, "I will be your shield and I will be your great reward." But Abram points out that he is very old and has no natural children (despite of all God's promises). In fact, any reward God might give Abram will go to his servant, Eliezer, whom Abram seems to have adopted. But the Lord says to him, "No, that's not the way it's going to be. Your descendants are going to be as numerous as the stars in the heavens." Notice how, each time Yahweh appears, He adds some detail to the promise He is giving. So here He speaks about the innumerable descendants Abram is to have. And we are told, in verse 6, the famous verse, that Abram believed God and it was accounted to him for righteousness.

What are we to make of that statement? Abram had already risked everything by following God to Canaan, and yet the text now says Abram believed God and it was "credited" to him for righteousness. Does that mean that he had not believed before? Not at all. I think he had faith, but it was faith that was deepening. This is one of the characteristics of the walk with God: The faith deepens and the commitment deepens and the understanding of the Other deepens. And along the way there are key points where what has been happening gradually is confirmed and solidified. In this fifteenth chapter, we have one of those points of confirmation, and God recognizes that with an act of covenant sealing. It is sealed with sacrifice and with a sign. And you will remember that sign is fire. Abram has now said to Yahweh, "How will I know that this is to take place?" And so, there comes the smoking pot of fire and the flame of fire, and that is God's signature, as it were.

Now, you do not have to use much imagination to see the beginning there of a motif that will run all the way through Scripture to the book of Revelation. Again and again, God shows Himself in fire: whether it is Moses at a burning bush or Moses on the mountain at Sinai, or whether it is Elijah on Mt. Carmel or Isaiah in the temple. If you go to the New Testament, you find it at Pentecost, and finally in the One who stands before John as a flame of fire in the book of Revelation. So this signature that is laid down here is the seal that is carried through the rest of the Scripture. Yahweh, the God of Scripture, has sealed the covenant with him.[52]

Now, in the next chapter we find Abram and Sarai saying, "We have waited ten years for the Lord to keep His promise . . . now we need to help Him out." And as I read that I ask myself how many times I have decided I needed to help God out and took my way instead of His way. And always, when I have done it, there have been problems that complicated my path. As far as we can tell, there was nothing immoral or illegal in what they decided to do. We have a prenuptial agreement from Nuzi in the area of Assyria, which shows that a wife was required to provide a substitute wife for her husband if she herself was unable to

---

[52] [Editor's note] It is also important to note that by the fire's passing between the parts of the animals, God was calling down a blood oath upon Himself if He should ever break this covenant (cf. Jeremiah 34:18). This is the point of the statement in Hebrews 6:13 that "He swore by Himself," there being none higher.

have children. So, Abraham had relations with Hagar, she conceived, and a child was born. And what was the immediate result of that effort to help God out? It was hatred between Sarai and Hagar, so that the angel of Yahweh, the messenger of Yahweh, had to move in and take care of Hagar and her child.

When we come to chapter 17 we find another place where the covenant is reconfirmed, as it were, and where it is spelled out in more detail. You will notice that it is here that Abram's name is changed to Abraham, and Sarai's name is changed to Sarah. This is also where God says, in effect, "Abraham, you made suggestions about Eliezer, and then you and Sarah made some about Hagar and about Ishmael, but I want to say, it is going to be Sarah who will be the mother of the child that will extend your progeny, through whom the rest of the world will find the possibility of blessing."[53]

In chapter 18 we are told the incredible story of God coming to visit Abraham with two friends. Abraham, like a good Oriental host, insisted on their having a meal with Him. While they were at the meal God said to him, "Where is your wife, Sarah?" And he replied, "She's in the tent." So God said, "Well, next year this time, she will conceive and have a child." In the seventeenth chapter, when God said that the mother would be Sarah, Abraham thought to himself, *Wait a minute, how can a woman who is her age and a man who is my age have a child?* And so, we are told, Abraham laughed. Now here in chapter 18, it is Sarah, being in a position where she could hear without being seen, who laughed. When God asked about it, she denied laughing. It is interesting that both of these people are capable of deceit. Having deepening faith does not guarantee spiritual maturity or entirely right behavior. It certainly ought to lead to those, but they are not requirements for getting in. We get a glimpse of that when God does not condemn Sarah, but responds in one of those incredibly great texts of Scripture, "Is anything too hard for [me]?" (Gen. 18:14).

When the child was born as reported in chapter 21, he was

---

[53] [Editor's note] It is in chapter 17 that Abraham is first given a direct command in regard to covenant obedience. It is hardly accidental that the sign of covenant obedience is circumcision. Here, after the tragic mistake with Ishmael, Abraham was symbolically surrendering his ability to reproduce himself into the hands of Yahweh, his covenant Lord.

named Isaac, which means, "He laughs." Now, for a long time I felt that what was being said was that the child was given a name that would be a perpetual reminder to Abraham and Sarah of their unbelief. But I did a good bit of work once on Ancient Near Eastern names and I found out that most of the names are sentence names and that the subject of the sentence was normally a god or goddess. Sometimes in common usage, the name might be shortened with the divine element left off, just as we sometimes shorten names in common usage and change Ronald to Ron. A clear example of that shortening in the Bible is in Ahaziah and Ahaz. The –iah element is a short form of Yahweh. So what does that mean about this name Isaac? Who is the subject? Almost without question it was Yahweh. So Isaac's full name was probably "Yahweh laughs," or maybe "God laughs." That puts the name Isaac in a little different light, doesn't it? Now, does God laugh in derision at Abraham and Sarah for their unbelief, or does he laugh in joy? I believe it is the latter, because every time "Isaac" occurs it is in a context of a promise for blessings for the whole world. So I think what you have in that name is God saying, "I want to tell you how to name him because we are big business together. We have a world that needs to be redeemed, and when this child is born, the messianic line is on its way." So with that name God already is looking down through the centuries to the day when the angels will sing in praise to God because the Son is born, a Savior has come, and He laughs in sheer joy.

Returning to chapter 18 and the three visitors, we find God ready to resume his journey and Abraham accompanying Him to the edge of the camp. When they reach that point a very significant conversation ensues. We pick it up at verse 16:

> When the men got up to leave, they looked down toward Sodom, and Abraham walked along with them to see them on their way. Then [Yahweh] said, "Shall I hide from Abraham what I am about to do? Abraham will surely become a great and powerful nation, and all nations on earth will be blessed through him. For I have chosen him, so that he will direct his children and his household after him to keep the way of [Yahweh] by doing what is right and just, so that [Yahweh] will

bring about for Abraham what he has promised him"
(18:16-19).

It is interesting to see the personal relationship that is developing between Abraham and Yahweh, to the point where Yahweh wants to share
the burden that is in His own heart and the pain that is there. Notice the
emphasis upon the family from the household, because for God to fulfill
His purposes, this family has to be in existence for the better part of two
thousand years.

> [Yahweh] said, "The outcry against Sodom and Go-
> morrah is so great and their sin so grievous, that I will
> go down and see if what they have done is as bad as
> the outcry that has reached me. If not, I will know."
> The men turned away and went toward Sodom, but
> Abraham remained standing before [Yahweh]. Then
> Abraham approached him and said: "Will you sweep
> away the righteous with the wicked? What if there are
> fifty righteous people in the city? Will you really sweep
> it away and not spare the place for the sake of the fifty
> righteous people in it? Far be it from you to do such
> a thing—to kill the righteous with the wicked, treating
> the righteous and the wicked alike. Far be it from you!
> Will not the Judge of all the earth do right?" [And Yah-
> weh] said, "If I find fifty righteous people in the city
> of Sodom, I will spare the whole place for their sake"
> (18:20-26).

There is an interesting textual variant in this passage, in verse
22, where the translation that we have says, "The men turned away and
went toward Sodom, but Abraham remained standing before [Yahweh]."
Now, one of the things that has fascinated me is the way the text of the
Bible, and particularly the Old Testament, was handed down from generation to generation. That text was looked upon as very sacred. It was so
sacred that when a scribe prepared to copy a manuscript he was required
to wash his hands. He was not supposed to let soiled hands touch holy
things. The reverse took place when he finished; he washed his hands,

because hands that had holiness on them were not supposed to touch common things.

That conviction of the text's intrinsic holiness meant that a scribe who was copying a manuscript was not permitted to change anything. So when you look at an ancient Hebrew manuscript you will find that certain fairly obvious copying mistakes have been left in place because a scribe could never correct a previous scribe's mistakes, no matter how obvious they might seem to be. So what did a scribe do in a case like that? He wrote the correct word in the margin. So you have what are called *Khethibh/Qere* readings, where you find the original written *(kethibh)* in the text and a note of how to read it *(qere)* in the margin. You would come to something unreadable in the text and you would look in the margin and there would be the clue as to what you were to do with it.

But there are about eighteen to twenty places where apparently the scribes did change the text. These are called *tiqqune hassopherim,* "emendations of the scribes." In these cases, despite the holiness of the text, the error seemed so glaring to the scribes that they simply had to go ahead and change it. One of those rare scribal emendations occurs here in verse 22. The best scholarship suggests that verse 22 was originally something like this: "The men turned away and went toward Sodom, but Yahweh remained standing before Abraham." Many of the scribal emendations were made to avoid potential problems in public reading. So references to bodily functions and the like would be replaced with euphemisms. But that is not the case here; here they actually changed the text. Instead of having God standing before Abraham, something that would obviously not be at all fitting, they had Abraham standing before God. But if we are right about the original, what was it saying about God and Abraham? God had just finished telling Abraham that He was going to destroy Sodom and Gomorrah. But now He stops and stands there looking at Abraham. It is almost as if Yahweh is saying to Abraham, "My friend, I told you where I'm going and I've told you what I'm going to do. Aren't you going to say anything? Are you going to let me go ahead without even a word?" Here is a picture of the eternal God, Yahweh the incomparable, standing in the presence of one of His creatures, virtually inviting that creature to voice an objection.

Now, I ask again why the scribes felt it necessary to change that. Every indication is that they changed it because they felt that the picture it presented of Yahweh was very irreverent. The one thing you knew in that ancient world was that no king ever stood in the presence of his subject. The king sat. The one making the petition stood or knelt. So here you have the text putting Yahweh in the unthinkable position of the petitioner before one of His creatures, something that is not only irreverent and disrespectful, but almost blasphemous. Yahweh, the eternal God, the Sovereign Lord of all, could never be represented as standing and petitioning one of His creatures. So they changed it.

But as the years have passed, and I have reflected on this text, it has become more and more significant to me. That is one of the things that fascinates me about the Old Testament. As you read it in terms of that ancient world, there is suddenly just a crack, and in that crack you get a glimpse of something that is to come. What is it that is to come? It is Jesus. And we have a glimpse of Him here in Genesis. But it is no easier for us to grasp the point than it was for the scribes. How hard it is for us to believe that God is the way Jesus presented Him to be. Remember that the disciples spent two-and-a-half to three years with Him and yet never really heard Him when He talked about the nature of His Father's kingdom. When Jesus said to His disciples, after the better part of three years, "Who do you say that I am?" Peter responded, "We know who you are, you are the Christ, the Messiah, the one we've been waiting for all these years." But when Jesus said, "That's right. Now you know. Now I go to Jerusalem and I will be crucified," Peter instantly reacted, "You don't know your lines, Lord. The Messiah is not going to be crucified. It is His enemies that are going to be crucified" (Mark 8:27-32). The disciples, after all those years with Jesus, could not conceive of a God who would sacrifice Himself for you and me.

If you will look at chapters 9 and 10 of the gospel of Mark, you will find that thesis is picked up and developed extensively. In the ninth chapter, as they are going along on the road, Jesus says, "Now we are headed for Jerusalem, and when we get there I will suffer at the hands of sinful men and will be crucified, and on the third day I will rise." And the text says that they did not understand what he was saying (9:32). They could not think those thoughts. In the same way, the scribes who read that Yahweh stood yet before Abraham could not think that thought, and so they dared to change the text.

Again in Mark 9, Jesus looked at His disciples at the end of the day and said, "I noticed you had a very animated conversation on the road today. What were you talking about with such vigor?" So John looked at Peter and Peter looked at John, and John said, "Peter, you tell Him." And Peter said, "No, John, you tell Him." But Jesus said, in essence:

> You don't need to tell me. I know what you were talking about. You were talking about who's going to be first in my kingdom. You envision the kingdom like a pyramid in which the business is to climb as high as you can among fewer and fewer people. But that's not the way my kingdom is. My kingdom's like this: what you want to do is move down in the kingdom. Because he that is first will be last and he that is last will be first, and if you keep your life you will lose it and the Son of Man came not to keep His life but He came to give it away, to lay it down.

But still, when they get to the Thursday night at the Garden, and the troops come to arrest Jesus, what does Peter do? He pulls a sword.

So contrast Abraham with Peter, or worse, with you and me. Think of all we know and how little Abraham knew. He did not have a page of the Scripture. He had never seen Christ, he had no church, no sacrament, none of the benefits you and I have, and yet some way or other there was something in him that was grasping and reaching out, and that God could connect with.

So, Abraham took his cue from God and said, "Well, now, let's talk a little about Sodom." As he does this, he is playing the role that a prophet, or a man or woman of God, or the elect people are supposed to play. That is a role of intercession, because election is not for privilege. Election, being chosen by God, is so a world can know the truth of the Gospel. So Abraham cannot sit by and say, "Thank God He's not going to destroy my camp." No, he has to say, "Wait a minute, Lord. Sodom is my concern. If there are fifty righteous people down there, are You going to destroy it?" And you know how he moves down to lesser and lesser numbers. Now, the intercession did not save Sodom, but it did save Lot and his two daughters and, temporarily, his wife.

Lecture 11

············

Abraham's Developing Faith

In this lecture we will continue to explore the nature of the faith as it develops in Abraham's life. Let me begin by reminding you that the biblical text places extreme importance on the patriarchs. There is apparently a special relationship between the God of Scripture, Yahweh, and the patriarchs. You find this in expressions like "the God of Abraham," so that the biblical God is identified with Abraham and Abraham is identified with Him, and you speak of the two at the same time. "The God of Abraham," you will remember, is the expression Jacob used, "the God of Abraham and the fear of Isaac."[54] Regularly, God is identified as the God of Abraham and of Isaac and of Jacob. You will remember that is the way God identified Himself when He came to Moses at the burning bush. He said, "Let me tell you who I am. I am the God of Abraham, the

---

[54] While the two different titles here may indicate a difference in the relationship of Isaac with Yahweh from that of Abraham with Yahweh, it is more likely that the two terms are simply intended to be synonymous, with each one informing the other in keeping with the forms of Hebrew poetry.

God of Isaac, and the God of Jacob."

This kind of thinking lies behind the term, "the God of the Fathers." When Scripture uses this term it is insisting that the God revealed in the Exodus or in the conquest or in the kingdom is the very same one whom the patriarchs knew. Later experience may flesh out the picture of Him more fully, but it is not a new picture. It is a part of a long process and it was started with "our fathers."

In Psalm 46 and 146, Yahweh is identified as the God of Jacob to whom one flees. He is also called the God of Israel. That title is not as common as "the God of Jacob," because "Israel" has a nationalistic and an ethnic connotation. I think that what the text is trying to say is that although He *is* the God of the nation, He is more than that—a personal God and a God of the individual. Elisha called Yahweh "the God of Elijah," because Elisha wanted the same anointing and the same relationship and the same assistance from Yahweh that his mentor, Elijah, had had. Yahweh is also called "the God of Hezekiah," and "the God of David."[55]

With a few exceptions as listed above, there is no name that is attached to Yahweh like that of the patriarchs. That common expression—the God of Abraham, the God of Isaac, and the God of Jacob—does not appear on every page or in every psalm, but recurrently it is there. When the Israelites came to worship, they recognized the One whom they worshipped as the God of Abraham and of Isaac and of Jacob. It

---

[55] There is one striking omission in this pattern: Yahweh is never called the God of Moses. This is despite the fact that Moses was the founder of Hebrew religion in the sense that he gave it its distinctive character. He was the instrument through which the basic character of Israel's religion was formed in its structured social, cultic way. Yet the Old Testament never once refers to God, Yahweh, as the God of Moses. I suspect that there is theological intention in that absence. Who was Moses? He is the giver of the Law, the one through whom it came. He is the leader, the deliverer of Israel through the Exodus. He is the one who, alone, spoke "face-to-face" with God and had even seen God's back. And he is the only human whom God Himself buried. God alone knew where he was buried. If ever there was a great man, it is Moses. But what do we do with great men? We tend to glorify great men, and Moses was such an incredible giant that it would have been very easy for people to build shrines to him or to have built a shrine where he was buried. But Yahweh says, "No, I am without rival and competitor and I hold Moses in higher esteem than you do, but I'm not going to let you slip into thinking that I belong to Moses as 'the God of Moses.' I want to protect you from yourself at that point. Moses is not your hope; I am your hope."

is interesting that he is not labeled as the God of the prophets in that same sense. We, in Western theological thought, have at times made the writings of the eighth-century prophets and their successors the most significant part of the Old Testament. And so we laud an Amos or a Hosea or an Isaiah. But the Scriptures never speak of the God of Isaiah or of Amos or Hosea, only of the God of Abraham, the God of Isaac, and the God of Jacob. He is the God of the Fathers and the Fathers are the patriarchs.

Abraham stands first in that list, and it is a legitimate question to ask why that is so. If Moses could be overlooked, why is Abraham so crucial? It is certainly not because he was perfect.[56] I used to wince over some of the accounts of Abraham's failures, but I do not anymore. I do not, because these passages remind us that the one who began it all was an incredibly human mortal. He was just like you and me, and the text does not present him as anything else. To be sure, some of the things he did were because he did not have the benefit of the Scripture and the tradition that we have. So, for instance, there is the point that William F. Albright makes in his *Yahweh and the Gods of Canaan*:

> In fixing relationships [among the gods] in the ancient Near East, we must remember that both in Egypt and Canaan the notion of incest scarcely existed. In fact, Phoenicia and Egypt shared a general tendency to use sister and wife synonymously. Such kings as Amenhotep III and Ramses II married one or more of their own daughters as late as the 14th and 13th centuries. Baal

---

[56] I am using the term "perfect" here in its modern sense of "absolutely flawless." But it is important to remember that the Old Testament has a somewhat different understanding. For instance in Genesis 17:1 God said to Abraham, "Walk before me and be thou perfect" (*KJV*); "Walk before me and be blameless" (*NIV*). Clearly, the biblical writers did believe that some sort of perfection was achievable in this life. The Hebrew word translated "perfect" by the *KJV* and "blameless" by the *NIV* is *tammim*, which is commonly used to describe the requirement for a sacrificial animal (Lev. 1:3 *KJV* "without blemish"; *NIV* "without defect"). That same word is put in the mouth of the Philistine king, Abimelech, to describe himself when he is talking to God in relation to the problem with Sarah (Gen. 20:5), and God confirms it (20:6). Clearly, what is being spoken of is Abimelech's motives lying behind his actions. His performance was not "perfect," but his motives were, in the sense that he was not doing anything that he knew was wrong.

was closely associated with two other goddesses. The relations between him and the goddesses Anat and Astarte were very complex. For example, Anat was not only Baal's virgin (*batultu*) sister, but also his consort. While she was in the form of a heifer, he raped her in an epic myth "77—even 88 times."[57]

So if Abraham told a half-truth about Sarah to protect himself, it *was* a half-truth. Abraham was living in his own world and was a part of that world, and God took a person like that to begin the messianic line, the line of redemption.

Not only do we find blemishes like that in Abraham's life, but the text also indicates that at certain times he was very slow to understand what God wanted and what He was after. So in the Sodom story it takes some time for Abraham to catch on that God wishes him to take on the role of intercessor. That is significant not only for persons training for some form of Christian ministry, but for every Christian believer. It is our business to fill that role of the intercessor, to stand between a God whom the world desperately needs, but whom the world does not know, and a God who deeply loves the world but is estranged by its offensive ways. We are the bridge between them.

But if Abraham was slow to catch on, he was certainly no slower than I. It took me a long time to realize that all intercession is initiated by God. As a seminary professor I do not like to admit it, but it is the reality: I have never been comfortable with my prayer life. So when I was pastoring and carrying the load of a pastorate, again and again I would find myself saying, "Kinlaw, you don't know enough about prayer, and you don't do enough intercessory prayer." So, sometimes I would get concerned and I would begin to intercede or at least to get as close to real intercession as I knew how. Then I would sort of pat myself on the back and say, "Well, you're beginning to learn, and you're beginning to do what you ought to do." But then one day it began to dawn on me: There is such a thing as prevenient grace. Before any one of us ever got concerned about anyone else, God had to put grace in our hearts to

[57] William F. Albright, *Yahweh and the Gods of Canaan* (Garden City, N.Y.: Doubleday, 1968), 128.

give us that concern. So what does that mean? It means that if I am not concerned about another person, it is because I have turned down and rejected God's concern. What God wants to do is put inside each of us the compassion and the care that He has for the world that He has made. So the initiative is with God.

Another way in which I think Abraham was slow to catch on, like some of the rest of us have been, is in the matter of Eliezer. There he said in so many words, "Lord, I will help you out. I have a servant and we can work out a way to fulfill the promise that you made" (Gen. 15:3). That is so much like the rest of us. We are perpetually trying to help God out and help him fulfill his promises, and when we do we simply complicate things. That is nowhere clearer than in the story of Hagar. Abraham and Sarah were helping God solve their problem, and they gave themselves a whole new set of problems.

Let me call your attention to something about the Hagar/Ishmael story that I never really thought about until recently. Do you realize that Abraham got everything that God promised him through Hagar, except Jesus? God had said to Abraham, "I will give you a son." Ishmael was a son. He had said, "I will make you a nation." Ishmael became a nation. "I will bring kings out of you." Ishmael had twelve sons that were called kings. "And I will make your progeny as innumerable as the stars." Who can count the progeny in the Arab world? But what did he not get? "All the nations of the earth will bless themselves through you." That is a very powerful way of saying something that is spelled out again and again and again and again in the subsequent pages of Scripture: There is no salvation in us. It is in God and God alone and in His action that grace and redemption come. We humans can seem to produce a total counterpart to God's work so that the world cannot tell the difference. But there is a difference: One is saving and the other is not. So Abraham's attempt to solve his problem through his own strength only created problems for himself and for his descendants. Later, Genesis tells us that Ishmael and his family lived in hostility with Isaac's family all of his days. And Paul's analogy between this hostility and that which exists between the flesh and the Spirit is completely apt (Gal. 4:21-31).

But of all Abraham's failures the one that hurts me most is the one found in Genesis 25 where we read the following:

Abraham took another wife, whose name was Keturah. She bore him Zimran, Jokshan, Medan, Midian, Ishbak and Shuah. [So, he had six sons in addition to Ishmael and Isaac.] Jokshan was the father of Sheba and Dedan, the descendants of Dedan were the Asshurites, the Letushites and the Leummites. The sons of Midian were Ephah, Epher, Hanoch, Abida and Eldaah. All these were descendants of Keturah. Abraham left everything he owned to Isaac. But while he was still living, he gave gifts to the sons of his concubines and sent them away from his son Isaac to the land of the east (Gen. 25:1-6).

The word translated "concubines" there is the standard Hebrew term for someone in that relationship. It is the same word used to tell us what Solomon had three hundred of, and it is the word that is consistently used through the Old Testament. In short, Abraham was a polygamist. To be frank, that is offensive to me. But do you know why it is offensive? It is because I have had the privilege of reading the Song of Songs and the New Testament and the book of Revelation. But Abraham never had that privilege. Now, as time has passed, I find myself glad that this information about Abraham was not omitted. Why? Because it reminds us that God has nowhere else to start with any of us than where we are. That is the beautiful part of the infinite grace of God. He does not set some standard and say, "Folks, when you have reached that then we'll start." No, God is ready to start at the present moment, anywhere a person is. How pertinent that is to a person who is going to be in ministry. Anywhere a person may be, God is ready to start at that point. This is the truth we find powerfully illustrated in Abraham.

Abraham was part of his world, but something had happened to him in relation to the living God, Yahweh, and he valued that. If there was much that he did not understand, and there was, there was still something inside him that said, "I cannot turn this loose. I have to go on." We get some sense of this in the gospel of John when Jesus was speaking to the Twelve after many of His disciples had left Him. He looked at them and said, "You do not want to leave too, do you?" But Peter responded, "Lord, to whom shall we go? You have the words of eternal life" (John 6:67-68). There was a great deal about Jesus that Peter surely did not understand. Indeed it was not until the illumination of Pentecost that he had any grasp of Jesus' essential mission in coming and how that mission was going to be realized.[58] But despite his lack of understanding, Peter knew that there was something in this Jesus of Nazareth that he could not live without. If he could not have whatever it was that he saw in Jesus, he was not sure he cared to go on living. Just like the patriarchs he was saying, "I've met Him and I don't want to lose Him."

So this is what makes the patriarchs so important. It was through them that that relationship that changed everything developed. What we are dealing with here is fairly subtle, so I hope you will stick with me in it because what I want to do is lead you into the biblical concept of *hesed*. The concept is not spelled out in the patriarchal accounts in great fullness, but it is implicit here, and if we are to understand how the covenantal relationship begins to develop in these accounts, we must recognize how central *hesed* is to every such relationship, that you cannot have a covenant unless there is *hesed* present.

With that said, let me try to lay some groundwork. What is the foundation of the covenantal relationship? I think it is fair to say that it is trust. And as I said earlier, there are two words used in the Old Testament that are often translated "believe" (or "trust"). One is the word from which we get "amen" = *he'amin* and the other is the word *batah*. *he'amin* is used occasionally and means "to make firm," while *batah*, which

---

[58] The disciples had no idea that the mission of salvation would depend absolutely on them. Jesus had made it crystal clear in the so-called "Upper Room Discourse" recorded in John 13–16, but they had not grasped it. In effect Jesus had put His arms around this motley crew and said, "You are mine. You belong to me and you belong to my Father. And we are one. If they receive you they get me and if they get me they get my Father." Isn't that amazing? "And if they turn you down they miss me and when they miss me they miss my Father." For years I would not consider the real implications of those statements. I just sort of mentally denied that they were there. Someone else's salvation hangs on me? No, thank you. For Him to say to me, "Kinlaw, if they accept you they get me and when they get me they get my Father," made me shudder in absolute horror. But that is what the text says. And who did Jesus say those things to? He said them to Peter, James, and John who, on the night before the Cross were arguing about their "pastoral appointments," about "who would get the biggest church," with all the envy and the jealousy implicit in those kinds of arguments. Yet it was to them that He said, "If they miss you they miss me. And when they miss me they miss my Father. And if they accept you they get me and when they get me they get my Father."

means "to trust" is found everywhere you turn. This is so because at the heart of the worship and the adoration and the praise, at the heart of the prayer, was this trust. It is both the product of and foundation for an interpersonal relationship. Without this inner confidence toward another, no real relationship is possible with that other person.

Finally, the evidence of any inner attitude is in behavior, so the Old Testament contains the 613 laws of the Torah. But it would be a mistake to think that it is only behavior that interests the Old Testament. In fact, the very opposite is true. Without the correct attitude, all that obedience is simply empty show. So the laws are the secondary thing. What is primary is this thing behind conduct. It is the attitude that leads to the right kind of conduct. It is that something that God approved of in Abimelech when Abimelech said, "I was perfect; I was innocent when I took Sarah," and God said, "Yes, I know that." Abimelech was speaking of an attitude or a condition and because of that right attitude or condition there was no judgment upon him.

This relationship between attitude and behavior is what is being spoken of in one of those great high points of the Old Testament, Hosea 6. God is speaking:

> What can I do with you, Ephraim?
>> What can I do with you, Judah?
> Your love is like the morning mist,
>> like the early dew that disappears.
> Therefore, I cut you in pieces with my prophets,
>> I killed you with the words of my mouth;
>> my judgments flashed like lightning upon you.
> For I desire mercy [hesed], not sacrifice,
>> an acknowledgement of God rather than
>> burnt offerings.
> Like Adam, they have broken the covenant—
>> they were unfaithful to me there.

What is it that God wants? In the heyday of the JEDP theory (see pages 86-87) it was popular to use passages like this to say that a sacrificial cult like that commanded in Leviticus was a later innovation of the priests. But even the most skeptical scholars today admit this is not the case. Rather, Hosea and the other prophets were condemning a pagan understanding of sacrifice in which the only thing that really mattered was not the attitude of the worshipper, but whether every detail of the performance was done correctly.[59]

Once again we go back to the fact that two people doing the same thing may not be doing the same thing. Two people may be performing the same ritual, but one is pleasing God, while the other is displeasing Him. The Old Testament never turns away from the importance of sacrifice, but you can sacrifice and do more damage to yourself spiritually than if you never sacrificed at all.[60] If you do it with the wrong attitude, attempting to manipulate God in your favor so you can live your life for yourself, you put yourself in terrible danger. The apostle Paul is thinking of the same thing when he warns the Corinthians about their attitude in taking the sacraments (1 Cor. 11:27-30).

The European Old Testament theologian, Edmond Jacob, reflecting on Hosea 6:6, says, "A sacrifice not inspired by *hesed* lacks the spirit to make it effective."[61] Now, this is very different from most of our religion. We don't even need to talk about Ancient Near Eastern religion. Did you see the Latin expression that Eichrodt uses: *Do ut des?*[62] The *Do* is "I give." That is where we get the word "donate." *ut* is "in order that." And *des* is "you will give." So, "I give so that you will give." I perform my

---

[59] Some years ago I learned why Presbyterians sit for Communion while Methodists kneel. I had a Scots Presbyterian friend who could conduct a Communion service like I have never experienced elsewhere. The sense of the numinous, the holy, was magnificent. But they always sat; nobody ever knelt. As I understand it, the reason is this: John Knox said the Roman Catholics knelt because they believed the bread and wine turned into God. So he said, "It would be an act of idolatry to kneel before the Communion elements, which only represent the body and blood." Thomas Cranmer, Henry VIII's man, knew he could not get away with that, so he began trying to work his way through it. Finally he said, "Well, no, the bread and wine are not divine. They don't turn into God, into Christ's body and blood. But there is a biblical promise that Jesus gave to us, that if two of us meet together in His name, there will always be a third person present with us, not as us, but with us. And so, we will kneel to the One whom we can't see who is with us."

[60] [Editor's note] This is the point of Psalm 51:16-17. The real sacrifice is a broken heart. Without that the outward sacrifice is worthless.

[61] Edmond Jacob, *Theology of the Old Testament*, tr. A. W. Heathcote and P. J. Allcock (New York: Harper, 1958), 176. Jacob here understands *hesed* to be the character and behavior of God, which the worshipper is seeking to imitate.

[62] Ibid., 47.

ceremony so you will reciprocate. Eichrodt refers to this as "a commercial relationship." In such a relationship personal submission and trust is not necessary.

In contrast, look at the life of Abraham and notice the way trust develops. The story takes thirteen chapters to spell out the development, and we still have to fill in a number of the blanks, but the growing trust is unmistakable. There are moments when Abraham slips. But the basic movement of the thirteen chapters is to a deeper and deeper trust in the One who has spoken to him. You see it in the fact that he left his country, and his people, and his father's house.

You see it when Lot and he find themselves discussing the conflict between their herdsmen, and Abram says to Lot, "You take what you want." He had to know that Lot would take the more desirable country. Why would Abram give him the choice? Abram was chieftain of the clan, so he had the right to first choice. I believe it was because he was saying, "I've left those kinds of questions in the hands of my Friend who promised me that He was going to give real estate to my descendants." If God has promised it to you, then you don't have to fight for it. That is a biblical principle. If you have to fight for something, it may be that you have put your hand on it and in so doing have hindered the hand of God. For if God intends to give that thing to you, He is going to do it in His own time, and nobody is going to stop Him. That is the reason you do not have to pull strings or play politics with regard to your pastoral appointment. Someone may say, "You're unrealistic." That is right from the world's perspective. It all depends on which set of standards you are operating under. If you do not believe that God can get you where you should be, I question whether you have the faith of Abraham that justified him.

A third evidence of this developing trust is the way he sought a wife for Isaac. Now, someone may say that I am relying heavily on the implications in these accounts. That is correct. But the other side is that these stories are what produced the faith that gave us the New Testament.

Here, in germ, is what is to come: In these narratives there are themes that appear and reappear, as in a symphony. One of those themes has to do with marriage. In chapter 21 when Hagar took a wife for Ishmael, she got one from Egypt. On the other hand, when Abraham knew that Isaac had to have a wife, he did not look to the Canaanite women around him. Now, this could be looked upon as ethnic prejudice, but it could also be a recognition of the fact that normally it is the mother's religion that is transmitted to the children. So in Abraham's heart there is something that says:

> A treasure has been given to me and I am responsible
> for seeing that it is perpetuated, because in it all the na-
> tions of the earth are to find their hope. And I must be
> very careful with this treasure that is committed to me.
> Isaac is not an ordinary child. He is a child of promise
> and my Friend wants to do something unique and re-
> demptive through him. And I cannot let there be in his
> life anything that will hinder if I can help it.

And so, you get that magnificent story of Abraham sending his servant to get a wife for Isaac.

The story of Jacob is a good bit more tangled with Rebekah's concern for her deceiving son's safety (Gen. 27:46). But in the end, Isaac is very forthright in saying to Jacob that he did not want Jacob to marry a Canaanite girl, and he linked that marriage to a continuation of the covenant (Gen. 28:1-4). Esau's decision to go to his uncle Ishmael and to get a Canaanite wife was an act of spite, but it also shows that he understood what the family did not want him to do (Gen. 28:6-8). You need to read the text carefully to find these little things, but they are there. Intermarriage is a significant motif in the book of Genesis. It is no accident that the longest chapter in the book of Genesis is about getting a wife for the son of Abraham, the son of promise. Is it possible that whoever put Genesis together understood Genesis 1 and 2, "And the two of them shall become one flesh"? "Flesh" as it is used there can almost connote one person, but it certainly connotes one social unit. And the redemption of the world hangs on the maintenance of that social unit in the case we are talking about here.

The fourth incident that shows the development of Abraham's faith, his trust in this Person whom he has met, is in chapter 22 when he is called upon to sacrifice his son, Isaac. This incident may be the capstone of that development; it is certainly the most poignant element in it. As we said earlier, Abraham's response to Yahweh's command was, "And he arose early in the morning and headed for the place of sacrifice." Why did he do it? How could he do it? I believe the answer to those questions is found later in the passage where Isaac looks at Abraham and says, "Father, we've got the fire and we've got the wood, but where is the sacrifice?" And Abraham responds, "God will provide the sacrifice." I do not think Abraham anticipated what was coming because faith rarely gives you a clue as to how the result of faith is going to be achieved. Nobody ever marches face-forward into the future. Everybody stumbles backward into it. You see yesterday, but you don't see tomorrow.[63] Faith does not enable you to see tomorrow, but faith determines how you are going to think and act now in relation to tomorrow. So what good sense it makes if He is the Eternal One, for whom there is no present, past or future, to put your hand in His and let Him lead you! You will still go stumbling because it's not natural for us to walk backwards. It is awkward. But that is where the trust comes out. Again Abraham did not know what God was going to do. In Hebrews 11:19 we are told that Abraham believed God would raise Isaac from the dead if that is what he needed to do. It was just that Abraham had lived with God long enough that he felt he could trust Him.

The final incident on Abraham's road of trust came with Sarah's death as reported in Genesis 23. Abraham has lost his companion of one hundred years or more. Who can imagine loss like that? And in all those years Abraham had never owned a square inch of Canaan. We know from contemporary documents that as an immigrant, he was forbidden to own any land. Yet, according to Hebrews 11, his faith never wavered. But surely as Sarah's loss struck him, there must have been a strong temptation to doubt if his children ever would possess the land. But that loss became the very means for God, almost as an aside, to give

---

[63] In Hebrew a person faces the east, because the word for "right" is the word for the "south" and the word for "left" is the word for "north." This is true in Arabic as well, with the country of Yemen (right, south) being as far south as one can go on the Arabic peninsula. But the word for east, *qedem*, is also the word for the past. So the Hebrew thinks of himself as facing the past. If that is so, I thought, then the word for "back," *'aher*, ought to be used on occasion for the west and for the future. Sure enough, that is the case. There are a few instances where that word is used for the west, and on occasion it is used for the future. So, in short, the Israelites backed into the future with their faces firmly fixed on the past.

Abraham a bit of a down-payment on the promise. The story is too complex to go into here, but just let me say that because of the intricacies of the legal system in Canaan at that time, the people who owned the cave where Abraham wanted to bury Sarah concluded that it was more in their interest to sell the whole field where the cave was rather than just give him the cave. In short, God turned the grief of Sarah's loss into the evidence that Sarah's children would indeed, as God had said, own the whole land.

Mrs. Richard Nixon was quoted as saying, "I may fall flat on my face and I may die trying, but I will never, ever, cancel out." I like that statement. You can count on a person like that; you can build on a person like that. That was Abraham's experience of Yahweh; He was not going to leave his friend in the lurch. Faith brings you to the place where you will keep going when you do not see and although there are plenty of fears, you are more afraid not to move in His direction than you are to let your fears control you.

Lecture 12

....

The Concept of *Hesed*

In the previous lecture we looked at the ways in which Yahweh showed Abraham how trustworthy He is. Yahweh can be depended upon to be passionately loyal to His creatures even if, and sometimes even because, they do not deserve it. The Hebrew word for that characteristic of Yahweh is *hesed*. In this lecture I want to consider this concept in detail.

In some older texts you will find *hesed* transliterated as *chesed*. That is because the first consonant of the word is a rough "h," rather like the opening sound in "Christ." Hebrew has two "h" consonants: a smooth one and a rough one. In more technical transliterations today, the rough one is usually represented by an "h" with a dot under it. Because that is a problem for typesetters, both consonants are represented in many texts [as here] with the simple "h."

As mentioned in a previous lecture, the translation of *hesed* is problematic. In the *Septuagint* it is most frequently translated with the

Greek word *eleos*, which means "mercy." For this reason the *King James Version* most commonly translates *hesed* with "mercy." Now, there is no question that mercy is one component of *hesed*, but when you have said "mercy" you have not begun to exhaust the richness and the fullness of what the Scripture wants to communicate when it uses this term. On another front the meaning of *hesed* is almost synonymous with "grace," although there is another Hebrew word for grace, *hen*. But there are many times when *hesed* is more equivalent to the Greek word for grace, *charis* than *hen* is. So, *hesed* is a powerful word. Thomas Torrance, a Scottish theologian at the University of Edinburgh, has said that this word *hesed* is the great sacramental word of the Old Testament.

While it is no longer believed as it used to be that *hesed* was a uniquely covenantal term [see below], it is still true that one of the most typical contexts in which *hesed* occurs is covenant. If two parties are in covenant with each other, they are obligated to do *hesed* with each other. They are required to be passionately loyal to one another come what may. This goes beyond mere literalistic fulfillment of the terms of the covenant to speak of the personal attachment of the covenant parties to each other.

We will get a feel for the word if we trace its occurrences in the book of Genesis. The first one is in 19:19. If you remember, this is the chapter that tells about the destruction of Sodom and Gomorrah. Verse 15 discusses the interaction between Lot and the angels who are the messengers of God sent to save the righteous in the city of Sodom. Lot was hesitating, and so they said to him, "Hurry! Take your wife and two daughters who are here, or you will be swept away when the city is punished." When Lot continued to hesitate, the messengers grasped his hand and the hands of his wife and his two daughters, and they led them safely out of the city. "For the LORD was merciful to them" (16). As soon as they had brought them out, one of them said, "Flee for your lives! Don't look back, and don't stop anywhere in the plain! Flee to the mountains or you will be swept away!" (17). But Lot wanted to equivocate. He was afraid. "No, my lords, please" (18). "Your servant has found favor in your eyes, and you have shown great *hesed* to me in sparing my life" (19). The *NIV* there translates it "kindness," while the *NASB* has "loving-kindness," and the *KJV* has "mercy." The fact of those multiple translations begins to give us a sense of just how rich the single Hebrew word is. Here we get the basic idea of the word. Lot knows that God has been much better to him than he ever deserved in getting him out of the city. What did God owe Lot? Nothing. Yet He went out of His way to be sure that Lot and his family did not suffer with the other inhabitants of the cities.

Now, look at chapter 20. This is the story of Abraham and Abimelech. Abimelech has taken Sarah into his harem, but has then found out the true relationship of Sarah to Abraham. So Abimelech has called on Abraham to explain himself. In the course of that explanation he says that when he and Sarah, his wife and also his half-sister, began their journeys, he had asked her, as an act of *hesed*, to represent herself as his sister (v. 13). Here you get a bit more of the covenant context. These are not two casual acquaintances, but two people in a formal covenantal relationship. Abraham was talking to his wife and was pleading the fact that since she was his wife, she owed him something.

Now turn to chapter 32. We are dealing here with Jacob as he is getting ready to meet Esau. He had naively assumed that Esau would have forgotten how badly Jacob had treated him, but now Jacob has heard that Esau is coming to meet him with a troop of armed men. So, in great fear and distress, he divides his people into two groups, hoping that if Esau gets one the other one can escape. Then he prays:

> O God of my father Abraham, God of my father Isaac, O [Yahweh], who said to me, "Go back to your country and your relatives, and I will make you prosper." [Jacob is reminding Yahweh that he is there because Yahweh told him to go there. He is trying to put leverage on Yahweh.] I am unworthy of all the *hesed* and the faithfulness you have shown your servant. I had only my staff when I crossed this Jordan, but now I have become two groups. Save me, I pray, from the hand of my brother Esau (32:9-11a).

Here, unlike the situation with Abraham and Sarah, Jacob cannot fall back on any obligation Yahweh might have to him. In fact, Jacob freely admits that Yahweh is under no obligation at all. Nevertheless, there is relationship and Jacob pleads that.

The next occurrence is in chapter 39:21. Joseph is in prison. He has had his experience with Potiphar's wife and has been thrown into prison because of it. But the text says that while Joseph was there in the prison, the Lord Yahweh was with him and showed him *hesed*. Again, the covenant with Abraham, Isaac, and Jacob is in the background, but there is no sense that God was only fulfilling a covenant obligation. That is not the reason He does it. Yahweh does *hesed* with people because it is Yahweh's nature to do *hesed!* This is the nature of the God who had become the friend of Abraham and had demonstrated that he could be trusted to do good to persons. Remember that before it was all over with, Joseph would say, "You meant it for evil, but Yahweh meant it for good." And that's part of *hesed*.

But there is another side to this, and I almost hesitate to say it, but it is so. If Abraham is confident that Yahweh will do *hesed* with him, Yahweh also has increasing confidence that Abraham will do *hesed* with Yahweh. The relationship between Yahweh and Abraham was one that developed into mutual confidence. When I say that, I shudder a little. To say that God should have confidence in you and me seems presumptuous. But He does. And He comes to where He knows there are certain things He can expect from Abraham. And He does expect them. Abraham does not always perform as well as he should, but at the big moments in Abraham's life, it is this covenant relationship based in *hesed* that determines how Abraham acts.

In chapter 40 we have the story of the cupbearer and the baker who were in prison with Joseph. You will remember they dreamed, and Joseph was gifted from God to interpret their dreams. He was able to tell the cupbearer that within three days he would be restored to his former position. And then Joseph says, "When all goes well with you, remember me and show me *hesed;* mention me to Pharaoh and get me out of this prison. For I was forcibly carried off from the land of the Hebrews, and even here I have done nothing to deserve being put in a dungeon" (40:14-15). He is asking for the cupbearer to show *hesed* to him.

It is clear that there is no formal covenantal relationship here. So what is the basis of the request for *hesed?* I wonder if this does not imply a larger covenant, one that exists between God and His entire creation, and therefore one that exists between the creatures. This would explain natural loyalty, natural good, or natural fidelity, brother-to-brother, one human being to another. It might also explain why I have a responsibility, say, for the poor, or why I have a responsibility for those who have never heard the Gospel of Christ.

The final occurrence in the book is found in chapter 47. Jacob has come down to Egypt and is with Joseph in Egypt;

> Now the Israelites settled in Egypt in the region of Goshen. They acquired property there and were fruitful and increased greatly in number. Jacob lived in Egypt seventeen years and the years of his life were a hundred and forty-seven. When the time drew near for Israel to die, he called for his son Joseph and said to him, "If I have found favor in your eyes, put your hand under my thigh and promise that you will show me kindness [*hesed*] and faithfulness" [64] (vv. 27-29).

This is a father asking a son to show *hesed* to him. He has some rights to ask some things of his son. He knows that and he is speaking of that when he speaks. "Show me *hesed* and faithfulness." But once again, this is more than mere legal obligation. The performance is the result of passionate, devoted loyalty.

The linkage of *hesed* and "faithfulness" (*'emet* "truth") here is very significant. These two terms are found together again and again in the Old Testament. They almost form a hendiadys, which is one idea expressed with two words, something like "passionately loyal dependability" or "dependable kindness," etc.

Now I want to return to the very important occurrence in chapter 24. There is the sense in which the entire chapter is a play on the word *hesed*. Abraham is old, advanced in years, and he wants to do what he should do about a wife for Isaac. So he gives his servant, the chief servant in his household, a charge. This is not just an ordinary servant. There is a sense in which this servant is Abraham's alter-ego. He is the one who can sign a legal statement for him. He is the one who can speak for Abraham. He knows him better than anybody else, and Abraham

---

[64] The sealing of an oath by placing a hand under the thigh also appears in Genesis 24. It may be emphasizing the seriousness of the oath by nearness to the genitals.

trusts him with everything he owns.

As we look at this servant I think we get an indication of the depth of Abraham's relationship with Yahweh. We see how deep it was because this servant has picked up the faith of Abraham. He believes in Abraham's God. In one sense it is a secondhand relationship because it came through Abraham to him. But you know, it is this man who gives us one of the greatest testimonies to piety in the book of Genesis, maybe the greatest one. It is a beautiful story of a man who expects God to lead him and who prays at every crucial step in the process. There is more praying done by this servant in one chapter than by any of the patriarchs. There is a beautiful naiveté in it; a simplicity. For many years I worked with college students and one of the things that is marvelous about them is their openness and naiveté. It is a beautiful thing. There is a freshness about it. That is what I sense in Abraham's servant. Where did he get that simple faith? He got it from Abraham. Abraham's faith was contagious.

We pick up the story in verse 3:

> "I want you to swear by the LORD, the God of heaven and the God of earth, that you will not get a wife for my son from the daughters of the Canaanites, among whom I am living, but will go to my country and my own relatives and get a wife for my son Isaac" (24:3-4).

Notice the way Abraham talks about God. He is the God who made what other people worshipped. The God of heaven and the God of earth. Notice that the patriarch is in tension with his culture. If we miss that, we miss a crucial part of the whole thing. Likewise Israel was in tension with their culture, in the same way the New Testament church was in tension with its culture.

> The servant asked him, "What if the woman is unwilling to come back with me to this land? Shall I then take your son back to the country you came from?" "Make sure that you do not take my son back there," Abraham said. "The LORD, the God of heaven, who brought me out of my father's household and my native land and who spoke to me and promised me on oath, saying, 'To

your offspring I will give this land'—he will send his
angel before you so that you can get a wife for my son
from there" (vv. 5-7).

Now that is a statement of faith. God has promised him. There
is more in that than Abraham saying, "I want to possess this land." Abraham now senses that what God is doing is of very great significance.
Some way or other God's purposes are tied up with this land that He is
going to give them. In that regard, read the Psalms and the references
to Zion. And it could be that if his son goes back and stays back there,
those purposes are going to be frustrated. So Abraham is sensing that
this land is important as is their tie with this land, because it is based on
this covenant with Yahweh. So he says, "Don't let my son go back there,
no matter what."

How does he know that God is going to send His angel? He
does not. It is an affirmation of faith. He says, "I know my Friend who
is in covenant with me, and I dare to believe." And he ventures on the
basis of that. And quite a venture it was, too. It is on that basis that he
says, "He will send his messenger before you." There is a trust relationship between Abraham and Yahweh. He is expecting Yahweh to do some
things. Now Abraham says:

> "If the woman is unwilling to come with you, then
> you will be released from this oath of mine. Only do
> not take my son back there." So the servant put his
> hand under Abraham's thigh and swore an oath to him
> concerning the matter. Then the servant took ten of
> his master's camels and left, taking with him all kinds
> of good things from his master. He set out for Aram
> Naharaim and made his way to the town of Nahor. He
> had the camels kneel down near the well outside the
> town; it was toward evening, the time the women go out
> to draw water. Then he prayed, "O [Yahweh], God of
> my master Abraham, give me success today and show
> *hesed* to my master Abraham. See, I am standing beside
> this spring, and the daughters of the townspeople are
> coming out to draw water. May it be that when I say to

a girl, 'Please let down your jar that I may have a drink'
and she says, 'Drink, and I'll water your camels too,'—
let her be the one you have chosen for your servant
Isaac" (vv. 8-14).

Is that naive faith? Apparently this fellow believed that he was in
divine order and that this God who had made a covenant with Abraham
would act. He expected something. "Let her be the one you have chosen
for your servant Isaac. By this I will know that you have shown *hesed* to
my master." God will have kept his covenant if the girl he speaks to says,
"Yes, I will give you some water and I'll water your camels, too." "Before
he had finished praying, Rebekah came out with her jar on her shoulder"
(15). And she played the role as if she had been taught!

Now go to verse 23 where he says:

"Please tell me, is there room in your father's house
for us to spend the night?" She answered him, "I am
the daughter of Bethuel, the son that Milcah bore to
Nahor."[65] And she added, "We have plenty of straw and
fodder, as well as room for you to spend the night." Then
the man bowed down and worshiped [Yahweh], saying,
"Praise be to Yahweh, the God of my master Abraham,
who has not abandoned his *hesed* and faithfulness to my
master. As for me, [Yahweh] has led me on the journey
to the house of my master's relatives" (vv. 23-27).

The Old Testament tells us that the key example of Yahweh's
leadership is the Exodus. But if God acts in a nation's life to redeem the
world, why should He not act in an individual's life too? And you will
find this kind of theme running all through these stories.

The final use of the word in chapter 24 is found in verse 49.
When the servant is brought before Rachel's brother, Laban, the servant
refuses to eat the food prepared for him until he has told his story and

---

[65] She was exactly the person he was looking for, and he did not know it.
Archbishop William Temple's comment is apropos: "I know that some of the things
people call answers to prayer are nothing but coincidences, but I notice that the
people who pray seem to experience more coincidences in their lives."

has learned what the response will be. In verses 34-48 he recounts the whole story word for word and concludes with these significant words, "Now if you will show *hesed* and faithfulness to my master, tell me." God has done his part in showing *hesed*, but there is also a human part, and if that is not carried out, the whole thing will be for naught: "and if not, tell me, so I may know which way to turn." The only true response to the divine *hesed* is for us to respond in kind. Fortunately, Laban, whom we know from later accounts was not particularly a paragon of virtue, was sensitive enough to the evidences of God's providence to respond, "This is from the LORD; we can say nothing to you one way or the other. Here is Rebekah; take her and go" (vv. 50-51).

Lecture 13

· · · · · · · · · ·

Hesed and the Nature of God

One of the interesting things in the Scripture is the development of the use of language. Recently a doctor, who is particularly caring for a group of patients who are fighting with cancer, spoke to me. She said, "I am trying to give a Christian witness to these people as I work with them. I want to tell them about the love of God. So, I started through the Bible and was astounded to discover how far you have to go before it says, 'God is love.'" That was troubling to her. I responded by saying, "Well, one of the reasons that you don't find it earlier is that we have so many misunderstandings swirling around the word we use for love. You have to have a whole new foundation laid before you can use the word."

That is what is going on with this word *hesed* that we talked about at such length in the previous lecture. For us *love* is primarily, and almost exclusively, a word about feelings. But the main truth about God is not that He feels in certain ways. The main truth about God is that He *is* certain things as revealed in how He acts. That is what is so significant about *hesed*. It is not about a way of feeling, it is about a way of acting. And when we discover that this is the way He *always* acts, that tells us about who He is. Then, when the Bible says that God is love, we have some new categories in which to put that statement.

I noticed that Edmond Jacob titled his chapter on *hesed*, "The Faithfulness of God."[66] That is one possible translation of the word. But as we said earlier, it can also be translated with "kindness," or "grace," or "fidelity," or "steadfast love," or "mercy,"[67] or any of several other possibilities. To rightly understand the concept you have to see it as encompassing all of those connotations.

In the previous lecture I called your attention to Torrance's suggestion that this word is the great sacramental word of the Old Testament. Before we finish this lecture I hope you will have a fuller sense of what that statement means and how incredibly important the concept is for biblical (not just Old Testament) theology. It is amazing that as important as this word is (occurring some three hundred times in all its forms in the Old Testament), there is no known cognate in any other

---

[66] Jacob, *Theology of the Old Testament*, 103.

[67] As we said in the previous lecture, the *Septuagint's* regular translation of *hesed* with *eleos* (Eng. "mercy") means that in the *King James Version* the word is commonly translated as "mercy." But "mercy," as we normally use it in English, conveys only one aspect of all that *hesed* connotes. Maybe we have to put new content into the term "mercy." Something of that idea is found in a book by Madeleine L'Engle (*The Rock that Is Higher: Story as Truth,* Colorado Springs: Harold Shaw, 1993) where she describes an automobile accident in which she was involved. She said, "I was being driven to an assignment to lecture and as we traveled, suddenly the windshield in front of us just became a configuration of broken glass." A large truck had gone through a red light and had side-swiped them. She was badly injured as was her companion. She said, "For the first time, really, I faced death. I had wondered, always, how I would feel at a moment like that. One of the wonderful things was the peace inside me. I found my response was one that had come out of my life. It was a prayer that I had prayed daily, which I felt was the best way to carry out the biblical teaching of praying without ceasing." It was just that expression which Bartimaeus used, "Lord Jesus Christ, have mercy on me" (Mark 10:48). And she said, "I found great peace and security in that." I suspect that what we tend to think of as mercy does not really express all that the biblical concept involves. It is not just that you want God to look upon you and let you escape the consequences that are negative in your life as far as He is concerned. The word has to do with far more than that. It has to do with the fullness of grace.

Semitic language.[68] It is as though the Hebrews have had to create a term for a concept that is unknown elsewhere in the world around them. But that does not mean that it was therefore restricted to certain limited, theological areas of their lives. No, its widespread usage indicates that the idea had penetrated every part of their thinking.

At the heart of the meaning of this term is the idea of reliability, and there are several passages that support the idea. For instance, there is Isaiah 40:6:

> A voice says, "Cry out."
> And I said, "What shall I cry?"
> "All men are like grass,
> and all their *hesed* is like the flowers of the field."

The *New International Version* follows the *Septuagint* and translates it "glory." But the *New Revised Standard Version* has "constancy," which is much better.[69] Humans are no more to be counted on than are the wild flowers, which wither and die overnight.

In Psalm 62, the psalmist says, "Strength belongs to Elohim; *hesed* to you, O Yahweh." Hebrew poetic parallelism would indicate that *hesed* is here being seen as somehow synonymous with "strength." However, it is enough to say that God's reliability or constancy is the equivalent idea. The same would be true of 144:2: "[Yahweh is] my *hesed* and my fortress, my stronghold and my deliverer, my shield, in whom I take refuge." Because of God's absolute reliability He is a secure hiding place and shelter.

This fundamental idea of reliability is supported by the frequent linkage of *hesed* with the Hebrew word *'emet*, which is the word for "truth." As we said in the previous lecture, they almost form a hendiadys. So when you speak of truth in relation to Yahweh, *hesed* is not far away. And when you speak of *hesed* with Yahweh, truth is not far away. In this

---

[68] As *New International Dictionary of Old Testament Theology and Exegesis* (2:211) points out, the equation with Arabic *hashada* proposed by *Hebrew and Aramaic Lexicon of the Old Testament* is very unlikely. The larger discussion of the term in *New International Dictionary of Old Testament Theology and Exegesis* (2:211-218) is an excellent brief treatment.

[69] *TNIV* has "human faithfulness."

respect, it is important that we understand the sense of "truth" in the Old Testament. It is not normally speaking of what we in the West call "objective truth," that is, something you believe. More frequently it is talking about something you *are* and *do*. If you are "true" in the Bible, then what you do and say is completely reliable. Moreover, *you* are reliable. Now, if the sole Creator of the universe is absolutely "true" both in what He says and does and in His person, it is not a very big jump to the idea that there are things in His universe that are absolutely so, regardless of whether we like it or not. That is where the Western world (and the Western world alone) has come up with the idea of "truth." But the key point here is that the concept of truth is secondary to the recognition that there is a Creator who is true. It is a logical deduction that is totally dependent on the first premise. Are you surprised that this generation of Americans, whose parents and grandparents have rejected the idea of an absolutely reliable Creator, are rejecting the idea of absolute truth and returning to the very same understanding of reality as the ancient Sumerians? You should not be.

Now let us return to the linkage between *hesed* and *'emet*. You will find in Psalm 85, interestingly enough, a beautiful little line that I first found in the *King James* as a student, "Mercy and truth are met together. Righteousness and peace have kissed each other." When I looked at that as a student, I was surprised, because I had never connected mercy and truth. I thought mercy was what you got in spite of the truth of the situation. And righteousness did not go with peace for me because of my own guilty conscience. But what the psalm is saying is that *hesed* and truth are met together and they belong together in the nature of Yahweh. Likewise, righteousness and peace have kissed each other and they have found their union in Him.

There are similar passages where the two words are linked in Psalms 25:10; 40:11; 61:8; and 138:2. But the occurrences in Exodus 34:5 and 6 are especially important. The context of Exodus 34 is the second giving of the tablets of the Law. When Moses received them the first time and brought them down the mountain, he found Israel was involved in idolatrous worship, and he became very angry. He became so angry that he threw the stone tablets down on the ground and they were broken. Now God is giving the tables of the Law, the heart of the covenant, again. When Moses had first pled with God not to annul his covenant with the Israelites in chapter 32, he had done so in a bit of ignorance. He had not yet seen what was going on at the foot of the mountain. But after he saw it, he realized just how serious the situation was and that God's very presence with them was in jeopardy. So in chapter 33, we have a lengthy dialogue between Yahweh and Moses in which Moses is saying that unless Israel has God's presence (his "face") with them, they might just as well stay at Sinai. Whatever "blessings" God might give them are worthless without Yahweh Himself. Clearly, God is gratified with this level of understanding on Moses' part and He promises to show His "face" to Israel. Moses then asks if he might see God's face, although what he actually asks for is to see God's "glory." God responds that Moses will be permitted to see his "goodness." I think the difference between those two words is very important. You can have a spiritual experience that is very exciting and yet is contentless. Or you can gain an insight into the character of the Eternal that will change you forever.

We break into the account at chapter 34, verse 4:

> So Moses chiseled out two stone tablets like the first ones and went up Mount Sinai early in the morning, as the LORD had commanded him; and he carried the two stone tablets in his hands. Then [Yahweh] came down in the cloud and stood there with him and proclaimed his name, [Yahweh]. And he passed in front of Moses proclaiming, "[Yahweh, Yahweh], the compassionate and gracious God, slow to anger, abounding in love and faithfulness, maintaining love to thousands, and forgiving wickedness, rebellion and sin" (vv. 4-7a).

Now, the order in which those adjectives is given is significant. You know, it is a moment when God would have had every right to be judgmental, when He would have had every right to say, "I'm giving you a second chance," but to do so grudgingly, angry with them because they had failed Him the first time. But that is not what we find here at all. He says, "Yahweh, Yahweh, the compassionate one." The term is *rahum*— the same three consonants appear in the word for "womb." So there is a sense of softness and tenderness and personal warmth in this word. It is far from the courtroom and any air of legality. The compassion of

Yahweh. Then he adds to "compassionate," "gracious." Here the word is *hen,* which has the idea of being favorably disposed toward someone. So often we assume that God basically does not like us and has to be persuaded to do anything good for us. In fact, He is the very opposite. His predisposition toward us is favorable.

So this is the way Yahweh starts this revelation of His essential character to Moses. He is the compassionate One, the gracious One. He doesn't start with His holiness. He doesn't even start with His righteousness and He doesn't start with truth. But He starts with the fact that He is compassionate and gracious. To those two He adds that He is slow to anger. He is very patient.[70] Then the text says, "He is abounding in *hesed* and faithfulness." The Hebrew word here translated with "abounding" is *rab,* which means "much, large, abundant." In other words, His character is full to overflowing with these qualities. But what does that mean? He has to say it again. It means He is very careful to extend *"hesed* to thousands, forgiving wickedness, rebellion and sin." Here in the setting of the first major breach of the covenant, Yahweh is at great pains to let Moses know that He is not merely characterized by justice and mercy, but rather that who He is goes far beyond that. He is absolutely loyal and dependable when the only reason for such behavior is just consistency with Himself. So, Israel is given a second chance, and the reason is because of Yahweh's nature as *hesed* and *'emet.*

From its earliest usages in Genesis and beyond, *hesed* is a word about relationships. Sometimes these are formal, as was the case with Abraham and Sarah. At other times, as with Lot and the angels, the relationship is not so formal. But there is some kind of social bond present, either explicit or implicit. What two strangers on the street might do for each other would not be defined as *hesed.* But there is a strange bipolarity about the word. On the one hand, it is behavior that is prompted by social obligation, and yet on the other hand, it goes far beyond mere technicalities of social obligation. The person who does *hesed* to another is going well beyond the expected. So Sarah's obligations as a wife hardly demanded that she lie for her husband and subject herself

---

[70] The Hebrew language prefers concrete expressions to abstract ones. So it does not say literally that He is slow to anger. Rather, it says, "He is long of nose." To be angry is to be "hot-nosed." So if one has a very long nose, it takes a long time for the heat to get all the way to the end.

to humiliation. But because she was a wife, that could be asked of her.

Nelson Glueck, an American Jew, wrote an interesting doctoral dissertation in Germany in 1927 on the word *hesed* in Old Testament usage. It was the first major scholarly treatment of the word. His conclusion was that the particular significance of the term was to be found in its usage in covenant contexts.[71] Ludwig Koehler, in his *Hebrew and Aramaic Lexicon of the Old Testament*, reflected a somewhat similar point of view when he defined *hesed* as "social obligation, association, solidarity—belonging." As a result of that sense of solidarity and that sense of belonging, the term has been translated by numbers of scholars simply as "loyalty."

Eichrodt, as we might expect, given his use of "covenant" as the unifying element in the Old Testament, sees *hesed* as a covenant word. He is very explicit about that.[72] He says that it speaks of the brotherly comradeship and loyalty that one party to a covenant must render to another, and he cites Glueck, who says that *hesed* is "the proper object of a covenant, and may almost be described as its content. The possibility of the establishment and maintenance of a covenant rests on the presence of *hesed*."[73]

You will find in the Old Testament a number of occasions where *hesed* and covenant, *hesed* and *b'rit*, go together and keep company. You find it in Deuteronomy 7:9 and 12: "Yahweh is the keeper of covenant *(b'rit)*, and *hesed*." You will find it when Solomon is praying at the dedication of the temple (1 Kings 8:23-26). He asks God to keep covenant and mercy with him the way He has with his father David. He wants him to keep *hesed* and *b'rit*. You will find it in Psalm 89, which sort of gives the

---

[71] Nelson Glueck, *"'Hesed' in the Bible,"* tr. A. Gottschalk, New York: Ktav Publishing House, 1975). [Editor's note] Two more recent studies of the term have appeared, and both agree that Glueck pushed the covenant connection too far (G. R. Clark, *The Word 'Hesed' in the Hebrew Bible*, JSOTSup 157 [Sheffield: JSOT Press, 1993]; K. D. Sakenfeld, *The Meaning of 'Hesed' in the Hebrew Bible: A New Inquiry*, HSM 17 [Missoula: Scholars Press, 1978]; see also F. I. Anderson, "Yahweh, the Kind and Sensitive God," in *God Who Is Rich in Mercy*, ed. P. O'Brien and D. Petersen [Grand Rapids: Baker, 1986]). The loyalty that is undoubtedly an aspect of the word does not necessarily arise from an understood legal obligation. Because Dr. Kinlaw's original treatment relied so heavily on Glueck's conclusions, which are now recognized to have been somewhat overstated, the present treatment reflects heavier editing than is the case elsewhere in this volume.

[72] Eichrodt, *Theology*, 1:232ff.

[73] Ibid. Glueck, *"Hesed,"* 47.

history of Israel and tells about Yahweh's covenant with David. Begin with verse 30:

> If [David's] sons forsake my law and do not follow my statutes, if they violate my decrees and fail to keep my commands, I will punish their sins with a rod, their iniquity with flogging; but I will not take my *hesed* from him, nor will I ever betray my faithfulness. I will not violate my covenant.

Notice the two things that are a part of covenant. One of them is *hesed* and the other is faithfulness. But notice that this is not merely performing the obligations of the covenant. *Hesed* and *'emet* recognize what the covenant calls for and then go beyond that. Nowhere is this more clearly expressed than in David's treatment of Jonathan's crippled son, Mephibosheth (2 Sam. 9). David's covenant with Jonathan had no remaining legal force after Jonathan's death. Furthermore, the house of Saul had been actively trying to prevent David from establishing his kingdom over all Israel. Nevertheless, David had the young man found, had him brought to Jerusalem, and gave him a lifetime pension. And why did he do it? "Is there anyone still left of the house of Saul to whom I can show *hesed* for Jonathan's sake?" (2 Sam. 9:1). The covenant between David and Saul provided the pretext for the acts of *hesed*, but the actions themselves far exceeded the expectations of that covenant. Psalm 18:50 says, Yahweh "will keep *hesed l*'*olam*—forever" to His anointed, David, and to his descendants. That is the nature of the relationship that He intends to have.

So I am saying that God's *hesed* is revealed, particularly, in the context of the covenant. It is by means of the covenant that He reveals His *hesed*. But when He reveals it, it is not merely an abstract quality. Rather, *hesed* is something you do, and something you do for another person. It is not something in isolation. This takes us back to one of the great facts of the Old Testament. At the end of Edmond Jacob's chapter on *hesed*, he says something about that which underlines the fact that the Old Testament is not interested in an abstract, systematic theological treatment of the nature of Deity. God is never presented in that way. Yahweh is always dealt with in relation to other persons or else in relation to His creation. And so, *hesed* is a description of the way He relates to people, not an abstraction. "Now the term *chesed* is particularly suitable for expressing that Yahweh was an active power in the midst of men, a power from which they could not escape."[74] Because doing *hesed* is in the very nature of God, a person who is in relation to Him has some things he or she can lay claim to. And there will be moments in your life, I suspect, when you will find yourself wanting to do that. You will say, "Lord, am I in covenant with you? If I am, a believer has some rights." I think that is what we see in Genesis 24—where Abraham's servant went to find a wife for Isaac. He counted on Yahweh's *hesed*, that He would protect him on his way, and when He got him there, that He would lead him to the right girl and that the people who were responsible for her would be gracious and let her go. And, furthermore, on the basis of the *hesed* of Yahweh, he would get back home safely. It was a marvelous thing. When we are in covenant with Him, we can expect Him to do some things.[75]

---

[74] Jacob, *Theology of the Old Testament*, 107.

[75] Two ladies, a doctor and a nurse, have spent their lives working among Bedouins in Jordan. Now, that is not the nicest place, normally, for a Christian missionary to go. And one said, "We often hear the sermons from the mosque about how these aliens have to be driven out, but over the years we've gotten to where we just go about our business. We couldn't preach outside the hospital, but in the hospital we could." She said, "Our mornings are so busy that we always have our prayers in the evening at 6 o'clock. Over the years [and I think she's been there almost fifty years] we've never had a great many converts. Some of the converts we've had we would never know about because in that culture there is no way you could know. These Bedouins, none of them can read or write. So, when they come to the hospital we have prayer together and we sing. We can't give them scripture because they can't read, so we took a set of scripture verses and set them to Arabic tunes. Once they've learned one of those tunes and the words to it, it's there forever because that's the kind of memory those people have—they live by it. It is funny, all the Christian groups that we know that are related in any way to us, their worship services are always at 6 o'clock in the evening because they figure that, from us, that's the canonical hour for the worship of God.

Occasionally we get an indication that God has used our witness. A Bedouin boy showed up one day, about eighteen, with TB—desperately sick. His father had watched him get sicker and sicker and finally his father, who had been in that hospital once before, said to him, 'You must go to the hospital where I went.' Now they were hundreds of miles away from it. This kid had never been away from his own little group, and there were three major transfers he had to make in the journey. So he said to his father, 'You will have to take me.' And his father said, 'We don't have enough money to take two of us so you will have to go alone.' But he said, 'The One that I heard about in that hospital will get you there.'" Think about that in

But you will never find out what God's *hesed* can do unless you dare to take risks. The only people who really know about His *hesed* are the people who intentionally reach beyond their own abilities and their own resources. If you play it safe, you will never know that He keeps covenant with you. But if you will risk everything for Him, you will find He keeps covenant, and more than that, does *hesed*, with those who belong to Him.

In the Bible the covenant is always initiated by Yahweh. That is an unfailing rule. No one enters into a covenant relationship with God on his or her own initiative. God always commits Himself first and then invites us into the relationship. That comes out of the fact that He is a God of *hesed*. What I am saying is that *hesed* is not a product of covenant. Rather, God's *hesed* is the reason why He offers a covenant to us, and why He will keep it until the bitter end.

Ah, but what is the bitter end? Now, we are dealing with human freedom and with the question: Can a person fall from grace? Yes they can, but hear me on this: If anybody ever falls from grace, it is not because

---

relation to the narrative in Genesis 24.

And then she told about how he made the transfers. At one place, he had gotten off a bus and he was standing and somebody came up to him and said, "Where are you going?" And he told him and he said, "Well, this is the vehicle that you take." He couldn't identify it, but that was it. He came to the next stop and he did not know how to go from there. An Arab came up to him and asked, "Where are you going?" He told him the name of the town and the fellow said, "I am a cab driver and I am going there on my next trip and as soon as I get four more customers I will take you." So, he crawled in the cab, the fellow got his four customers and they started on their trip. He began to cough and he said, "I was terrified. I did everything I could do to cover up my cough because I was afraid that the cab driver, when he realized how sick I was, would throw me out. So I was horrified when the cab driver turned and said, 'Are you sick?' I tried to make it as small as I could. The fellow said, 'You need to go to the hospital,' and named the hospital the kid was trying to reach. 'I will take you there.'"

So, he showed up at the hospital. And they took him in. He was very sick, but he had not been there long when he said, "When do you sing?" And they said, "What do you mean, when do we sing?" "Well," he said, "my father told me that you sing. I want to hear you singing because I hear that you sing about Jesus."

That illiterate father had come home, having heard the hymns, or the songs that had Scripture in them. He had stopped praying to Allah, had begun to pray to Christ, and now his son, at eighteen, was a believer. All I could think about was, that's almost like Abraham, isn't it? No Bible, none of the things that we have, but in his heart there was that faith and that providential guidance that got him there.

Yahweh has abandoned him. The thrust of Scripture is that He does not abandon those with whom He is in covenant. He may discipline, chasten, withdraw His face, etc., but again the metaphors that are used illustrate the strength of that covenant. Parent and child; king and His people; shepherd and His flock; spouse and spouse.

If a person falls from grace I think it is fair to say he or she walks out of the relationship deliberately, intentionally. So, "fall" is a somewhat misleading expression for this condition. It is a biblical expression; Paul uses it, so we certainly can. But we are not talking about an accident or something that happens against a person's will. If a person has "fallen away" it is because that person jumped. It is the mindset that results in a person beginning to move away from the Gospel.

What *hesed* teaches us is that the arms of Yahweh are wide open, waiting. Sometimes it is difficult to reconcile scripture with scripture. For instance, the prophet Jeremiah will say that Judah has come to the end, that the Babylonian conquest is inevitable; but a few verses later he will be calling upon the people to repent so they can escape the coming judgment. Likewise in the Psalms, you will find one that begins with seemingly inevitable judgment, but then throws the door wide open for repentance and return. He says, "I have to punish you, I have to chasten you, I have to deal with your sin," and then before He finishes the sentence His arms of compassion and forgiveness are spread wide open. Why is this? Because it is His will that none of us should perish. The reason for the election of the Hebrew people in the Old Testament is that God has elected the whole world. And *hesed* is at the heart of that.

We have already spoken of the connotations of firmness and fidelity in *hesed* and how this idea is underlined by its linkage with *'emet* (to be true to, faithful to). In the modern world the concept of fidelity in marriage seems to be rapidly disappearing, but it is certainly not so in the Bible. For an illustration of this, the prime example is Hosea, where God continues to love His adulterous bride despite the fact that she "does not know" Him. Jacob says that in Hosea the term *hesed* reaches its greatest significance as a figure to show the relationship of Yahweh to His people, people to Yahweh and people to each other.[76]

One of the beautiful illustrations of the person-to-person aspect

---

[76] Jacob, *Theology of the Old Testament,* 105.

of *hesed* is to be found in the relationship of Jonathan and David. What a pity it is that we have reached a day in America where it is difficult to deal with that relationship. It is a magnificent thing when a man loves a man. And there is nothing biological in it. That is what you have in that story. It is a *hesed* story. It is not an *'ahab* story or a *dod* story; *'ahab* is one Hebrew word for "love" and *dod* is another word for "love," the kind you have in the Song of Songs. What existed between David and Jonathan was not that kind of relationship. It is a *hesed* relationship, one in which each was committed to the other at whatever cost to himself.

Micah sums up much of what we have been saying in a well-known statement found in Micah 6:8: "He has showed you, O man, what is good. And what does [Yahweh] require of you? To act justly and to love *hesed* and to walk humbly with your God." You will notice there is no abstraction in that statement. It is: You act justly—it's something you do; you love *hesed*—the attitude and disposition of your being that determines how you act and the result is you walk humbly with your God.

Later in the Old Testament, in the prophets, *hesed* is extended, interestingly enough, to those who are outside of the covenant. Or else, to those who have sometime, somewhere, broken the covenant. You will find it in Hosea 2:1:

> Say of your brothers, "My people," and of your
>   sisters, "My loved one," (*ruhama*).
> Rebuke your mother, rebuke her,
>   for she is not my wife, and I am not her
>   husband. Let her remove the adulterous look
>   from her face and the unfaithfulness from
>   between her breasts.
> Otherwise, I will strip her naked
>   and make her as bare as on the day she was
>   born; I will make her like a parched land,
>   and slay her with thirst.
> I will not show my *hesed* to her children,
>   because they are the children of adultery
>   (vv. 1-4).

That is the background. You see how strongly He stated His

point: "I am no longer her husband, I have divorced her." Now come
down toward the end, to verse 16.

> "In that day," declares [Yahweh],
>> "you will call me, 'my husband';
>> you will no longer call me 'my master,' [my *baʿal*].
> I will remove the names of the *baʿal*s from her lips;
>> no longer will their names be invoked.
> In that day I will make a covenant for them
>> with the beasts of the field and the birds of
>> the air and the creatures that move
>> along the ground.
> Bow and sword and battle
>> I will abolish from the land,
>> so that all may lie down in safety.
> I will betroth you to me forever;
>> I will betroth you in righteousness and justice,
>> in love [*hesed*] and compassion [*raḥᵃmim*].
> I will betroth you in faithfulness ['*emet*],
>> and you will acknowledge [Yahweh].[77]
> In that day I will respond,"
>> declares [Yahweh]—
> "I will respond to the skies
>> and they will respond to the earth;
>> and the earth will respond to the grain,
>> the new wine and oil,
>> and they will respond to Jezreel.
> I will plant her for myself in the land;
>> I will show my love to the one I called 'Not my
>> loved one.'
> I will say to those called 'Not my people,'
>> 'You are my people,'
>> and they will say,
>> 'You are my God'" (vv. 16-23).

---

[77] Note the key theological words: righteousness, justice, love, compassion, faithfulness.

God extends His *ḥesed* even to those who in no way deserve it and the effects of that act will reach out to nature as well, and ultimately to the world.

Now, look for a moment at Isaiah 54:

> "For a brief moment I abandoned you,
>> but with deep compassion I will bring you
>> back.
>
> In a surge of anger I hid my face from you for a
>> moment, but with everlasting kindness [*ḥesed*]
>
> I will have compassion on you,"
>> says [Yahweh] your Redeemer.
>
> "To me this is like the days of Noah,
>> when I swore that the waters of Noah would
>> never again cover the earth" (vv. 7-9a).

Yahweh's promise to Noah was given before there was a chosen people. That was before Israel existed. It was Yahweh in relation to the whole creation. Once again, we see that it was not the covenant with Israel that was the basis of *ḥesed*. Rather, it is God's *ḥesed* that makes the covenant possible. And that means that His compassionate, committed, undeserved love, His *ḥesed*, is available to His whole creation. It is that *ḥesed* that gives strength and endurance to the covenant.

In these passages we get beyond the legal conception of *ḥesed*. In a legal relationship, I can fight for my rights and you can fight for yours, and each one has a legal, technical obligation. But in this covenant shaped by God's *ḥesed*, the basis of it is not a legal obligation. The basis of it is the very character of Yahweh. And that is the character He wants to produce in you and me.

I hope I am clear in this. These passages from Hosea and Isaiah and some others show us that the covenant that God works out is not just a legal document—two equals fighting with each other and staking out their claims, sort of like Lot's herdsmen and Abraham's herdsmen in Genesis 13. Rather, what we have is One who wants to be in a personal, committed relation with each of us. This is no contract, but a giving of self to self without limitations. Why does He want this? It is because we are valuable to Him. As we said earlier, you and I are *sᵉgulla*, we are a prized possession. We are a priceless jewel to Him. And He loves us and wants us.

As I said at the beginning of the lecture, later in Scripture we will find those words of natural affection, *'ahab* and *dod*, being used of Yahweh. But that does not occur often in the earlier parts. It is absolutely necessary to set the stage for them. God's love is not like the world's love. If somebody will love me, then I will love him or her—maybe. If someone has a personality that clicks with mine and seems kindly disposed toward me, then I find a certain degree of affection for that person rising in me. That is the world's love—that is the love of the gods. That is *not* the love of Yahweh. So you have to start with a term the Canaanite does not even know to talk about, a reality that is right outside of a fallen, sinful world. Once you have laid the groundwork with *hesed* you are ready to hear about divine love with that sense of natural affection. He sees us and He responds, because He loves us. We are desirable to Him. That is an astounding thing. We are infinitely desirable to God. In the Song of Songs, the longest and most ecstatic passages are those where the Lover speaks of his Beloved. In our case the Lover is the Eternal One, and that means He has capacities for joy that go beyond anything we can imagine, and the incredible thing is that you are an object of joy to Him. You and I are objects of joy to Him.

In the light of all this it is not surprising that sometimes *hesed* is used of unexpected works of God, like miracles that break the natural pattern of life. Look at Psalm 107. This is one of those psalms that deals with the history of Israel. Notice how it begins:

> Give thanks to [Yahweh] for he is good;
>> his *hesed* endures forever.
> Let the redeemed of the LORD say this—
>> those he redeemed from the hand of the foe,
> those he gathered from the lands,
>> from the east and west, from north and south.
> Some wandered in desert wastelands,
>> finding no way to a city where they could settle.
> They were hungry and thirsty,
>> and their lives ebbed away.
> Then they cried to [Yahweh] in their trouble,

and he delivered them from their distress.
He led them by a straight way
    to a city where they could settle.
Let them give thanks to [Yahweh] for his *hesed*,
    and his wonderful deeds for men,
for he satisfies the thirsty
    and fills the hungry with good things (vv. 1-9).

Now, the context shows that we are talking about the return of the exiles and all the miraculous and providential things that God engineered to bring that about. These are acts of *hesed*. Look in the same psalm at verse 13:

Then they cried to the Lord in their trouble,
    and he saved them from their distress.
He brought them out of darkness and deepest gloom.
    and broke away their chains.
Let them give thanks to [Yahweh] for his *hesed*
    and his wonderful deeds for men,
for he breaks down gates of bronze
    and cuts through the bars of iron (vv. 13-16).

Wonderful works of Yahweh, these acts of mighty power. Look at verse 19:

Then they cried to [Yahweh] in their trouble,
    and he saved them from their distress.
He sent forth his word and healed them;
    he rescued them from the grave.
Let them give thanks to [Yahweh] for his *hesed*
    and his wonderful deeds for men.
Let them sacrifice thank offerings
    and tell of his works [of *hesed*] with songs of joy
    (vv. 19-22).

Then you come down to verse 28 and it repeats:

Then they cried out to the Lord in their trouble,
> and he brought them out of their distress.
He stilled the storm to a whisper;
> the waves of the sea were hushed.
They were glad when it grew calm,
> and he guided them to their desired haven.
Let them give thanks to [Yahweh] for his *hesed*
> and his wonderful deeds for men.
Let them exalt him in the assembly of the people
> and praise him in the council of the elders
> (vv. 28-32).

So, you find that the word is used not just to speak of His attitude and His nature, but it is used to describe His mighty works. This, I believe, is why the term *hesed* occurs most frequently in the Bible in the book of Psalms. Out of a total of 247 occurrences more than 150 are found in the Psalms. Now what are the Psalms about? They are about worship, about prayer, about the Israelites' communion with Yahweh. They are talking with Him and they are reminding Him and thanking Him and praising Him for the relationship. And what is at the heart of the relationship? It is *hesed!* Without the *hesed* of God, there would be no relationship. There would not have been one in the beginning, and there most certainly would not have been one in the end. Thus the praise of God in the Bible is rooted in His *hesed.* Nowhere is that made more explicit than in Psalm 136, whose twenty-six verses constitute a brief review of the Creation, the Exodus and the Conquest. Every one of the twenty-six verses ends with the refrain, "His *hesed* endures forever." In other words, both the world and Israel exist, creation and redemption, for one reason: the eternal *hesed* of God.[78]

That *hesed 'olam*—the eternal *hesed,* means that *hesed* is future as well as past and present. It is something you can count on in the future, just as you counted on it in the past. And that, I suspect, is something that was very close to the heart of Abraham's faith. He came to believe that Yahweh had acted in *hesed* to him in the past, and he said, "It will

---

[78] This is probably why Torrance calls *hesed* the sacramental word of the Old Testament.

be interesting to see what He does in the days ahead." It is easy enough to look back and recognize what God has done, but if all of this is true, then *hesed* is as much before as it is behind. And the best is yet to be.

Lecture 14

....

His *Hesed*
Endures Forever

At the end of the previous lecture, I was saying that if *hesed* is forever, that means that *hesed* is something you can count on in the future. And as you have had it in the past and you look back and you see that Yahweh has been gracious, then that is one of your assumptions now about the future. He will be in the future what He has been in the past, because that loving-kindness, that sheer concern, is there forever.

If that is so, that gets to the heart of what I think may have been Abraham's faith. He had come to believe that this One would be in the future as He had been in the past. I wonder if this is one of the reasons he found himself able to respond when Yahweh said to him, "I want you to sacrifice Isaac." He may have said, "I don't know what this means, but I know the One who is asking me to do it, and I can trust Him."

I believe that the following illustration originated with Dr. H. C. Morrison, one of the great preachers of the late nineteenth and early twentieth centuries:

The Trinity were looking on at the sacrifice of Isaac. One member of the Godhead said to another one, "This is not the last time we're going to be on this mountain, is it?" And the First Person of the blessed Trinity said, "No, it will be about two thousand years and we will be back, right here." And the Second Person of the blessed Trinity said to the First Person of the blessed Trinity, "And when we come back next time, it's not going to be one of them on that altar, is it?" And the First Person of the blessed Trinity said, "No, when we come back the next time it won't be one of them—it will be one of Us." And then the Second Person of the blessed Trinity said to the First, "And when they put me on that altar of sacrifice, are you going to say, 'Stop, don't touch the lad?'" And the Father said, "No. We never ask them to do in symbol what we haven't been willing to do in reality."

That is a different concept of the Godhead. And that is getting right at the heart of what I think the Old Testament means when it talks about His *hesed*, His loving-kindness. How far will He go to redeem us and how far will He go to help us? He will go as far as necessary, even to His own death, because He cares about us. Now, none of that is explicit in these accounts. You can only get intimations of it here. But, at the same time, there is nothing here to conflict with that understanding when it appears later in the biblical narrative. And that to me is one of the beautiful things about the unity of Scripture.

I mentioned Psalm 136 in the previous lecture. As I said, each verse ends with the same refrain. It was probably sung antiphonally, with one choir singing the refrain. But when the same line is repeated twenty-six times, you get to the place where you know what is coming, and it is fairly easy to cut yourself off and miss the richness that is there. I want you to notice the progression that appears in the initial part of each successive verse:

Give thanks to [Yahweh], for he is good . . .

The psalmist has found that He is good, and so it is appropriate to give thanks to Yahweh because of that fact.

> Give thanks to the God of gods . . .

Whatever the Canaanites might call "gods," this One is God over them. He is another category of being.

> Give thanks to the LORD of lords . . .

Notice that *lords* is lower case. Whatever "lord" might pretend to have power, Yahweh is over him.

> to him who alone does great wonders . . .

Notice the word *alone*. There is something that can be said about Yahweh, and there is no one else about whom it can be said.

> who by his understanding made the heavens . . .
> who spread out the earth upon the waters . . .
> who made the great lights . . .
> the sun to govern the day . . .
> the moon and the stars to govern the night . . .

In short, He is the God, the LORD of Genesis and He is the LORD, the God of creation. He created it. And His mercy endures forever. So the creation is an expression of that *hesed*.

Now, it is love, in a sense, that wants to reproduce itself and produce another—that it can pour its love upon it. The great tragedy is when a person has no one to love. So creation is a product of, and the object of, the love of God.

Now, notice verses 10 to the end of the psalm:

> To him who struck down the firstborn of Egypt . . .
> and brought Israel out from among them . . .
> with a mighty hand, an outstretched arm . . .
> to him who divided the Red Sea asunder . . .

and brought Israel through the midst of it . . .
but swept pharaoh and his army into the Red Sea . . .
to him Who led his people through the desert . . .
who struck down great kings . . .
and killed mighty kings . . .
Sihon king of the Amorites . . .
and Og, king of Bash . . .
and gave their land as an inheritance . . .
an inheritance to his servant, Israel . . .
to the One who remembered us in our low estate . . .
and freed us from our enemies . . .
and who gives food to every creature . . .
Give thanks to the God of heaven.

You will notice that after the introduction the writer identifies Yahweh as the God of creation. But then, when you get to verse 10 he shifts and says He is the God of history. He is the LORD whose hand is sovereign both *over* time and space and over what takes place *within* time and space. The illustration he uses is the history of Israel from the Exodus from Egypt through His provision in the wilderness to His bringing them to the Promised Land giving the place that He promised to Abraham—to his descendants, Israel. But then at the end (v. 25) he shifts back from history to God's relationship to the creation—"Who gives food to every creature." So when the wild animal eats its food, or the pet in your house or anyone else, all of this is an expression of "his *hesed* endures forever" (*hesed ʿolam*).

Now, as we continue on in our thinking, I want to pick up that reference to history. This is, again, one of the unique things about the religion of Israel. Perhaps you have had the experience as I have, of suddenly becoming aware of the significance of something that you have seen a thousand times before. For instance, there is the Apostles' Creed. It was said every Sunday in my home church so even as a child I could say it without one conscious thought. Then one day, I decided to look at it to see what it is that the Christian church, in this the earliest of the great creeds, believes. We say:

I believe in God the Father Almighty, maker of heaven

and earth; Jesus Christ his only Son our Lord who was conceived by the Holy Spirit, born of the Virgin Mary, suffered under Pontius Pilate, was crucified, dead and buried.

What? It suddenly dawned on me that every Sunday morning millions of Christians stand up and say that we believe in God the Father, God the Son, God the Holy Spirit, the Virgin Mary and Pontius Pilate. That is an interesting quintet, is it not? As I thought about it I could understand, I think, something of why Mary got in there, because we do not need to elevate her to semi-divine status to recognize the absolutely unique role she played in the Incarnation. But how did Pontius Pilate get in? I doubt if even Pontius Pilate's mother believed that two thousand years after her son died there would be millions of people every Sunday morning who would stand up and say, "I believe in Mrs. Pilate's son." Yet that is what we do. Why? Why does almost the entire Christian church affirm Sunday after Sunday that we believe in the existence of Pontius Pilate?

As I have reflected on this fact it has become very precious to me. Furthermore, it is profoundly biblical because there is a sense in which if you could prove that Pontius Pilate never lived, you would have pulled a major cornerstone out from under the Christian faith. This is so because the faith that we hold is rooted in something that happened in time and space, which you can date fairly closely on a calendar. That is a religion that has moved beyond rational abstraction. It is also a religion that has moved beyond great pious truths. It has an anchor point right in the middle of time and space.

Why is this rootage in history so important to the Christian faith? It is because Christianity rests squarely on the Old Testament, and rootage in time and space is at the very core of the Old Testament's faith in God. The Old Testament insists that God made time and space, that when He made them they were good and His purposes for them are good, and those purposes will be realized.

That means that time is not something you want to run away from. And how different that is from the Greek world, where reality was to be found in the world of the eternal ideas untouched by the pettiness and the decay of time and space. Only in escaping time and space was there real deliverance. I suspect that it was precisely to confront those ideas that Pontius Pilate was put into the creed. For the Bible says that the heart of our faith is to be found right in the middle of that world of time and space. God does not call us to try to escape this world in our search for him. Rather, He comes into our world in search of us.

H. Wheeler Robinson, a British Old Testament scholar, said that there is a sense in which history is the sacrament of the religion of Israel.[79] In saying that, he is trying to put his finger on the significance of time for biblical religion. The reality is that from its earliest periods, Israel felt that its experiences in time and space had meaning. Furthermore, they came to believe that those experiences were not merely going around and around in endless circles, but that they were leading beyond themselves to new experiences yet to be. The germ of the idea of history lies right in those two convictions. If you believe those two things, you will write history. If you do not, you never will.

Now, there are many peoples in the history of the world who look back fondly at some golden age in their past to which they hope to circle back. But here was a people who did not have a golden age in the past, but who said, "We have a golden age to come." They were future-oriented. Where did they get such an orientation? I suspect some of it may have come from that concept that "his *hesed* endures forever." If His *hesed* has been so good in the past, what will it be in the future?

You sense that future-orientation from the very first words of the Abraham narrative, because the text begins with a promise from God to the patriarch about the future. And that promise is repeated in one form or another eight more times in the next thirteen chapters. So Abraham's experience with God was built around that promise and its progressive fulfillment. And the promise was not merely for Abraham. It was for his descendants. Thus the fulfillment stretched out over centuries. That progressive fulfillment of the promise to Abraham not only gave direction to Israel's experiences in time and space, but it also gave coherency to those experiences. They were not just discrete, disparate elements, but they cohered with one another in a great unity. This is one of the reasons the Israelites interpret Scripture the way they do. They

---

[79] H. Wheeler Robinson, *The History of Israel: Its Facts and Factors*, 2nd ed., rev. L. H. Brockington (London: Duckworth, 1964), 1.

expect that the component parts will form part of a larger whole.

When we think about history, there are two elements that are foundational. The first of these is unique events. While some might say that history always repeats itself, that is not really true. A truer statement is the old aphorism, "You can't step into the same stream twice." It is precisely because events do not happen again that it is important to record them with care. So, if God is to reveal Himself in time and space, it is not going to be by doing the same thing over and over again and in an identical way so that one can say, "there." But rather, as He reveals Himself, He will have to do it through individual, separate events in the course of time. Crucified under Pontius Pilate.

The second element that is necessary for revelation in history is interpretation. In the past, the scholars have tended to have less of a problem admitting the veracity of the events themselves back as far as the Exodus. There was more doubt about the supposed events of the patriarchs' lives. But I doubt if there would be that interpretation of the Exodus if it had not been for the fact that the Abraham story is there behind it and the faith that was beginning to develop in someone's individual life.[80] The Bible insists that the explanation of the meaning of the events is as revelatory as the events themselves. So it is impossible to separate event and interpretation, the event and the word. I do not think it is an accident that the Hebrew word for "word," *dabar*, also means "event." You cannot separate the thing from the expression of the thing. They go together. That is what lies behind John 1:1: "In the beginning was the Word . . ." and the divine "Word" is both of these, the eventness and the spokenness.

The happenings that take place, these events, provide the objective base on which our faith stands. And that objectivity, that objective base, saves the faith from abstractions and keeps it focused on daily life and on human persons. But the interpretation of the event explains the particular significance of the event, and the Old Testament puts these two together

---

[80] [Editor's note] Unfortunately, the level of skepticism toward the Bible's historical veracity has grown exponentially in recent years, to the extent that Thomas Thompson, a professor at the University of Copenhagen, can say that the only thing we know for certain about the history of Israel is that it was utterly unlike the one narrated in the Old Testament (unpublished lecture). A position like this makes those who deny the Exodus and the Conquest but permit the possibility that there might have been a David look conservative today.

in a unique way. There are two special examples of this combination that have engaged a good bit of scholarly attention.

The first example is found in the sixth chapter of Deuteronomy. In this book we are getting the word of Moses to Israel at the end of his life, before he is taken from them. He gives them again the Decalogue, the Ten Commandments, the heart of their covenant. In Exodus, the Decalogue is immediately followed by specific examples working out the implications of the commandments (Ex. 21–23). But that is not the case in Deuteronomy. Here the Decalogue is given in chapter 5 and the specific examples are found in chapters 12–26. Between the two we have Moses attempting to give the people an understanding of the significance of their covenant and what it will mean to truly live it out. One of his concerns is how and whether the covenant will be transmitted to the next generation. And he is not only concerned about the covenant itself but about the prior history upon which it rests. He is concerned that these texts or traditions, this truth, this knowledge will be transmitted to subsequent generations. And I think one of the authentic marks of a work of grace in a person's heart is the concern to share it, and the concern to see that that truth is maintained and transmitted.[81]

Now, Moses is feeling that and feeling it intensely. Yahweh had given to Israel the knowledge of Himself. And along with that knowledge, He had now given them a system of worship and the Law. He had done this so that their life might be acceptable to Him and they might walk with Him, and so that they might live together as a social group. It was a Law that was so encompassing that it affected every part of the Hebrew's life. There is no separation between the sacred and the secular

---

[81] There was an Australian young man who was living in a drug colony in the Outback in Australia, and in a very unusual way he heard the Gospel and found Christ. He knew nothing, really, about Christian faith, but Christ came to him and his life was transformed. The person who led him to Christ was the most unlikely of all creatures—and so often that is the case: God does not send the person you would expect—nevertheless, he found himself, his life, changed—transformed. He said, "I talked to the gentleman for a few moments and suddenly I thought, 'My buddy, my buddy . . . I've got to tell my buddy.'" I suspect that is the most authentic mark of true grace. When Christ has found you, there is something within you. It transforms you. It turns you inside out. And instead of continuing to live for yourself, now suddenly you are living for others and you have to tell them. That is not only true for your own generation but also for those to come. You want your children and your grandchildren to hear this word of the transforming Cross. It must be passed on.

in this ancient literature. In fact, we might go so far as to say that there is no concept of the secular to be found here. There is no area of life that the sacred does not touch.

So how is this knowledge, born out of experience, to be transmitted? In chapter six, Yahweh envisions the day in the next generation when the child will do what is inevitable. The child will look at his father and say, "What is the meaning of all these things that we do? Why do we do these things and why do we do them this way?"

Notice what Moses says the father should answer, beginning with verse 20:

> In the future, when your son asks you, "What is the meaning of the stipulations, decrees and laws [Yahweh] our God has commanded you?" tell him: "We were slaves of Pharaoh in Egypt, but [Yahweh] brought us out of Egypt with a mighty hand. Before our eyes [Yahweh] sent miraculous signs and wonders—great and terrible—upon Egypt and Pharaoh and his whole household. But he brought us out from there to bring us in and give us the land that he promised on oath to our forefathers [to Abraham, to the patriarchs]. [Yahweh] commanded us to obey all these decrees and to fear [Yahweh] our God, so that we might always prosper and be kept alive, as is the case today. And if we are careful to obey all this law before [Yahweh] our God, as he has commanded us, that will be our righteousness" (Deut. 6:20-25).

What you have here is the historical statement, the testimony. It is the inspired interpretation of the events of the Exodus. There is not a line of systematic theology in it. And yet virtually every line is pregnant with incredibly great systematic theology. The history means something about God and about the Hebrews and about life and about hope. Now, that kind of expression of faith is right at the heart of biblical religion. It is history. Personal history, national history, world history, it does not make any difference. It is history.

There is a similar passage found at the conclusion of the

covenant stipulations in chapter 26. It is almost as if Moses were saying, "If you didn't catch on when I started my sermon, let me repeat my first point for you." Here Moses is using the context of worship. It is the festival of first fruits. After they are in the Promised Land and God has blessed them, they are to bring some of that harvest before Yahweh as an expression of gratitude. It is right that you express gratitude to Yahweh for His blessings to you. Now, those blessings are natural. They are in the realm of nature. That is, Yahweh's activity as the creator in nature.

> The priest shall take the basket from your hands and set it down in front of the altar of [Yahweh] your God. Then you shall declare before [Yahweh], "My father was a wandering Aramean, and he went down into Egypt with a few people and lived there and became a great nation, powerful and numerous. But the Egyptians mistreated us and made us suffer, putting us to hard labor. Then we cried out to [Yahweh], the God of our fathers, and [Yahweh] heard our voice and saw our misery, toil and oppression. So [Yahweh] brought us out of Egypt with a mighty hand and an outstretched arm, with great terror and with miraculous signs and wonders. He brought us to this place and gave us this land, a land flowing with milk and honey; and now I bring the firstfruits of the soil that you, O LORD, have given me." Place the basket before the LORD your God and bow down before him. And you and the Levites and the aliens among you shall rejoice in all the good things [Yahweh] your God has given to you and your household (Deut. 26:4-11).

Now, don't miss the fact that, as in Psalm 136, there is the link between the creation and history. He is the Creator and as such He is the Lord of this world of time and space.

Again, you will notice that this is a history recital. The faith of the Hebrew is based on what Yahweh has done, His saving acts in history as interpreted by God through His prophets. And when you come to the New Testament, you find that expressed in what is found in the first five books. In the Gospels are the appearance of Christ and His acts. Words and acts. You have the Passion, the Crucifixion, the Resurrection. Then in the fifth book in the New Testament, the book of Acts, there is the history of the early church. And if you take the witness of Stephen when he is on trial for his life, you will remember he gives them a history lesson with which they are very familiar. It is not systematic theology, but it is profoundly theological. It is just that the theology emerges from the recounting of the history. I am not opposed to systematic theology. God knows we need all we can get, and we need infinitely better than most of us have. But the witness here is to the eventness of what God has done, and linked with it and out of it comes that theology as interpretation. In contrast to their neighbors, whose gods are inseparable from nature, Yahweh is the Creator and the source of nature, but He is more. He is the Lord of history.

Now, this has left its impact on the Old Testament, and you can find the evidence everywhere. Apart from Yahweh Himself, you could say that the main subject of the Old Testament is history. As you run through the book, look at how much is devoted to that. Take the first seventeen books of the Old Testament according to the arrangement in our English Bibles. You get the Pentateuch and Joshua and Judges, 1 and 2 Samuel, 1 and 2 Kings, etc. The first seventeen books of the Old Testament are basically dealing with the history. And even when you come to the Psalms, the worship, you will notice that right in the middle of the worship is the historical emphasis: "We are a people for whom God has done something great." You do not have to make much of a jump to go from here to the doctrine of election, do you? The basis of that doctrine of election is this Old Testament concept of the unity of history and that Yahweh is sovereign in it and sovereignly working redemptively. The Israelites are the illustration of truth of those convictions about God's revelation in history.

But what about the prophets? Surely you do not find a lot of historical narrative in them. No, you do not, but the context in which the prophets moved is history. Let me illustrate this with an example. Amos is one of the earliest of what we speak of as the classical eighth century or the writing prophets. You will remember that Amos was a herdsman. He said, "I was neither a prophet nor a prophet's son, but was a shepherd, and I also took care of sycamore-fig trees. But the LORD took me from tending the flock and said to me, 'Go, prophesy to my people Israel'" (7:14-15). "The lion roars; don't blame me if I tremble. Yahweh spoke, don't blame me if I have showed up here in your square and am preaching to you. Yahweh spoke and I don't have any option" (see 3:8). Amos was under a compulsion that had come from God.

Notice how the book begins: ". . . two years before the earth-quake, when Uzziah was king in Judah and Jeroboam, son of Jehoash, was king in Israel"(1:1). It is like Pontius Pilate. What Amos is dealing with is anchored to the clock and to the calendar. He is going to speak timeless truth, but it *is* timeless precisely because it came in a specific historical context. The prophet then launches into eight prophecies of judgment. Each one is prefaced with, "For three sins of . . . even for four . . ." That is the way of expressing plurality in Hebrew. The plural is three and above. To ante it on up to four is a bit like squaring a number in English. So it is "for the multiple sins of . . ."

Notice to whom the first six are addressed. According to chap-ter 7, verse 13, Amos was preaching at Bethel, the royal chapel of Israel, the northern kingdom, and his message, as 7:15 says, was to the people of Israel. But he says, "for three transgressions of Damascus and for four." Then he tells you what is going to happen to Damascus. "For three transgressions of Gaza and for four." Then he tells you what is go-ing to happen to Gaza. "For three transgressions of Tyre and for four." And he tells you what is going to happen to Tyre. Then he does the same with Edom; he does the same with Ammon; and he does the same with Moab.

Every one of those states had its own system of gods. And Amos is standing up and saying their problem is not Chemosh or Baal. Their problem is Yahweh because Yahweh, the God of Israel, determines the destiny of these six nations. Now 760 B.C. is a long time before Christ. You find a man standing up in this little country of Israel—very small state—saying, "The God we worship is the One who determines the destinies of these nations that are around us."

Then he turns on Judah and says, "For three transgressions of Judah and for four . . ." And then he turns on the people to whom he was immediately speaking: "For three transgressions of Israel and for four, judgment is going to come."

In each of the cases he speaks in the name of Yahweh and proclaims Yahweh's judgment on all lands because Yahweh is the Lord of all of these. He is the God of the nations. And as such, He is the righteous God, the righteous Judge. You remember Abraham's question, "Shall not the Judge of all the earth do right?" He is the righteous Judge because He is going to pour out His wrath on all eight of these peoples, and He will pour it out because of their multiple transgressions. He does so because a central aspect of His holiness is righteousness and justice.

The charges that God makes against Damascus, Gaza, Tyre, Edom, Ammon and Moab are very interesting. He does not judge them in terms of the specific covenant standards of righteousness. Look what He does judge them for: "For three sins of Damascus, even for four, I will not turn back my wrath. Because she threshed Gilead with sledges having iron teeth" (1:3). Now, if you understand the metaphorical language, what He is saying is, "She not only defeated Gilead but did it in the most cruel and inhumane way." The judgment is for unnecessary cruelty of man to man. This is what the Lord says about Gaza: "Because she took captive whole communities and sold them to Edom [enslaved them and sold them to an enemy]" (1:6). Tyre: "She sold whole communities of captives to Edom, disregarding a treaty of brotherhood" (1:9). That is, she broke a covenant. Edom: "Because he pursued his brother with a sword, stifling all compassion because his anger raged continually and his fury flamed unchecked" (1:11). Edom is judged for undue cruelty. Ammon: "Because he ripped open the pregnant women of Gilead, in order to extend his borders, I will set fire to the walls of Rabbah that will consume her fortresses" (1:13-14). Moab: "Because he burned, as if to lime, the bones of Edom's king" (2:1). The judgment is for disrespect to an enemy's body. So, we might say that Yahweh judges the other nations by natural law.

But notice what happens when he comes to Judah. "For three transgressions of Judah, even for four, I will not turn back [my wrath]" (2:4). Who is this Judah? She is a part of the chosen nation. Yahweh is their particular God. But Yahweh is so just and righteous, He will deal with the sins of His favorite just the same way He will deal with the sins that are distant from Him. He is no respecter of persons in this sense. Judah will not be exempted from the wrath of Yahweh, "Because they have rejected the law of [Yahweh] and have not kept his decrees, because they have been led astray by false gods, the gods their ancestors followed." So the reason for judgment is much more particular here. She has not kept the covenant law that was given at Sinai, and she has been guilty of idolatry. Judah is not being judged more lightly because she is Yahweh's favorite. Just the opposite is true. The Judeans have a greater responsibility because more has been revealed to them. Remember Jesus' words, "From everyone who has been given much, much will be demanded" (Luke 12:48).

Then He comes to Israel, which was really where He was heading:

> [My wrath will be poured out because] they sell the righteous for silver, and the needy for a pair of sandals. They trample on the heads of the poor as upon the dust of the ground and deny justice to the oppressed. Father and son use the same girl and so profane my holy name. They lie down beside every altar on garments taken in pledge. In the house of their god they drink wine taken as fines. I destroyed the Amorite before them (2:6b-9a).

God had told Abraham in his dream recorded in Genesis 15 that he could not give the land to Abraham at that time "because the iniquity of the Amorites is not yet full." But the day came when it was full and God had given the Israelites the land in fulfillment of His covenant promises. But Israel's subsequent history, as reported in Amos 2:10-12, shows that the Israelites had not kept their covenant promises, so God says, in effect, "What happened to the Amorites can happen to you." The Israelites are God's chosen people, but they are not exempt, as the rest of Israel's history was to show. Here you see that moral element that runs down through history. And the biblical view of history cannot conceive of history apart from that moral element.

So it is history that provides the context for Yahweh to work and the context for Yahweh's word. So when the prophet speaks, the context of his message, the message of Isaiah, Jeremiah, Ezekiel, and the Twelve, is the context of history. That fact is represented in the way Israel organized its Canon of Scripture.[82] It includes Joshua, Judges, Samuel, and Kings along with Isaiah, Jeremiah, Ezekiel, and the Twelve (what we call "the Minor Prophets") in a section called "Prophets." Why is that? It is because those books of history are really books of prophecy. Israel was again and again told by the prophets (like Joshua; see also Judges 2:1-3; 1 Sam. 2:27-36) that they had a choice as to what their future history would look like. And the historical narratives tell us about the outworking of those messages and those choices. Now, dare I suggest that that is not inconsistent with this *hesed l'olam*, His loving-kindness forever? They believed that the One who had been good in their past would reign in the future. As He had guided and led them in the past so He would guide and lead them in the future. And so, they felt, as we said, other people may have their golden age behind them but for these Hebrews, their golden age was in front of them.

Now, is there a connection between that idea and Jesus' words about the kingdom of God? A lot of time and energy have been spent debating the question as to whether the kingdom is present or future. But ultimately one has to say there is an element of both in His teaching. You cannot rule out the future. And what is the last book in the New Testament? It is a book of Revelation, which has to do with the future. For a long time I did not know what to do with the book of Revelation. I read all those visions and tried to historicize them the way a lot of people do. But one day it dawned on me. Do you know what I think is primary in the book of Revelation? It is like the Old Testament; when the book of Revelation talks about the future it does not tell you the *what* in your future, but it tells you the *who*. Who is central in the first chapter of the book of Revelation and then again in the fourth and the fifth chapters after the letters to the churches? It is the exalted Christ. And there He is, central to whatever is in the future. That is a part of what you find

---

[82] I was taking an examination at Princeton, and one of the questions was: What are the former prophets and what are the latter prophets? I hate to admit it but at that stage of my education, I did not even know what the question was talking about. So I thought, "We divide them between the Major Prophets and the Minor, I wonder if that can have anything to do with it?" I honestly had never heard about the Hebrew order before. So, when I was told about it, I looked at the professor, Henry Snyder Gehman, and said, "Why under the sun do they call prophecy what is obviously history?" "Well," he said, "they believed their history was going somewhere." That is as good a brief answer as you will find.

implicit, beginning to be developed, in the earlier pages of the Old Testament.

Now, I do not think there is any question but that students of intellectual history consider the development of the concept of history itself one of the major breakthroughs, intellectually, in the history of human thought. Here are these people, this very small nation. You did not have to walk too many days to be outside of it, and it was an inconsequential nation most of the time. Where did it get that concept of history?[83]

These questions about the Bible and history are not merely academic ones. If we can accept the validity of the biblical accounts, then we know some things about God that have a profound impact upon pastoral ministry. We can know that on the widest level God is interested in universal history; every nation on the earth is His concern. But on a somewhat narrower level, God is interested in the chosen people; He wants to involve Himself in their life as a nation. But there is a still narrower level: God is interested in you. Why do I say that? Because the whole thing begins with a single individual: Abraham.

That means there is no such thing as an inconsequential person in whom God is not interested. The history of every one of those individual persons is significant to this God, and every person's life is to be, if it is related to Him properly, not a set of accidental, disparate events, but according to a way—a way that is good. So you never know what the shadows are going to be from any individual life. You do not find much about Jesus of Nazareth among the Roman historians. The historians of the day missed Him. And if you were appointed as a pastor in Nazareth, you would think you had come to the end of the road. But this is the kind of God who can raise up the Savior of the world out of that. In the world of this God of the Bible there is no such thing as an inconsequential spot or an inconsequential person.

---

[83] [Editor's note] This question has exercised Old Testament scholars increasingly in the last three decades. Because of the historical skepticism mentioned above in note 2, there has been an unwillingness to grant any uniqueness in the Hebrew understanding of history. There have been attempts to show that Israel's neighbors also thought of their gods as acting in history, that Israel's history writing and Greek history emerged at the same time with Israel's suffering by comparison. But the points that Reinhold Niebuhr made sixty years ago (cited in the following lecture) remain valid. Despite superficial similarities, Israelite history writing is essentially different from anything else in the ancient world.

Lecture 15

· · · · · · · · · ·

The Transcedent Element in History

In the previous lecture we were dealing with the emergence of the sense of history in Israel. We said that this sense of history developed very early in comparison to other cultures. And it arose so early that it made Israel unique in its world.

The question comes to scholars and people who observe with questioning minds, Why did this sense of history arise among these people when it did not arise among the Edomites or the Ammonites or Moabites? But it did arise among these Hebrews. Claus Westermann is one of the major Old Testament scholars in the world in our generation, educated at the University of Heidelberg. And he has written a little book called *Elements of Old Testament Theology*.[84] He has this to say about the

---

[84] Claus Westermann, *Elements of Old Testament Theology*, tr. D. W. Stott (Atlanta: John Knox Press, 1982).

emergence of the concept of history among the people of God. He says the historical element occurs in Israel because, first of all, Yahweh has bound Himself to a particular people, to Israel. And it comes out of that covenant relationship (Eichrodt's term). Now, Westermann says Old Testament theology cannot use the nineteenth- and twentieth-century concept of history as the standard for what is history in the Old Testament. Because, he says, modern historiography has an a priori commitment that excludes the central fact in Israel's history.[85] That central fact is a Yahweh and His integral involvement in human experience.

In the Old Testament, Yahweh's acts and words belong to every event that He picks for revelational purposes. Furthermore, He is behind every event. Reality without the working of Yahweh did not exist for the Old Testament true believer. Yahweh was the major participant in everything. What moves history takes place between Yahweh and humankind. It is a relationship, as Martin Buber would say, of dialogue. It is a dialogue in which God is speaking to us even in events as well as in word, and we are responding. Claus Westermann places a great emphasis upon the necessity of and the reality of the response. The roots of this dialogical relationship are in the Creation. God created humankind in His own likeness, and when He made us, He made us in a sense as a counterpart to Himself. So, you get the passage where He has made man a little lower than God (Psalm 8:6), and on occasion you wonder if He is calling us "gods" with a little "g". He made us in His likeness to correspond to Him so that the two of us can dialogue. Yahweh wants dialogue with His people, with His creatures, and Yahweh has made us so that is possible. All this is summed up or symbolized in that phrase in Genesis, "walk with (or before)" Yahweh (5:32; 17:1).

Here the modern concept of history, Westermann says, is at variance with Israel's concept. Modern historiography deals only with the documentable, that which is historically demonstrable. And he said for you to be able to do that, for that kind of science to exist, it assumes a level of culture that was not present in Israel's beginnings. Modern historiography also has another characteristic about it that is different. Modern historiography works in terms of forces or factors that are internal to the historical process. These include things like the political, or

---

[85] Westermann, *Old Testament Theology*, 12.

the sociological, or the ethnic, or the economic, or the religious, or the geographical. So there are histories written from each of these perspectives: political history, sociological history, etc. And sometimes you will find histories that are written using a combination of these elements. But you will notice that every one of those elements is, in a sense, an immanental. Each of them is a factor from within history itself.

So, the role of the divine has no place in typical, modern historiography or historical writing, because the historian has no scientific means of identifying and demonstrating divine involvement. That means that you will have people who will write in terms of the development of history with never a reference to biblical texts. What happens in modern historiography is that we separate the historical from the religious to the degree that religion posits a transcendent God who is outside of the machine and who acts in relation to it. For the believer in Yahweh, that kind of thinking was inconceivable because Yahweh was the major factor in their life, as far as they were concerned. It is ironical to me that it was these believing Hebrews who first began to give the world the first intimations of what we know today as historical thought or historiography, yet their texts are excluded from being historical by many scholars.

Westermann believes that this kind of historical way of thinking first arose with Yahweh's word of promise. Yahweh speaks to Abraham and gives him a promise, and then He repeats that promise, and over a period of time it is repeated until after a twenty-five-year span part of that promise is clearly fulfilled. That promise is given to his descendants and that promise is, four hundred years later, more fully fulfilled in something else. So, he says, a promise was given that necessitated the recipient to think in what Westermann calls a "context of time." He is differentiating that from an event.[86] "A context of time," a length of time.

The time between the promise and the fulfillment became what Westermann calls "an organic whole," so that the promise in Genesis 12 and the birth of Isaac twenty-five years later are not two separate events. In one sense they may be two separate events, but they are part of a larger whole and are related to each other.

The period between the promise and fulfillment became for the Israelites a unit of time. The relationship was seen between the word

---

[86] Ibid., 13-14.

that was given and the event that developed. There are other cases where you get an event and then a word that comes out of the event. But in the patriarchs what you get primarily here is a word and then the event comes later. The relationship was seen between the word and event, and out of such thinking Westermann says, "historical consciousness began to emerge."[87] He says another factor in this, though he does not develop it as much as he does the previous points, is the fact of genealogies. And if you go through the book of Genesis you will remember the genealogies put in at strategic times. What they do is to group the narratives in units of time instead of single, individual lives.

From this kind of experience developed the concept of linear time. This was a break from the normal, cyclical manner of thinking in relation to time, which was found in the ancient world. That way of thinking was basically rooted in the seasonal cycles of nature. It is not that the Old Testament does not recognize the validity for that kind of thinking. The cyclical paradigm is not one that the biblical believer automatically rejects, because you will remember that after the Flood, God came to Noah and, recognizing the validity and the goodness of these rhythms of nature, God made a promise to Noah that in the future, after the Flood, that rhythm would not be disturbed again. Yahweh promises that never again will He curse the ground because of man and his sin, nor will He ever again destroy all living creatures, but "as long as the earth endures, seed time and harvest, cold and heat, summer and winter, day and night will never cease" (Gen. 8:22). So God says that is a valid and a good thing. But God's purpose with humankind goes beyond mere perpetuation of the status quo. When it comes to His human creatures He has a goal that means that progress is possible, and it is even possible for something new to develop.

In this regard, note that the Hebrew word for "new" is *hadash*, which has the same consonants as the word for "a new moon." Now, how original is the new moon? You get the view, you know, that the cycle turns and comes back to where it was. It is new in the sense that it has been absent for a while, but it is the same moon that was there before. There were many people in the ancient world who believed that to be a valid philosophy of history. Aristotle says that if you will wait long

---

[87] Ibid., 18.

enough, everything that happens will happen again.[88]

But that is not how the biblical writers thought. So here again, with "new" is an illustration of the way that biblical thought has to re-shape linguistic categories. We mentioned that above in relation to the word *holy*. The Bible sees something that no surrounding culture saw: the possibility of something truly new, something that had never occurred before. So it could use a word related to "new moon" and fill that word with a previously unheard of meaning. For the Bible sees a future ahead that is going to be better than the present. So there is a concept of new-ness. To be sure, the future will be in harmony with the past, but it will not be merely repetitive of the past; it will go beyond it in something brand-new. So when you come to the new covenant in Jeremiah 31 and Ezekiel 36, or when you come to Isaiah as he speaks about the Suffering Servant and the kingdom that He will bring, it is not just a reformulation of something that already was before, but it is something new in a richer, fuller, creative, original sense.

As I said above, the cyclical understanding is related to the world of nature and is expressive of the idea that, if you want to get in touch with reality, you do so in the recurring cycles of nature; God is the world of nature. But when you come to God's relationship to us human be-ings that Genesis sets as the climax of the Creation, it is clear that God has a goal, a purpose, an end to which we are to move. That purpose is reflected in His promise of blessing. I cannot expound everything that is implied in that word, but you can count on it, that when that word *blessing* is used, the implication is that there is something to come that is incred-ibly rich and good and better than what is present. The best is yet to be.

God promises that blessing to His creatures, and that blessing is not just more of the same. But notice that that idea involves an element that transcends both nature and time. Yahweh comes from outside of time, and if a blessing is because of a relationship to Him, we are deal-ing with the factor that is not immanental to history, nor immanental to nature but with the transcendent element that is above and beyond, outside.

Reinhold Niebuhr taught for many years at Union Theological

---

[88] Cited in Reinhold Niebuhr, *The Nature and Destiny of Man: A Christian Interpretation*, 2 vols. in one (New York: Scribners, 1941), 10.

Seminary in New York City and at that time (the 1940s and '50s) he was considered by many people to be the best theological mind in the United States. He was invited to give the Gifford Lectures at Yale University on the topic of "The Nature and the Destiny of Man."

One of the interesting conditions of the Gifford Lectures is that they cannot be an exposition of Scripture. They are to address a theological subject. As such, they may utilize Scripture, but that cannot be the starting point. So the lecturer must lean heavily on what has been called natural revelation. If you will recall the previous lecture, you will remember that this is what Amos did when he pronounced judgment on Israel's and Judah's neighbors. He did not judge them on the basis of the Mosaic legislation, but on the basis of what we speak of as natural standards of decency and law. It is from that perspective that the scholar must work when he comes to the Gifford Lectures.

Niebuhr's study was eventually published as a massive two-volume work, and it is well worth any amount of time you can spend with it. At the core of his study is an examination of the different views of humanity and its relation to history from ancient until modern times. Here are a couple of the things he says: "It is in fact impossible to interpret history at all without a principle of interpretation which history as such itself does not yield."[89] Did you link that with what I said earlier about biblical Hebrew? The biblical mind-set is different from modern historiography in that modern historiography can only deal with immanental principles, immanental factors.

Here is Niebuhr saying it is impossible to interpret history at all without a principle of interpretation, which history itself does not, cannot, yield.

> The various principles of interpretation current in modern culture such as the idea of progress or the Marxist concept of an historical dialectic, are all principles of historical interpretation, introduced by faith.[90]

---

[89] Ibid., 141.

[90] Ibid., 141. Remember this was done about 1940 and in those days there were basically two competing philosophies of history that had moved through the earlier part of the twentieth century. One of them was the idea of inevitable progress. If you just wait long enough everything would be better. It was an ideological carry-over of

They are not introduced by science, but by faith. These are hypotheses. Let me remind you of what I said earlier of Archbishop Sheen's claim that while communism may be the enemy of Christianity, it is also a child of Christianity. Niebuhr is saying the same thing, that the very philosophy that informed Marxism is a by-product of Hebrew belief.

Niebuhr goes on to say:

> They claim to be conclusions about the nature of history at which men arrive after a "scientific" analysis of the course of events, but there is no such analysis of the course of events which does not make use of some presupposition of faith, as the principle of analysis and interpretation.[91]

So, it is not a question of whether you are going to have some principle of faith by which you interpret history. Niebuhr is saying that a person just has to make a choice as to which principle it is going to be. And it is better if you acknowledge your choice rather than pretending that you are purely scientific and totally objective and have no presupposition of faith.

Let me quote another passage from the same work: "The idea of progress is possible only upon the ground of a Christian culture."[92] Here he is explaining the origin of the idea of inevitable progress, or of the Marxist historical dialectic. He says, "[The idea of progress] is a secularized version of biblical apocalypse, and of the Hebraic sense of the meaningful history, in contrast to the meaningless history of the Greeks."[93] Now remember, this is not a fundamentalist saying this, nor even an evangelical. He says that it was among the Hebrews that a concept of a meaningful history developed; something that the Greek world never quite grasped. The Greeks could never quite see where human life was headed. Was it to oblivion, or was it to absorption into the Divine?

---

the doctrine of naturalistic evolution. The other philosophy was the Marxist concept of the historical dialectic.
[91] Ibid., 141.
[92] Ibid., 24.
[93] Ibid.

In either case, our present life, our history, is reduced to meaninglessness.

Now, let me give you one more quotation from Niebuhr: "Nothing is so incredible as an answer to an unasked question."[94] I was very interested in his terminology. He is saying that when you present someone
with an answer to a question they have not asked, their response is incre-
dulity, or unbelief. "Nothing is so incredible as an answer to an unasked
question." One half of the world has regarded the Christian answer to
the problem of life and history as foolishness. It has done so because it
has no questions for which the Christian revelation was the answer, no
longings and hopes for that revelation to fulfill. You have a feeling of
some of that when you read the story of Paul's preaching on Mars Hill.
The cultures of that half of the world were non-messianic and they were
non-messianic because they were non-historical. Their failure to regard
history as basic to the meaning of life may be attributed to two primary
methods of looking at life, methods which stand in contradiction to each
other.

One of these methods regards the system of nature as the final
reality to which man must adjust himself. The other regards nature from
the human perspective. One regards man from the perspective of nature,
the other regards nature from the human perspective as either chaos or a
meaningless order from which man will be freed, either by his reason or
by some power within him that is higher than reason. Now, he says the
two most consistent methods of denying meaningfulness to history are
to reduce it to the proportions of nature or to regard it as a corruption
of eternity.[95] The latter is reflected in the Platonic view that the flesh is
evil and time is bad, so that you want to get out of both. You want to get
into eternity and into the realm of eternal ideas. In that world, Niebuhr
concludes, "There is no yearning for fulfillment in history; there is only
a desire to be freed from history."[96] The origins of that view of history
as progressive were in the Hebrew scriptures and in the biblical stories
where the very concepts that Niebuhr was communicating had their origin.

Consequently there is another aspect of ancient thought that

---

[94] Ibid., vol. 2, 6.
[95] Ibid., vol. 2, 7.
[96] Ibid., vol. 2, 11.

we need to notice. This is the idea of fate—inexorable, unpredictable, and uncontrollable fate. In the ancient world where one did not know Yahweh, there was an almost universal belief in it. I want to read for you a quotation from Jack Finegan, who used to teach New Testament History and Archaeology at the Pacific School of Religion at Claremont in California. He published a book called *Myth and Mystery: An Introduction to the Pagan Religions of the Biblical World*.[97] If you want a good introduction to the religions and peoples around Canaan, it is one of the best that I have found. It is very well researched and documented but also written understandably. In this passage Finegan is dealing with the concept of fate in that ancient world. He presents the Olympian deities of Greece as particularly illustrative: "Powerful as [they] are, they are not always able to accomplish their will. Nor are they exempt from inevitable results that come from their actions."[98] They have to pay the price for their misconduct too, so that there is a power beyond them. As I read that, I found myself thinking about Yehezkel Kaufmann and the whole concept of the meta-divine. "In fact the gods themselves as well as human beings are in the last analysis subject to fate."[99] The Greek word for "fate" is *moira*. In the Liddell and Scott Greek-English lexicon *moira* is entered with a capital "M" because it is the name of a goddess. She is the ultimate determiner of destiny. Here, the concept of fate was being expressed mythologically. "Fate is a goddess bearing the several names of Ananke (necessity), Tyche (fortune), Heimarmene (allotted portion), Dike (justice), and Nemesis (retribution). Again there are three fates and these three fates are pictured as weavers."[100] This is a common picture in Greek mythology. The first of these is Lachesis, which comes from the word *langchano*, which means to obtain by lot or by fate, by the roll of the dice, and she is the measurer to tell you how much you are going to have. The second is Clotho, who is the spinner who spins out your life. And then, Atropos, from which we get a pharmaceutical name Atropine. She is the cutter of the thread of life. So Lachesis measures you a portion, Clotho spins it, and Atropos, when she takes a notion, cuts it.

It is interesting that Liddell and Scott's comment on Nemesis is

---

[97] Jack Finegan, *Myth and Mystery: An Introduction to the Pagan Religions of the Biblical World* (Grand Rapids: Baker, 1989).
[98] Ibid.,162.
[99] Ibid.
[100] Ibid.,162f.

that she is the one who brings down all immoderate good fortune. Are you familiar with that concept, immoderate good fortune? There was nothing that bothered the gods on Olympus more than if you were too lucky. If you were too lucky, sooner or later Nemesis would take care of you and even things out. That is a bit different from the Yahweh who is looking for an opportunity to bless, is it not?

In a world where there is no transcendent element exerting its will on history and nature from beyond this world, the forces of life are both implacable and inexplicable. All we can do is to personalize those forces (mythology) in an attempt to understand them and control them to some degree. But in the end it must be admitted that the raw power behind everything, Kaufmann's meta-divine, dictates the final outcome of everything, even the direction of those natural forces we have invested with human-like masks.

In Israel a radically different faith emerged. Yahweh is absolute and ultimate, the source and cause of all. He is the transcendent Lord. When He created the world He made us and placed us over against Himself so that there is a sense in which we transcend the natural order because we are made in His image. This is what makes the Incarnation possible. He made us and placed us over against Himself. Among the other gifts He gave to us was freedom, and this means that He made us as persons. I wish I could spell out what I am going to say next with more precision, but I cannot yet. But notice that the one thing you never find below the human level is personhood. When you introduce the element of the person, you have the element of freedom, and you also have the element of reality. To be a person means you can make free choices; and if you can make free choices, you are a person. Freedom is not a concept that you use in the same way with the lower levels of the creation. And ultimately there is no meaning apart from the moral and the personal. So, when a person does not have a concept of that, the sense of meaning begins to go. And, of course, as I said, we get that concept from God and not from ourselves.

Yahweh gave to us the power to reject Him, and the power to choose our own way, even when He made known to us His way. This puts an element of contingency into history, and that element of contingency cannot be erased. It is an element that leaves a degree of ambiguity and uncertainty, so that we do not know all of the factors and cannot make ironclad predictions. But it is this that makes possible the glory of the realm of the personal, which is the moral and the ethical. It is there that real value and meaning are to be found. And with this we come to know that the religious and the historical cannot ultimately be separated, because nothing is ultimately unrelated to Yahweh.

Now, what difference does this kind of thing make? Is this of interest just to the philosopher or the student of antiquities? No, this has had an incredible impact on the church. Let me give a Wesleyan illustration.

I have read Wesley's Aldersgate testimony many, many times. I would read about how he felt his heart strangely warmed and felt that God, for Christ's sake, had forgiven his sins, even his, and how he was delivered from the law of sin and death and so forth. But then one day I noticed something I had never paid any attention to previously. He not only tells us that the event took place on May 24, 1738, but he also tells us what time in the evening it happened: at about a quarter before nine. When the divine and the human met, time and eternity intercepted. That was important enough to Wesley to drive a stake down right there.

You will find that element all through Scripture, and you will find it all through Christianity. What is Wesley most famous for in terms of writing? He wrote his sermons, biblical exegesis; he wrote his books on theology, his journal. But how many of you are familiar with *Wesley's Veterans*? You need to know that work (often seen in multi-volume editions). You will never be a good Methodist (if you are a Methodist) or a good Wesleyan (if you are a Wesleyan) if you have never read *Wesley's Veterans*. The book is composed of autobiographical witnesses of Wesley's lay preachers. A stonecutter gets converted and called to preach and you get his story. If you have never read Thomas Walsh's story, you have missed one of the gems of human literature. But in virtually every one of them, you have that time element. Something happened so that time became important and they began to take note of it.

Let me give you another example from beyond the Wesleyan world. Blaise Pascal was the Einstein of the 1600s—a brilliant mathematician. When he was sixteen he was doing creative and original work in mathematics. He was recognized by the French Academy of Arts and Sciences because of that. But the scholarly world never knew quite what to do with Pascal because although he had been the brightest intellectual star on the Parisian scene, he had become "religious" and he gave us his *Penses* and some other remarkable stuff. After he died, his servant was checking one of his jackets and felt something in the lining. So he unstitched it and took out a crumpled piece of vellum. By the date on it, it had been transferred by Pascal from jacket to jacket, for eight years. What was written on that vellum was:

> In the year of grace, 1654, on Monday the 23rd of November, Feast of Clement, Pope and martyr and of others in the martyrology, the vigil of Saint Chrisoganus, martyr and others, from about half past ten in the evening until about half past twelve, FIRE. God of Abraham, God of Isaac, God of Jacob, not of the philosophers and scholars. [And he was both a scholar and a philosopher.] Certitude, certitude. Feeling joy, peace—God of Jesus Christ, My God and Your God, Thy God shall be my God and you will be my people. Forgetfulness of the world and of everything except God. He is to be found only by the way he is taught in the Gospel; greatness of the human soul. Righteous Father, the world has not known thee, but I have known thee. Joy, joy, joy, tears of joy. I have separated myself from him. My God, wilt thou leave me? Let me not be separated from him eternally. This is eternal life that they might know thee, the only true God, and the one whom thou has sent, Jesus Christ. Jesus Christ. Jesus Christ. I have separated myself from him, I have fled from him, denied him, crucified him. Let me never be separated from him. We keep hold of him only by the ways taught in the Gospel. Renunciation, total and sweet. Total submission to Jesus Christ and to my Director. Eternity and joy for a day's exercise on earth. Do not let me forget your word. Amen.

You have the privilege of preaching the kind of Gospel that can make that kind of difference in a two-hour span that somebody will mark on his calendar and say, "There is where it started."

Lecture 16

· · · · · · · · · ·

Yahweh as the Holy One

In an earlier lecture we introduced the concept of holiness.[101] Now we need to think about it in more detail before we proceed further.

In the Old Testament it is very clear that Yahweh is the Holy One. In fact, I think it can be safely said that the primary word of Scripture about God is that He is holy. I am aware that there are many who say that the primary thing about Him is His sovereignty. One of the theologians who has been of most help to me says the first thing about Yahweh is that He is sovereign and the second thing is that He is holy. But I have come to the place where I am ready to say the primary thing is His holiness, not His sovereignty. I say that because His holiness determines the nature of His sovereignty, not vice versa. Please keep that in the back of

---

[101] Lecture 4, 60ff.

your mind as we proceed.

The New Testament supports this contention that *holy* is the primary word in Scripture about God. Notice the first petition in the Lord's Prayer. Notice that the prayer does not begin, "Dear Lord," but it begins, "Our Father," which is a personal relationship, not a legal relationship or a political relationship. It is a kind of blood relationship. That is followed with, "which art in heaven," which underlines His transcendence. Then comes the first petition, ". . . hallowed be thy name." And what follows that? "Thy kingdom come . . ." I do not want to make too much of that order, but I believe it is significant. God's holiness precedes His sovereignty. It is significant that this aspect of His being is referred to before the royal aspect, the kingly aspect, is mentioned.

In the New Testament, the holiness of God is not so much argued for as assumed, as is true with a number of other Old Testament truths. When you read through the Old Testament you are aware of how common it is. In the New Testament it is not as explicit that God is the Holy One.[102] In fact, there is a sense in which it appears that the New Testament is more concerned to affirm the holiness of the Holy Spirit than of God, per se. You do have "Holy Father" once in John 17:11, and Jesus is called "the Holy One" a few times (Mark 1:24; Luke 4:34; Acts 3:14), but how often do you have "holy" linked to the Spirit? Dozens of times. So, in the New Testament the Spirit is holy, and so is the church, which the Spirit inspires, supposed to be holy. We might say that since the distinctive holiness of God has been established in the Old Testament, the New Testament is concerned to show by Whom and in what way the people of God will share that holiness.

How are we to understand "holy"? The fundamental act in all religion seems to be that of worship. And when we say "worship" the implication is worship of the Holy, whatever the Holy is.[103] At bottom, the least common denominator, *holy* connotes that awesome, terrifying quality of the divine that separates it from ordinary, human life. This

---

[102] [Editor's note] It seems significant that the holiness of God is affirmed several times in the book of Revelation, the last book in the Bible (3:7; 4:8; 6:10; 15:4).

[103] [Editor's note] It is no accident that the roots of the word *worship* are in the Old English "worth-ship." The Holy One is the one to whom we ascribe ultimate worth. He is worth all we are and have. And the ultimate offense is to make Him appear worth-less.

was what Rudolf Otto was trying to express in his influential book, *The Idea of the Holy*,[104] when he used words and phrases like *the numinous*, or *the mysterium tremendum* to try to convey this sense of awe. It is interesting the way we go to Latin to say the things that we do not think English says quite strongly enough. But that is what Otto is trying to convey: this tremendous mystery about God when we meet Him, the otherness that separates the divine from the human. The divine world is different from ours. That much is true whether you are in Greek mythology or in the Old Testament.

In one of the stories from Greek mythology a god fell in love with a human maiden. He visited her, but he only came to see her at night in the dark. She lived for those night visits, and her whole world was turned into a Garden of Eden because of his blessing on her. But he would not let her see him. So, one night, when he was asleep [that is interesting, the gods sleep], she took a candle and lit it and held it up to see, and it was a god. She was so captivated by his beauty that she moved down to get a closer look. A drop of hot wax fell on his face. He woke up, and she was turned into stone immediately. A human cannot cross the barrier between god and human.

So the chief word in religion for our subjective experience of the divine is *reverence*. The Old Testament defines this reverential awe as "the fear of God." You do not treat the Other casually or disrespectfully. But if *reverence* is the chief word to speak of our subjective experience, the primary word from the objective point of view is the *holiness* of the Divine. So all religions have some concept like this, whatever terminology they may use, and the Old Testament is similar. But as in other areas we have talked about and will talk about, it is not the similarities that are essential, it is the differences. Now, I confess that I am tempted to wonder if that is really true. Am I only seeing these differences as essential because I want to? But I take comfort when I find great scholars like Eichrodt, or von Rad, or Jacob, who have spent their lives with the Old Testament and the comparative religions of the Mediterranean, saying that the Old Testament is qualitatively different in its understanding of holiness. And the difference, they agree, is that in the Old Testament you

[104] Rudolf Otto, *The Idea of the Holy: An Inquiry into the Non-Rational Factor in the Idea of the Divine and Its Relation to the Rational*, tr. J. Harvey, rev. (London: Oxford University Press, 1936).

are not first of all dealing with the holy, or holiness, but with the Holy One. We are back to that personal character. There is a sense in the mythology of the ancient world that the gods partook of holiness so that holiness could be abstracted from the gods. That is not true in the Old Testament. There, holiness is defined by the one Person who has a right to be called Other. Holiness resides in Him and is defined by Him. It is in Yahweh, the Holy One.

In the religions of the world, this element of holiness can be attached to all sorts of objects. The same thing is true in the Old Testament. If you look up the occurrences of "holy" in a concordance of the Old Testament, you will find that most of the occurrences are adjectival, describing things. There are holy pots and holy pans. There are holy instruments and holy altars. There are holy places and finally a Holy City and a holy temple. That is not unlike what you will find in the other religions of the ancient world. But in the Old Testament, nothing except Yahweh is holy in itself. Everything that merits the adjective "holy" does so because it is in a special relationship to Him. He is the source of it all. Nothing in the Old Testament is holy in itself except Him.

This means that the holiness of Yahweh is not a quality. You will find this discussed in systematic theologies: Is holiness an attribute? Is it on a par with His omniscience, His omnipotence, or His omnipresence? It is not. A quality, or an attribute, is not essential to the being of a thing. That is not the case with Yahweh's holiness. Holiness is not a quality He possesses in common with other beings; it is His nature. This which distinguishes Him from all else. He *is* holy; it is not something He possesses. It is similar to what you finally arrive at in 1 John 4:16 where it says, "God is love." It is not something He does, it is what He is. There is a sense in which about sixty books are leading up to that statement. Holiness is in the same category.

The origin of the concept of holiness in the ancient world seems to be in some notion of separation. Thus the holy instruments in the temple could not be put to common ordinary use. In that sense, *holy* connoted "otherness." This idea is reflected in the first and second commandments. There is an incredible theology implicit in those deceptively simple statements when you look at them in the light of that ancient world. Yahweh was to be worshipped alone, by Himself; nobody with Him; without rival or competitor. That is the first commandment.

What about the second? There is nothing in the created order that is adequate to symbolize Him. So, in the first commandment you have the exclusiveness. He wants our exclusive devotion. And in the second commandment He is saying, "There is nothing in the creation that I have made that can be identified with me. I am radically other than all of it."

This is in striking contrast to all of the rest of the religions of the Ancient Near East. Gerhard von Rad, in his Old Testament theology, says that this is a:

> most abrupt affront to this concept of deity [the one common to Israel's world]. Here becomes manifest something of the mystery of Israel, something of her nature as a stranger and a sojourner among the religions.[105]

What he is saying is that because Yahweh is so different from all the rest of the gods as humanly conceived, when you relate to Him the way He wants you to, you automatically become a pilgrim and a stranger, a sojourner in your world. So Israel is not at home in its world. It is interesting that this is taught in a book where the doctrine of Creation is so central and where you get the clearest teaching of the importance of the creation and its goodness. Yet there is no holiness in the best of the creation. Neither is there in you and me, though we are made in His image; there is no holiness in us of ourselves. He is distinct from us. And the radical strangeness of Israel's understanding of reality made them seem alien to everybody else.[106]

---

[105] von Rad, *Old Testament Theology*, vol. 1, 214.
[106] Either God will separate us from the sin of the world, or the sin will separate us from Him. Fifty or sixty years ago there was a preacher in Vermont named Arthur Wentworth Hughie, who wrote a book called *Jerusalem the Golden*. If you can ever find it, it is worth buying. There are some priceless things in it. One of those is an illustration of the way sin blinds us to God and separates us from Him. He tells about the old man who loses his hearing to the point where he is stone-deaf. But his family is lovingly caring for him, and he can still see them. But then he loses his sight. He can't hear anything and he can't see anything. So he can't hear them when they speak to him, and he doesn't see them. One day the family, thinking to do something kind for him, took him for a drive in the mountains. He had always loved the beautiful Vermont mountains, and if he could not see them, he could at least smell them. But the old man thinks, "They have wearied of me. They have

von Rad continues:

> Anyone who seriously devotes himself to a study of
> religions as they appear and to their worship of images
> can find absolutely no way of transition from them to
> Israel's prohibition of images.[107]

Through the years the European theologian, Emil Brunner, has
been of great help to me. He was a contemporary of Barth; not as well-
known as Barth and did not write as voluminously as Barth, but oftentimes I have the feeling he wrote more clearly. One of his books was
titled *The Christian Doctrine of God*. In it he says:

> The whole conflict between Yahweh and the Baalim
> of the Near East raged around this essential Transcen-
> dence of God; the conflict raged between the God who
> is the "Wholly Other" and the nature gods, who were
> only hypostatized forces of nature.[108]

In the Hebrew realm, in Israel's religion, you got the "Wholly Other"
in Yahweh, the personal God. But in the other religions you got natural
forces personified and hypostatized. He goes on to say:

> We might therefore paraphrase the Biblical idea of ho-
> liness thus: the Divine Nature, as it is peculiar to God
> alone. "I am God, not man; the Holy One in the midst
> of thee" (Hos. 11:9), that is, "I am he with whom none
> can be compared.[109]

---

wearied of caring for me. They are taking me away to put me in an old-folks' home.
My family has forsaken me, and from now on I'm among strangers." Shortly after
that, even though his family continues to care for him lovingly, he dies of a broken
heart, because in his head, he has been abandoned to strangers. Wentworth says, that
is what sin does to you. You could be right in the Father's house and never know it.
You can be above, on the golden throne of God, and yet be farther from God than
the limits of time and space.

[107] von Rad, *Old Testament Theology*, vol. 1, 214ff.

[108] Emil Brunner, *Dogmatics*, tr. O. Wyon (Philadelphia: Westminster, 1950),
vol. 1, 159.

[109] Ibid.

Accordingly, when you confront true holiness you have confronted God. And when you confront the true and living God, you have confronted holiness, and this takes us back to that incomparability.

Now, if the aniconic nature, the antagonism to physical representations, to idols, reflected in the second commandment, is unique in the ancient world, there is no question but the exclusiveness demanded in the first commandment was equally so. Von Rad says,

> This intolerant claim to exclusive worship is something unique in the history of religions, for in antiquity the cults were on easy terms with one another and they left devotees a free hand to ensure a blessing for themselves from other gods as well. Why, even the various sanctuaries were quite often regarded as common ground, for in a temple cultic gifts were quite often offered to other deities as well as to the god to whom the temple belonged—a fate which on occasion befell even Solomon's temple (II Kings XXIII. 4, 11f.).[110]

Here he says the characteristic of exclusiveness is attributed to Yahweh which is, according to him, another reflection of Yahweh's holiness. As you know, the commandments occur in Exodus 20 and again in Deuteronomy 5. These passages are anchor points in the biblical data on this concept of holiness. Look at Exodus 20: "And God spoke all these words: 'I am [Yahweh] your God, who brought you out of Egypt, out of the land of slavery.'" Notice that the first thing in the presentation of the covenant, the Law, is the historical context. Who is Yahweh? He is the Lord of history who has redeemed them from Egyptian bondage. He is the God who is sovereign over history. "I am the Lord your God." Admittedly, there are scholars who use this kind of statement to try to drive a wedge between the Bible's theology of redemption in history and its theology of nature, or creation. Do not fall into that trap. You will find the two theologies held together if you look at the whole of the Old Testament text. But here He is speaking about Himself as the God who transcends nature and is sovereign over history.

---

[110] von Rad, *Old Testament Theology*, vol. 1, 208.

"I am [Yahweh] your God. . . . You shall have no other
gods before me. You shall not make for yourself an idol
in the form of anything in heaven above [Not even in
heaven is there anything adequate to represent him.] or
on the earth beneath or in the waters below. You shall
not bow down to them or worship them; for I, [Yahweh]
your God, am a jealous God, punishing the children for
the sin of the fathers to the third and fourth generation
of those who hate me, but showing *hesed* to those who
love me and keep my commandments. You shall not
misuse the name of [Yahweh] your God, for [Yahweh]
will not hold anyone guiltless who misuses his name.
Remember the Sabbath day by keeping it holy. Six days
you shall labor and do all your work. But the seventh
day is a Sabbath to [Yahweh] your God. On it you shall
not do any work" (Ex. 20:2-10a).

Then He goes on with the remaining six commandments. But
you will notice that He is talking about Himself. There is no one else to
be before me, nothing to represent me. And then He says, "Be careful
about my name." And if you will go through the Old Testament, you
will find that one of the most common usages of the term "holy" is in
reference to Yahweh's name, his "holy" name.[111] Then you come to the
fourth commandment, and He talks about a "holy" day. And so you see
that in the beginning of the Law, He is operating from the basis of His
holiness.

You find the same thing in Deuteronomy 5.

Moses summoned all Israel and said: Hear O Israel, the
decrees and laws I declare in your hearing today. Learn
them and be sure to follow them. [Yahweh] your God

---

[111] [Editor's note] In Hebrew thought, one's "label" (name) and one's character
were inseparable. There is nothing sacred about the label "Yahweh"; it has no
magical power. But that label is inseparable from the one holy being it identifies.
God's "name" is His character, and as such He is the one holy being in the universe.
To do anything to Him that diminishes His holy character in the eyes of others is a
terrible offense. It makes them take lightly the One before whom we will all stand
one day, and the only one who can deliver us from judgment on that day.

made a covenant with us at Horeb. It was not with our fathers that the Lord made this covenant but with us, [because this is an eternal covenant] with all of us who are here alive today. [Yahweh] spoke to you face to face out of the fire on the mountain. (At that time I stood between [Yahweh] and you to declare to you the word of [Yahweh] because you were afraid of the fire and did not go up the mountain.) And he said, "I am [Yahweh] your God who brought you out of Egypt, out of the land of slavery. You shall have no other gods before me. You shall not make for yourself an idol . . . for I, [Yahweh] your God, am a jealous God" (Deut. 5:1-9a).

Yahweh says simply that "I am the holy one, and as an aspect of that, I am jealous." Let me go back to Brunner for a moment. He says:

Thus the divine holiness is inseparably connected with that character of absolute intolerance which distinguishes the biblical Idea of God, and differentiates it from all other ideas of God. God will not tolerate the recognition of any other.[112]

Now, in connection with this divine intolerance you find two important concepts. One if them is "glory," represented by the Hebrew word *kabod*. The other concept is "wrath." There are different words used for that, one of them *hemah* and the other *'ebrah*. But for "glory" there is one primary term. The idea that God is jealous for His glory, that He wants all glory to come to Him, and that He becomes wrathful over any attempt to dilute His holiness are concepts that many of us in the modern secularized world tend to have difficulty with. Oftentimes these ideas that God should be jealous or that He should want everything to redound to His glory or that He should become angry are dismissed as being only primitive anthropomorphic conceptions. But the reality is that they are intrinsic to the picture of Yahweh that is presented in the Old Testament. They are vital parts of that picture. And if they are

---

[112] Brunner, *Dogmatics*, vol. 1, 160. See Isa. 42:8; 48:11.

rightly understood, if we see what the Scripture means by them, they add immeasurably to the greatness of the biblical concept of God and the greatness of Yahweh Himself.

Let me speak for just a moment about the concept of jealousy. This is a part of the Old Testament understanding of God that is developed extensively in the Old Testament and in the New Testament, as well. It is taken from the sphere of marriage, and if you look carefully at the Bible you will find that marriage is one of the most prevalent themes in the Book, in both Testaments.[113] There is passage after passage that assumes this metaphor that sees Israel's election in terms of that and the church's role likewise. Now, a married person, by definition, guards

---

[113] I remember once I was preaching through the Gospels, and I came to the wedding at Cana of Galilee. I was young and I thought, "Why did he begin his ministry here, in an out of the way place with some unknown, nameless people?" Furthermore, the only apparent reason for this first miracle was to solve a social problem of personal embarrassment because the refreshments had run out. Nevertheless, that is the way the Lord began the redemption of the world, and I knew enough to know that if it is in the inspired Word, it is not there by accident and I ought to try to figure out what it was there for.

I remember I was getting ready for a wedding and I wondered if there could be something in the passage that is applicable to a wedding. And as I thought about it, I suddenly remembered that was the way human history began: with a wedding. That brought me to a second thought: that is the way human history ends, with a wedding, the marriage supper of the Lamb. I had done enough Old Testament study by that time that I was aware of a passage like Ezekiel 16 with its gripping parable of Israel as the prostituted bride of Yahweh. And that immediately called to mind Hosea, and the way his prostitute wife symbolized Israel. In fact, when I began to really think about it, I realized the theme is all through the Old Testament.

Then I began to think that you find it in Jesus, too. Of course you find it in Paul in places like Ephesians 5, but look at John 3:26-29 from the life of Jesus. I confess I missed it for years. You remember when they came to John and said, "Master, that fellow you baptized has stolen your crowd. How do you feel about that?" And John the Baptist said, "Should the best man be upset when the bridegroom upstages him at the wedding announcement party?" I read that for years and it did not make much sense to me. But when I began to back into the biblical thrust on marriage I began to say, "Wait a minute. Does John the Baptist understand human history in terms of marriage?" And then I remembered the three passages in the Synoptic Gospels where they came to Jesus and reported that John's disciples had good religion; they fasted when they prayed. And they said, "Your disciples don't fast." Jesus responded, "Is it appropriate for the friends of the bridegroom to fast at a wedding announcement party? No, at a wedding announcement party they feast. The day will come when their bridegroom will be taken from them and then they will fast" (Matt. 9:15; Mark 2:19; Luke 5:34). And I thought, apparently Jesus had a nuptial view of history, too.

the exclusiveness of his or her marriage relation. And just as a married person, in any biblical understanding of marriage, is unwilling to permit a third person into that relationship, so God defends the uniqueness of His divine being and that exclusive relationship with Israel consistent with His election of her. So, when He speaks of His jealousy, it is not the carnal kind of jealousy that we often speak about. It is an inevitable reflection of election love. So, it is not something to be looked upon as a primitive anthropomorphic concept to be outgrown. In fact, you find it in the last pages of the book of Revelation.[114]

The emphasis on His glory is an indication that from God's point of view it is not a matter of indifference to Him. It is not a matter of indifference to Yahweh, whether we know falsehood or truth about Him, and whether we know who He is and what He is like. God cares about me and wants me to know that He is not like anything in His creation and that my only hope is in a right relationship, a *batah* relationship, a trusting relationship with Him and Him alone. He is to be there first.

So, God is not indifferent to this, and that is the reason He is concerned about what we worship because what we worship determines what we are. Our well-being is in worshipping the true God, and our lostness is in worshipping something else. You see, His jealousy and His glory, if they are seen correctly, are simply reflections, expressions, of that holiness that you find in Yahweh and in Yahweh alone.

The wrath of God should be understood from the same perspective. The Old Testament says it is "holy" wrath. It is not an emotion like anything we know in human experience when we get peeved and explode or our self-interest is offended and so we are angry to defend our rights. It is not that at all. It is the inevitable and the necessary reaction to evil by a holy God who is a person—to that which opposes His will and to that which is destructive to human persons or to His good creation.

---

[114] [Editor's note] The Hebrew word translated "jealous" is *qanah*. This word has a larger pool of meanings than does the English word *jealous*. It means to be passionately concerned for. Thus, in the *KJV* it was often translated with the now archaic "zealous." We see this in the Gospel account of the cleansing of the temple (John 2:12-22). The disciples remembered the Old Testament passage (Ps. 69:9), "Zeal for your house will consume me." So we are not talking about a selfish, petty concern for one's own rights and prerogatives (which the English word tends to connote). We are talking about a passionate concern for what is right and true and in the best interests of all concerned.

His wrath is a reaction. I think it is part of being a person, because persons have emotions and He is a holy person. He has feelings about right and wrong. "The Force" of the *Star Wars* movies does not care what happens. "The Force" is not a person.

One of the issues here is that some of us want Him to get emotional over what is right, but we do not want Him to get emotional over what is wrong. Perhaps that is because we find ourselves too much in the wrong, and we feel there is a better hope for us if He is not too antagonistic to something out of His will. But you cannot separate those two things. His commitment to the good is countered by commitment against that which is destructive. It is the Old Testament foundation of Paul's "God is not mocked" in Galatians 6:7. And it is the background for the fury of God, which is portrayed in the book of Revelation, in that final conquest of the kingdom of evil and the triumph of the New Jerusalem.

Now, we want good to triumph. But the only way good can ultimately triumph is for God to be opposed to evil. The Old Testament way of expressing that is "the wrath of God," a holy wrath. Here it is that the moral nature of holiness begins to be definitive. We want a God who undergirds a dependable moral order, but sometimes we recoil at the idea that He would become angry if that moral order is violated. But these two things go together. Here it is that the moral nature of the holiness of Yahweh is made definitive. The first four commandments establish the unassailable holiness of God. As both Brunner and von Rad made so clear, there is no other being in the universe who is holy in and of himself. But then what follows? There are six commands about how we treat other people. "I am the one who put you in families, so do not fight the family. I am the one who gives you life so do not take it. Human sexuality is a gift I give to you, so honor it and do not defile it. As for your neighbor's property, respect it." Did you know that you can not have democracy and freedom without property rights? And did you know that you cannot have charity without property rights? If I do not own anything, I cannot give anything. On the other hand, do not ever believe that you would really be happy if you just had the stuff your neighbor has.

I lived a long time looking upon these things as simply legal matters. But what you are dealing with are rudimentary basic principles of human existence. A recent report argues that the thing that really distinguishes democratic societies from others is not free enterprise, but social institutions. One of the first things Hitler did when he came to power was get rid of the Boy Scouts, because the Boy Scouts were a threat. Stalin did the same thing. Another distinction was that democratic societies have patent laws. That surprised me. I would never have thought about that. But you see, if you do not have a right to the fruit of your own labor, then why labor? If, on the other hand, you do have the right to the fruit of your own labor, you can be charitable. So, in these principles, in these laws that are laid down, there are incredibly profound philosophical and theological issues.

Now why are they so profound? Are they not just arbitrary commands from the lips of the Sovereign of the universe? No they are not. Just as the first four commands establish the holiness of God's essence, His otherness from all of creation, the last six establish the holiness of His character, the absolutely consistent moral and ethical nature of the Creator. One of the purposes of the covenant was to be a teacher. How were former Egyptian slaves to learn that Yahweh, unlike any other god they had ever known, was absolutely faithful and reliable? They were to learn it as they sought to embody it in their own lives. Why did He command truthfulness and faithfulness? Because that is what He is, through and through. Thus, far from being a morally neutral term as it had been in the beginning, *qadosh* came to have an inseparable moral and ethical connotation. The Only Holy One is self-denying, self-giving Love, true and faithful to a fault.

I said in an earlier lecture that since all the gods were other than human, then all the gods were holy. But that meant that *qadosh*, "holy," as it was originally used had no particular moral or ethical qualities to it, for not even the most beneficent gods could be counted on to do the right thing when they did not consider it in their best interests to do so. Beyond that, the cruel gods, and the gods of death and pestilence were holy too.

But something happened as a result of the first two commandments and the rest of the Sinai Covenant. The Israelites came to realize that there is only one Being in the universe who can truly be called "holy." He is "Wholly Other" in ways that the human creators of the gods could not even imagine. He was not continuous with the creation, like the gods. But if there is only one Holy Person, then there is only one holy character. And the wonder was that this God whom Abraham had come to know as the God of *hesed* proved Himself to be absolutely dependable and committed to do right no matter what the cost to Himself. He would neither lie nor steal; He would not manipulate people for His own ends. Not only is Yahweh "other" in essence, but He is also "other" in character. He is not a "super-sized" projection of humanity, possessing all our qualities, good and bad, but just written large.

That all became clear when Yahweh called upon His people to "be holy as [he is] holy." Could they share His essence? Of course not! Were they to be holy simply by being "separated" to Him in some sense? That is not what the context of the covenant conveys. When Yahweh calls on His people to share His holiness, as in Leviticus 19, it is inseparably linked with unselfish moral and ethical behavior. All of that came to be contained in *qadosh*, which had once been morally neutral. Yahweh's holiness burst the word open with new meaning.

All of this helps to explain a very odd feature of the *Septuagint*. When the scholars of Alexandria came to translate the Hebrew scriptures into the Greek language, the language of culture throughout the Roman world, they had a number of terms that on the surface seem as though they would have been good options for translating *qadosh* and its related terms. But in fact they chose a term that was almost unknown in classical Greek and the connotations of which were almost neutral. Why did they do that for such an important concept? It was because of what had happened to *qadosh* in the course of the biblical revelation, and that was the problem the *Septuagint* translators faced.

Just like *qadosh* had been originally, there was no Greek word in existence that captured what *qadosh* now conveyed. It is not that they lacked possibilities; there are at least five different Greek words that might have been pressed into service. But none of these terms as they were used in the literature of Greece meant to a Greek speaker what *qadesh* or *qadosh* conveys in biblical Hebrew. The reality is that the concept of the holy that you find in the Old Testament appears nowhere else in human thought. The best that either Latin or Greek had to use to convey the ultimate nature of Yahweh were terms that represented things like the sublime, the consecrated, the religious, the venerable, that sort of thing. But just as with *qadosh* in Canaan originally, none of those terms had any moral element in them. I believe the solution to the problem that the *Septuagint* translators chose represents one of the significant steps in human intellectual history and one of the significant steps in theological history.

The first of the possible terms, *hieros*, had to do with what is set apart for sacred service. We get words from it like "hieratic," meaning "priestly," and "hieroglyph," meaning "priestly writing" (because the strange Egyptian picture writing was thought to be sacred). It is used in Greek literature from the earliest time to speak of that which relates to the gods, to the divine. It is the Greek equivalent of the Latin, *sacra*, from which we get "sacrifice" and "sacred." In Homer, *hieros* means "marvelous," "mighty," "divine" and "sacred." The neuter singular noun *hieron* is used for a temple, as it is in the New Testament some sixty times for the temple in Jerusalem.

There was a whole family of words in Greek that developed from this root. The Liddell and Scott Greek Lexicon has between one hundred twenty-five and one hundred fifty entries for words beginning with *hiero-*, because the sacred was very much a part of Greek life. In all of these expressions, it is speaking of something related to the gods, something sacred or something religious. This would have seemed to have been the most obvious counterpart to *qadosh*. And forms of it do appear with some frequency in the apocryphal books of the Old Testament. Yet the *Septuagint* has hardly any occurrences at all. This may say something about their attitude toward the apocryphal literature. In any case, the translators of the *Septuagint* clearly did not consider *hieros* an adequate equivalent of *qadosh*, and it is almost non-existent in the Septuagint. So, the most common way in Greek of expressing that which related to the gods, is virtually absent.

The second term, *semnos*, also seems like a viable possibility, because it is a religious term too. It comes from a root "seb" which means "to worship." The root idea was reverential fear, which comes close to the Old Testament concept, the fear of Yahweh. And in relation to the gods it meant to "honor with holy awe." The question is, what was meant by "holy" in that case? The real understanding of the concept can be seen in two developments.

One is *asebeia* which is the opposite of godliness. It consists of the negative *a* joined to *sebeia* which means "religiosity," etc. *Eusebeia*, with the *eu-* element meaning "good" prefixed, meant "god-fearing," full of holy and devout reverence. It is used in Plato. *Semnos* is used in classical Greek to refer to the gods. It is used of things divine. It is used of things that relate to the gods and of human persons when they are noble, majestic or revered. Liddell and Scott list some forty terms developed from this root. The noun *eusebeia* occurs fifteen times in the New Testament, while the noun *semnoteis* occurs three times. They occur together once in 1 Timothy 2:2 where Paul urges that prayers be offered for kings and those in authority so that Christians may live their lives in *eusebeia*, all godliness, and *semnoteis*, which is translated in the *NIV* as "holiness." So, it is used once in the New Testament in a place where modern English translators used the word *holiness*. Yet, that word never occurs in the *Septuagint*. Once again the reason seems to be that like *hieros*, *semnos* could not be made to carry the basic connotations that the translators felt were essential to a communication of the biblical concept of holiness. And I would argue that what was missing was that moral ethical element, which was originally not even found in *qadosh*.

Now, a third possibility was *hosios*, which denotes in classical Greek that which is consecrated or hallowed through divine or human law. When it is used of persons it can mean pious, devout. It can mean sinless, and it can mean pure. The noun form, *hosioteis*, was used as a title in ecclesiastical Greek in the early Christian church, where we speak of "his holiness." The verb form expressed the idea of making holy and freeing from guilt by expiatory offerings. The septuagintal translators were not opposed to the root, using it at times to translate *hesed* or *hasid*. It was also used to translate, on occasion, *shalom* for "whole," *tahor* for "clean," *yashar* for "right," and *tam* and *tammim* for "perfect." But it was never once used for *qadosh*.

The fourth possibility was *hagnos* from which we get the name Agnes. It is a root that originally signified that which awakens religious awe. Etymologically it is linked to an old Indian root that means to reverence or to sacrifice. It is a religious term that could have been used to represent what we speak of as taboo. Its history, though, brought it to mean ritually clean, then chaste, and finally, morally blameless. Yet it seldom occurs in the *Septuagint* and was at no point seen as an adequate term for *qadosh*.

The word the septuagintal translators did pick was *hagios* with its nominal and verbal accompaniments. The surprising thing is that this term was very seldom used in classical Greek. Homer lived about 900 B.C. and gave the first great literature of the Greeks. It never occurs in Homer. Hesiod lived in the eighth century and gave to us the best literature we have on the nature of Greek religion. But *hagios* never occurs in Hesiod. It never occurs in the tragic poets; the dramatists either. Why use such a rare word, when there were others that were much more common, and, on the surface, at least, seemed to be perfectly functional?

What seems clear is that the Greek translators of the *Septuagint* considered that the classical Greek language in all its richness had no term that in itself was adequate to convey the meaning of "holy" as it came to be used of Yahweh. The lack was not in a sense of the religious nor a sense of the sacred nor in the sense of the separated. There was no lack in these terms of a sense of the numinous or of the sublime. The lack was in what was of the essence of Yahweh's character.

So what did they do? They took a term that was relatively un-known, which had almost neutral connotations. That way when they used it in the context of the Old Testament, the Old Testament could do to *hagios* exactly what it had done to *qadosh*—transform it. *Hagios* would not have the excess baggage of those other terms, which would constantly obtrude itself on the mind of the reader and cause him or her to read the text in the wrong way. Instead the text would tell you what the word meant.

Let me conclude with a quotation from von Rad. He is talking about holiness in general. He does not have in mind here the distinctive Hebrew understanding. But what he says is even more true of that con-ception than of the concept in general.

> Both in the history of religion in general and in Israel in particular, the experience of the holy is a primeval religious datum; that is, the concept of the holy cannot in any way be deduced from other human standards of value. It is not their elevation to the highest degree nor is it associated with them by way of addition. The holy could be much more aptly designated the great strang-er in the human world, that is, a datum of experience

which can never really be co-ordinated into the world in which man is at home, and over against which he initially feels fear rather than trust—it is, in fact, the "Wholly Other."[115]

Now if holiness is the central characteristic of Yahweh, as I have argued, Wesley was on target when he said, "I conceive as the purpose, as the goal, in the order of salvation, what we speak of as entire sanctification."

---

[115] von Rad, *Old Testament Theology*, vol. 1, 205.

Lecture 17

· · · · · · · · · ·

Form and Experience: Integral Components of a Religious System

I want to turn our attention today to the matter of what Eichrodt calls the cultus, or cult. We tend to think of *a* cult as some special marginal group that has developed a particularistic, maybe faddish, interest in some aspect of religion. But the dictionary defines "cult" as "the external expression of a religious system." Thus, you will find cult in every religious system there is. Eichrodt, following the German scholar Georg Quell, defines it as "the expression of religious experience in concrete external actions performed within the congregation or community, preferably by officially appointed exponents and in set forms."[116] You will notice that that is a definitional sentence consisting of five elements.

---

[116] Eichrodt, *Theology*, vol. 1, 98.

And those are the five basic elements you will find in any religious system anywhere that has any group of people of any size.

The definition includes four external elements. The first is the actions of the group whereby they express their religious faith externally. Second, you need a congregation or a community in order to have cult, and it is such a group's external actions—whether they are a trespass offering or a votive offering, or Passover, or the Lord's Supper, or baptism, or a Quaker silent meeting, or a Pentecostal celebration with speaking in tongues—that form that "cultic" expression of their faith. The third element Eichrodt mentions is religious officialdom. These are the priests, or ministers, the ones who are officially sanctioned to perform those public actions and ceremonies. The final element in that definition is that these external expressions that may be labeled cult are "in set forms." There are many public expressions of religion that are not in set forms. Those are not cult. But there are others that are set. And they do not have to be written down either. The most anti-ritualistic country church will have a set way of worshipping, and woe betide the young preacher who comes in and tries to change it. So these are the four external elements of cult, and even a minimal acquaintance with the Pentateuch will reveal that a significant part of those five books is given over to discussions of those elements.

For many of us in the pietistic tradition, this attention to cult is a problem. We are more comfortable with private, individual worship than with formalized community activity; my quiet time as opposed to the Eucharist. But much of the Pentateuch is devoted to the latter, and that is one of the reasons a lot of us have not been very interested in reading the Pentateuch through. It is all right until we get to the latter part of Exodus, say about chapter 20. But then comes the rest of Exodus and all of Leviticus and most of Numbers and Deuteronomy—and it is all a bit strange and alien to us. But what you find there is very much like what you will find in a great deal of literature in the Ancient Near Eastern world. It was commonplace with religion in that time and place.

But you may have noticed that I initially said there were five elements and then talked about four. When I first looked at that definition, that is what I focused on: four external elements. There are the actions that he speaks about. They are performed within the congregation or the community. They are performed by officially appointed participants.

And they are performed according to set forms. But in my initial analysis of the definition, I missed the first element that he mentioned. What is that first element? Cult is the expression of religious experience. Without personal religious experience there can be no cult.

So, there is an internal subjective basis for what you find externalized and objectified in the cult. For us in our day, and for the typical person in the typical Protestant church, there is an incredibly long jump from the Feast of Unleavened Bread, the Passover, and the Day of Atonement to Holy Week and to Good Friday and to the Eucharist. But there is a continuity from the first set of practices to the second set. So the reality is that if we are going to understand the New Testament expressions and practices, we need to have some grasp of those Old Testament expressions and practices.

Now, this religious experience that Eichrodt says is the basis for cultic behavior is both supremely important—you will not understand the meaning of the expression correctly if you misunderstood the experience—and supremely difficult for us to understand. One of the reasons for that is the degree of continuity that exists between Ancient Near Eastern cults outside of Israel and Hebrew cult inside Israel. A careful comparison of cultic practices will show that Israel's practices were remarkably similar to what can be found among the Canaanites, the Egyptians, or the Babylonians. In fact, I suspect you can find something very comparable to almost any religious practice in Israel in one of the other religions of the Ancient Near East.

But here again, I remind you of Eichrodt's comment that I have alluded to before: Two people doing the same thing may not be doing the same thing. Beyond the observation of what is being done you have to make an evaluation of why it is being done and for what purpose. There is no place where that is more obvious than in the area of sacrifice. One of our problems is that nowhere in the Old Testament is there a direct, specific exposition of the biblical understanding of sacrifice. It is not theologized for us the way we would like to have it theologized. There is a statement here and a statement there, but one of our Old Testament theologians says, "We have to work at this kind of material a posteriori"—we have to look back to find the meaning. And as we look back into it we discover a number of gaps. The Bible will give you examples of what the Israelites were supposed to do, but it is not a total system. If you get to know an orthodox Jew, you will learn that Judaism as it developed in the intertestamental period and later, felt it necessary to fill in many of those gaps.

Many scholars say that if we look to comparative religion, we can find the keys to filling in the gaps. This follows from the basic assumption that everything that happened in Israel happened somewhere else, and everything that happened somewhere else might well have happened in Israel. So if we find a gap in the biblical information, we assume that we can fill it from any Ancient Near Eastern source that comes to hand. As I have already said, there is no question but that there is a continuity between the forms of religion in the Ancient Near East, including Israel. But the introduction of Yahweh into that sacrificial system makes a radical difference. The difference is not in the Hebrews; they were part and parcel of their world. Nor is the difference in the commandments regarding the practice of sacrifice in the Law. The difference is in the presence of Yahweh in it all. One of the great things about Eichrodt's work is his treatment of the covenant. When I read other Old Testament theologies I keep feeling a greater appreciation for Eichrodt's emphasis upon the covenant. But you see, not even the fact of the covenant makes the difference in the biblical understanding of sacrifice. It is the nature of Yahweh that determines the covenant. It is the nature of Yahweh that brought the covenant into existence, and so it is He who is central in it and central to its understanding. I have belabored that theme of the centrality of Yahweh before and you will probably hear me belabor it again, but there it is. When we come to the sacrificial system, if there is a difference between Israel and her neighbors, the significant difference is in the One who is being worshipped, not in the external expressions of that worship.

Now, if you take sacrifice itself, the scholars in the realm of comparative religion argue that there were certain fundamental understandings of sacrifice anywhere you found it in the ancient world. Eichrodt refers to these.[117] The first of these understandings is that sacrifices were a means of feeding the gods. You will notice how much of the sacrificial material is edible. Nor is it just any kind of food. Typically, it was of the most desirable sort the worshipper could procure. Furthermore,

---

[117] Eichrodt, *Theology* vol. 1, 141ff.

there was often some idea of a communal meal with the priests and the worshippers eating some portion of the sacrifice together.

The second common element is the offering of gifts. The sacrifice was understood to be a gift to the deities. As you know, we give gifts for a lot of different reasons, and gift-giving is a part of human relationships. You do not have to think very far to recognize that there can be a great variety of motives for the giving of gifts. The third understanding of sacrifice is what the scholars call sacral communion, the establishment of fellowship between the worshipper and the deity. The fourth one is atonement or propitiation, to keep God from being angry with you, to satisfy any degree of unsettledness He might have toward you.

As Eichrodt addresses cult in the Bible he is constantly stressing two things: the commonality between Israel's cult and the nations around it, and also the differences. Do not miss either one. When he talks about sacrifice as the feeding of a god, he says the most primitive idea is that first one, giving nourishment to the deity. One gives nourishment to the deity to renew his or her strength. In one version of the mythical flood story, the reason for the gods' displeasure with humans is that the humans were not feeding the gods well enough. So also in the Babylonian story of origins, humans were made as an afterthought to feed the gods when Marduk had fixed the gods in heaven as stars and they could no longer freely range the earth. The assumption in this understanding is that the deity has needs that the worshipper can meet. In that understanding there was a reciprocal relationship, and indeed a reciprocal need for each other, between the gods and the worshippers.

So sacrifice becomes the prime means of influencing the deity for human purposes, and as a result you find sacrifice everywhere in that ancient world. Are there traces of this understanding of sacrifice in the Hebrew cultus? Eichrodt says it is significant that all of the materials used in Hebrew sacrifice are edible. That in itself suggests nourishment. Moreover, you even add salt and oil to make them more tasty. Then we add wine to the equation, presumably to make the communication convivial. Another example that might point in this direction is the *lechem panim*, the "bread of the face," or "bread of the presence" (*KJV* "showbread") that was always kept fresh in the tabernacle and later in the temple. That would suggest that we are feeding Yahweh. The story of Noah is used sometimes to confirm that this was the understanding of sacrifice in the Bible. We are told that when Yahweh smelled Noah's sacrifice, He found the aroma pleasing and He promised not to curse the ground again.

So Eichrodt raises the question: Are we finding in Israel this concept of sacrifice as a feeding of the Deity? His answer is that it does not. What you have are similar externals, the materials, the practices, even some of the language, but when it comes to the meaning and the purpose of sacrifice, he argues that there is a profound difference. His reserved comment is this, and let me quote it, "It is extremely doubtful whether this conception, that of feeding the gods, was still a living reality in Israel."[118] I think he would say there is no question about it having been a reality in their forefathers' thinking, but that in some way or another they had reached the place where they said, "This God that we worship, unlike their gods, does not need our offering."

One of the things that contributes to the degree of commonality in the cultic forms is that a common language is being used. The Hebrews spoke Canaanite, so you would hear the same language used in a Canaanite sacrifice as you would in a Hebrew sacrifice. But Eichrodt says that the commonality of language between the Canaanite world and Israel can be misleading. His illustration of that is Yahweh's smelling the aroma of Noah's sacrifice. He believes that it had become a figurative expression to express the idea that God is pleased with the sacrifice. He also notes that in Leviticus 21, the expression "the offerings made to Yahweh by fire, the food of their God" occurs three times. But just as it is true that two people doing the same thing may not be doing the same thing, it is also true that two people using the same language may not be saying the same thing. No better example of this can be found than the fact that the early Roman/Greek world listened to the Christian language of the Eucharist and said that the early Christians were cannibals. "This is my body, which is broken for you. Take, eat, feed on me within your heart. This is my blood, which was shed for you." Eichrodt believes the same dichotomies existed among the Canaanites and the Israelites.

Eichrodt concludes that the whole tenor of ancient Israel's belief in Yahweh is irreconcilable with the idea that God is fed by sacrifice,

---

[118] Eichrodt, *Theology*, vol. 1, 143.

bound up as this is with God's dependence upon man.[119] The doctrine of Creation destroyed that possibility of divine dependence.

In fact, the central teaching about covenant in the Pentateuch is that Yahweh existed a long time and demonstrated His power in many ways to Israel before the Israelite sacrificial system was ever instituted. So, you have the existence of Yahweh in His power and in His *hesed*, in His grace before Israel ever began a pattern of formal sacrifice. I have not worked this out thoroughly enough to talk about it with any authority, but I wonder if the reality of the unique experience with Yahweh did not come first, and then the adaptation of certain common religious forms and language second, much as happened with Christmas and the Saturnalia—the Roman holiday at the end of December—or with Easter and some of the customs of spring fertility festivals.

Eichrodt's approach to the idea of sacrifice as giving gifts to the deity is similar; there are great similarities between Israel and her neighbors, but at heart there are fundamental differences. He says that the idea of gift-giving is a normal way for an inferior, a vassal, to express his relationship to his superior, his lord. As such, it can be an expression of subjection or fealty or even gratitude. Now, for a gift to be given to the deity, it is rather obvious that it should be something valuable to the one who is sacrificing. The Hebrew term most commonly used for this is the first term used in the Old Testament for a sacrifice. It appears in Genesis 4 when Cain and Abel made their sacrifices. It is the Hebrew *minkhah*, which is the word for a gift. Cain and Abel were giving a gift to God, an expression of gratitude, identification, and self-surrender.

In this matter of gifts, you get what is called the votive gift. *Votive* may not be a word you commonly use, but what it means is a gift given to fulfill a vow. This is what Hannah, the mother of Samuel, did when she gave her son for service in the tabernacle. She had made a vow to God, "If you will give me a son, I will give him back to you." So Samuel was a votive gift. Eichrodt points out that votive giving has in it all sorts of potential for perversion. It can be used as a threat; it can be used as a means to exert compulsion; it can be used from a bargaining motive to buy favor from God. There is little question that these perversions play a significant part in the religion of much of the world. And undoubtedly it

---

[119] Ibid.

was true in Israel as well. Such motives seem to have played an important part in Jacob's early relationship with Yahweh. In Genesis 28, after God has graciously reaffirmed His covenant promises to Jacob, Jacob promises that *if* God keeps His promises, he, Jacob, will magnanimously give God a tithe of the profits.

But the votive gift does not have to be perverted. Eichrodt points out that in all the prophetic diatribes against unworthy sacrifices, they never attack votive offerings—vows. Apparently the prophets believed they were legitimate. The Hannah story may be an illustration of that kind of thing at its best. There she is expressing her gratitude to God, not just in words but in a sacrificial act.

Unlike the votive offerings, the "thank offering," the *todah*, has no strings attached to it. The offerer is simply expressing voluntary gratitude for some great blessing, some marvelous benefit, some great answer to prayer, some special deliverance. A good example can be found in Genesis 46 where Jacob, having found out that his lost son is certainly alive, makes a spontaneous *todah*, thank-offering. Many of the psalms were written to fit some occasion like that, where a person has had something special happen, or has experienced a special deliverance from God. There even existed a special form, the individual song of thanksgiving, to be used for such expressions of praise and adoration to God.

Eichrodt mentions one other group of what he calls free-will offerings. These are dedicatory gifts to the sanctuary. He has listed the Scripture references for all that he identifies as such.[120] Some of them are the sword of Goliath, which had been given by David to Yahweh; the gifts of silver and gold and bronze, often gifts that had been given to an Israelite king by another king and then given in turn to God; the golden shields that were made by Solomon and hung in the temple for Yahweh; the jar with the manna in it; the ephod of Gideon made from gold taken from the Midianites, etc. The stone that Samuel set up between Mizpah and Shen called Ebenezer was one of these dedicatory things.

But there are two kinds of dedicatory gifts given elsewhere that are not found among the gifts given to Yahweh. The first of these is human sacrifice. You will remember that this was practiced in pre-Israelite Canaan. And child sacrifice was even practiced in later Israel on several

---

[120] Eichrodt, *Theology*, vol. 1, 147, nn 8-11.

occasions. But the Hebrews practiced it contrary to the instructions of Yahweh. It was explicitly condemned in the Law. There are a number of references in Deuteronomy and Leviticus that specifically condemn this kind of thing. And when any renewal or revival came, this practice was one of the first things to be attacked and rooted out. The prophets always opposed it as in the days of Manasseh, Ahaz, and Hoshea.[121]

I think it is significant that in the passages where it speaks against child sacrifice, we find that divination, sorcery, omens, witchcraft, spells, mediums, spiritism, and necromancy are also spoken against. This suggests to me that there is a connection we should not overlook. The purpose of those other practices is to obtain spiritual power, and I suspect the same thing is at work in child sacrifice. But at the least, child sacrifice is being grouped together with other practices that the biblical understanding of reality rules out of bounds on the grounds that they conflict with the identity and nature of Yahweh, the Creator.

It is interesting that there was a widespread revival of child sacrifice in Israel in the eighth and seventh centuries B.C. Notice the dating, at least five or six centuries after Moses. That reminds us that there is always the possibility of the world shaping us instead of us influencing our world. And that battle was fought all the way through the Old Testament. Under the circumstances, surrounded as they were with the very opposite understanding of reality, it is astounding that in the end the Hebrews won it as well as they did.

Now, in the eighth and seventh centuries this was part of a

---

[121] But what about the sacrifice of Isaac? My own feeling is that there is no question but that Abraham's background made this action less offensive to him. His neighbors were doing it. But that did not make it less offensive to him personally because this was the son of promise. All of the future that God had promised, that he had come to believe in so deeply, was tied up here. And somewhere in his spirit he had come to believe that the well-being of the whole human race was tied up here, as well. So, it was an incredibly heavy load that was put on him, and apparently from the text, he felt that the Lord had specifically told him to do it. Now he must have had a conflict in his mind, "Is this the kind of Friend I've been walking with all this time? Does He expect this? If He does, knowing what I know about Him, the only thing I can do is trust Him." And so he apparently did. And God honored it. I certainly cannot prove from the text that this is the way Abraham thought. But to me, the way the rest of the Bible develops it, I do not think it is unfair to the text to say that here is a person who says, "This runs counter to everything I have believed about Him, but if He asks me, it is my place to trust Him." We are back to the absolutely foundational nature of trust.

renaissance of Canaanite heathenism and the influx of the foreign cult
practices that characterized that period. It was especially associated with
the Phoenician god, Melech, which is the Semitic word for "king." This
god is called Molek in the Bible. There are those who think that "Molek"
is the result of the biblical writers taking the vowels of the Hebrew word
for "shame," *boshet*, and combining them with the consonants in the
name of the Phonecian god, Melech.

Cultic suicide was coupled with child sacrifices in the other religions, and like child sacrifice, was forbidden. For the biblical writers,
human life in the image of God is a trust from God to us. It is not ours
to do with as we wish. In paganism, individual human life virtually is of
no worth at all. You are only of value to the extent that you replicate the
ideal. You are a bubble on the surface of the ocean. If you are absorbed
back into the ocean, what is lost? The Old Testament will have none of
that. The Creator knows His creatures by name, and the death of even
one of them is very costly to Him. Neither we nor our children are at our
own disposal to do with as we wish.

The second gift that Eichrodt finds is never to be sacrificed to
God among the Hebrews is chastity. That is, sacred prostitution is everywhere condemned. The sacrifice of personal chastity was firmly en-
trenched throughout the Ancient Near East, especially in Babylonia. It
had its roots in sympathetic magic designed to ensure increased fertility.
Here again the worshipper is seeking to access the power that animates
the cosmos. This practice was engaged in by both men and women, and
it took the form of selling themselves either on a one-time occasion at
the beginning of married life, or else on a vocational base as permanent
prostitutes in the sanctuaries.

If you are going to give your best gifts to a god, why should
a woman not give her virginity so that before the woman marries her
husband, she gives herself in a temple to some man and that is a sacrifice
to the deity? And surely it would be an even greater gift to dedicate
your sexuality on a vocational, or permanent basis. Such a person was
called the *hieros* (sacred, relating to the gods) *gamos* (wedding). The sacred
bride, or the sacred groom, the *hieros gamos*, was felt to secure for you
a share in the divine power from the divinity or apotropaically to buy

off the jealous malevolence of some demon.[122] You see, you have done something (that may be unknown to you), and there is somebody or something out there that is upset with you. So how do you avert it? The sacred wedding was one of the possibilities. If you had had ritual sex with the god or goddess, they were less likely to try to kill you. This, of course, was all dependent on the idea of continuity, whereby you could become the god and the prostitute, the goddess, and you could thereby participate in that divine power.

But if God is not to be identified with this world and cannot be manipulated through this world, such ritual prostitution is useless. So we find ourselves coming again and again to the fact that the determinative force in this Old Testament religion is the character of Yahweh. He Himself transcends the distinctions of the creation, so there is no sexual differentiation in Him and thus no sexual need. However, the sexual qualities He has placed in His creatures are very precious to Him. So there is a fierce reaction in Yahwism against what Eichrodt calls the shamelessness common among Israel's neighbors. For them sexuality was a power to be exploited. But not so in Israel; it was a gift to be treasured. So we find Yahweh saying to Moses, "I don't want you to live like the Egyptians, where you've been; and I don't want you to live like the Canaanites where you are going." One very interesting example of this has to do with the nudity of the priest. Such nudity was relatively common in Egypt and some of the other countries, but God makes a point of specifying that the priests of Israel were not only to wear all the special clothing identified in Exodus, but also that they must wear underwear so that they would not expose their nakedness when they stand upon the altar. In this same vein, it is interesting that the Greeks, who thought the body was bad, made a point of uncovering it, whereas the Israelites, who knew the body is good, carefully covered it.

Before we leave this discussion of sacrifice as gift, we should

---

[122] The basic idea of that word *apotropaic*, is "to avert or turn aside." *Apo* means "from," while the *tropaic* comes from the Greek word "to turn," *tropos*. So an *apotropeon* is something that was believed to avert evil like an amulet, a charm, a symbol or a votive offering. This thing was in some way linked to the meta-divine and had the power to make the god do something or not do something. The dictionary definition of *apotropy* is "the magic or religious science and art of averting or overcoming evils, usually by ritual acts or by incantations or by both combined."

mention two other types. One is first-fruits which was found very early. It is a recognition of the fact that all of the fruitfulness of the earth comes from God and is an expression of His blessing. So the first-fruits are given out of gratitude but also in what Eichrodt calls the "sanctification of all of one's possessions." So the part you give is representative of the whole. Put another way, the offerer is acknowledging that God is really the owner of it all. We express this in the words of the hymn, "We give thee but thine own, whate'er the gift may be. All that we have is thine alone, a trust, O Lord, from thee."

The last illustration of sacrifices as gifts is the tithe. It was evidently a practice of great antiquity. You will remember Abraham giving tithes to Melchizedek. And this enabled everyone, Eichrodt says, to be involved in support for the sanctuary so that the tithe was a means of pulling Israel together as a people as they gave to the sanctuary and the sanctuary became central to their life. It was also a means of expressing solidarity with all the rest of the nation.

Deuteronomy tells us that every third year the tithe was to be made available to the priests and to the needy, and you get that three-fold classification of people—the widows, the orphans, and the strangers or foreigners—that become so commonplace in the rest of the Old Testament.

Lecture 18

· · · · · · · · · ·

Sacral Communion and Atonement

We turn now to the third and fourth functions of sacrifice as Eichrodt defines them. The third function is what he calls, "sacral communion." This is the idea of fellowship together with your deity as well as with those who are worshipping with you. Eichrodt says this is the concept that makes sacrifice truly sacramental. Israel had no easy task in moving from the thinking of their fathers (not to mention their neighbors), who had been pagans and polytheists, into the kind of thinking that Yahweh wanted in terms of sacral communion. So, let me deal with some of what Eichrodt has to say here.[123]

Among Israel's neighbors, sacrifice was attended by the belief that there was a power resident in the sacrificial victim. And it was believed that that power would strengthen the god to whom it was offered

---

[123] Eichrodt, *Theology*, vol. 1, 154ff.

as well as the person who was offering it. When the sacrifice was shared by a group, then all of the members became participants in that power. Since the deity and the group shared in this meal, then the worshippers and the god himself or herself entered "the same system of living power [a very interesting phrase] indicated by the victim's blood."[124]

Perhaps you are like me when I first began reading this kind of material. It was totally alien to any thinking I had ever done, and it was not easy for me to even hear what Eichrodt was saying here. But if you stay with him and pay close attention, you will begin to sense what he is after and begin to understand some of his comments, which may at first seem to be going too far. So he goes on to say, "[the fact that both deity and worshipper drank the same blood] meant that God and Man were united by the strongest possible bonds."[125] And so, sacrifice was a means of uniting the worshipper and the god in a mystical way, so that the worshipper is almost sharing in the life of the deity at that point.

We may look at this in one of two ways: Did the worshipper thus become a sharer in the god's divine life, or did they become participants together, god and worshipper, in a meta-divine or magical power that the god himself needed and could use? In any case, the power that was to be gained was very different from that which Yahweh longed to impart to His worshippers. Eichrodt makes an important point here when he says,

> Moreover, the consuming holiness of his nature constantly breaking in on human life further excludes any thought of presuming on the bond of blood-brotherhood.[126]

Thus, the power that was to be gained in communion with Yahweh was very different. What we find when Yahweh becomes central is neither physical participation, in which human nature becomes divinized so that now God is within us and our life becomes His and His becomes ours, nor is it an involvement in magic, producing certain automatic results. It is rather the expression of a personal relationship of an ethical,

---

[124] Ibid., 155
[125] Ibid.
[126] Ibid., 157

moral character that has a quality of pure sacredness about it. Those are not Eichrodt's precise words, but I think they catch the sense of what he says.

The emphasis here is on the personal character, because Yahweh comes through as a person to Israel. He is not a force that has been personified but a Person. Too often that personal element gets lost in religion. If there is any genius in evangelicalism it is that the personal relationship comes back into the center. And that is, as far as I can see, the only way to explain what really took place and developed in Israel in that ancient day. God stepped out of the shadows and became personal. You will remember that in the opening lectures we dealt with knowing God and that it is not an intellectual, cerebral knowing about Him, but it is a personal encounter and a personal communication.

What Yahweh offers is for the worshipper to know Him personally in a context of blessing and fellowship. In such a relationship, the true worshipper receives in that relationship forgiveness, cleansing, and fellowship, as well as revelation and life. The sacrifice becomes sacramental in that way. I find myself going back to 1 John and to that intimate personal relationship that is expressed in 1 John 1:7, where he says,

> If we walk in the light, as he is in the light, we have fellowship one with another [and if with one another, then with Him], and the blood of Jesus, his Son, purifies us from all sin.

I suggest that there is more continuity between the Pentateuch and that understanding in 1 John than there is between the Pentateuch and the blood sacrifices of much of the Ancient Near East.

The fourth function of sacrifice is that of atonement, and I suspect here is the place where we need to do our best and hardest thinking. When Yahweh began to try to reveal Himself to His people, He had to find a way to enter into their lives through words, concepts, and practices that had old associations, alien to His purposes, which did not contain within themselves the truth He wanted to communicate. You will remember that I spoke about the development of the word *hesed* in the Old Testament. That is an illustration of how God has to put new content into language if He is to be able to communicate what He wants to say to us. And so, old words develop new meanings, and there is a counterpart to that in the New Testament when it speaks about us as new creations. There is a clear connection to the past, but that connection is not determinative.

If God wanted to communicate, He was going to have to use the language, cult, and thought life with which the people were familiar. But these had to be cleaned up by disassociation and/or transformed by being filled with new meaning that had not been thought or experienced before. We miss what really took place in Abraham and Moses if we do not recognize the incredible intellectual revolution that took place there. I say, it was an incredible intellectual revolution. Nowhere was this more tricky for the Lord than in the area of sacrifice, and especially sacrifice that had to do with expiation or atonement.

The ancient world around Israel had its lustration rites, its washings. It had a wide variety of uses of blood. You will find the same things in Leviticus. Likewise, there were rites in which hands were laid on persons or animals as with the scapegoat. Then they had their special words and practices that were again not unlike those we read about in Leviticus. But the reality is that in Israel you get a revolution in the thinking that takes place when using the same materials and doing very similar rites.

The cultic world of the Ancient Near East sought protection from and favor with two worlds. The one was the world of the gods, and the other was that meta-divine world that empowers and shapes everything. They needed protection to keep the power in those worlds that were beyond them from harming them. So, a lot of their religion was defensive, because they needed the favor of those two worlds just to survive in the struggles of daily life. If an individual did something that was wrong; acted in such a way as to displease one of the gods or to get himself in trouble with the meta-divine world, he needed a way to appease those powers and to avert inexorable judgment. Notice the word I used there: *powers*. The primitive person was dealing with forces and powers that were basically impersonal. Although those powers may have been given names and figures, personification, in an attempt to make them more understandable and controllable, they were, nonetheless, simply powers.

That being the case, the right words and the right ceremonies were thought to work mechanically in a naturalistic cause-and-effect manner. You may be familiar with the Latin phrase *ex opere operato*. It is interesting that when we want a terse, precise statement of something, we have to go back to Latin to get it. That phrase literally means "out of the work working." That is, "the work produces the work." The idea is that if I do this right, I will get the right benefit. If I have the right coins to put in the machine, and push the right buttons, the machine will kick out the right product. How I feel about the machine, or whether I have a good relationship with it, has absolutely nothing to do with the process.

And so, it is a mechanical, an automatic, way of working. You do it right and you get the right benefits from it. There is nothing at all personal involved in it. But do you know, when my wife tries to work me that way, I resent it, almost as much as she does when I try to work her that way. We are persons and we do not want to be used or mechanically controlled. But that was at the heart of much of the sacrificial system of the Ancient Near East. The right words, the right ceremonies, should work automatically in a naturalistic cause-and-effect manner. These same ideas are found around the world. Studies of Polynesian culture have made a couple of their terms—*taboo* and *mana*—part of the English language. Both of them are that *ex opere operato* kind of thing. It does not matter what your motive was; it does not matter what the circumstances were. If you did it so that it is wrong in terms of that other world, then the consequences are automatic. The only way to avert those consequences was for you to do something to counter them.

Perhaps the nearest approach to that kind of thinking in the Old Testament is found in the treatment of retributive justice. You will remember how the Old Testament sometimes seems to treat disease as a result of sin. You do wrong and you contract a disease. We will come back to that. But in the larger picture of biblical religion there is a personal relationship between Yahweh and His people that vastly complicates this whole discussion. Eichrodt says that Yahweh stepped into this polytheistic world, with what he calls its "demonistic" practices, as a Person, bringing a whole new set of ideas that were contradictory to the magical and the mechanistic conceptions that were associated with the old practices and the old language.

This means that sin for the Hebrew is not primarily associated with "taboo." It is not associated with some destructive power that has been unleashed and that you must magically counter or suffer its consequences. Rather, you have a God of *hesed*, a divine Friend who has been offended. That creates a radically different understanding of what was done and what needs to be done to correct it. Sin is now against a personal God whose character is marked by *hesed*. It is no longer in relation to an external force out there, but it is in relation to a divine Friend. Atonement, therefore, is not a magical manipulation of demonic powers. That is the meaning of the word *apotropaic* that we used in the previous lecture. Atonement in the Old Testament is not apotropaic. It was not a negotiation with demonic power for protection from their wrath, but instead atonement is a means of restoring personal fellowship with that divine Friend. "The formulas of magic and incantation, which formerly constituted the liturgical texts," Eichrodt says, "are now replaced by prayer and confession of sin."[127] Now, incantation can look to one like a prayer, but to the Hebrew, it was something different. It was not an automatic means of diverting an unwanted consequence, but it was a restoring of a personal relationship with a divine Friend. So now, prayer and confession and faith become central, in place of magic and incantation. Eichrodt says, in one of the most significant passages in the whole work:

> We are dealing here with two quite different systems of concepts, two types of action which are qualitatively distinct and which cannot be derived the one from the other or interpreted as the stages of a linear development in time.[128]

When Eichrodt wrote that, he was running counter to the great majority of Old Testament scholarship in the world. The concept of evolution, of progress from the simple to the complex, had come to rule the field. So it said, "Those passages in Leviticus that are so boring to us reflect a very primitive stage, which biblical faith eventually outgrew. That kind of thinking was common in all the other religions, and so Hebrew religion emerged out of that background." But Eichrodt is saying that

[127] Ibid., 159.
[128] Ibid.

there is a radical discontinuity here. These two different understandings of atonement cannot be interpreted as different stages in a linear development in time. So he goes on to say, "They correspond to two different experiences which are different in kind."[129] Now, as Wesleyans, with our understanding of the importance of personal experience, we ought to have some understanding of what he means when he says that. What happened in Abraham's life was not just a rational conclusion, it was a personal encounter that made a difference with very significant and radical intellectual consequences. We are not dealing with an evolutionary emergence. We are dealing with something radically unique in man's intellectual history and in his spiritual development.

Now, how did such a revolutionary development take place? Eichrodt responds with a statement that I appreciate a great deal. He says,

> About the possibility or impossibility of [these experiences] in any particular period of civilization no completely satisfactory opinion can ever be formed on the basis of purely scientific investigation.[130]

We would say that the answer is divine revelation. But it is important that when we speak of revelation, we keep two things together: the personal encounter and the intellectual consequences. If we separate those two, I think we have not been fair to what is taking place here. Yahweh is not merely communicating content, concepts. He is revealing Himself. What Eichrodt is saying is that Yahweh made Himself known. The Divine Person stepped into His creation and an "other," a qualitatively distinct "other," is introduced. The result is that while the materials involved in the expiatory offering and ritual of its presentation may be very similar in both Ancient Near Eastern religions and in the Hebrew cult, the actual function of the two is very different. And an analysis of the difference puts the focus not on what they did or what they used, nor even what they believed or understood, but it puts the focus on who Yahweh was and, thus, what he wanted. The divine demands in worship,

---

[129] Ibid.
[130] Ibid.

in law, in custom, in morality, all stem from the fact that God's "personal will is present to control all human conduct."[131]

Turn with me to Psalm 32. This is one of the seven psalms that the early Christian church listed as penitential psalms. It has to do with the forgiveness of sins. It was the favorite psalm of St. Augustine, and Luther called it Pauline. He said that in this psalm we are dealing with basic New Testament faith. It begins with a statement of what a blessed man is. "Blessed is He whose transgression is forgiven, whose sins are covered. Blessed is the person whose sin [Yahweh] does not count against him and in whose spirit is no deceit."

Notice the four different words used for sin here. The first is the word *transgression, pesha'*. It can also be translated with "trespass" and "rebellion." There is a sense in which that is the strongest word for "sin" in the Old Testament, because it speaks of intentional refusal to do God's will. I knew what I ought to do, the law was there, and I went ahead and did it anyway—rebelled.

The second word for sin, "Blessed is the man whose sins are covered," is the word *hata'*. This carries the idea of missing a target. You can miss it intentionally or unintentionally, but you have missed it all the same. The bowman pulled his bow and shot it at the deer; he did not pull it quite hard enough and the arrow fell short. You tried and you did not quite make it. This is the most general word for sin, because it covers all the bases of the concept. It is usually translated into English, as here, with the word *sin*.

The third word for sin in this psalm is *'awon*. It is dispositional, speaking of an inner condition. The basic idea is twistedness. So it can be translated with the archaic "iniquity." There is a twist in your spirit, and so you are out of joint and what you do comes out of that. The covenant relationship with the person that you are iniquitous toward has been forgotten, and so you are out of sorts and work against it. It can also be translated with "guilt," speaking of the twistedness in the soul that is a result of doing something wrong.

The fourth word is *r'miyyah*, which can be translated with "guile" or "deceit." It is a lack of candor, where you are just not really honest or straightforward. For whatever reason, you decide that to be truthful

---

[131] Eichrodt, *Theology*, vol. 1, 160.

would not be to your advantage, so you compromise the truth.

Now, notice that each one of these is said to be dealt with differently. I do not think this is just artistic variation or that the psalmist just said the first thing that came to mind in each case. In fact, I think he was writing very deliberately under the inspiration of the Spirit, choosing the most appropriate method for correcting each kind of behavior. He says, first of all, "Blessed is he whose transgressions are forgiven," and the Hebrew word translated "forgive" is very concrete. It is *nasa'*, which means "to carry (away)." Second, "Blessed is he whose sins are covered." The word there is *kipper* which may have the idea of wiping something away or blotting it out (this is the term regularly translated "atoned for" in *KJV*). Third, "Blessed is the man whose iniquity is not reckoned against him." The person who has been wronged by the behavior springing from twistedness is not holding that behavior against the sinner. He is not holding a grudge. The last one, "deceit," is treated a little differently since it is stated positively. The truly blessed person is the one who does not have a deceitful spirit. He or she is not playing games. This person is candid.

So the last one does not exist. The third one is not held against the sinner, and the second one is covered over or blotted out. But the first one, someone is carrying on his back. *Pesha'*, "transgression," is deliberate, willful rebellion. It is not forgiven in the sense of just being forgotten. It does not simply go away. It is not covered over. It cannot just be dismissed. Someone has to carry it. To get the full implications of this you have to go to other parts of the Old Testament and ultimately to the New Testament.

When you see this in the light of the whole Scripture, what you are going to see is the Cross, because this is what is described in Isaiah 53; the Servant bears our griefs, our sins, and our transgressions. They are not spoken away. They are moved from the back of the person who committed them to the back of one who did not commit them, much as was true of the scapegoat in Leviticus 16.

We often have a wrong conception of what forgiveness involves. We think of the sin as merely an abstraction, so that if we deny its existence it is gone. If you forget it, then it is gone. No Hebrew could think that way. When you sinned, above all in the sense of trespass, you had brought something into existence. You had borne a child that you could not abort. It was there with an objective existence of its own, which was going to have to be dealt with. Thus, in order for the sin to be covered over, or blotted out, in order for the iniquity to be no longer counted, in order for a person to have a true and transparent spirit, somebody had to carry away that offense against reality, to nullify it. And that could only be done by taking the consequences away.

But that is not just an antique, Hebrew way of thinking. We live in a cause-and-effect world. One of the most deadly things you can do to your children is always to shield them from the consequences of their actions. They will grow up living in a fairy-tale world that does not exist. And they will never be able to cope with the real world where actions have inevitable consequences. We depend on that fact, as does science. What kind of a world would it be if we never knew what the effects of our actions would be? We, in our fallenness, insist on getting the just rewards of all our good (or almost-good) actions, but assume that the consequences of all our bad actions can just be forgotten. It is not true. For forgiveness to exist in the cosmos, there has to have been created some mechanism whereby the just consequences of sin can be fully suffered. Jesus Christ and His Cross are that mechanism, and so much more than a mere mechanism.

Continue on in Psalm 32. In verse 3 the psalmist becomes personal. He has told who is the blessed man, the person most to be envied in the world (for that is what "blessed" means). It is not the person with the most wealth, or the most education, or the person in a position of political power. The person who is most to be envied is the person the consequences of whose sin have been thoroughly dealt with. That is biblical.

But there was a time, he says, when that was certainly not true of me. "I kept silent," he says. Silent about what? About my sin, my trespasses, my iniquity, my deceit. I thought I could deal with the consequences of my actions by just denying them. But what was the result? "My bones wasted away." I love the *King James Version* of this verse: "My bones waxed old through my roaring all the day long." That means that the sinner is a person who has a cacophony inside himself or herself. They have noise inside instead of harmony. He said, "I was going to keep quiet about my sin on the outside. But what happened? It got awfully noisy on the inside. And besides the uproar, there was an ache in my soul." The worst thing about getting old is your aching bones. You feel it all the way through. And he is probably not merely speaking metaphorically. We know enough these days to know that there is a direct connection between the physical body and the spirit. A sick spirit will produce a desperately sick body.

He says in verse 4, "For day and night your [Yahweh's] hand was heavy upon me; my strength was sapped as in the heat of summer." Now that is a fascinating description of guilt. We might use different images today, but that is what he is talking about here, and I think it communicates very powerfully. He knew what he should do, but he did not do it; he ran counter to it. The load came and he found he could not live with the guilt. He was like a wilted plant without even the strength to stand up.

But, "Then I acknowledged my sin to you and did not cover up my iniquity. I said, 'I will confess my transgressions (*peshaʿ*) to [Yahweh].'" There are the three key words again, and I rather think they are in rank order. "Sin" is the general term; "iniquity" is what accounts for my sin; and "trespasses" is the most blatant expression of it all. And what did Yahweh do? "You forgave the guilt of my sin." Here is the other side of *ʿawon*. It is "guilt," the inner pain of a grinding conscience. So what we have in this verse is the testimony of a person who repented and confessed and found inner release.

Now, what happens after that? He testifies in verses 6 and 7 about God's care and protection, and it is very personal. Notice the second-person pronouns in reference to Yahweh: pray to you (6); you are my hiding place and you will protect me from trouble (7). He seems to be saying by implication that the most awful thing about his sin was that it deprived him of God's personal care.

Then in verses 8 and 9 Yahweh is speaking, and again it is very personal. He wants to give instruction and guidance to His faithful ones, and He wants them to be eager to follow that instruction, rather than being like a stubborn animal. In the context, I suspect the point is that He wants us to confess sin instantly and not allow it to destroy us and our relationship with Yahweh as it had begun to do in the psalmist's case.

Finally, we come to the conclusion of the thought in verse 10. Here we are ready to see why Luther said this psalm was Pauline. First of all, did you notice anywhere in the psalm any reference to the Law?

There is not a reference in this ancient poem to any kind of legalistic obedience. It is a personal matter between the psalmist and Yahweh. To be sure, it is the teaching of the Law, the Torah, that has been given to him that shows him he has offended Yahweh. But he is not dealing with the Law. He is not trying to get right with the Law. He is trying to get right with Yahweh on a personal level.

Now verse 10: "Many are the woes of the wicked, but [Yahweh's] *hesed* surrounds the [person] who trusts in him." Notice the contrast between the wicked and those who trust in Yahweh. It is not between the wicked and the righteous, although that occurs plenty of times in the Old Testament. What is the point here? The psalmist is saying that the real question is: What determines whether a person is wicked or not? And the answer is whether the person put his trust in Yahweh or not. So, you see how personal this thing is? The opposite of wicked is trust. Trust. You have two kinds of people: the wicked and the people who trust. You can see why Luther would say this is a great Protestant psalm. But more than that it is a great biblical psalm; it is a great Christian psalm.

Now when you read Leviticus, especially those long, boring passages about sacrifices, don't fall into the trap of modern higher criticism, saying that dull, priestly types wrote those passages, while saintly believers wrote the Psalms. It was people who were faithfully carrying out those Levitical practices who wrote this kind of psalm! What you get in that Levitical legislation, when you understand it correctly, is not opposed to this kind of spiritual religion. It was those practices that made this kind of thing possible, and this kind of thing infused those practices with an entirely different meaning than that found in the not-so-different practices of the Canaanites.

I believe you see how the two fit together in Psalm 51. You will notice that the writer, identified as David in the superscription, begins with his plea. One of the differences between Psalms 51 and 32 is that in 51 the author has not yet found resolution; he has not yet reached the blessedness described in 32:1-2; he is seeking to get there. So we have the process of repentance and confession laid out more fully here. He cries out, "Have mercy upon me." And the Hebrew word there is the word from which we get the word *grace*; it's a plea for grace. He knows that if he gets what he deserves he is under judgment, so he wants grace. "Have mercy on me, O God, according to your *hesed*." He is appealing to the *hesed* that is ever-present in the Old Testament. Whenever people need God in the Old Testament, you will find it a part of their thought. "Have mercy on me, O God, according to your *hesed*; according to your great compassion, blot out my transgressions." There is *pesha'*, that willful, deliberate act of rebellion. "Wash away all my iniquity." There is *'awon*, the twistedness in our character. "Cleanse me from my sin." There is *hata'*, the shortcomings, the missed targets in my life. "For I know my transgressions, and my sin is always before me."

Now, pay careful attention. "Against you, you only, have I sinned and done what is evil in your sight." Once again, you see, Yahweh stands right at the center of the situation. The big issue everywhere you turn in the Old Testament is Yahweh. It is not first of all about truth, or about the Law. It is not first of all about power, or about guilt. It is not first of all about sacrifice. The central, overriding issue is: Who is Yahweh and how do I relate to Him? That personal character is at the heart of this psalm as it was in Psalm 32.

In verse 7 we begin to get some language that we might call cultic or sacrificial. "Cleanse me with hyssop, and I will be clean; wash me and I shall be whiter than snow." But notice he is not saying that the sacrificial system will do it. He is saying to Yahweh personally, "*You* cleanse me with hyssop and I will be clean. *You* wash me and I will be clean. *You* wash me and I will be whiter than snow. Let me hear joy and gladness; let the bones *you* have crushed rejoice." Now, when I read that I remember that passage in Psalm 32 where he speaks about when he kept silent; when he didn't confess his sin. He said, "Your hand was heavy upon me . . . and my bones wasted away through my groaning all day long." There was a roaring inside of me.

"Hide your face from my sins." I cannot overemphasize the importance of Yahweh's face in the Old Testament. If His face is toward you and He approves, then everything is fine. If His face turns away from you, you have problems. And what is the most personal of relationships with Yahweh? It is a face-to-face relationship (Ezek. 20:35). So if Yahweh will not look at our sins, they are truly gone.

"Create in me a pure heart, O God." The word *create* here is the Hebrew word *bara'*, which is the word used in Genesis 1. It is used exclusively for an act of God. Humans do not do this; they may make, *'asah*, but they cannot create. Only God can. So, the psalmist is asking

God to do something He alone can do. Then here comes "face" again. "Do not cast me from your face [Heb., Eng. "presence]." If I lose your face, I have lost everything. In Psalm 16 the writer says, "I have set you, Yahweh, always before me." Yahweh's face is what he is wanting to see, and that is much the same thing Moses was asking when he said to Yahweh, in essence, "You are sending me, who is going to go with me?" (Ex. 33:12-16). And Yahweh said, "My [face] will go with you" (Ex. 33:14). You cannot get more personal than that in Hebrew. "Presence" is fine, but it is an abstraction. How much more powerful is, "My face will go with you."

So, he says, "Don't cast me away from your face or take your Holy Spirit from me." Now look what he has done here. He has paralleled the personal presence of God with the Holy Spirit. How much did David know about the Holy Spirit? He certainly did not know very much. He had never read John chapters 14–16, had he? But this is an example of one of the beautiful features of Scripture. First a concept or a theme is just touched on, as here. Then later you will get a little more, and then later still more. And finally you will begin to get the full picture. But in this case, whatever the writer may know about the Holy Spirit, he knows that something has happened inside him that is a work of God, and he attributes it to that breath of God that breathed on the deep and brought order out of chaos. That breath of God has breathed in him, and he says, "Please don't take that away from me or my insides will continue to be chaos. So, don't take that breath, your breath, away from me."

But then he goes on. "Restore to me the joy of your salvation and grant me a willing spirit, a free spirit, to sustain me." This is not a New Birth text. This is a believer's text. He has known this "joy of salvation," this spirit that leaps up to do the Lover's wishes, and he has lost it. This is a person inside the covenant who has sinned. Then he says, if God will restore my salvation and grant me a willing spirit, I will teach transgressors His ways. I will do that because I have been there and I can tell them the way out. And if I have that joy and that free spirit, "sinners will turn back to you."

"Save me from bloodguilt, O God, the God who saves me, and my tongue will sing of your righteousness. O Lord, open my lips, and my mouth will declare your praise." Now, it is interesting that all through the psalm, it is "God." And here it is not the personal name, but the title,

"Lord." I wonder if it is because his experience was like mine. When I have sinned I find that there is a distance introduced between me and God. Before the truly personal relationship can be enjoyed again, there is some legal business that has to be conducted between the petitioner and the Judge.

Now we come to a passage that in the last century and a half in Old Testament studies has had a great deal written about it. "You do not delight in sacrifice, or I would bring it; you do not take pleasure in burnt offerings. The sacrifices of God are a broken spirit; a broken and contrite heart, O God, you will not despise." One of the results of the higher critical approach to the Old Testament at the end of the nineteenth century was the view that early Israel, up until the exilic period, had a very simplistic cult, where sacrifice and ritual were insignificant and fairly unimportant. The complex, standardized practices of Leviticus, this view held, were only created and instituted after the return from exile. They looked to passages like this one and certain others from the eighth-century prophets like Amos and Micah for support of that view. Those prophets, the critics said, pioneered the idea that God was ethical and moral and spoke sharply against the emerging cultic practices.

In that light, look at the last two verses of this psalm. "In your good pleasure make Zion prosper; build up the walls of Jerusalem. Then there will be righteous sacrifices, whole burnt offerings to delight you; then bulls will be offered on your altar." When I was in seminary fifty years ago, one of the most common things taught was that verses 18 and 19 were not a part of the original text and that they were added later, because this looks contradictory to verses 16 and 17. So, it was argued, originally the psalm must have ended with verse 17. But the people who later transmitted this psalm to us lived in that later, priestly period where sacrifice was an established part of the worship. And so they added this postscript on the importance of sacrifice.

But there has been an interesting shift in thinking over the last forty or fifty years. There were already people like Eichrodt in the 1930s and von Rad in the 1950s who, without denying the higher critical dictum that Leviticus may have taken its final form late, were beginning to say, in the light of comparative studies, there is no way that you can conceive of early Israel without the kind of ritualistic sacrificial system that is described in the book of Leviticus. As a result, it is much more common now to see Psalm 51:16-19 as complementary rather than contradictory. Seen in that way, they give us the heart of the Yahwistic understanding of cult. That understanding is that sacrifice can never be made to function *ex opere operato*—a means in itself to bring forgiveness and salvation.[132] That is the point of the Amos and Micah passages. The prophets are seeking to call the people back away from the pagan understanding to the true, original understanding. God does not want sacrifice and never did. What He wants is the human heart. And when the Israelites sought to placate God with sacrifices, while keeping their hearts for themselves, God found sacrifice deeply disgusting. That is also the point of Psalm 51:16-17. God does not want sacrifice as a substitute for genuine contrition, repentance, and submission.

But if all that is true, what is going on with Leviticus? If God really does not want sacrifices, why are they commanded so forcefully as part of the covenant? If he really does not live in a house, why the meticulous directions for one in Exodus 25–40? I believe the answer lies in the nature of humanity. We are finally an inseparable melding of body and spirit. Therefore we need to represent invisible spiritual realities in tangible ways. And if we are unwilling to represent the realities in tangible ways, there may just be a question about whether the realities are realities at all. If I am unwilling to give the best sheep in my flock to God as an expression of real gratitude for His continual atonement for my sins, maybe I have not really repented and received His forgiveness. I think that is exactly the point of Psalm 51:18-19. When God has confirmed to me that He has indeed seen my broken heart and crushed spirit and has heard my cry of genuine contrition and has done all those things I asked Him to do in restoration and new creation, what will I do? I will gladly represent the reality of what has taken place in the very tangible

---

[132] [Editor's note] This understanding of sacrifice is as inherent in the worldview of transcendence as the other understanding is inherent in the worldview of continuity. If God is truly absolutely other than His creation, there is nothing that can be done in creation that will automatically produce a change in Him. On the other hand, if the gods are simply the powers of the cosmos with masks on, and if all parts of the cosmos are inseparable from all other parts, then of course what is done in one part of the cosmos must be done in every part of the cosmos. If we ask when the distinctive Israelite understanding of cult had its beginnings, we must ask the prior question: When did its understanding that Yahweh is not His creation come into being, for the two are inseparable?

ways He has laid out for me.[133]

There is one more thing I want to call to your attention before we leave this psalm. Notice that those last two verses are related to Jerusalem. That is not an accident. The writer knows himself to be a person inside the covenant, and the whole Old Testament doctrine of election is implicit here. This understanding of God and the critical importance of personal relation to Him has implications for the nation and not just for the individual. And I wonder if even corporate expressions are significant until they become that personal. But notice that the Law was given after election, not before. The Israelites did not become God's people because they had the Law; they were given the Law because they were God's people. The same thing can be said about sacrifice. The sacrificial system was not given to Abraham, it was given through Moses to the descendants of Abraham, the people of God. What came first to Abraham was the personal relationship with the Yahweh of *hesed*. Only later came those external ways to live out that relationship. What the psalmist is saying is, "If you will take my sin away and restore our relationship, we can put the covenant back in operation and we can go through the regular acts of worship the way they ought to be gone through." I do not go to the Communion table to get forgiveness. I go to the Communion table because He has died for me and forgiven me.[134]

Having said all these things, I want to remind you that this psalm is a prayer, not a systematic theology treatise. It was written a long time ago by a person who had no interest in trying to answer all of my theoretical questions or yours either. He is a man who is trying to get his soul right with his Lord and get back into the covenant the way he should

---

[133] The church has long argued over the right language to express what is taking place in the sacraments. The reformers rightly contested the idea of transubstantiation, with its strong overtones of continuity. On the other hand, there seems to be more than mere symbolism at work. There were appropriate ways to represent the work of God, and there were inappropriate ways, which suggests a more essential connection between the inner reality and the outer expression than the word *symbol* may quite represent.

[134] None of this should be taken to say that we should only carry out the forms of worship when we feel deeply moved by God's prior activity on our behalf. We should participate in the forms of worship because our Savior has commanded us to do so. Many times it is only when we have dutifully obeyed Him that the wonder of what He has done for us will fall upon us. But we should never worship *in order* to get God to do something for us.

have stayed all along. But in some ways, that is exactly my point: Old Testament religion is not about some abstract concepts; it is about the real experience of the face of Yahweh in your life. So, it is a beautiful psalm from that point of view.

Lecture 19

. . . .

Festivals as Instruments of Theology

In the previous lectures we were thinking about the Israelite cultic practices and the issues of continuity and discontinuity. There are clearly materials and actions in Hebrew ritual that correspond with the pagan Canaanite ritual. But the significant thing is the difference in meaning and in what the people are thinking and doing in their hearts.

Now, we know that Israel was enough like its world that historians of religion can deal with Israel as one of the religions of the Ancient Near East. But at the same time Israel was unlike many of her neighbors. There was a uniqueness in her. The enticing questions are: How did the Israelites become so different? How did they break the mental paradigm of the world in which they were living? How did they break out of those thought forms?

We use key words like *revelation*, but the interesting thing to me is that when Genesis goes to explain it, all it says is, "Yahweh said to

Abraham." That is all that we have in the book of Genesis to explain what took place there, and the same is true in Exodus; when Moses was on the mountain, very simply, Yahweh spoke to him.

But whatever that speaking involved, there is no question that out of it a new people emerged, a new nation. And they were different. And in that difference was the potential for the redemption of the world. It was not in how they looked so much as it was in what they had come to know. But beyond the mystery of how they came into existence, there is an equal mystery over how they were maintained as a people—how they survived. There was little in their culture to encourage them and plenty in their culture to leech out the faith that was there. You find that evidenced as you go through the Old Testament, with the lapses that came over and over again. Cultural gravity was against them, and oftentimes they yielded to that.

If you take the time to stop and think, they had very little to help them maintain their identity. We, on the other hand, have masses of things to help us that they never knew anything about. There were no publishing companies, so nobody had a library at home. I do not know what I would do if I did not have books. And I do not know how a preacher would preach if he did not have books. But they did not have them. There was obviously writing, and we are told that things were written down from Moses' day onward. So there obviously were texts, but they were not for common consumption. The ordinary Hebrew taking care of his sheep and living with his family did not have a family Bible, let alone a personal one.

There were no churches there either, in the sense that you and I know them. When we go into a town we find them everywhere we look. There were no educational programs, no Sunday schools, no vacation Bible schools, no Bible classes. Think of the Bible classes that we have in our culture to help us. In the early days, there was not the temple establishment that came later after David and Solomon. So, it was not easy for them to survive, but the amazing thing is they did survive.

I had the opportunity to go to a prayer meeting in Canton, China, in 1982. They had just opened four churches in that big city. The first break for the church, other than the house churches, was beginning to come in China. And so, on a Wednesday night we had an opportunity to go to one of those churches that had been opened. A translator sat behind me and translated into my ear so I had a chance to know what was taking place. It was a very moving experience for me because in the 1940s, before China closed, I took a year of Mandarin, hoping that one day I could go to China. The teacher was an elderly gentleman; he was as old as I am now. It was a forty-five- to fifty-minute Bible class. Everybody in that audience sat there with a Bible in one hand and a list of questions he had given them in another. It was like a great InterVarsity Christian Fellowship Bible study, and I was deeply stirred.

Afterwards I got a chance to have tea with the pastor. He knew English, and my friend, the translator, was with me, so we could converse. I said to him, "I have a question. It looked to me like this crowd had two hundred fifty to three hundred people in it." He nodded his head. I said, "And it looked to me like about sixty percent of them were under thirty years of age." And he smiled and nodded his head. I said, "If that's true, they were born under Mao. They were born in a society where the government was committed to the obliteration of the Christian church. Where did they become Christians? How did they become Christian?" He looked back at me and smiled, you know, with that enigmatic Oriental smile, as if he had a secret that he did not know whether he wanted to share with me or not, and finally he said very quietly, "They are children of believers, or else their friends are children of believers, or else they are friends of friends of children of believers." Then I realized it was not the church that survived in China, it was the Christian families, and that was the base.

I suspect that was true in Israel too; faithful families passed the faith on through waves of apostasy and periodic revivals. If you read the book of Judges, you will find that it oftentimes depended upon a leader. You have a judge who appears who is in touch with the Lord and is obedient to Him, and he gives the right kind of leadership, and the people turn and follow. Then he dies and you have a period of backsliding, turning away. Then another leader will arise and there is a coming back. So, as you go through the Old Testament you have something like wave-action, with a wave of fidelity and then a trough of apostasy. We look with horror at a Solomon, recognizing that he introduced the pagan elements right into his court. That means that when you come to the accounts of Hezekiah and Josiah, one of the things they have to do is to remove the sacred prostitutes from the temple. They had to remove the images and the occult practices from the temple because they were all there. Canaan had moved into the very house of Yahweh. How did they survive in that kind of world?

A major contributing factor, I believe, was their annual pilgrimage festivals. You will remember that they had three great festivals a year. In the section dealing with sacred season you find they deal with the Sabbath, they deal with the Feast of Trumpets, they deal with the Day of Atonement, but there are three major feasts. One is the Passover, which is very familiar to us. It is closely connected with the Feast of Unleavened Bread. The second of these is the Feast of Weeks, which we know as Pentecost, because it comes fifty days after the giving of the first sheaves, which was at the time of Passover. And then the Fall Festival, the Feast of Tabernacles, or the Feast of Booths.

It is of interest to me that in the Pentateuch we get three different discussions of these festivals. One of them is in Exodus 34 where all three are mentioned. Another is in Leviticus 23 where all three are mentioned. The third is in Deuteronomy 16. When you go back to Exodus in chapters 12 and 13, you get the initial Passover, and the beginning of the background for the Passover, and the Feast of Unleavened Bread initiated in Egypt.

The Hebrew word for a feast is *hagg*.[135] The Hebrew word has a different connotation from our word *feast* because there is implicit within it the concept of pilgrimage. If you go back you will remember that these were pilgrim feasts when all of Israel came together and they traveled. They were told first to go wherever Yahweh chose to put His name, and ultimately, of course, that meant Jerusalem.

Look at Exodus 34. You are probably beginning to get familiar with Exodus 34, at least I hope you are.

> The Lord said to Moses, "Chisel out two stone tablets like the first ones, and I will write on them the words that were on those first tablets, which you broke. Be ready in the morning, and then come up on Mount Sinai. Present yourself to me there on top of the mountain. No one is to come with you or be seen anywhere on the mountain;

---

[135] The Arabic cognate is *hajj*, which like Hebrew *hagg*, means "pilgrimage."

not even the flocks or herds may graze in front of the mountain." So, Moses chiseled out two stone tablets like the first ones and went up Mount Sinai early in the [morning, carrying] the two stone tablets in his hands. Then [Yahweh] came down in the cloud and stood there with him and proclaimed his name, [Yahweh]. And he passed in front of Moses, proclaiming, "[Yahweh, Yahweh], the compassionate and gracious God, slow to anger, abounding in love and faithfulness, maintaining love to thousands, and forgiving wickedness, rebellion and sin" (Ex. 34:1-7a).

Now, you will notice that what is taking place here is the re-establishment of the covenant. You are getting a repetition of what happened in chapters 20–24. So what happens?

Moses bowed to the ground at once and worshiped. "O Lord, if I have found favor in your eyes," he said, "then let the Lord go with us. Although this is a stiff-necked people, forgive our wickedness and our sin and take us as your inheritance." Then the LORD said: "I am making a covenant with you. Before all your people I will do wonders never before done in any nation in all the world. The people you live among will see how awesome is the work that I, [Yahweh], will do for you. Obey what I command you today. I will drive out the Amorites, Canaanites, Hittites, Perizzites, Hivites and Jebusites. . . . Be careful not to make a treaty with those who live in the land, for when they prostitute them-selves . . . they will lead your sons to do the same. Do not make cast idols" (Ex. 34:8-17).

Clearly, following the golden calf incident, Yahweh is focusing this re-establishment of the covenant with the people of Israel on the issue of idolatry. If they had a problem out here in the desert, what will it be when they are surrounded by the Canaanites? So what comes next is quite significant.

"Celebrate the Feast of Unleavened Bread. For seven days eat bread made without yeast, as I commanded you. Do this at the appointed time in the month of Abib, for in that month you came out of Egypt" (34:18).

Then in verses 19-21 he talks about redeeming the firstborn and the Sabbath. In verse 22 he says:

"Celebrate the Feast of Weeks [the second great festival] with the firstfruits of the wheat harvest, and the Feast of Ingathering at the turn of the year. Three times a year all your men are to appear before the Sovereign [Yahweh], the God of Israel. I will drive out nations before you and enlarge your territory, and no one will covet your land when you go up three times each year to appear before [Yahweh] your God" (34:22-24). [In other words, you do not have to be afraid to go because no one is going to take your property while you are gone.]

The conclusion, which appears beginning in verse 27, leaves no doubt that this is a covenant ceremony.

"Write down these words, for in accordance with these words I have made a covenant with you and with Israel." Moses was there with [Yahweh] for forty days. . . . And he wrote on the tablets the words of the covenant—the Ten Commandments (34:27-28).

Now, notice how the commands to keep these festivals are interwoven in this re-establishment of the covenant. Clearly, keeping these festivals was a significant part of the covenant relationship with Yahweh.

The direct connection with the covenant is not as explicit in Leviticus 23, but it is certainly implicit. Look at verse 33: "The Lord said to Moses, 'Say to the Israelites: "On the fifteenth day of the seventh month, [this would be the Feast of Tabernacles] . . . the first day is a sacred assembly.''''' And in that word *assembly* is a connotation of pulling together the congregation of Israel.

Now, look at verse 37 and you will get a similar thing: "These are the LORD'S appointed feasts, which you are to proclaim as sacred assemblies for bringing offerings made to the LORD by fire—the burnt offerings and grain offerings, the sacrifices and drink offerings . . ." and so forth.

Now turn to Deuteronomy 16 where you will find that Moses, at the end of his life, is repeating the instructions for the three festivals. You will notice at the beginning of the chapter, "Observe the month of Abib and celebrate the Passover of the Lord your God because in the month of Abib he brought you out of Egypt by night. Sacrifice as the Passover. . . ." That is a one-day family festival, but then, as he goes ahead to the Feast of Unleavened Bread, that is a seven-day solemn assembly.

Now look at verse 5: "You must not sacrifice the Passover in any town the Lord your God gives you, except in the place he will choose as a dwelling for his Name. There you must sacrifice the Passover."

Then in verse 11, you will get a comparable statement, "Rejoice before [Yahweh] your God at the place he will choose as a dwelling for his Name."

Then in verse 16, "Three times a year all your [people] must appear before [Yahweh] your God at the place he will choose: at the Feast of Unleavened Bread, the Feast of Weeks and the Feast of Tabernacles."

So there were three times a year that these people, who did not have newspapers or telephones or radios, had to get in touch with one another. In New Testament times you are aware that the city of Jerusalem would fill with the crowds of Jews who came from all over the Mediterranean world for those festivals. The Passover is recorded in all three of the Gospels. You will remember that John 7 tells us about the Feast of Tabernacles. And one of the things that was done in connection with the Feast of Tabernacles was that they would go and bring water into the temple and, you will remember, it was in that kind of context, probably at the same time of day, some scholars say, on the eighth day of that festival. It was probably at the same time when the priests brought the offering of water from the pool of Siloam that Jesus stood and said, "If any man thirsts let him come unto me and drink."

So the Feast of Tabernacles was a part of Jesus' life. And what about the Feast of Pentecost? Jesus said, "Don't depart from Jerusalem until my Spirit comes." And the day the Spirit came was the Feast of Pentecost.

Now, there are plenty of gaps in our history and in our knowledge, between the Pentateuch and the New Testament. And so there may have been periods when all of Israel did not celebrate all three of the festivals. There are passages like the one in 1 Samuel, in the story of Hannah and Elqanah and Samuel, where the impression is given that there was only one major festival at Shiloh.[136] We do not have enough data to cover that kind of thing, and so scholars have a good time with that. But the reality is that the Pentateuch lays down the three, and no matter what the ebb and flow of the religious life and the fidelity of Israel in between, when you come to the end of the Old Testament and into the New Testament, there those three festivals are as an established part of Israel's life.

Now, what did these festivals do, and why did God order the people to come? I think if you will just stop to think, you will understand something of how the faith of Yahweh survived through those centuries between Moses and Jesus. And I think there is something there for us to learn about how the faith will survive when it is in periods of spiritual decline and in periods of opposition.

The first thing I want to say is, it gave all of these people a sense of belonging to one another. Now, later we can talk about it as a national consciousness, and I am sure that developed. I assume it developed, to some extent, very quickly. But normally, for a nation, you need a government. Yet it is not until you get to Saul and David that you have a king and not until David that you get a centralized government, really. And after that you had a nation with people with a national consciousness. But in the centuries before when they would meet together and look at each other, they would say, "Ah, we belong to each other." You see that in 1 Samuel. Look at the first chapter of 1 Samuel:

---

[136] [Editor's note] Second Kings 23:22 says that there had not been a Passover celebration since the time of the judges like the one Josiah led. But 2 Chronicles 30 tells of a Passover led by Hezekiah, which was unlike any since the days of Solomon.

> There was a certain man from Ramathaim, a Zuphite
> from the hill country of Ephraim, whose name was
> Elkanah son of Jeroham. . . . Year after year this man
> went up from his town to worship and to sacrifice to
> the Lord Almighty at Shiloh [Jerusalem is not there yet],
> where Hophni and Phinehas, the two sons of Eli, were
> priests of the Lord. Whenever the day came for Elkanah
> to sacrifice, he would give portions of the meat to his
> wife (1 Sam. 1:1-4).

What you have here is, I think, a picture of what held Israel
together—one of the factors that held Israel together during those years
when there was no political structure. It was neither their ethnicity nor
natural geographical boundaries that bound them together. It was the
fact that they had a common God, Yahweh, and a common history. They
had a common law that had been given to them at Sinai, and they had a
common cult, a common worship experience. So, when they came and
broke bread together, that is where their sense of identity and belonging
were. I do not believe anybody ever makes it alone, and God knows that.
You need me and I need you. We need each other, and this is one of the
ways God did it in the Old Testament.

Given all the possibilities for fragmentation and disintegration,
it really is an astounding thing that they survived. And there were clearly
plenty of times, if you read the text, when their survival seemed very
much in doubt. But they did survive, and I believe that is part of the
sovereignty of God, the work of His Holy Spirit in human history. His
church is not going to die, and His people are not going to die. But he
used these festivals as one of the ways of keeping them together.

Now, let me say a second thing about the festivals. I think they
had great pedagogical value, and the Old Testament makes that clear.
The festivals were teaching occasions and teaching instruments. You will
remember, in connection with the Passover, when it was established in
Exodus 12, God told Moses about the establishment of the festival, the
Feast of the Passover and then the Feast of Unleavened Bread. Now,
look at verse 24 of Exodus 12.

> "Obey these instructions as a lasting ordinance for you
> and your descendants. When you enter the land that

the Lord will give you as he promised, observe this
ceremony. And when your children ask you, 'What
does this ceremony mean to you?' then tell them, 'It
is the Passover sacrifice to the LORD, who passed over
the houses of the Israelites in Egypt and spared our
homes when he struck down the Egyptians.'" Then the
people bowed down and worshiped. The Israelites did
just what the LORD commanded Moses and Aaron (Ex.
12:24-28).

Remember that the Passover was a family affair. They were to
come to the central sanctuary, but they were to celebrate this part of the
festival in family groups. I think of that story from China when I think
of that. As I sat there that night and listened to this man and he said,
"They are children of believers or else they are friends of children of
believers or else they are friends of friends of children of believers," in
my imagination I could see a father and a mother in the evening pulling
the blinds so nobody on the outside could see, and bringing out of a hidden place, maybe from under the floor, a Bible. And then they sat with
their children and taught them.

Now, when they sat down to the Passover feast, like children
everywhere, the children would automatically say, "Why are we doing
this?" And there was the opportunity for teaching. You will find that that
was true of each one of these. Look at Deuteronomy 16:3 for a moment,
where the festivals are discussed. They are sitting at the table or planning
for the Passover. "Do not eat it with bread made with yeast, but for seven
days eat unleavened bread, the bread of affliction, because you left Egypt
in haste—so that all the days of your life you may remember the time of
your departure from Egypt."

What was wrong with leaven? I suppose if you left yeast long
enough in a bit of dough it would ferment and you did not want that.
One explanation is given here in Deuteronomy, and I think this is the
only place where this one occurs. He says it will just remind you how fast
you had to move that night. Your life was at stake, and God gave you
a chance and saved you. So, again, you see the pedagogical function of
that.

Now, turn to Leviticus 23 and you will find a little word about this in dealing with the Feast of Tabernacles. At the end of 23:

> "So beginning with the fifteenth day of the seventh month, after you have gathered the crops of the land, celebrate the festival to the Lord for seven days; the first day is a day of rest, and the eighth day also is a day of rest. On the first day you are to take choice fruit from the trees, and palm fronds [and] leafy branches. . . . Celebrate this as a festival to the LORD . . . a lasting ordinance for the generations to come. . . . Live in booths for seven days: All native-born Israelites are to live in booths [Why?] so your descendants will know that I had the Israelites live in booths when I brought them out of Egypt" (Lev. 23:39-43).

So the Feast of Tabernacles was an object lesson for the children, for the families, for Israel, to remind them of those forty years that God sustained them in their wilderness wandering.

Let me go back to that passage in Exodus 34 where Yahweh is graciously re-establishing the covenant on the other side of Israel's repudiation of it. Israel is still the elect; they are still the chosen people. Yahweh has chosen them. They are His. It is in that context of the giving of the covenant that He gives them the three festivals. There are some scholars who suggest that at each one of these festivals there was a public renewal of the covenant. I do not know of any evidence to prove that, but it makes sense in that keeping the feasts was an act of covenant obedience. And since the feasts were an instrument to let Israel know that they were in a covenant with Yahweh, it may well be that at every one of these, major portions of the covenant were read. We can think of Exodus 20–24, of Deuteronomy, and other passages that would remind them who they were.

Now, you and I would get a bit bored—that is not a part of our life. We would not enjoy going to church and sitting for several hours while somebody reads. But in the ancient world it seems to have been much more common. In ancient Greece they would read Homer by the hour to the public. It is a different world. But they were there to hear.

So I do not think there is any question but that this was part of the oral tradition. And as these people sat and listened, the parents listened and heard. Then they came home and for the next three or four months talked with their family about what they had heard there, and they checked each other out. The Lord wants us to know Him and where He did not have the means that we have today, He used other means like these.

There were three elements in all of these feasts. One was a historical element. There are scholars who will say that the historical element was not original, but you can only say that by creating a hypothetical reconstruction of the text, because that element is clearly there in what we have. The second element, because they were covenantal, was a future element. That was so because when you looked back to the history, the covenant had promise in it. God had chosen Abraham in Genesis, and in Exodus He chose Israel. He elected to enter into a covenant with them. He delivered Israel from Egyptian bondage, brought them to Sinai and gave them His law. He provided for them marvelously through the wilderness: quail on the wind, manna out of the air, water out of the rock. He blessed them with His word, which He gave at Sinai, and He gave them a future; there was a land before them. But in that covenant also was a mission. "Out of you is to come blessing for all the peoples of the earth."

I think back to how long I lived before I could find anything in the Old Testament as a basis for preaching missions. Of course, it was there all along. I was just too ignorant to see it, but there was this mission. They were a people with a future. That was one of the things that differentiated them. They were people with a role. They were people with a purpose; a nation with a purpose.

The third element to be found in all of the festivals was the naturalistic element. There was a natural element. There is a sense in which each one of these was a nature festival. You and I may not think too much about that, but if you will read the literature you will find that the historians of religion will find Canaanite roots for all three of these. And they will tell you very quickly that the Passover and the Feast of Unleavened Bread started in pre-Hebrew Canaan with the Shepherd's Festival. And so a Lamb was the central figure. Then a second nature element was joined to it in the Feast of Unleavened Bread, which was an agricultural festival because it came at the time when the first grain was coming in.

The Feast of Weeks came after the barley harvest had been completed, and the wheat harvest was beginning. And so now you had grain so you could live another year. And, of course, the Feast of Tabernacles was the final harvest festival at the end of the grape harvest.

But as the Bible reports these feasts, they are not nature festivals at all. To be sure they took place at the same time as the Canaanite nature festivals, and that may be intentional, but they are not nature festivals. That is, there is nothing in these feasts about plugging into the power of fertility, gaining a good harvest, and ensuring that the plants would come back from the dead in the spring. The fascinating thing is that Israel took these feasts that Canaan had and added another element to them that totally changed their character. They historicized all three and made them thanksgiving festivals for what God had done in redeeming them. And that changed the whole approach to nature.

Following is a quotation from Theodore Vriezen, in his *Outline of Old Testament Theology*:

> In contrast to the Canaanite feasts, the harvest festivals are no longer naturalistic in character. No longer devoted to the devotion of fertility, but linked with historical events, and insofar as they remained agricultural feasts, they were stamped as harvest thanksgiving festivals by the offerings of the first fruits.[137]

But notice an important point here. The Israelites did not abandon nature. Yahweh is not only the Lord of History, He is also the Lord of Nature. There is nothing wrong with having a harvest festival in the church. There is nothing wrong with us having Thanksgiving. There is nothing wrong with us celebrating the fact that we are going to have food to eat this winter. Do you know how many millions of people in the world are not sure of that or are not going to be sure? Let us not separate the doctrine of creation from the doctrine of redemption. In a remarkable way, the Hebrews pulled these together, and it meant that their festivals were different, but they did not lose, they gained.

---

[137] Vriezen, *Outline of Old Testament Theology*, 285-85.

Lecture 20

* * * * * * * * *

Prophetic Charisma
in Israel

You will notice that Eichrodt, when he comes to deal with leadership in Israel, begins with what he calls charismatic leaders. Now most of us think of that term *charismatic* in terms of the so-called "Pentecostal" revivals that took place in various segments of the church during the twentieth century. But the reality is that the term *charismatic* was not actually given to the twentieth century by the church, but by a German sociologist by the name of Max Weber. In 1920 he wrote a book called *The Protestant Ethic and the Spirit of Capitalism.*[138] This book is what he is best known for outside of sociological circles, but he did a great deal to promote the sociology of religion, which is one of those hot areas of interest today.

---

[138] Max Weber, *The Protestant Ethic and the Spirit of Capitalism*, tr. T. Parsons (New York: Scribner, 1958).

Now, when Max Weber used "charismatic," he used it to describe
the power of attraction that a person with a magnetic personality or with
great gifts of leadership has; the way he or she is able to draw together
a body of followers. When he gives examples, he lists such persons as
Alexander the Great, Napoleon, Buddha, Moses, Jesus, the apostle Paul,
and Mohammed. So you get an interesting perspective there.

The *Dictionary of Sociology* defines *charisma* or *charismatic leader* in
this way: "The supposed possession on the part of some individuals of
exceptional or superhuman powers, frequently so indicated by a sign,
perhaps by a miracle, and indicated to such a degree that individuals are,
from the standpoint of believers, properly regarded as leaders deserving
of absolute trust and devotion."[139] So that is a social scientist defining
what charisma is and what charismatic leadership consists of.

When Eichrodt begins to talk about the "seers,"—the early
prophets in Israel—you will find that he compares these seers,[140] these
people who can see, with similar figures in other Ancient Near Eastern
religious and national groups. One of those he refers to is Balaam in the
book of Numbers (24:3ff).[141] And then he refers to people that have a
gift of clairvoyance. He says this often takes place during "ecstatic disturbances of consciousness."[142] And so, in those moments or periods of
ecstatic disturbances of consciousness, the word *frenzy* will oftentimes
be used. In those periods the person will have visual or auditory revela-
tions. They will see a vision or hear a voice. They may be fully conscious
at the time, or it can be that they are asleep. You will remember that
Samuel heard a voice in the night, and when he awakened to that voice
he thought that Eli had called him. So, this "seeing" can come in full consciousness, or it can come in a state of frenzy or ecstasy, or it can come
in sleep.

In the Bible you have clairvoyance or pre-vision indicated in
a case like Samuel. Saul's servant persuaded him to go and ask Samuel
where his father's lost donkeys were. But Samuel knew that Saul was
coming and that Saul was to be the king of Israel. He had knowledge

[139] Henry P. Fairchild, *Dictionary of Sociology* (New York: Philosophical
Library, 1944).
[140] The Heb. word is *ro'eh* which is a participle of the verb "to see," *ra'ah.*
[141] Eichrodt, *Theology*, vol. 1, 296.
[142] Ibid.

ahead of time. (1 Sam. 9:15-16).

Eichrodt goes on to say that all of these features are found in heathenism [sic] as well as in Israel. Then he makes an interesting statement that fits with what we have been talking about—the question of continuity and discontinuity. "The soil from which Israelite religion springs is the same as that of other Oriental peoples."[143]

Here is an example of what we are talking about from the Ancient Near East. It is from Egypt. It can be found in J. B. Pritchard's *Ancient Near Eastern Texts*.[144] It is the story told by an Egyptian by the name of Wenamon. Wenamon was sent by the Egyptian court to Byblos in Phoenicia to get wood to make a boat for the Egyptian god Amon-Re. The cedars of Lebanon were prized all over the ancient world, from Egypt to Solomon to the Assyrians. Wenamon was a hard-luck character. Before he ever got to Byblos, he had been robbed and lost both his money and his ship. When he did get to Byblos, he found some of the Tjekker people, of the same ethnic group as those who had robbed him, so he seized a cache of money from them. All this infuriated the king of Byblos, so he told Wenamon to get out. Wenamon replied that he would as soon as the king would get a ship for him. This went on for twenty-nine days.

But one day something different happened. Here it is from Pritchard:

> Now, while the prince of Byblos was making his offering to his gods, the god seized one of his youths and made him possessed. And [the lad] said to [the king], "Bring up the god. Bring the messenger who is carrying him. Amon is the one who has sent him. He is the one who made him come." While the possessed youth was having his frenzy on this night, I had already found a ship headed for Egypt. . . .[145]

The result was that the king's attitude toward Wenamon changed radically, and eventually the Egyptian got his lumber. But notice that the

[143] Ibid., 297.
[144] Pritchard, *Ancient Near Eastern Texts*.
[145] Ibid. 26.

message came while the servant boy was in a frenzy.

W. F. Albright, the archeologist and biblical scholar from earlier in the twentieth century, in his *From the Stone Age to Christianity*,[146] discusses the Wenamon text and ecstacism in the Ancient Near East. He says that in Assyrian descriptions from the first millennium, we frequently find references to the *makhkhu*. He says this is a kind of priest or diviner. Notice that he equates the two. In Assyrian there is an adverb that comes from this noun, and that word, *makhkhutash*, means "madly" or "like a madman" or "in a state of madness."

The same kind of thing could be found in other cultures. In the Greek world you had what was called a Dionysiac frenzy. It was associated with the god, Dionysius, who was thought to act like that. This phenomenon is first reported in Asia Minor. Toward the end of the second millennium, it swept through Greece and eventually into Syria-Palestine. Here is what Socrates says on this theme of a person being taken out of himself in a kind of madness. Socrates is speaking to the orator Ion, who was an artist at speaking and influencing an audience.

> I perceive and I will proceed to explain to you what I imagine to be the reason for what we are talking about here. The gift which you possess of speaking excellently about Homer is not an art, but, as I was just saying, an inspiration; there is a divinity moving you, like that contained in the stone which Euripides calls a magnet, but which is commonly known as the stone of Heraclea. This stone not only attracts iron rings, but also imparts to them a similar power of attracting other rings; and sometimes you may see a number of pieces of iron and rings suspended from one another so as to form quite a long chain: and all of them derive their power of suspension from the original stone. In like manner the Muse first of all inspires men herself; and from these inspired persons a chain of other persons is suspended, who take the inspiration. For all good poets, epic as

---

[146] William F. Albright, *From the Stone Age to Christianity: Monotheism and the Historical Process,* 2nd ed. (Garden City: Doubleday, 1957), 304.

well as lyric, compose their beautiful poems not by art, but because they are inspired and possessed. And as the Corybantian revelers when they dance are not in their right mind, so the lyric poets are not in their right minds when they are composing their beautiful strains: but when falling under the power of music and meter they are inspired and possessed; like Bacchic maidens who draw milk and honey from the rivers when they are under the influence of Dionysius, but not when they are in their right mind. And the soul of the lyric poet does the same, as they themselves say: for they tell us that they bring songs from honeyed fountains, culling them out of the gardens and dells of the Muses; they, like the bees, winging their way from flower to flower. And this is true. For the poet is a light and winged and holy thing, and there is no invention in him until he has been inspired and out of his senses, and the mind is no longer in him: when he has not attained to this state, he is powerless and unable to utter his oracles. Many are the noble words in which poets speak concerning the actions of men; but like yourself when speaking about Homer, they do not speak of them by any rules of art: they are simply inspired to utter that to which the Muse impels them and that only; and when inspired, one of them will make dithyrambs, another hymns of praise, another choral strains, another epic or iambic verses— and he who is good at one is not good at any other kind of verse: for not by art does a poet sing, but by power divine. Had he learned by rules of art, he would have known how to speak not of one theme only but of all: and therefore God takes away the minds of poets, and uses them as his ministers, as he also uses diviners and holy prophets, in order that we who hear them may know them to be speaking not of themselves who utter these priceless words in a state of unconsciousness, but that God Himself is the speaker, and that through them He is conversing with us. And Tynnichus the Chalcidian affords a striking instance of what I am saying: he wrote nothing that anyone would care to remember but the famous poem which is in everyone's mouth, one of the finest poems ever written, simply an invention of the Muses as he himself says. For in this way the God [sic] would seem to indicate to us and not allow us to doubt that these beautiful poems are not human, or the work of man, but divine and the work of God. And the poets are only the interpreters of the Gods [sic] by whom they are severally possessed. Was not this the lesson by which the God [sic] intended to teach when by the mouth of the worst of the poets he sang the best of songs? Am I not right, Ion?

Ion. Yes, indeed, Socrates. I feel that you are: for your words touch my soul and I am persuaded that good poets, by divine inspiration interpret the things of the Gods [sic] to us. . . .

Soc. I wish you would frankly tell me, Ion, what I am going to ask of you: When you produce the greatest effect upon the audience in the recitation of some striking passage, such as the apparition of Odysseus leaping forth on the floor, recognized by the suitors and casting his arrows at his feet, or the description of Achilles rushing at Hector or the sorrows of Andromache, Hecuba or Priam—are you in your right mind? Are you not carried out of yourself and does not your soul in an ecstasy seem to be among the persons or places of which you are speaking, whether they are in Ithaca or Troy or whatever may be the scene of the poem?

Ion. That proof strikes home to me, Socrates. For I must frankly confess that at the tale of pity my eyes are filled with tears, and when I speak of horrors my hair stands on end and my heart throbs.

Soc. Well, Ion, and what are we to say of a man who at a sacrifice or festival, when he is dressed in holiday attire, and has golden crowns upon his head,

of which nobody has robbed him, appears weeping
or panic-stricken in the presence of more than twenty
thousand friendly faces, when there is no one despoil-
ing or wronging him—is he in his right mind, or is he
not?

> *Ion.* No, indeed, Socrates. I must say that strictly
speaking, he is not in his right mind.[147]

Euripides tells us of a similar eruption among the devotees of
Bacchus and, of course, it's not hard to understand that, since Bacchus
was a god of wine. W. F. Albright, in commenting on all of this, notes
that in 1 Kings 18 the prophets of Baal work themselves into a frenzy
as they try to combat the challenge of Elijah. As a result of these kinds
of things there are those who want to major on the similarities between
the ecstatics of the Ancient Near East and the biblical prophets. They
would draw a straight line from Dionysiac frenzy to Isaiah; it is a sort of
evolutionary development; there is a continuity between the two. The
second stage may be better than the first, but there is an essential continuity between them.

But I want to take you back to Eichrodt. A moment ago I
quoted him to the effect that Israel's religion sprang from the fertile soil
of "heathenism." Now, here is his next line: "But in Israel the form is
pressed into the service of quite different ideas and aims; it is filled with
new meaning."[148] With that in the background I want to do something
different today. Go back to my theme that two people doing the same
thing may not be doing the same thing. Couple that with the idea that
God meets us where we are, using what is familiar to us, and what communicates to us. Think of how the word of God comes to us as well as
what the word of God is.

I want to pull out an incident from the Wesleyan heritage.[149] It
was on May 20, 1738. Charles Wesley said,

---

[147] *The Dialogues of Plato,* 2 vols., tr. B. Jowett (New York: Random House, 1920), vol. 1, 288-90.
[148] Eichrodt, *Theology*, vol. 1, 296.
[149] The following account is taken from *The Journal of the Rev. Charles Wesley M. A.* (Taylors, S. C.: Methodist Reprint Society, 1977).

I waked much disappointed and continued all day in great dejection, which the sacrament did not in the least abate. Nevertheless, God would not suffer me to doubt the truth of his promises [about peace of heart and forgiveness of sins]. Mr. Bray [remember that name], too, seemed troubled at my not yet believing and complained of his uneasiness and want of patience. "But so it is with me," says he, "when my faith begins to fail God gives me some sign to support it." He then opened a Testament and read the first words that presented, Matthew 9:1, "And he entered into a ship and passed over and came into his own city and . . . they brought to him a man sick of the palsy, lying on a bed, and Jesus seeing their faith said unto the sick of the palsy, 'Son, be of good cheer, thy sins are forgiven thee.' And behold, certain of the scribes and pharisees said within themselves, 'This man blasphemes.' And Jesus, knowing their hearts, said, 'Wherefore think ye evil in your hearts? For whether it is easier to say, Thy sins be forgiven thee, or to say, Arise and walk? But that ye may know that the Son of Man hath power on earth to forgive sins, then sayeth he to the sick of the palsy, 'Arise, take up thy bed and go into thine own house.' And he arose and departed to his house. And when the multitude saw it they marvelled and glorified God which had given such power unto man."

It was a long while before he could read this through for tears of joy: and I saw herein, and firmly believed, that his faith would be available for the healing of me.[150]

At this time Charles Wesley was suffering seriously from pleurisy. He had been in great pain, and the physicians had bled him, and he had bled himself to try to get rid of the pain. Now remember, Charles Wesley is the Oxford graduate. Mr. Bray is

---

[150] Ibid., 145.

at the other end of the educational spectrum, but it is Mr. Bray who is showing the Oxford priest how to find Christ. Here is Charles' journal entry for the following day

> *Sunday, May 21, 1738*—I waked in hope and expectation of his coming. At nine my brother and some friends came and sang an hymn to the Holy Ghost. My comfort and hope were hereby increased. In about half an hour they went: I betook myself to prayer; the substance as follows: O Jesus, thou hast said, "I will come unto you;" Thou hast said, "I will send the Comforter unto you;" Thou hast said, "My Father and I will come unto you and make our abode with you." Thou art God who canst not lie; I wholly rely upon thy most true promise: accomplish it in Thy time and manner.
>
> Having said this, I was composing myself to sleep in quietness and peace, when I heard one come in (Mrs. Musgrave, I thought, by the voice) and I heard her say, "In the name of Jesus of Nazareth, arise, and believe, and thou shalt be healed of all thy infirmities." I wondered how it should enter into her head to speak in that manner. The words struck me to the heart. I sighed, and said within myself, "O that Christ would speak thus to me!" I lay musing and trembling: then thought, "But what if it should be him? I will send at least to see." I rang, and Mrs. Turner coming, I desired her to send up Mrs. Musgrave. She went down, and, returning, said, "Mrs. Musgrave has not been here." My heart sunk within me at the word, and I hoped it might be Christ indeed. However, I sent her down again to in-quire, and felt in the meantime a strange palpitation of the heart. I said, yet feared to say, "I believe. I believe." She came up again and said, "It was I, a weak, sinful creature spoke; but the words were Christ's. He com-manded me to say them, and so constrained me that I could not forebear."
>
> I sent for Mr. Bray. I asked Mr. Bray whether

I believed. He answered, I ought not to doubt it; it was Christ spoke to me. He knew it; and willed us to pray together: "but first," said he, "I will read what I have casually opened upon: [If I did that, I do not think I would find the will of God. But when Mr. Bray did, it is interesting what took place.] "Blessed is the man whose unrighteousness is forgiven and whose sin is covered: blessed is the man to whom the Lord imputes no sin, and in whose spirit is no guile." Still I felt a violent opposition and reluctance to believe; yet still the Spirit of God strove with my own and the evil spirit, till by degrees he chased away the darkness of my unbelief. I found myself convinced, I knew not how nor when; and immediately fell to intercession.

Mr. Bray then told me, his sister [Mrs. Turner] had been ordered by Christ to come and say those words to me. This she afterwards confirmed, and she related to me more at large the manner of her believing. At night, and nearly the moment I was taken ill, she dreamt she heard one knock at the door: she went down, and opened the door; saw a person in white; caught hold of and asked who he was; was answered, "I am Jesus Christ," and cried out with great vehemence, "Come in, come in!"

She waked in a fright. It was immediately suggested to her, "You must not mind this: it is all a dream, an illusion." She continued wavering and uneasy all Friday till evening prayers. No sooner were they begun than she found herself full of the power of faith, so that she could scarce contain herself, and almost doubted whether she was sober. At the same time she was enlarged in love and prayer for all mankind and commanded to go and assure me from Christ of my recovery, soul and body. She returned home, repeating with all joy and triumph, "I believe, I believe": yet her heart failed her, and she durst not say the words to me that night.[151]

---

[151] Ibid., 146-48

Do you know the social chasm between Mr. Bray's sister and Charles? Do you know the cultural chasm and the audacity that a woman like this would have to have to speak to a priest of the church in such a way as that?

> On Sunday morning she took Mr. Bray aside, burst into tears, and informed him of the matter; objecting she was a poor, weak, sinful creature, and should she go to a minister? She could not do it; nor rest till she did. He asked whether she had ever found herself so before. "No, never." "Well then," said he, "go. Remember Jonah. You declare promises, not threatenings. Go in the name of the Lord. Fear not your own weakness. Speak you the words: Christ will do the work. Out of the mouths of babes and sucklings hath He ordained strength."

> They prayed together and she then went up, but durst not come in till she had prayed again by herself. About six minutes after she had left him, he found and felt, while she was speaking the words, that Christ was with us. I never heard words uttered with like solemnity. The sound of her voice was entirely changed into that of Mrs. Musgrave. (If I can be sure anything sensible). I rose and looked into the scriptures. The words that first presented were, "And now, Lord, what is my hope? Truly, my hope is even in thee." I then cast down my eye and met, "He hath put a new song in my mouth, even a thanksgiving unto our God. Many shall see and fear and shall put their trust in the Lord." Afterwards I opened upon Isaiah 40:1, "Comfort ye, comfort ye my people, saith your God: speak ye comfortably unto Jerusalem, and cry unto her, that her warfare is accomplished, that her iniquity is pardoned, for she has received of the Lord's hand, double for all her sins."

> I now found myself at peace with God, and rejoiced in hope of loving Christ. My temper for the rest of the day was mistrust of my own great, but before

unknown, weakness. I saw that by faith I stood; by the
continual support of faith which kept me from falling,
though of myself I am ever sinking into sin. I went to
bed still sensible of my own weakness. (I humbly hope
to be more and more so), yet confident of Christ's protection.[152]

That is the conversion of Charles Wesley. Here is what we find
in his journal for the next day:

An old friend called to see me, under great apprehen-
sions that I was running mad. His fears were not a little increased by my telling him the prayer of faith had
healed me when sick at Oxford. He "looked to see the
rays of light about my head," he said, and more to that
purpose. I begged him for his own sake not to pass
sentence till he had his full evidence concerning me.
This he could not promise, but faintly prayed me to flee
from London, and in despair of me, he took his leave.
It was morning before I could get to sleep. Many emotions of pride arose, and were continually beaten down
by Christ my King. The devil also tempted me to impa-
tience through pain; but God turned it into an occasion
of resignation. *Tuesday, May 23,* [the second day after
his conversion.] I waked under the protection of Christ
and gave myself up, soul and body, to him. At nine
I began an hymn upon my conversion. But was persuaded to break off, for fear of pride. Mr. Bray coming,
encouraged me to proceed in spite of Satan, I prayed
Christ to stand by me, and finished the hymn.[153]

You see, in his thinking for him to affirm that he had been forgiven of
sins, would be the ultimate arrogance. So, he is in that double world, as it
were. Now, let me read for you from one year later, June 4, 1739:

[152] Ibid., 148-49.
[153] Ibid., 150-51.

I had some conversation with Mrs. Stonehouse, surely a gracious lovely soul; then with him. We joined in prayer; and I was better reconciled to their sudden marriage. I met Mr. Shaw, the self-ordained priest. He was brim-full of proud wrath and fierceness. His spirit suited to his principles. I could do him no good; but was kept calm and benevolent towards him; therefore he could do me no harm. I stood by George Whitefield while he preached on the mount in Blackheath. The cries of the wounded were heard on every side. What has Satan gained by turning [Whitefield] out of the churches?

Tuesday, June 5—I was with [Whitefield] at Blendon. Bowers and Bray followed us thither, drunk with the spirit of delusion. [Remember, Bray is the one who helped Charles find saving faith. It is interesting in the *Journal* to see the indications of Bray's increasing fascination with what we might call "manifestations" of the Spirit during that spring of 1739.] George honestly said, "They are two grand enthusiasts."

Wednesday, June 6—Above 60 of the poor people had passed the night in Mr. Delamotte's barn, singing and rejoicing. I sang and prayed with them before the door. George's exhortation left them all in tears.

At the society in the evening, Shaw pleaded for his spirit of prophecy; charged me with love of preeminence; with making my proselytes twofold more the children of the devil than before. Fitch said he looked upon me as delivered over to Satan, etc. They declared themselves no longer members of the Church of England. We were kept tolerably meek; and parted at eleven. Now am I clear of them. By renouncing the Church, they have discharged me.

Thursday, June 7—Many of our friends have been pestered by the French Prophets, and such-like *pretenders* to inspiration. J. Bray is the foremost to listen to them, and often carried away with their delusions. Today I had the happiness to find at his house the famous

Prophetess Lavington. She was sitting by Bowers; and Mrs. Sellers on the other side. The Prophet Wise asked, "Can a man attain perfection here?" I answered, "No." The Prophetess began groaning. I turned and said, "If you've anything to speak, speak it." She lifted up her voice like the lady on the tripod [sic] and cried out vehemently, "Look for perfection; I say, absolute perfection!" I was minded to rebuke her; but God gave me uncommon recollection, and command of spirit so that I sat quiet and replied not. I offered at last to sing, which she allowed, but did not join. Bray pressed me to stay, and hear her pray. They knelt; I stood. She prayed most pompously, addressing to Bray with particular encomiums. I durst not say Amen. She concluded with an horrible hellish laugh; and endeavored to turn it off. She showed violent displeasure against our baptized Quaker saying, "God had showed her, He would destroy all outward things."

Whit Sunday, June 10—I read the Society my account of the Prophetess. All were shocked but poor J. Bray. He now *appeared*, and strongly withstood me, and vindicated that Jezebel. I gave no place to him, no, not for a moment. My natural temper was kept down, and changed into a passionate concern for him, which I expressed in prayers and tears. All besides him were melted down. I kissed him, and testified my love; but could make no impression.

Tuesday, June 12—I heard more of my Prophetess, who told a brother that she could command Christ to come to her in what shape she pleases, as a dove, an eagle, etc. The devil owed her a shame by bringing her again to Bray's. Wise, her gallant, came first; whom I urged with a plain question whether he had or had not cohabited with her. He was *forced* to confess he had. J. Bray was vehement in her defense; when she came in, she flew upon us like a tigress; tried to outface me; insisted that she was immediately inspired. I prayed. She cried, "The devil is in [Charles Wesley]. [He] is a fool, a blockhead, a blind leader of the blind, put[s] out the people's eyes, etc." She roared outrageously, said that it was the lion in her. (True; but not the Lion of Judah.) She *would* come to the Society in spite of me. If not, they would all go down.

I asked, "Who is on the Lord's side? Who for the old Prophets rather than the new. Let them follow me." They followed me into the preaching room. I prayed, and expounded the lesson with extraordinary power. The women, several of them, gave an account of their conversion through my ministry. Our dear Brother Bowers confessed himself convinced of his error. We rejoiced and triumphed in the name of the Lord our God.

Wednesday, June 13—My brother returned. We had over the Prophetess's affair before the Society. Bray and Bowers were much humbled. All agreed to disown the Prophetess. Brother Hall proposed expelling Shaw and Wolf. We consented, *nem. con.*, that their names should be erased out of the Society-book, because they disowned themselves members of the Church of England.[154]

Now, let me share with you some of the hymn that Charles Wesley wrote the day after his conversion.

Where shall my wandering soul begin?
How shall I all to heaven aspire?
A slave redeemed from death and sin.
A brand plucked from eternal fire.

How shall I equal triumphs raise
or sing my great Deliverer's praise?
O how shall I the goodness tell,
Father, which thou to me hast showed.

[154] Ibid., 234-38.

That I a child of wrath and hell,
I should be called a child of God.
Should know, should feel, my sins forgiven,
blessed with this antepast of Heaven.

I hope you know that hymn. It was written on May 22. He was
converted on the 21st. One year later, on May 21, he wrote a hymn in
honor of his conversion, his spiritual birthday. That hymn begins:

Glory to God and praise and love
be ever, ever given.
By saints below and saints above,
the church in earth and heaven.
On this glad day the glorious sun
of righteousness arose.
On my benighted soul he shone
and filled it with repose.
Sudden expired the legal stripe,
was then I ceased to grieve,
my second real, and living life
I then began to live.
Then with my heart I first believed,
believed with faith divine,
pow'r with the holy ghost received
to call the Savior mine.
I felt my Lord's atoning blood
close to my soul applied.
Me, me he loved. The Son of God,
for me—for me he died.
O for a thousand tongues to sing
my dear redeemer's praise,
the glories of my God and king,
the triumphs of his grace.
My gracious Master and my God,
assist me to proclaim,
to spread through all the earth abroad,
the honors of thy name.

The poem continues for twelve more stanzas. Now, that is what he wrote on the anniversary of his conversion. The whole story is a little different from some of our simplistic approaches to conversion, is it not? But the one thing that is essential here is that each of us hears the word of God. I am so grateful that all that Genesis tells us is, "And the Lord said to Abraham, 'Leave your country.'" We do not know how he did it, we do not know where he did it, we do not know what the circumstances were. And that is good, because if we were told those details, we would always be trying to reduplicate them. That is one of the unfortunate by-products of our human condition; we keep thinking that if we pay proper attention to the physical and the external—the bodily—the spiritual can be left on its own. The very opposite should be the case.

I have taken the time to rehearse this story for you in order to underline this point: God may work in many different external ways, but the question is, is He speaking through them? No matter what the pattern may be culturally or otherwise for the living God, if He is in it, He will transform it. Notice that there were two experiences of "divine" inspiration in this account, one from Miss Bray and one from Miss Lavington. Each of them claimed to have a message from God. But one was confirmed by the events and the other, though it could even take in someone like Mr. Bray for a while, was proven false. The final issue was not the outward manifestations, but is God manifestly in it?

It is because of that sort of thing, I imagine, that Eichrodt felt compelled to give such a long treatment to ecstasy in his work. He was writing at a time when there was a great fascination with comparative religion and when the evolutionary explanation for Israel's religion was quite strong. By comparison, you will notice that Childs in his *Biblical Theology of the Old and New Testaments* gives very little consideration to this. One of the reasons was that Albright and his students were very successful in the 1940s, '50s, and '60s at showing the weaknesses of the evolutionary model. But in Eichrodt's day, in the '20s and '30s, it was still necessary to take account of that whole approach. It is to his credit that he was able to break out of that mindset. But to do it he had to take account of it.[155]

---

[155] [Editor's note] Already by the time Dr. Kinlaw first delivered these lectures, the pendulum had begun to swing back in the evolutionary direction. That swing has

One of the most important books written on the subject of the prophets is by Jewish scholar Abraham Heschel. It is simply called *The Prophets*.[156] Writers before him had sought to deal with the psychology of the prophets, but Heschel was able to link the psychological and the spiritual in the most helpful ways. So he has a section on whether the prophets were mad and whether that was what enabled them to give to us the oracles they did. That sounds a little like Socrates, does it not?

But it is not the psychological questions that interest me. It is the meaning of what was taking place. That was my purpose for reading you the excerpts from Charles Wesley's journal. It is not the "how" that interests me. It is the "what," that is, whether a person has really encountered the living God. That is the big issue, because salvation is in Yahweh alone. You may have an experience that is a near duplicate of the experience of a person who has met Yahweh, but if you have not met Yahweh, no matter how much the experiences are alike, the differences are greater than the similarities. One of them is a contact with ultimate reality and ultimate truth, and the other is probably a contact primarily with ourselves.

---

only increased in the years since. This makes Eichrodt's approach, now some eighty years old, all the more valuable.

[156] Abraham Heschel, *The Prophets* (New York: Harper & Row, 1962).

Lecture 21

. . . .

"The Word" as Divine Revelation

In this lecture I want to move on in our treatment of Israelite prophecy to a discussion of "the word." In Hebrew religion and in the Old Testament, the primary way Yahweh reveals Himself is by the word. It is confirmed, Edmond Jacob says, by every book in the Old Testament.[157] This is Yahweh's prime method for demonstrating that He is the living God and that He is a Person, that He is personal. In fact, He is the ultimate personal. This makes Him different from the other gods of the world. In the diatribes against the gods in Isaiah 46 and Jeremiah 10, one of the things they say about these gods that we make with our own hands and our own minds is that these gods cannot move or speak. The same is true elsewhere in the Old Testament; the gods cannot move—you have to carry them—and they cannot speak. So, when Yahweh, the Person,

---

[157] Jacob, *Theology of the Old Testament*, 127.

speaks and says, "Listen," that is different. And when He says, "Walk before me and be thou perfect," that is very different from the rest of the gods of the world.

Now, in that ancient world the understanding of the concept "word" was far different from what it is in our world. In our world words come and go very easily. We are drowning in a sea of words and most of them mean very little. Too often they are just sounds. But in that world, a word was more than just a sound. Jacob expresses the difference in this way: "A word was an operative reality."[158] It is more than just a sound. It represents a reality, and because it does it becomes a reality itself, with its own operative power. Thus, when a word was spoken, the ancient world looked upon it as something that came into existence, had a life of its own and a power of its own, as if it had that existence and that power apart from the one who spoke it. So when Yahweh speaks to the prophet and gives him a word, a message, you can write a history of that message and its influence that is, in a sense, separate from Yahweh Himself, though it is His word.

That explains the emphasis in the Old Testament, as well as in the rest of the ancient world, on blessings and cursings. Remember that plea from Balak, king of Moab, to Balaam, "Now come and put a curse on these people. . . . For I know that those you bless are blessed, and those you curse are cursed" (Num. 22:6). Balak believed that if he could just get the prophet to speak the curse, however Balaam may have felt about it, it would have its adverse effect on Israel. We do not feel that way. We call certain kinds of speech "profanity," but it is just considered a matter of bad manners or poor taste to use it. We do not really think it means anything. But what if it does? What if the ancients had it more right than we do? What would you do with an expression like, "God damn it!" if you really believed that words have that kind of power? Their world looked upon words as having a sort of sacredness, a sanctity, and also a dynamic character. That is what Edmond Jacob meant when he said a word was an operative reality.

There is validity in that concept. Have you ever gotten into a conversation where you felt you were under great pressure? You were not aware you were being pressured until suddenly you found yourself in

---

[158] Ibid.

a corner and you said something you would rather not have. But after it was said, you realized that for the foreseeable future, every time you met that person there were going to be three of you instead of two? If there was any way you could have, you would have pulled it back, but if you said anything to clear it, then there would be *four* of you instead of three? There is power in a word.

I was doing doctoral work at Brandeis University in Waltham, Massachusetts, a suburb of Boston, and pastoring in northeastern New York State, traveling about 380 miles each weekend and sweating. I had a marvelous secretary. It was a growing church, and I was hanging on by the skin of my teeth, and my secretary was the one who kept me hanging on. She was a very gifted administrator. She handled all of my finances because Elsie had just delivered twins and that made five children, and Elsie definitely did not have time to take care of finances. One day I knew I had a bill that would have to be paid that week, but I did not know how much it would be. So, I signed a check and put it in the bottom of the left drawer in my desk in my church office. I put everything in the drawer on top of it and it was down underneath everything. I left a note for her and told her where it was and that she was to fill in the amount and send it off when the bill arrived.

When I came back that next weekend, I got a phone call from my bank. The manager said, "Did you write a check for $438 to Mr. So and So?" I said, "No, I've never heard of such a person." He said, "Well, we think you did." And I said, "You are kidding." And the manager said, "No, you better look at this." So I went down and looked and there was my name on that check to a man I had never heard of. Now, what happened was that a man from Montreal, Canada, was headed for Florida, and he came down U.S. 9 and passed right in front of our church in the middle of the night. Somehow or other he got into the church, read that note, and found that check in the bottom of that drawer. And do you know what he did? He wrote it for the exact amount of the balance in the checkbook. He cleaned me out. And the banker said, "We've already honored it because it's your signature." Now, you see, there is a sense in which a word is an expression of a reality, a hypostasis, as we know the term from the Trinitarian discussions.[159] So when that fellow took that

---

[159] *Hypostasis* literally means "to stand under." In some parts of the church

check to the bank in Florida, there were two of us there because I was there bearing witness that that was my check.

All this illustrates how "word" is understood in the Old Testament. And when God gives you His word, there is a sense in which it is an hypostasis. We don't have time to go into that now, but there is a direct logical line and development from that to John 1:1. And there is a direct line of development from that to our looking at the Bible and calling it the Word of God. We don't worship the Scripture, but my name on that check had a stronger sense and power about it than my voice would over the telephone. So, keep this kind of thinking in mind when you read the simple statement in the Old Testament, "And the word of the Lord came unto. . . ."

The most common term for "word" in Hebrew is *dabar*. Edmond Jacob, noting that there is a verbal root having the same three consonants, which means something like "to come behind," has suggested that *dabar* can be defined as a projection forward of something lying behind, thus a projection from the one speaking. He goes from that to suggest that *dabar* represents a transition from what is first of all in the heart to the external act.[160, 161] and so you can take my word and, in a sense, separate it from me, and if I lie to you, you will separate the two and say, "Those are two different things, very clearly."

Whether we agree with Jacob or not, we do know that in Hebrew, interestingly enough, this word *dabar* not only means "word," but also, "thing," "event," or "matter." That tends to substantiate the idea of hypostasis, that the speech becomes something that has existence in

---

it has been used to speak of the three persons being differentiated and yet being essentially one. In other parts it has been used more to speak of the persons. I am using the term here somewhat in the sense of "to stand in for." I am not suggesting that the Scriptures are of the same essence as God any more than my signature was of the same essence as me. However, I am saying that the Scriptures stand in for God and represent Him as though He were actually present. And when you follow this theme out all the way, the Word of God (John 1:1ff.) is *indeed* of the same essence as God the Father and God the Spirit.

[160] Jacob, *Theology of the Old Testament*, 128.

[161] [Editor's note] This is not a common understanding today. The normal verb form is found in the Piel stem, indicating that it is formed from the noun. Thus, "He worded." For a good treatment see *New International Dictionary of New Testament Theology*, vol 2, 912-15. The article contains a helpful bibliography, including treatments of "word" as a hypostasis.

itself. This is also reflective of the Hebrew reluctance to distinguish between thought and action.

There are two other terms that are used. Both of them are noun forms of the verb *'amar*, "to say or speak." They are *'imrah* (37 occ.) *and 'emer* (48 occ.). Interestingly, neither of these terms occurs in prose, but only in poetry. They refer to that which has been spoken, while *dabar* is used both for the written word and the spoken word.

These two roots (*dbr* and *'mr*) are commonly found together in the introductions to the prophetic oracles. So you find Jeremiah saying, "Hear the word, *dabar*, which Yahweh spoke, *dibber*, to you, O house of Israel. Thus says, *'amar*, Yahweh." So, you get two usages of the *dbr* root and one of the *'mr* root in one sentence, or in one opening communication. You will find Jeremiah saying in the next chapter, "The word, *dabar*, which came unto Jeremiah from Yahweh, saying, *le'mor*. . . ." So, these two roots form a pair that is used again and again in Scripture to speak about the fact that God, Yahweh, is a speaking God.

This is not to say that it is only among the Hebrews that the Divine was thought to speak. This idea is found, to some extent, in the other literatures of the Ancient Near East. It appears in Sumerian hymns, in Egyptian decrees, and in Babylonian oracles. But as in other areas, it is a case of superficial similarities and essential differences. The big difference, in the light of my earlier illustration, is whose name is on the check. In the other countries of the Ancient Near East, the word that had this "hypostasization," this life of its own, this word that came in its power and its mystery, was multiplex. It was not one word, it was many words, because you had many speakers, not a single one. But in the Old Testament you can speak of the word of Yahweh, of the Lord God. That message was unified, with all parts related to the other parts. In the rest of the world you had words that dealt with isolated, unrelated events. So, there was no possibility of pulling the whole thing together with a sense of unified history and of a unified creation. There are divine words from the different gods, so there are many words, but in Israel, something different occurs. The word of Yahweh comes to be related to His revelation of Himself. And that revelation is in history, a single history. It is Yahweh's word that brought the creation into existence in the beginning. "And God said *vʾamar 'elohim*. . ." and there it was. Along with His creative word, there is His interpretive word: He is the one who speaks and gives meaning to our history so we understand what is taking place. That is what you have in so many of the prophetic oracles where you find a Jeremiah speaking about the relationship of Israel to Babylon or the relationship of Israel to Egypt or to Nebuchadnezzar or whoever it might be.

The prophets, the seers, the visionaries, play a unique role in Israel's history. That is because they are primarily persons of the word. So, when Israel confronted a true prophet, there were, as it were, three possible elements—the messenger who carries the word, the message that is carried, and the sender, who is Yahweh Himself. The important thing about the Israelite prophet is not the way he or she gets his or her message or even the way it is delivered. It is not the ecstasy, the vision or the dream, but it is the word of Yahweh. It is not enough to simply say, "He is a person of the word." It must be, "He or she is a person of the word of Yahweh." That is so because the prophet was the special recipient of the word of God. And he or she was the bearer of the word of God.

There is a key passage on this. Turn with me to Deuteronomy 18:9, one of the pivotal passages in the Old Testament for this concept of the prophetic word. In Deuteronomy, Moses is both looking back and looking forward. He will not be a part of what he is looking forward to, but he sees it clearly in the light of what he has been through with these people.

> When you enter the land the Lord your God is giving you, do not learn to imitate the detestable ways of the nations there. Let no one be found among you who sacrifices his son or daughter in the fire, who practices divination or sorcery, interprets omens, engages in witchcraft, or casts spells, or who is a medium or spiritist or who consults the dead (18:9-11).

That is a remarkable catalogue, and it is a catalogue of the alternatives to the word of God. These are what other societies turn to in order to get an insight into life and to what lies in the future. So, he is not just speaking accidentally. That is a preparation for the next passage.

The nations you will dispossess listen to those who practice sorcery or divination, but as for you, the Lord your God has not permitted you to do so. The Lord your God will raise up for you a prophet (18:14-15a).

So, you do not need a diviner, a magician, or someone who can cast spells. You do not need mediums or spiritists or interpreters of omens or sorcerers. God will give you a prophet in the place of all of those.

The Lord your God will raise up for you a prophet like me [Moses] from among your own brothers. You must listen to him. For this is what you asked of [Yahweh] your God at Horeb on the day of the assembly [when the Ten Commandments were given] when you said, "Let us not hear the voice of [Yahweh] our God nor see this great fire anymore, or we will die."

[Yahweh] said to me, "What they say is good. I will raise up for them a prophet like you from among their brothers; I will put my words in his mouth, and he will tell them everything I command him. If anyone does not listen to my words that the prophet speaks in my name, I myself will call him to account. But a prophet who presumes to speak in my name anything I have not commanded him to say, or a prophet who speaks in the name of other gods, must be put to death" (18:15b-20).

Notice what the prophet is to do: He is to stand between a society that is scared to death of Yahweh and Yahweh, who wants to get near to them. So, the prophet is the link between the two. But it is not the vision that is significant. It is not the ecstasy that is significant. It is not the means that is significant. It is whether the word of God is there or not.

You can look at 1 Kings 14 where the son of Jeroboam is sick, and he wants a word from Yahweh. He cannot go himself, because he and the prophet have had too much conflict, so he tells his wife to disguise herself and go. That idea that the king's wife could disguise herself and the prophet would not know who it was perhaps reflects a pagan idea of prophecy where the prophet only knows as much about the future as his magical activities will permit. To her surprise and chagrin, she discovers that this prophet, a prophet of the transcendent Creator, is not limited to magical devices. He knows who she is and he gives her a word, but it is not the word that either she or Jeroboam were eager to hear.

Jeremiah, in 18:18, characterizes the various ministries of Israel as they were understood in his day. He mentions the priests, the sages, the wise men, and the prophets. He says that the priests are the teachers of the Law, the wise men give counsel, and the prophets give the word. So, the prophet is particularly the bearer of the word and there is an immediacy between the prophet and God that is not common with either the wise man or the priest (though it is possible to have a priest who is also a prophet: Jeremiah, for instance). But the essence of prophethood is that there is an immediacy in the relationship with Yahweh that is different from His other servants. That may be some of what is implied in 1 Samuel 3 when the author speaks of the boy, Samuel, who is later to be a prophet. At the beginning of the chapter he says, "Nor had the word of the Lord yet been revealed to him." And at the end of the chapter (v. 21) we read, ". . . and there [Yahweh] revealed himself to Samuel through his word." In the interim there had arisen that intimacy of relationship between Yahweh and his young prophet.

There are three principal forms in which that word of Yahweh comes. The first is promise; the second is law; and the third is oracle. There are other categories as well, but these three are the most evident in the biblical text. We have already commented on the promise with Noah. God's word is that He is never again going to destroy the world and the human race with water as He did in Noah's day. Again, as we have said previously, the divine promise is central and crucial to the Abraham narrative where you see God's threefold promise starting and developing and being reiterated again and again. The promise and its fulfillment is the backbone of the *heilsgechichte*, the "salvation-history," that begins with Abraham and carries on right through the Bible. This idea of promise is the basis of the doctrine of the election.

The second category for God's word in the Old Testament is law. We see that preeminently, of course, in Moses and in the Pentateuch. And you notice how Exodus 20 begins: *vaydabber 'elohim*, "And God spoke" *'et kol hadd'barim ha'elleh*, "all these words," and the Ten Commandments follow. In fact the Ten Commandments are regularly referred to as "the ten words." An example is found in Exodus 34:28 where we read, "And [God] wrote on the tablets the words [*d'barim*] of the covenant—the ten words [*d'barim*, *NIV* "Ten Commandments"]. Remember that these ten words are not the "case law," the specific examples stated in "if-then" language (in Ex. 21–23 and Deut. 12–26). Rather they are what has been called the "apodictic" laws.[162] These "ten words" are an unchanging revelation of the very nature and character of God.

The philosopher Friedrich Hayek argues that there is a fundamental difference between "law" and "legislation." It was wrong to kill someone long before some king prohibited it or some assembly passed a bit of legislation condemning it. It was wrong to steal before any state in the United States passed a law against it. There are certain things that are wrong in and of themselves. Now, if you do not come within the biblical tradition, you have to explain that phenomenon in terms of "natural law." But however you explain it, I suspect there are very few groups of people across the course of human history that have not intuitively recognized this difference. There are some things that are absolutes, that are binding—they are wrong in themselves. What the Old Testament does that is so striking is that it roots these "laws" in the very character and nature of the Creator of the universe. It is wrong to violate these ten "words" because these ten "words" reveal the nature of the ultimate God.

But these words are not merely commandments; they are the heart of the covenant that God and Israel made with each other. In this sense, they are Israel's vows in her marriage contract with God. Yahweh had chosen Israel in grace, had elected her, and this was to be her response, a response that would be appropriate to the nature and character

---

[162] A term probably originated by Albrecht Alt, a German Old Testament scholar of the early twentieth century. He observed that the law codes of the rest of the Ancient Near East were all stated in the "if – then" form, including a protasis: "If so and so does such and such," and an apodosis: "then you shall do such and such to so and so." But, he further observed, the foundational statements of the Hebrew law were different, containing only an apodosis. There was no conditional element. So, as we said above, the cases in the Hebrew system are not based on a pragmatism that is relative. Rather, they rest on principles that are absolute.

of her Groom. Given these circumstances these words carry for Israel the very authority of God Himself. When He says, "Thou shalt have no other gods before me" that is not a wish on Yahweh's part or just an expectation. It is a statement of reality; it is the state of affairs if you are going to walk with Him in a marriage covenant.

The third form that the word takes in the prophets is what the *NIV* calls "oracles." The *KJV* uses the term *burden*. The Hebrew term, *massa'*, comes from a Hebrew root, *nasa'*, which means *to bear*.[163] This noun *massah* becomes a technical term in the later prophets in the Old Testament. It appears in Jeremiah (ch. 23, eight occ.) and in Nahum, Habakkuk, Zachariah and Malachi, but it is especially frequent in Isaiah. Turn to Isaiah 13:1 for an example, "An oracle concerning Babylon that Isaiah, the son of Amoz, saw . . ." As I said, the *KJV* and some other translations say, "The burden concerning Babylon that Isaiah, the son of Amoz saw . . ." If we turn to Isaiah 14:28 we find another literary segment beginning: "This oracle came in the year king Ahaz died. . . ." So Isaiah had something to say when the word had come that Ahaz had died. The term occurs again at the beginning of chapter 15, of chapter 17, and of chapter 19. It occurs three times in chapter 21, and again at the beginnings of chapters 22 and 23. Each of these is a distinct pronouncement about or against a specific nation or people.

The entire book of Nahum is a pronouncement against Nineveh and Assyria, so it is not surprising that it is titled, "An oracle of the prophet Nahum." But the books of Habakkuk, Malachi, and Zechariah are not pronouncements against a nation. Yet we find that Habakkuk and Malachi begin with *massah*, while Zechariah, chapter 9 begins with it, as does chapter 12. All this suggests that what started out as a specific kind of self-contained word addressed to a nation became broadened out to any kind of a message that was an expanded treatment of a single subject.

Not all the prophets used *massah*. Others used other expressions. For instance, Amos will say, "Thus saith the Lord," *koh 'amar 'adonai* (1:3, etc.). You will also find him saying, "Hear this word which the Lord has spoken" *sh'ma' 'et dabar hazzeh 'asher dibber 'adonai* (3:1, etc.). But notice the

---

[163] *Nasac* is one of the most interesting Hebrew words in the Old Testament in that while it means to carry in a physical sense, it also has a spiritual sense with the meaning of "to forgive."

two terms there that are crucial. "Thus saith the Lord," means, "Yahweh has spoken and I am telling you what he has said." Likewise, "Hear this word which the Lord has spoken," means "Yahweh has spoken and I am giving to you His word." The *NIV* translates *koh 'amar 'adonai* as "This is what the Lord says." In his first two chapters Amos uses this phrase very similarly to the way Isaiah uses *massah* in that he uses it several times to introduce charges against different nations. So, in verse 3 of the first chapter, "This is what the Lord says: 'For three sins of Damascus . . .'" Then in verse 6, "This is what the Lord says: 'For three sins of Gaza . . .'" In verse 9 it is Tyre. In verse 11, Edom. In verse 13, Amon. In 2:1 the word is about Judah, and then in 2:6 he gets to his major concern, where he says, "This is what Yahweh says: 'For three sins of Israel . . .'"

So, you find seven times at the beginning of his book where Amos has a special word for a particular city, a particular nation, a particular people. And in each case the essential thing is that the Lord has spoken and the prophet has heard what He has to say. *How* he got that word he never even bothers to tell us. It was evidently a matter of no concern to him. What is important to him, he says, is that "Yahweh spoke and I'm telling you what He said."

Now, one of the most interesting passages related to this idea of a message from God is found in the prophecy of Jeremiah. Turn to Jeremiah 23. This is of particular interest to me because here he deals with false prophets. So you have a general category of prophets, but within that category there are two subcategories. The first of these is that group called false prophets. The second group is those of whom Jeremiah is one, the true prophets. People in both groups call themselves prophets of Yahweh. So what is the difference? As this passage demonstrates, especially as we get to the end, the only difference is whether the prophet has truly been intimate with Yahweh and has indeed heard His voice or has, in fact, been manufacturing the whole thing.

We begin at verse 9, concerning the prophet:

> My heart is broken within me;
>> all my bones tremble.
> I am like a drunken man,
>> like a man overcome by wine,
>> because of Yahweh and his holy words (23:9).

Jeremiah has become a party to what Yahweh is thinking. He is party to what Yahweh is feeling. He is party to what Yahweh is planning. Yahweh has spoken to him and that word puts him in terror so that his bones tremble. He is like a drunken person, and all because of the word. Now he says,

> The land is full of adulterers;
>> because of the curse the land lies parched
>> and the pastures are withered.
> The prophets follow an evil course
>> and use their power unjustly
>> (23:10).

The term for prophets here is *nebi'im*, a group in which Jeremiah includes himself. These false prophets are not of a different professional category and not without power. What makes them false is how they use their position and power.

> "Both prophet and priest are godless;
>> even in my temple I find their wickedness,"
>> declares [Yahweh].
> "Therefore, their path will become slippery;
>> they will be banished to darkness,
>> and there they will fall.
> I will bring disaster upon them
>> in the year they are punished,"
>> declares [Yahweh].
> Among the prophets of Samaria
>> I saw this repulsive thing;
> They prophesied by Baal
>> and led my people Israel astray.
> And among the prophets of Jerusalem
>> I have seen something horrible:
> They themselves commit adultery and live a lie.
>> They strengthen the hands of evildoers
>> so that no one turns from his wickedness.

They are all like Sodom to me;
        the people of Jerusalem are like Gomorrah."

Therefore, this is what [Yahweh of Heaven's Hosts]
        says concerning the prophets:
"I will make them eat bitter food
        and drink poisoned water,
because from the prophets of Jerusalem
        ungodliness has spread throughout the land."

This is what [Yahweh of Heaven's Armies] says:
        [*koh 'amar 'adonai tseba'ot*]
"Do not listen to what the prophets
        are prophesying to you;
they fill you with false hopes.
        They speak visions from their own minds,
        not from the mouth of [Yahweh]"
(23:11-16).

Now, you will notice that the prophets in Samaria prophesied by Baal, by false gods. Jeremiah does not make that charge of the Jerusalem prophets. As the next verse shows, they were prophesying in the name of Yahweh. The problem was that they were not in Yahweh's inner councils. They were speaking for themselves, not for Him.

They keep saying to those who despise me,
        "[Yahweh] says: You will have peace."
And to all who follow the stubbornness of their
        hearts, they say, "No harm will come to
        you."
But which of them has stood in the council of
        [Yahweh] to see or hear his word?
        Who has listened and heard his word?
See the storm of [Yahweh]
        will burst out in wrath,
a whirlwind swirling down
        on the heads of the wicked.

The anger of [Yahweh] will not turn back
> until he fully accomplishes the purpose of his
> heart.
In days to come you will understand it clearly.
> I did not send these prophets,
> yet they have run with their message;
I did not speak to them,
> yet they have prophesied.
But if they had stood in my council,
> they would have proclaimed my words to
> my people and would have turned them
> from their evil ways and from their evil
> deeds (23:17-22).

Notice that the essence of what he is saying is that the true prophet would not so much tell them in detail what is going to happen but would give them the pure word of God so they would turn from their evil ways. So, it is a moral word that comes from a holy God, and its purpose is to turn us from our sins and from our evil. Of course there is prediction in the true prophets, but the purpose of that prediction is something very different from divination. Divination seeks to let you know what the future is so you can escape it. The purpose of true prophecy is to let you know who God is so you can get right with Him, and in that way guarantee your future.

"Am I only a God nearby?" declares [Yahweh],
> "and not a God far away?
Can anyone hide in secret places
> so that I cannot see him?"
"Do not I fill heaven and earth?
> [I am everywhere.]"

"I have heard what the prophets say who prophesy in my name. They say, 'I had a dream!' How long will this continue in the hearts of these lying prophets, who prophesy the delusions of their own minds? They think the dreams they tell one another will make my people forget my name, just as their fathers forgot my name through Baal worship. Let the prophet who has a dream tell his dream, but let the one who has my word speak it faithfully. For what has straw to do with grain?" declares [Yahweh]. "Is not my word like fire . . . and like a hammer that breaks a rock in pieces?" (23:23-29).

Remember what we said above about the word when it is spoken being an operative word, a dynamic word. The word of God is like a fire that burns, like a hammer that breaks the rock in pieces.

> "Therefore," declares [Yahweh], "I am against the prophets who steal from one another words supposedly from me. Yes," declares [Yahweh], "I am against the prophets who wag their own tongues and yet declare, 'Yahweh declares.' Indeed, I am against those who prophesy false dreams. . . . They tell them and lead my people astray with their reckless lies, yet I did not send them or appoint them. They do not benefit these people in the least," declares [Yahweh] (23:30-32).

Now look at verses 33-40. It is a fascinating passage. It is full of terms that have to do with something that Yahweh says or speaks.

> "When these people, or a prophet or a priest, ask you, 'What is the oracle of [Yahweh]?' say to them, 'What oracle? I will forsake you, declares [Yahweh].' If a prophet or a priest or anyone else claims, 'This is the oracle of the Lord,' I will punish that man and his household. This is what each of you keeps on saying to his friend or relative: 'What is [Yahweh's] answer?' or 'What has [Yahweh] spoken?' But you must not mention 'the oracle of [Yahweh]' again, because every man's own word becomes his oracle and so you distort the words of the living God, [Yahweh of Heaven's Armies], our God. This is what you keep saying to a prophet: 'What is

[Yahweh's] answer to you?' or 'What has [Yahweh] spoken?' Although you claim, 'This is the oracle of [Yahweh],' this is what [Yahweh] says: 'You have used the words, 'This is the oracle of [Yahweh],' even though I told you that you must not claim, 'This is the oracle of [Yahweh].' Therefore, I will surely forget you and cast you out of my presence along with the city I gave to you and your fathers. I will bring upon you everlasting disgrace—everlasting shame that will not be forgotten" (23:33-40).

In the Hebrew of this passage *massah* (burden, oracle) occurs eight times; the word *'amar* (he said) occurs nine times; the word *dabar* appears five times. The word *nahum*, which is a technical term for the utterance of Yahweh, occurs twice, as does the word *answer*. As I count it, there are twenty-nine different instances in eight verses where there is a reference to the communication between Yahweh and His people, and that is the thrust of what He is getting at. The word. Yahweh's concern is that we should have His word, not a message of some self-styled diviner, because that word makes the difference between life and death.

The *KJV* translation of *massah* as "burden" is helpful in getting a feel for some of the cost of being a prophet and receiving a word from Yahweh. You can understand something of why that was significant to Jeremiah, because Jeremiah found his own relationship to that word interesting, to say the least. In Jeremiah 15:16, he finds receiving God's word to be a delight: "When your words came, I ate them; they were my joy and my heart's delight, for I bear your name, O [Yahweh, God of Heaven's Armies]." The same thought appears even more graphically in Ezekiel 2:8 and 3:3, where the prophet sees himself literally eating a scroll with God's word on it. The same images appear again in Revelation 19:9-10. So here the prophet is saying that it was a joyous thing to be the recipient of God's word.

But now turn to chapter 20. Pashur, chief officer in the temple, had listened to Jeremiah prophesy about the coming victory of Babylon over Judah. Pashur was infuriated, so he had Jeremiah beaten and then put in stocks at the upper gate of Benjamin, for all to see. The next day Jeremiah was released from the stocks and told Pashur what was going to happen to him. It was both a predictive word and a prophetic word, as I distinguished those two above, and it was not good. But then Jeremiah had a conversation with Yahweh. He had just been beaten and publicly humiliated. So he says,

> "[Yahweh], you deceived me . . .
>> you overpowered me and prevailed.
> I am ridiculed all day long;
>> everyone mocks me.
> Whenever I speak, I cry out
>> proclaiming violence and destruction.
> So the word of [Yahweh] has brought me insult
>> and reproach all day long."

Do you see what I meant about "burden" being appropriate?

> But if I say, "I will not mention him
>> or speak any more in his name,"
> his word is in my heart like a fire,
>> a fire shut up in my bones.
> I am weary of holding it in;
>> indeed, I cannot.
> I hear many whispering, "Terror on every side!
>> Report him! Let's report him!"
> All my friends are waiting for me to slip,
>> saying, "Perhaps he will be deceived;
> then [when we can prove him wrong]
>> we will prevail over him and take our revenge on him."
> But [Yahweh] is with me like a mighty warrior;
>> so my persecutors will stumble and not prevail.
> They will fail and be thoroughly disgraced.
> O Lord Almighty, you who examine the righteous
>> and probe the heart and mind,
> let me see your vengeance upon them,
>> for to you I have committed my cause (20:7-12).

Now look at verse 14, which sounds a little like the book of Job.

Cursed be the day I was born!
May the day my mother bore me not be blessed!
Cursed be the man who brought my father the news,
who made him very glad saying,
"A child is born to you—a son."
May that man be like the towns
the Lord overthrew without pity.
May he hear wailing in the morning,
a battle cry at noon.
For he did not kill me in the womb,
with my mother as my grave;
her womb enlarged forever.
Why did I ever come out of the womb
to see trouble and sorrow
and to end my days in shame? (20:14-18).

This experience of hearing Yahweh and speaking for Him has indeed become a heavy, heavy burden. But now look at the first verse of chapter 21. We do not know whether these materials are chronologically sequential or not. But I am certain that they are ideologically sequential. Jeremiah will not be allowed to wallow in his frustration and self-hatred. He has been called and he has a mission to perform.

The word came to Jeremiah from [Yahweh] when King Zedekiah sent to him Pashhur son of Malkijah [not the same person as in ch. 20] and the priest Zephaniah son of Maaseiah. They said, "Inquire now of [Yahweh] for us because Nebuchadnezzar king of Babylon is attacking us. Perhaps [Yahweh] will perform wonders for us as in times past so that he will withdraw from us" (21:1-2).

What a sudden reversal. One day they put him in stocks and beat him publicly, and the next day the king has sent a politician and a priest to see him and say, "Could you give us a word? Nebuchadnezzar is out there, and we need the word of God."

So for Jeremiah there was something overwhelming about this

word that burned in his soul; it was a burden that demanded the total surrender of his total being. It demanded everything there was about him, his total life, to proclaim that word that came to him and all it implied. The man who speaks from his own spirit can live as he pleases, so "the prophets follow an evil course and use their power unjustly. Both prophet and priest are godless, even in my temple I find their wickedness" (Jer. 23:10-11). But it is a different story for the one to whom that word comes: "I can't keep quiet and I have to speak it, even if it costs me my life." What is it that makes a person sacrifice himself like that? It was not because of those fleeting moments of pleasantness; it is because of the insistent reality of Yahweh in his heart and mind.

Lecture 22

· · · · · · · · · ·

The Prophetic Limitation on Royal Power in Ancient Israel

In this lecture I want to use the interchange between the prophet Nathan and King David reported in 2 Samuel 12 to transition from our discussion of the prophets to a discussion of the place of the king in ancient Israel. Let me just remind you of the events leading up to the encounter of Nathan and David. David had seen a beautiful woman bathing in the courtyard next to his palace, had her brought to him, had sex with her, and sent her home again. Maybe he thought that was it. But that was not it. She got pregnant. So David tried to cover his tracks. He had her husband brought home from the battlefield, ostensibly to give a report, and then sent him to spend the night with his wife. But the husband felt that would be unfair to his buddies back on the battlefield who did not have such a privilege and would not do it. So David sent him back with sealed orders to the general to put him in a place in the battle where he would be killed. When that happened David married Bathsheba, and again probably thought it was all over.

Now, you have to remember that what David did was next to nothing in that world of Oriental despots. If you wanted something, you took it, and that was the end of the story. That is the way Jezebel thought when her husband wanted the vineyard of Naboth, the man next door. Naboth refused the king's offer and Ahab was frustrated. He was frustrated because he knew perfectly well that Naboth was within his rights as those rights were spelled out in the covenant, and that he, though king, could do nothing about it. That was totally confusing to Jezebel, the daughter of a Canaanite king. She simply went out, bought a couple of lying witnesses, had Naboth convicted of blasphemy, had him killed, and his land sold at an auction where she was the only bidder. We can almost hear her say to Ahab, "What is the big deal? You are the king!"

Maybe David was infected with that kind of thinking for a while, we do not know. But in a world where there is a single Creator, who is Himself morally consistent, and whose world only functions properly when that same moral consistency is carried out, no king is absolute. That point is underlined in one of the most powerful literary moves in the Bible. It is found in 2 Samuel 11:22. Throughout that chapter the narrator has very dispassionately described the rapidly deepening moral swamp into which David seems intent on hurling himself. There is no moralizing, no pious questions as we see this good man covering himself with shame. But then come the final seven Hebrew words, brief, sledge-hammer words: "The thing (*dabar*!) that David had done was evil in the Lord's eyes." In Jerusalem it did not matter who David was, or how successful (apparently) his cover-up was, or how legal his subsequent marriage was. One thing mattered: the word of Yahweh, and David, mighty king, man after God's own heart, darling of the people, had violated that word.

But that presented the prophet Nathan with a problem. How was he to get this self-assured young man to see the truth? Sometimes the most pious people are the ones most difficult to convince that what they have done is a sin. Their very piety is a kind of armor. They know, or think they know, God too well. They know all the theological answers as well as all the theological dodges. Because of the way the text is set

up, it is easy to overlook the fact that there were at least nine months between the initial event of adultery and Nathan's confrontation of David.
Chapter 11 gives all the details, and then chapter 12 begins immediately
with the account of Nathan. Without careful reading we might think that
Nathan confronted David a few days after the adultery and the second-
handed murder. But that is not true. The confrontation took place at
least nine months after the first tragic incident, and perhaps six or seven
months after Uriah's death, because the child that David had fathered
with Bathsheba had already been born.

We do not know why it took so long for Nathan to act, but it is
apparent that David had a good long time to steel himself against any
charges that anyone, including Nathan, might make against him. I think
that is why the word God gave to Nathan took the form it did. David the
theologian might have been able to rationalize his behavior if confronted
directly. But the large-hearted David would not sit by and see one of his
"little people" be preyed on by some overbearing rich man.

The story that Nathan told was fairly simple. A certain poor
man in David's kingdom had one ewe lamb. It was the sum total of his
possessions, but it was much more than a mere possession. It was family. It was like a daughter to him. Next door was a rich man who had
innumerable flocks and herds. But when a traveler came to the rich man,
instead of taking one of his own many sheep or cattle to prepare a meal
for the stranger, the rich man took the ewe lamb that belonged to the
poor man. David responded in self-righteous anger, "Where is that rich
man so I can straighten him out and deal with him? He deserves to die."
Nathan replied, very simply, "You are the man."

How could Nathan get away with that? Why would an absolute
monarch like David not just put this troublesome little man out of the
way? Why would he be moved to the kind of paroxysm of repentance
recorded in Psalm 51? The answer to those questions surely lies in the
radically different understanding of the relationship between king and
God that existed in Israel. Here is a passage from the book by Abraham
Heschel that I mentioned in an earlier lecture. He says,

> God and king are two conceptions so nearly coupled
> in the oriental mind, that the distinction is constantly

blurred between God and the king.[164]

Heschel is quoting from a work titled *Ideas of Divine Rule in the
Ancient Near East*, written by a British scholar named C. J. Gadd.[165] Heschel
goes on to say that Re, the sun god in Egypt, according to mythology,
was the first king in Egypt. So Egypt felt that its royal lineage went back
to a divine being. And gods were among the rulers in Samaria after the
flood. Thus in historic times, the king's majesty was equaled to that of a
god. The king was held to be a god, begotten by his heavenly father, the
sun god Re, who assumed the form of the living king for the purpose
of procreation of an heir to the throne. So sacrifices were offered to
the kings, and their worship was celebrated in special temples by special
priests.[166] Indeed, the worship of the king sometimes cast worship of
the gods into the shade. Thus in the reign of Merenra, in Egypt, "a
high official declared that he had built many holy places in order that
the spirits of the king, the ever living Merenra might be invoked, more
than all the gods."[167] The king was also the high priest of each god,
although for practical purposes the king delegated his functions to the
professional priesthood.

In Mesopotamia the king, while not begotten by a god, was regarded as a man who became divine as the adopted son of the god. He
was nursed and reared, and educated by the different gods and goddesses.

It was not uncommon for rulers of Samarian cities to
claim that a god was their parent. And the belief of having been nourished by the holy milk of a divine nurse
was professed by rulers as far apart as Eannadu about
(probably before 4000 B.C.); and Ashurbanipal (died
633 B.C.). A few kings called themselves "husbands" of
goddesses. The king, who was also a priest, was always

---

[164] Heschel, *The Prophets,* 474.
[165] C. J. Gadd, *Ideas of Divine Rule in the Ancient Near East* (London: Oxford,
1948), 33.
[166] We are not so far from that today. In the latter part of the 1980s the dictator
of Romania, Ceaucescu, had the university choirs in Romania singing hymns to him
in political meetings.
[167] Heschel, ibid.

upon the point of stepping over into the gods, and yet he is always subordinate. The courtly phrase for the demise of the crown was the late king "became a god."

Among the Hittites, in Anatolia, the king was also the high priest. He sustained the cult, deposed and instituted priests. Though not recognized as a god during his lifetime, he was deified after his death. Similarly, Parthian monarchs of the Arsacid dynasty called themselves brothers of the moon and brothers of the sun, and they were worshipped as gods. The conception of kingship, going back to primitive times when the chief was regarded as charged with mysterious *mana, orenda* or *dynamis* and was *tabu* to his subjects, has remained the potent motive in political and religious history in many civilizations down to the 20th century.[168]

Now, that was the view of what a king was like in the world in which Israel lived. But when you come to Israel, how different things were there. To the true Hebrew, deification of kings was unthinkable, at least in theory. Edmond Jacob says that, "if elsewhere the king was god, in Israel it was God who was king."[169] So, Ezekiel chides the king of Tyre for assuming divinity (ch. 28). For a similar attack on a king's attempting to take the place of God, see Isaiah 14.

The king in Israel was the ruler who was appointed by God. You will remember that the king was anointed and that anointing had special significance in terms of the political role of the king. And he was to reign according to the will of Yahweh, and according to the *mishpat*, the justice, of Yahweh. The heart of the social order was neither king nor priest. Heschel says:

> The heart of the social order in Egypt was the throne. But in Israel the heart of the social order was the covenant between God and the people at the center. That was the center for their social life.[170]

[168] Ibid., 474f.
[169] Jacob, *Theology of the Old Testament*, 238ff.
[170] Heschel, *The Prophets*, 477.

That understanding of the separation between king and King went very far back. When the people tried to make Gideon their king during the period of the judges, he refused, saying, "I will not rule over you. . . . [Yahweh] will rule over you" (Judg. 8:23). That is certainly a very interesting response in the light of the understandings common in the rest of Gideon's world. The words translated "rule" have the same three consonants as the noun "king" (*mlk*). So he is literally saying, "I will not be king over you, but Yahweh will be king over you."

The same concept can be found in the Psalms. Psalms 93, 97, and 99 all begin with the same phrase: *'adonai malak*, "Yahweh reigns." This entire section of the book of Psalms is made up largely of what are called royal psalms, psalms that are saying, "Yahweh is our King." These were used in the temple worship; they were sung in the temple; they were a part of the worship life of the nation. So you can see how the worship ties in with the theology and the political structure of Israel.

Now, here you get an interesting echo of something else in the Old Testament. You will remember that at Sinai,

> Moses went up to God, and the Lord called to him from the mountain and said, "This is what you are to say to the house of Jacob and what you are to tell the people of Israel: 'You yourselves have seen what I did to Egypt, and how I carried you on eagle's wings and brought you to myself. Now if you obey me fully and keep my covenant, then out of all nations you will be my treasured possession [my *segullah*, which we have mentioned before]. Although the whole earth is mine, you will be a kingdom of priests and a holy nation.' These are the words you are to speak to the Israelites" (Ex. 19:3-6).

God called them to be a kingdom, but it is a different kind of kingdom, and that is central to Israel's election. They were called to be a kingdom of priests. The king would not be a priest, acting as God to them. They would themselves be priests to the Only King.

You will remember a similar passage in Samuel when Samuel was getting old and facing death. Knowing that he was going to disappear from the scene, Israel's elders came to him and asked him to appoint a king for them over the people. Samuel was not happy with that request. But he prayed to Yahweh about it and Yahweh told him to go ahead, that it was not Samuel they were rejecting, but that they were rejecting Yahweh as their king (1 Sam. 8:1-7). But the appointment of a human king in Israel in no way diminished the ultimate kingship of Yahweh. Neither did it suggest that in some way the divine kingship of Yahweh could be absorbed into the human king. In part that is what the struggles between Samuel and Saul were about (1 Sam. 12–15). In the end the distinctions were crystal clear; the king who sat on the throne was a king under a King and had a responsibility to his Overlord, who was Yahweh.

The kings of Egypt, Assyria, and Phoenicia, as Heschel said, possessed priestly authority, and they acted as priests. To combine the royal and the priestly functions in one person was common in the Ancient Near East. That meant that the king was the expert on religion as well as the person of supreme power. And so, the priests were subordinate to him, just as the army was subordinate to him, and just as the political figures were subordinate to him. This gave the king, as you can understand, a concentration of power that put him in a position of dictatorial control. Remember in Genesis 14 when Melchizedek was introduced, he was said to be the king of Salem and also the priest of *El Elyon*, the god most high (Gen. 14:18). That combination was common in Canaan as well as the neighbors around them. You can imagine something of the advantage that meant to a ruler in terms of freeing him to do what he wanted to do without challenge.[171]

---

[171] One of my professors at Brandeis University was Joseph de Somogy. I will never forget the first class I was in under him. The course was on Islamic History and Institutions, and the first lecture was titled, "What Is Europe?" I was intrigued; he spent two hours telling us what Europe was. What he was dealing with was political philosophy and religious philosophy. He said, "You have no problem knowing what the western border of Europe is; the Atlantic Ocean does that for you. But where is the eastern border?" And he drew it out. He said it was not a geographical line. He said it is an ideological line, and that ultimately it is the difference between the Eastern church and the Western church. In the West, he said, you had two authorities. You had the crown, the holy Roman emperor, and you had the pope. Periodically these two would square off against each other. You may remember that an emperor stood barefooted in the snow for three days outside the papal residence, waiting, waiting for someone to let him in and give him an

But here in Israel, in a world where church and state went hand in glove, you have this remarkable separation. Instead of one major social institution you have two: the throne and the temple, and they are separate. That separation was made clear at the beginning, when Saul, impatient for God's blessing, offered a sacrifice and was condemned for it (1 Sam. 12:9-14). It was underlined later in the case of Uzziah, whom the book of 2 Kings represents as a good king. He tried to enter the temple to make an incense offering and was struck with leprosy (2 Kings 15:3-5; 2 Chron. 26:16-21). The separation of these two institutions gave stability in that each had the capacity to check and correct the other.

One element that contributed to this stability was the fact that both institutions were hereditary in nature. There could be problems coming from that, but instability was not one of them. One of the sons of the king became the next king so you knew who your next ruler was going to be. There was no anxiety about that. You were protected from the upheaval, at the least, or bloodbath, at the worst, that could accompany the changing of government. If you want to know the cost of dynastic instability, look at the last decades of the northern kingdom of Israel, where a king would be assassinated and the assassin would take the throne for a few years, but then he in turn would be assassinated. So you had four different dynasties in the last thirty years of Israel's independent existence. There was tremendous instability, and that was the prelude to Israel's collapse before Assyria.

The same thing was true of the priesthood. It was a family affair, with the temple functionaries all coming from the same tribe, the Levites. And the high priests were all from a family within that tribe, the descendants of Aaron. So it was not like the ministry of the Protestant churches or even of the Roman Catholic church that we know today.

What was it that brought about the separation of powers? It

audience with the pope, so he could seek forgiveness. At that point it was very clear which one was on top, was it not? "But," de Somogy said, "that never happens in the East. The orthodox church and the czar, the throne and the church, were hand in glove. And you were not always sure which one was which because the church was the servant of the throne. The end result was, there was never freedom in Russia, and in any other part of the East where the church reigned." He said, "You never have political freedom unless you have to make a choice as to who your ultimate authority is and as to who your ultimate lord is." If that choice is taken from you, there is no chance for political liberty.

was the covenant. The covenant was the relationship that defined Israel. Every other institution in the nation was subsidiary to that relationship. The Levites were the ministers of that covenant, and when the king came, it was under the terms of the covenant, and there was a book of the kingdom that was given to the king that told about the limitations on his power and authority.

But despite the official separation that existed between throne and temple, there was still the danger, especially given the understanding of the relationship of them to each other in the rest of the world, for a very cozy arrangement to come into existence between the two, where neither one was likely to correct the other. That could be further heightened by the hereditary factor. Why were you king? Was it because you were a divinely inspired leader? No, it was simply because of who your father was. Why were you a priest? Was it because God was moving in your heart to surrender your life to Him for His service? No, it was because you were born a Levite.

This is where the third typical institution of Israelite life comes into play. Now, I am a little reluctant to use the word *institution* here, because prophecy in Israel was distinctly *not* institutional in nature. Yes, there were "schools of the prophets" that we see mentioned in Samuel and in connection with Elijah and Elisha, and there were royal prophets maintained by the kings, but these were not, by and large, where the distinctive Hebrew prophets came from. They were definitely not hereditary. They were the ones who had heard a word from Yahweh and were responding to Him rather than fulfilling some familial or professional assignment.

These prophets were like Amos. The priest of Israel, the northern kingdom, told Amos at the royal chapel of Bethel that if he wanted to earn a living by prophesying some place, he should go home to Judah. Amos responded that he had no "need" to prophesy as though he were a professional. He was just a working man, but Yahweh "took me . . . and said to me, 'Go, prophesy to my people Israel'" (Amos 7:15). In other words, Amos was there, challenging both the temple and the throne, because he had no other option. He was there because he was more afraid of displeasing the One who called him than he was of what anybody in the northern kingdom could do to him.

There is that *ad hoc* character about this institution so that a

Nathan, though he was a counselor to the king and certainly had ties with the temple, did not have his ministry defined by either of those relationships. He was responsible to Yahweh, and the other institutions, when they were at their best, recognized that fact and were capable of being corrected by Yahweh through the prophet.

There is a fascinating example of all that I have been talking about reported in 1 Kings 12 and 13. You remember the sad end of Solomon's life and then the unwise advice that his son, Rehoboam, followed, with the result that the kingdom split in two and Jeroboam became the king in the northern part in Israel. Now clearly, Jeroboam faced a lot of problems in trying to get this new kingdom stabilized. One of those problems was the attraction of the glorious temple in Jerusalem and the three pilgrimages that the people were supposed to make there each year. Imagine that you are Jefferson Davis in May of 1861 and that all the people of the Southern states have been accustomed to making three trips a year to great family gatherings in Washington, D.C. Would you think you had a problem?

So, what did Jeroboam do?

> After seeking advice, the king made two golden calves. He said to the people, "It is too much for you to go up to Jerusalem. Here are your gods, O Israel, who brought you out of Egypt." One he set up in Bethel [on the southern border of his kingdom], and the other in Dan [on the northern border]. . . . Jeroboam built shrines on high places and appointed priests from all sorts of people, even though they were not Levites. . . .
>
> He instituted a festival on the fifteenth day of the eighth month, like the festival held in Judah [but one month later], and offered sacrifices on the altar. This he did in Bethel, sacrificing to the calves he had made. And at Bethel he also installed priests at the high places he had made. On the fifteenth day of the eighth month, a month of his own choosing, he offered sacrifices on the altar he had built at Bethel. So he instituted the festival for the Israelites and he went up to the altar to make offerings (1 Kings 12:28-33).

You see the throne and the temple united here in a most disastrous way. So what happened? Yahweh sent a prophet. The report of the encounter is found in chapter 13. The prophet found Jeroboam in the very act of making an offering and announced that one day a Judean king named Josiah would desecrate that very altar. Jeroboam was incensed and pointed at the prophet and called for him to be arrested. But the king's pointing arm was shriveled and frozen in place, and at the same time the altar split open as the prophet had predicted. Jeroboam's attitude underwent a dramatic change. He begged for the man of God to intercede for him, which he did [the amazing grace of God], and invited the prophet home to lunch [which the prophet refused]. So here we have the remarkable power of the Israelite prophets to confront both throne and temple and call them to account.

Now, the role of the prophet in the proper maintenance of the temple and the throne is one of the most significant things in the Old Testament. You will never find the prophets asking that the priesthood be abolished or the temple be abolished. They may predict their destruction, but they never call for it. And the same is true for the throne. For all of the conflicts between the prophets and the kings, the prophets never suggest that it would be well to dismantle that apparatus of the state. Rather, what you have is these *ad hoc* prophets who come along and tell the king to stay in his place, in his limited scope, and who tell the priests that their business is not political, but spiritual. And so, you get the voice of God coming as the perpetual corrective.

We are not merely talking about ancient history here; we are not merely talking about some academic concepts. There are eternal principles involved here that are as relevant to the end of the twentieth century and the beginning of the twenty-first century A.D. as they ever were back then. Let me go back for a moment to our previous discussion of apodictic law versus case/casuistic law, or between *law* and *legislation*. I asked a young lawyer of my acquaintance whether he had had a course in Philosophy of Law in law school. He answered that none was taught. I think what we have now in our legal circles, what shapes the thinking of our judiciary, is what is called positive law. It is an understanding that has no metaphysical, ontological frame of reference. So that whatever the *vox populi*, the voice of the people, decides, that is law. But that is wrong, you see. Even the ancient Greeks, void of the biblical revelation, but gifted with tremendous powers of analysis and logic, concluded that beyond the voice of the people, there is this absolute word that comes. So it is wrong to kill whether there is a law against it or not. The same is true for adultery, stealing, lying, etc. What the Bible does for us is to explain why this is so. It is so because these things are a violation of the character and nature of the sole Creator of the universe. So whatever the temple or the throne might say, if it is contrary to what God says, it will not stand.

What I am belaboring here is that we are not dealing with something remote way back in Israel. We are dealing with basic principles that are very applicable today. I have had the privilege of meeting the man who is the head of the Romanian Baptist Alliance. His name is Vasily Talosh. He was a law student and was halfway through law school when he was converted to Christ. The day after he was converted, when he gave his witness, he was expelled from the law school for being a Christian. So he became a Baptist pastor. In the early 1970s, some eighteen years before the collapse of communism in Romania, he did something very illegal and very dangerous. He got together first with one, and eventually with three or four, other Baptist pastors to pray. They began to ask God to give them the courage to take their stand and to be the witness that they ought to be. They began to ask the government for the privilege of pulling together all of the Baptist pastors in Romania in a conference. There was no way that a communist government was going to do that. But the pastors kept asking over the years. Finally, as the years wore on and the situation in Russia began to change, the Romanian government decided that they needed to make some concessions. So they said, "You can pull fifty together." So fifty Baptist pastors met together for a conference. They met on December 11, 1989, and on December 12, three of those pastors sat down and wrote an open letter to the president, Mr. Ceaucescu. It began with a statement from a dissenting minister in England, who wrote to James the First in England, saying, "Your Majesty, you are but dust and ashes and have no authority over our souls." That is how they began their letter to Ceaucescu. I call people like that prophets. On December 13 that was on his desk. On December 21, his own people shot him down. His death was caught by a television camera. Pastor Talos said, "I saw it on television. And I watched while this man, who had had the university choirs singing hymns to him, collapsed on his knees with his face up and both hands lifted, empty, toward heaven. And I thought, yes, Jesus *will* reign forever." He will reign. The Hebrew of that is *malak*. Now, if you do not believe that He will reign, you are not going to risk your life to confront what this world thinks of as absolute power.

One of the other pastors in that group is named Joseph Tson. He had written a paper in the late 1970s that showed how, although all the promises of Marx had failed, all the promises of Jesus are being kept. The authorities got a copy of it and called him in for questioning. They interrogated him up to six days a week, fourteen hours a day, over a long stretch of time. They would on occasion do it with a loaded, cocked revolver between the interrogator and him. Finally, the interrogator looked at him and said, "Joseph, you are stupid. You will never learn. All we can do is kill you." Joseph Tson looked back at the interrogator and said, "I understand that your ultimate weapon, when everything else has failed, is to kill. But I have an ultimate weapon. And when you use yours I get to use mine." So the interrogator said, "And what's your ultimate weapon?" "Well," he said, "mine is to die. Yours is to kill. But when you kill me, you are not going to be better off. Because every tape of every sermon that I've preached that is scattered across Romania is going to be sprinkled with my blood, and you are going to have much more trouble with me dead than you have with me alive." The interrogator said to the guard, "Get him out of here!" Some time later he was exiled from the country. "Tson's gone berserk," they said. "He wants to be a martyr, and we're not going to give him that privilege."

So what do you do? You are a man without a country. If you are a Joseph Tson who believes that there is a God who is greater than all the institutions of man, you start the Romanian Missionary Society and begin to fill a warehouse in the Netherlands with Christian literature translated into Romanian. Now remember, this is the early 1980s. Communism seemed ascendant, unstoppable. But Tson said, "I knew it would fall. It could not last." And the instant the borders began to open in 1990, the trucks were on the road. A prophet.

Now what do you think makes a person do that? I was talking yesterday to somebody on Leighton Ford's staff about evangelism in the church, particularly in terms of Methodism and some of its problems. "Well," he said, "we've just recently been in Malaysia. There is nothing wrong with the Methodist church in Malaysia. We found ourselves out in the public square witnessing where it is against the law in a Muslim country. I got anxious. But the Malaysian Methodists looked at us and said, 'We've longed to have this freedom, and we will get it, but we may have to pay a price for it. Some of us will probably have to die.'" My friend said, "I was ready to go get on my plane and come home."

Now, if you do not believe God reigns, you're not going to do that kind of thing. But if you do, and some way or another, this word of God comes alive in you, there are going to be some confrontations. It can even happen to priests. Jeremiah and Ezekiel were priests. In the period of the greatest corruption of the temple, you had priests that were prophets. And when that word comes, it makes ordinary people into extraordinary people who will challenge all the secondary authorities in the name of the Primary Authority.

Now, that did something to keep the society free. And we need that in our society. Institutions will petrify society if they are not constantly challenged. That's what John Wesley did in the Anglican church and that's the kind of thing that is going to have to take place in our society, where people can be *ad hoc* instruments of the living God. The word they speak will not be conditioned on their security, their relationship to an institution, or to anything else, for they have heard from God.

When I was young, I had one of the most definitive experiences of my life, while preaching in a Swedish Baptist church in Brooklyn, New York. I was young and thought the only way you could be saved was to kneel at a Methodist altar. They did not have an altar in this church, so I invited people to kneel at the front row. Well, God blessed and that night we had about eight of those Swedish Baptists down on their knees at the front row. I thought that was great. But there was an old man who watched me and waited for me. He had a mustache and was very distinguished, straight as an arrow. When he came up to me, he came around so that when he spoke to me, nobody would hear what he said. So I turned to speak to him and I put out my hand to shake hands with him. But instead of taking my hand, he took me by the shoulders. I was a lightweight in those days, so he could rock me back and forth, and he stared me straight in the eye. I wondered what was coming. He said, "Son, what these people need to hear is not what Dennis Kinlaw thinks, but what God says. For goodness sakes, go home and get down on your knees, with your Bible, and stay there until you know what God has to say. And the next time you stand up to speak, tell people what God has to say." And he just kept rocking me back and forth.

You know, the incredible thing is, I did not feel that he was trying to rebuke me. I felt he loved me and cared about me. So instead of being hostile and offended, I found myself drawn to the old guy. His name was Reed Burr. Everybody called him Unc Rebur. He ran a city mission there in New York, and he was a blue blood of blue bloods. The next morning when I got up, I rolled out of my bed with my Bible, and my life has been different ever since Unc Rebur. There is something about the Word that, when it is preached, has a life and a power of its own. But one of the great things is what it does to you, the preacher.

Lecture 23

· · · · · · · · · ·

The Demonic in the Old Testament

In the previous lecture we talked about the impact that the word of God had on those to whom it came. I said that it produced some incredibly noble people, people who could stand in the face of all sorts of opposition, hostility, and could keep their consciences clear and say what they felt God had given them. There can be no question but that there was an incredible moral force released in human history through these people who had heard Yahweh speak, had met Him, and who in their encounter with Him and in the reception of the word were transformed.

At the end of the lecture we talked about the fact that prophecy had a political impact in that all political absolutism was challenged by a man who had received a word from Yahweh. Yahweh transcends all political authority, and so a Nathan could speak to a David the way he did; or an apostle Paul could do what he did; or a Martin Luther could do what he did. And so there are the political forces that come from it.

And we said that these may well have laid the background for some of our separation of powers in the United States in order to protect liberty. It is only when you have restrained power that people can be free.

But now I would like to turn our attention to something that is, perhaps, even more intriguing to me than that subject. It is one that oftentimes we miss when we think about the Old Testament and its influence on us. Prophecy was an incredible force in delivering the human spirit from superstition. And you get echoes of this as you go through the Old Testament. Eichrodt makes reference to this when he talks about how Yahwism restrained magic, sorcery, witchcraft, necromancy, familiar spirits, and all of that sort of thing.

What I would like to talk about today is the demonic in the Old Testament. This topic came sharply to my attention during the 1960s. I received a telephone call one day from the president of the Christian Medical Society and he said to me, "We have the possibility of a grant to put together a conference on the demonic. Would that be worthwhile? Would that be a worthwhile expenditure of Christian money?" At that time I was teaching the Old Testament on the seminary level and was just beginning to get my own feel of what the Old Testament has to say on some of these things. So I replied, "Yes, I think it would, as long as you will see to it that one lecture is given on the demonic in the Old Testament." The next thing I knew I had an invitation to give the opening lecture. We met at the University of Notre Dame, and it was a fascinating group. There were about seventy people present, of whom eighteen were psychiatrists, if my memory serves me correctly. There were sociologists, biblical scholars, and medical doctors. There were missionaries from all over as well.[172]

As I was preparing for that address, the thing that caught my attention was this: How many cases of demon possession do you have in the Old Testament? There are none, are there? In the case of Saul, the text says it was an evil spirit from Yahweh. Whatever we do with that, it is not an expression of demon possession. On the other hand, what happens when you get into the Gospels? There in the very first chapter of

---

[172] I developed a friendship with one of the men in that group who was the head of the Department of Psychiatry at Duke University Medical School. Another one whom I got to know a bit, I learned years later, was assigned to work with Jim Bakker when his empire collapsed.

Mark, which many scholars believe was the first gospel, Jesus is disturbed by what the text tells us is a demon-possessed person. And then you get it all through Mark and all through Matthew and all through Luke. It seems to be everywhere.

There are only two examples in Acts. In 8:7 there is a reference to those who were possessed being freed by the preaching of the apostles, and in 16:16 we hear of a possessed girl being used to tell fortunes. And how much is there about demons in the epistles of Paul? There is no reference to demon possession. He may talk about Satan (Rom. 16:20, etc.) and demons (see e.g. 1 Cor. 10) and principalities and powers (Eph. 6:12, etc.), but there is nothing about actual possession. Furthermore, there is no reference to exorcism and no instruction on how to perform one. In the book of James, there seems to have been a liturgy that is assumed to be used for healing, but nowhere in any of the Epistles, Pauline or otherwise, do you find anything comparable for dealing with demonic possession.

In the book of Revelation the situation is not the same. While there is no reference to demon possession, per se, the demonic realm is everywhere, and the final conflicts of history are seen as conflicts with that realm.

I think that lets you see the question that was spinning in my head. You have thirty-nine books of the Old Testament in which you get one account of a person who could be said to have an evil spirit within him. As for Satan himself, how much does the Old Testament have to say about him? Not much. What about the serpent in the third chapter of Genesis, is this Satan? The Old Testament does not answer the question, does it? Have you noticed how many of our questions the Old Testament does not answer? As the years have passed, that has become one of the great things about the Old Testament to me. There are things we do not need to know, and the Old Testament is not going to waste its precious space merely satisfying our curiosity. I hope to say more about that before the end of this lecture.

But let us assume for a moment that the serpent is Satan. What is the first thing said about him in the text? He is one of God's creatures. Here is the agent through whom sin makes its entrance into the world. But the first thing that is said, and said very clearly, is that this agent of temptation is a creature that Yahweh, God, had made. Whatever and whoever Satan is, he is like all the other creatures.

Where else in the Old Testament do you find any treatment of Satan? It is in the opening chapters of Job. Turn to Job 1:6:

> One day the angels [literally "sons of God"] came to present themselves before [Yahweh] and Satan also came with them. [Yahweh] said to him, "Where have you come from?" Satan answered [Yahweh], "From roaming through the earth and going back and forth in it." Then [Yahweh] said to Satan, "Have you considered my servant Job? There is no one on earth like him; he is blameless and upright, a man who fears God and shuns evil." "Does Job fear God for nothing?" Satan replied. "Have you not put a hedge around him and his household and everything he has? You have blessed the work of his hands, so that his flocks and herds are spread throughout the land. But stretch out your hand and strike everything he has, and he will surely curse you to your face." [Yahweh] said to Satan, "Very well, then, everything he has is in your hands, but on the man himself do not lay a finger." Then Satan went out from the presence of [Yahweh] (Job 1:6-12).

Is there any question who is charge here? Is there any ambiguity? Now turn to Job 2:

> On another day the angels came to present themselves before [Yahweh], and Satan also came with them to present himself before him. And [Yahweh] said to Satan, "Where have you come from?" Satan answered the Lord, "From roaming through the earth and going back and forth in it." Then [Yahweh] said to Satan, "Have you considered my servant Job? There is no one on earth like him; blameless and upright, a man who fears God and shuns evil. And he still maintains his integrity, though you incited me against him to ruin him without any reason." "Skin for skin!" Satan replied. "A man will give all he has for his own life. But stretch out your hand and strike his flesh and bones, and he will surely curse you to your face." [Yahweh] said, "Very

well, then, he is in your hands; but you must spare his life" (Job 2:1-6).

It is significant that in this, the longest statement in the Old Testament about Satan, Yahweh is the one who sets the conditions for the game—and sets them ineluctably—and there is no indication that Satan has any capacity to go beyond that.

So that was my problem. The Old Testament acknowledges a world of evil, but it tells us very little about it. Then you pick up the Gospels and start reading, and you run into case after case of demon possession, as common as can be.[173] But then in the book of Acts and the Epistles, while it is there, it is relegated to a very minor role.[174] Then you come to the book of Revelation and it is as though the cover is pulled off of hell itself. And that is the concluding note of the Scripture on the subject. So, there is a large section in which the demonic is almost absent; then a section in which it is very common; then a section in which it is there but not developed; and in the final section it is one of the major players in the game—the demonic and hell.

Now, my question was, Why that difference in the Scripture, and what is going on in the Gospels? So I went back and looked more carefully at the data in both testaments.

The situation in the Old Testament becomes much more dramatic when you set it against the backdrop of the Ancient Near East. If you will look at the Egyptian literature in the second and the first millenniums B.C., the period comparable in Egyptian history to everything from Abraham down to the close of the Old Testament Canon, you will find that the demonic played a massive role in that culture. The same is true in Mesopotamia. In both Babylonian and Assyrian literature you will find a great deal about the demonic world and its activity and the activities of humans to try to escape the effects of the demonic in their lives. The same is true with Greek or Roman or Hittite literature. Yet here stands the Old Testament with hardly a reference to what was a major concern for everybody else.

It is as though you have a five-hundred-page novel written about

---

[173] The term "devil" appears forty-two times in the Gospels.
[174] "Devils" is used six times in Paul's letters, and "devil," speaking of Satan, appears an additional five times in them.

people living in New York City at the present time, and there is not a reference in it to automobiles, the telephone, television, or computers. Unthinkable, is it not? Yet that is what we find in the Old Testament. You would not have to go too many miles from Jerusalem in any direction to find people who, having a cow lose its calf, or having a wife who miscarries, would immediately explain it and try to deal with it in terms of the demonic.

So with that thought in mind, I went back to the Old Testament trying to see what traces there are and what references there are. Turn to Deuteronomy 32:15-17. This is the song of Moses:

> Jeshurun [Israel] grew fat and kicked;
>> filled with food, he became heavy and sleek.
> He abandoned the God who made him
>> and rejected the Rock his Savior.
> They made him jealous with their foreign gods,
>> and angered him with their detestable idols.
> They sacrificed to demons, which are not God—
>> gods they had not known,
>> gods that recently appeared,
>> gods your fathers did not fear.
> You deserted the Rock, who fathered you;
>> you forgot the God who gave you birth.

The Hebrew word translated "demons" is *shedim*. The same word occurs in Assyrian and Babylonian, where it is a standard term for "demons." Here it is occurring in Deuteronomy.

Now turn to Psalm 106:34-37.

> They did not destroy the peoples
>> as the LORD had commanded them,
> but they mingled with the nations
>> and adopted their customs.
> They worshiped their idols,
>> which became a snare to them.
> They sacrificed their sons
>> and daughters to demons (*shedim*).

When they did not remove the temptation posed by pagan neighbors properly, they picked up their customs, worshipped their idols, and sacrificed their sons and daughters to the demons. But those two are the only occurrences in the Bible of that typically Ancient Near Eastern word for demons.

Now turn to Leviticus 17:7 and you find another interesting word: "They must no longer offer any of their sacrifices to the goat idols [literally "he-goats," *śᵉirim*] to whom they prostitute themselves." Other translations of the *NIV* phrase "goat idols" are "devils" (*KJV*), "goat demons" (*NASB, NRSV*), or "demons" (*NKJV, REB*). *REB* has a note "or satyrs." In Greece "satyrs" were part of the retinue of Bacchus, the Greek god of wine. They had a human head and chest, but had goat horns and the body of a goat from the waist down. They were symbols of high sexuality and fertility. Now, you can see why the use of the term "he-goat" in what is clearly a context of worship would suggest the term "satyr" here.[175]

Now, turn to 2 Chronicles 11:13-15. This is the story of Rehoboam, after he had ascended the throne after Solomon's death.

> The priests and Levites from all their districts through-out Israel sided with [Rehoboam]. The Levites even abandoned their pasturelands and property, and came to Judah and Jerusalem because Jeroboam and his sons had rejected them as priests of the Lord. And he ap-pointed his own priests for the high places and for the goat and calf idols he had made.

Literally, the text says, "for the he-goats and the calves that he had made."

There are two more occurrences of this word for goat where it is apparently being used for a god. Both of them are in Isaiah, and both occur in similar contexts, that of abandoned pagan cities. The first is in 13:21:

---

[175] [Editor's note] There is a bas-relief of the Canaanite fertility goddess Asherah/Anat showing her bare-breasted holding up sheaves of grain in her hands with a goat rearing up on either side of her. Here, as in Greece, the connection to sexuality is very clear.

But desert creatures will lie there,
> jackals will fill her houses;
there the owls will dwell,
> and there the wild goats will leap about.

The second occurrence is found in 34:13-14:

She will become a haunt for jackals,
> a home for owls.
Desert creatures will meet with hyenas,
> and wild goats will bleat to each other;
there night creatures will also repose
> and find for themselves places of rest.

In both cases the *NIV* translates the word we are looking at, *s^eir-im*, as "wild goats," although there is nothing in the term itself to specify "wild." What makes it look as though the word is intended to connote more than just a wild animal in these two contexts is the word the *NIV* translates "night creatures" in 34:14. The Hebrew word there is *lilit* and this is the only time it occurs in the Bible. The *Jerusalem Bible* transliterates it and capitalizes it as if it were a proper noun. Eichrodt has this to say:

> [In Isaiah 34:14] a female night-phantom *lilit* is men-
> tioned in conjunction with [the *s^eirim*]. This figure plainly
> derives from Babylonia, where a rich selection of such
> fiends was available. Under the same name, Lilith, she
> appears there as a storm demon dwelling in the wilder-
> ness, from which she bursts forth to attack men.[176]

The Interpreter's Dictionary to the Bible gives a very graphic description of a female demon who is responsible for a good deal of the sexual activity that takes place in the world.[177] Yet the figure appears only once in the Old Testament, and in this obscure context no one quite knows what to do with it.[178]

---

[176] Eichrodt, *Theology of the Old Testament*, vol. 2, 224.
[177] *The Interpreter's Dictionary of the Bible*, ed. (New York: Abingdon).
[178] J. Oswalt, *The Book of Isaiah*, New International Commentary on the Old

These are all the references to the demonic in the Old Testament. But I noticed that the minute you get to the Apocryphal literature and especially in the Pseudepigraphical literature, and get out of the biblical material, after the Canon is closed, you begin to get an amazing development of the demonic in which the demons are given personal names. They are ranked and located as far as their territory is concerned. You are given a formula as to how to handle them, and suddenly that whole world becomes very massive and a very active part of every person's life.

Now, with all that in my mind, let me tell you what I began finding myself coming to. The Old Testament never says it isn't there. But it never plays it up. And the reality is that what were symbols for other people of the demonic became natural for the Hebrew, so that you looked at the fire or the Canaanite looked at the fire and said, "There is a demon in there and that is what is doing that." But the Hebrew, as Moses instructed them or as Yahwism said he ought to do it, looked at the fire and said, "No, that's what I cooked my beans with." And so what you've got is an incredible demythologization of the worldview that is found in the Old Testament.

Now, the people in Eichrodt's time came from that period when everybody was concerned about finding all the parallels in the nations around Israel and in the literatures around Israel. So, they find a Lilith in the Assyrian literature and say, "If it's in the Old Testament it must be a personal demon," when maybe it is not a personal demon but a natural creature. When you see *resheph* in the pagan literature, it is a god who plagues you. But when you come to the Old Testament, it may be nothing more than fire. When you find a satyr in the pagan literature, but the word is also the word for "goat," what do you do when you come to that word in the Old Testament? Is it "goat" or is it something more? What you have in the Old Testament is demythologizing, saying that goat is a goat and don't think anything more about him, and above all, don't fear him.

Testament (Grand Rapids: Eerdmans, 1986, ch. 1–39, 616, says this: "*He-goat* and *night-bird* are interpreted by some as demonic figures (*RSV* satyr, night-hag), and this meaning is possible. However, since both the preceding and following verses speak of regular animals, it seems best to remain with that interpretation (as do *NEB* and *NIV*, but not *JPSV*)."

Let me point out to you the kind of thing that comparative religion has led us to. Look with me at Proverbs 30:15-16:

> The leech [*'luqa*] has two daughters.
>   "Give! Give!" they cry.
> There are three things that are never satisfied,
>   four that never say, "Enough!":
> The grave, the barren womb,
>   land, which is never satisfied with water,
>   and fire, which never says, "Enough!"

Now here is what Eichrodt says about verse 15:

> The *'luqa* of Proverbs 30:15 seems to be a spectre of a
> similar kind [as Lilith]; as a monster of the vampire type
> it belongs to the same class of beings as the *lamia* of the
> Romans or the ghoul of the Arabs. It is not impossible
> that the *m''arbim*, or "liers in wait" who according to 2
> Chronicles 20:22 at the prayer of the Israelites caused
> discord in the host of the allied Ammonites, Moabites
> and Edomites, also represent demonic beings of this
> kind.[179]

As a matter of fact, this occurrence of *'luqa* in Proverbs 30:15 is the only one in the Hebrew Bible, so there are no other usages to check it against. Both *Brown-Driver-Briggs Hebrew and English Lexicon Old Testament* and the *Hebrew and Aramaic Lexicon of the Old Testament* define it as "leech" and nothing more on the basis of an Arabic cognate that means to cling to something, or to hang suspended clinging to something. I checked the *Jerusalem Bible* which is more influenced by the *Apochrypha* than our Protestant versions (so they translate "goats" in those two places in Isaiah as "satyrs"), and even they read "leech" in this verse. So why does Eichrodt say what he does? (Note that he does not cite any evidence.) It is simply because of the effect on him of comparative religion studies. Is it theoretically possible that this Hebrew term was used for a demon

---

[179] Eichrodt, *Theology*, vol. 2, 224.

elsewhere in the ancient world? Of course. We have seen that with the earlier examples. But the key point here is that there is absolutely nothing in the context of Proverbs that would cause us to think that. If there ever was a mythological usage, it has been thoroughly strained out of the present text. The text says *leech* and we are given no reason to see it in any other light.

As I thought about these things we have talked about, I found myself saying, "What we have in the Old Testament is—no question about it—a massive demythologization of the pagan worldview." And that is still true even if you were to accept all of Eichrodt's suggestions and add to them all that *The Interpreter's Dictionary of the Bible* brings in on top of them. Even if you were to accept all of them (although I see no need to do so), you still have an incredibly demythologized book in the Old Testament.

While I was thinking about these things, I came across two statements that interested me. One of them was from G. K. Chesterton, who said, "Why is it so difficult to write a good Christian novel?" This, I think, is one of the more perceptive comments I have ever heard. He answered his question in this way:

> Well, the reason it's so hard to write a great Christian novel, is because the Christian is at a disadvantage when he starts. And that disadvantage is this: that evil is so much better in imagination than in reality, while good is so much better in reality than it is in imagination. So in the novel, whose scene of operations is the imagination, evil has it over good all the time.

Then I found this thought in Dorothy Sayers. Sayers says that if a playwright introduces the Devil into her cast of characters, she immediately has a great problem on her hands. The problem is how to keep the Devil from becoming the hero. Since the human spirit is so attracted to evil, even if you just make Satan one of the minor characters, you are going to have trouble keeping him from getting center stage. That is the reason, according to Sayers, that playwrights put red pajamas on the devil, give him a forked tail, and put a pitchfork in his hand. They are trying to make him ridiculous in order to strip him down to size so the human imagination will not play him up for greater than he is.

With those thoughts and my study of the Old Testament in mind, I came to this conclusion. Since Israel lived in the world it did, where everybody was deeply concerned about the demonic and the evil and how to keep the evil spirits off one's back, so to speak, the Old Testament had to go to extremes to make its point or every Hebrew would have been slipping behind a bush somewhere, making sacrifices to propitiate the demons. Even as it was, that tendency was a problem. Think how much greater the problem would have been without that incredible playing down of the demonic.

But what about the Gospels? Why do they make so much of the demonic? Do you know what I noticed? There is a factor present in the Gospels and in the book of Revelation that is not present in the Old Testament or the Epistles. What is that factor? It is the presence of the living Christ, the radical presence of Jesus Christ. That means you can read the story of Legion to a six-year-old before he goes to sleep, and he will not have nightmares because there is something about the living Christ that pulls all the teeth out of the demonic, so you do not have to worry about it. He is in total control. And when you come to the book of Revelation and the lid is taken off hell, who is the central figure in the book of Revelation? It is the Christ. And when He is there, our imaginations are brought into subjection to Him, and the Evil One loses his power to come in and dominate our imaginations. It is no accident that when the seduction of evil is first introduced in Genesis 3, it is represented as being entirely under the control of Yahweh.

In that light there is one more verse that we must look at before we close this lecture. It is Isaiah 45:7:

> I form the light and create darkness,
> I bring prosperity [*shalom*] and create disaster [*ra'*].

Notice that the *NIV* translates the last word with *disaster*. That is not an incorrect translation, but if you are not aware of the Hebrew word behind it, you will miss some of the force of what is being said. That word is *ra'*, which is fairly close in meaning to English "bad." It speaks of everything from misfortune to the most intentional moral degradation. What this text is saying is that a whole range of possibilities exists for one reason alone. They exist because Yahweh, the sole Creator, made it a possibility. Now, what is being said? The Old Testament says that if it is there, there is only one person to blame, and that is Yahweh.

It is almost impossible to overemphasize the importance of that thought. Paganism sees existence as a struggle between chaos and order, with chaos being "bad" and order being "good." These two principles have always existed and always will, and we simply need to face the fact that disorder, evil, is as necessary a part of existence as order, good, is. It is all right to attempt to maximize order and to minimize disorder, but disorder is always going to be there, and you are just going to have to learn the tricks to try to hold it at bay. So the universe is full of these forces of disorder. To all of that the Old Testament says a resounding "No!" Evil is nothing more nor less than the results of a refusal to submit to the creative purposes of our Father. In the sense that He made a world where that refusal is possible, He is responsible for the existence of evil in the world. That means that when you face the realm of evil within you and without, He is the only One you need to deal with, and if you have Him in the right place in your life, you can forget about your fears.

There is an illustration of this point that has been helpful to me. Notice that in much of the Old Testament there is no distinction between primary and secondary causes at all. It was absolutely critical to make the overriding point that there is one single cause for everything: Yahweh. But that raises a question. Did Yahweh *cause* Satan to tempt Eve and Adam? Did He cause them to choose to disobey Him? If so, how can He justly punish them? No, God was not the immediate cause of their sin. He was the ultimate cause, but not the immediate cause. On this point Aristotle was very helpful to us as he distinguished among the various levels of causation.

Here is an illustration of this differention of causes. Probably none of you here is old enough to remember what a scourge polio was in the 1950s. It was very common and very deadly; two of my closest associates ended up paralyzed for life with it. So, when Dr. Jonas Salk developed an effective vaccine against it, it was as if you were to develop a vaccine for AIDS today. As you can imagine, Jonas Salk got a lot of acclaim. They started a crash program to produce vaccine so they could inoculate the whole country, and eventually just about everybody was. But there was a laboratory on the West Coast called Cutter Laboratory. And Cutter, in the haste to produce large batches of this vaccine, developed a bad batch that instead of inoculating people against polio, gave people polio.

And so, of course, Cutter Laboratory was very quickly shut down, but it created quite a stir. Now, I can hear a good Hebrew talking to a good Greek. The Hebrew says, "Dr. Salk was a great man, wasn't he?" And the Greek would say, "Oh yes, he's a great man." And the Hebrew would say, "He delivered us from polio. He saved us from polio, didn't he?" The Greek would say, "Yes, he saved us from polio." Then the Hebrew would say, "And he gave a lot of people polio, too, didn't he?" And the Greek would say, "Oh, for heaven's sakes, no. He didn't give anybody polio. He saved us from it." And the Hebrew would say, "Well, what about that Cutter Laboratory bad vaccine?" "Yeah," the Greek would say. "That bad vaccine gave a lot of people polio." And the Hebrew would say, "Yes, that's right. Dr. Salk gave a lot of people polio, didn't he?" But when the Greek protests, the Hebrew would say, "Well, whose vaccine was it Cutter was making?" And the Greek would answer, "Well, it was Salk's vaccine." And the Hebrew would answer triumphantly, "That's what I said. Dr. Salk gave a lot of people polio!"

So do you see my point? Yes, it is true that there were people who might not have gotten polio if Dr. Salk had not invented that vaccine. But he bore absolutely no moral culpability for Cutter's failure. And so, what is established in the Old Testament, it seems to me, particularly in the early part of it, is that there is one God and one alone. One original source of everything and one alone.

What the Bible then goes on to say is that when God created us as persons with our own identities, He created creatures that were out of His control. He was making an other over against Himself. And if I dare use the language, He was creating a partner for Himself. What He wanted was a relationship of trust and faith and personal affection, of personal love. But for us to have the freedom to respond to Him in those ways, He had to make a person who was capable of rejecting Him. From that first cause you get all the rest of the flow of evil in the Old Testament. It comes because someone, misusing the freedom God has given, has shut the door on the source of light and virtue and goodness and righteousness.

Lecture 24

· · · · · · · · · ·

The Promise of Redemption: God's Approach to Evil

I would like to begin today in reverse; that is, I want to tell you where I expect to end up at the end of our lectures. I do this in hope that this will help you be patient as I work my way through some things. Many of these thoughts are heavily shaped by Eichrodt, for whom, as I have said before, I have a great appreciation.[180]

---

[180] Although there is a good deal of what seems like "clutter" to me on the surface of Eichrodt's treatment, underneath that clutter there is great, profound wrestling with theological truths. If you will look at his footnotes, you will find that almost every verse in the Old Testament is referred to at one time or another. I have never read another writer on the Old Testament who reaches that standard. I may not always accept his interpretation of the biblical data, but at least he has looked at the

Let me give you some propositions. The first proposition is: God wants to save the world. The second is: The world is not going to be saved from the throne. I have heard some interpretations of Calvinism that gave the impression that God could sit on His throne and pick one person out and reject another. But as I read the Scripture, not even God can sit on His throne and save. This may seem to be an oxymoron since we are talking about the throne, God's sovereignty, and then in the next breath talking about what He cannot do. But at the least we must say that God *did not* save the world from the throne.

The third proposition is that salvation is not going to be accomplished without us. Some may get uneasy with me on that point and think I am headed into Pelagianism,[181] but not even Calvin can reject that statement, if it is understood correctly. Salvation is not accomplished without human involvement. Why does He need us? There are several passages in the Old Testament where God looks for one single person and says, "If I could have found one single person, my circumstances would have been different."[182] He was shocked when He could not find the person. One does not expect omniscience to be surprised,[183] or that sovereignty has circumstances, because circumstances are those things around you that condition you. But in these passages the Unconditioned One is conditioned.[184]

The fourth proposition is that while He is not going to save without us, there is nothing saving in the human. That understanding saves me from heresy, or at least from some heresy. There is nothing

---

data, which is more than some of us who claim a high view of Scripture have done.

[181] Pelagius was an opponent of Augustine (circa 400 A.D.) who seems to say in some of his writings that we humans have the capacity to save ourselves by imitating the example of Christ.

[182] Isa. 51:18; 59:16; 63:5; Jer. 5:1; Ezek. 22:30.

[183] This is not to use "surprise" in any absolute sense. I have no wish to qualify God's omniscience. I do not believe God was surprised in the Garden of Eden. The Lamb was slain from before the foundation of the world (Rev. 13:8). This is not to say that there was some primeval crucifixion, but that God knew about the fact of sin and was fully committed to redemption before Creation. Rather, I am speaking about "surprise" as it relates to the emotional side of God's being, the pathos of His character. When He says, "I need somewhere to start, and I need somebody to start with, and I am amazed that there is not a one in this crowd who will go with me," you feel the pathos in God.

[184] For a fuller explanation of this argument, see below.

saving in us. If there is anything clear in Scripture it is that there is no salvation from the human level, in us. So, our four propositions are: God wants to save the world; salvation is not going to be accomplished from heaven, from the throne; it is not going to be accomplished without human involvement; but there is no salvation in us. So, my question is: Is this not the Old Testament demand for the Incarnation, for the God/man? One of those statements I mentioned above is twice repeated in Isaiah (59:16; 63:5). It says that God sought for a person, an intercessor, and could not find one. And He was shocked when He could not find one. So, He said that His own arm brought salvation. The first verse of Isaiah 53 identifies the Servant as the "arm of the Lord." In fact, in the last twenty chapters of Isaiah, you will find that "the arm of the Lord" becomes almost a technical term for the Messiah. So, if that is true, when He is looking for a person and cannot find one and says, "My own arm brought me salvation," is He not saying, "When I couldn't find one I had to become one"? That means then that salvation did not come from outside of history, but from inside, and that makes history incredibly important.[185]

And this brings us to our opening question as to whether this is part of the Old Testament promise of the God/man, where heaven and earth meet in a human person, and in that human person redemption is provided. Indeed, was the greater portion of the Old Testament necessary to enable people like you and me to comprehend what Jesus was saying and what He came to do? When I was in the pastorate, a Sunday school teacher who was trying to teach the Old Testament to intermediates said to me with some frustration, "Let me ask you, why didn't Jesus just come in Abraham's day? Then we wouldn't have to deal with all this Old Testament stuff." It would have been far simpler from her point of view. But the chances are, if He had come then, He would not have been understood at all. We had enough trouble recognizing Him when He did come. His disciples lived with Him three years, and

---

[185] This is not to say that God did not originate salvation. It is only to say that the means of salvation came through Someone who had a mother, and some brothers and sisters, and hurt when He cut Himself. Salvation came from Someone who looked like us. Two important resources on this point are Gene Edwards, *The Divine Romance* (Auburn, ME: Christian Books Pub. House, 1984) and Charles Williams, *The Descent of the Dove* (London: Longman's, Greene, 1939).

even until the last night they misunderstood what He had come to do. So, our darkness may be deeper than we think it is. And because of that He had to spend a lot more time in preparation to make clear what He wants to do. [186]

<hr/>

[186] If it is true that the Old Testament exists to prepare for Christ, why did so many of the Jewish people miss Him? Look at the twelve disciples; they had spent the better part of three years with Jesus. They had heard everything He had to say. Yet when He told them of the Cross, Peter said, "Never." A person has to be pretty dense to have a teacher like Jesus and still miss it. But Peter was not alone. In Mark 9 and 10 there is story after story where the disciples simply cannot grasp the Cross. It is incomprehensible to them. And the night before the Cross when Jesus stooped to wash their feet, Peter said, "Lord, you will never learn your lines. You don't know how you are supposed to act." We are masters at instructing God in how to be God, because we want Him to play the role we think God ought to play. So they missed Him and we miss Him. Yet, somewhere in this Old Testament it is plain enough so that Jesus could take His two disciples, His two friends, on the road to Emmaus and, starting with Moses and all the prophets, explain that everything that had happened had been anticipated in the Scripture.

So why did they miss Him? Why did His disciples miss Him? But above all, why did the temple miss Him? One day I noticed that there are four pictures of Jesus in the gospel of John that are the exact reverse of what I always thought the Messiah ought to be. I thought that, like the disciples and the temple leaders, I started from a sovereignty concept. God is in control. He can straighten things out if He wants to.

The first picture is implicit in the first chapter where He says, "He came unto His own and His own received Him not." That idea is picked up in Revelation 3 in the Laodacian letter where He says, "Behold I stand at the door and knock." And that image has been translated into Christian art; in Holman Hunt's painting, "The Light of the World." The Christ figure with a crown on His head, royal robes on His body, stands knocking at a door, which has obviously not been opened in a long time, which has no handle on the outside. Now, there is one thing a king never does; that is, to knock at anybody's door, because knocking is a sign of weakness. And He is especially not going to knock on a door that may not be opened to Him.

The second image is on Palm Sunday when He came into the city. And you will remember He chose a donkey. Zechariah 9:9-10 says, "See, your king comes to you . . . gentle and riding on a donkey, on a colt, the foal of a donkey." But verse 10 says, "I will take away the chariots from Ephraim and the war-horses from Jerusalem." Not only is He coming in great humility (Do you think any Roman general ever rode a donkey through Jerusalem? In the Rose Bowl parade, the only people that ride donkeys are the clowns), but He is explicitly denying the key sources of military power. The horse was the military instrument that all the nations in the world were bargaining for, the way the nations want our jets today. They were the equivalent of tanks or greater. But the eternal King rejects all that and comes riding on a donkey.

The third picture is seen on Thursday night before the Crucifixion. On that night He knelt at the feet of His disciples and washed their feet. Human history is the story of mortal men kneeling at the feet of their gods. But there is never in human history the story of a god who knelt at the feet of his people, his worshippers,

Now with that introduction, let me work through the Old Testament data with you. God has this concern for the world. He is a Father. He was a Father before He was Lord,[187] and He will be a Father in the end. And when He created us He put us in families. In other words, He put us together like Himself and He wants us to have that kind of paternal relationship with Him. But He is a *holy* father. And His holiness, His otherness, is especially expressed in an ethical purity unlike anything found in humanity. As such, He is offended by wrong; it repels Him. But that repulsion does not make Him want to let us go. Rather, it makes Him want to get His arms around us and not let us go, because He knows that when we have chosen wrong, we have chosen something detrimental to us, the ones He loves. He wants to deal with the evil, not just to punish us as a Judge.[188] So, what is it that creates evil? It is when I shut the door on

---

the way Jesus did. Peter said, "Never, Lord." And Jesus said, "If you won't let me be me, if you won't let me be Christ, if you won't let me be God, then you can have no part in my kingdom." That was beyond anything they could comprehend.

Of course, the fourth picture is the Cross. And it is a sacrifice. Human history is full of sacrifice, but it is men sacrificing to their gods, not God sacrificing Himself for His people.

But notice how all of those images are turned around in the book of Revelation. In Revelation He does not come knocking; He comes like lightning from east to west. Every eye sees Him simultaneously and there is no door that can shut Him out. In the book of Revelation He does not come on a donkey, He comes on a great white horse with a two-edged sword coming out of His mouth, and with the armies of heaven following Him. In the book of Revelation, He does not come kneeling at our feet, but all the nations of the earth are on their faces at His feet. And the chief men, the mighty men, the captains, are calling for the mountains to fall on them and hide them from the face from the Lamb who sits on the throne. For in the book of Revelation He does not come on a cross, but sits on a great white throne.

But what makes possible those powerful images in Revelation that, if we are honest, we are much more comfortable with? It is the images of self-sacrifice in the gospel of John. Phillipians 2 makes that crystal clear. It is *because* the Second Person of the Blessed Trinity denied Himself and became a servant even unto death that He has been given a name above every name before which every knee will bow. But the fallen human spirit is very good at blocking out every suggestion that the only way to victory is through loss. We have a filter built into us that blocks us from seeing what the Old Testament says as it prepares us for Christ. And it seems as though that filter has to be torn down again in every age. Assisi had to do it in his age. Wesley had to do it in his age as he went out into the fields to preach to miners. Who will do it in our age?

[187] That is, He was Father in the Trinity before there was a creation to be Lord over.

[188] Eichrodt frequently uses the term "juristic" to express this limited aspect

the Source of life. When I shut the door on God, when I shut my heart on God, then evil develops because the source of virtue, the source of righteousness, the source of holiness, is cut off. By my shutting the door on Him, I have created something alien to Him, something that will be my destruction.

So how does He deal with evil? Can He do it by power? You can accomplish a lot with force. And since He is sovereign, He has the power —all power. But the interesting thing is that righteousness cannot be produced by force, and He wants us to be like Himself; he wants us to be righteous. If righteousness could be produced by force, hell might be the most righteous place in existence. But righteousness cannot be produced by force, because you depersonalize people when you deal with them by power alone. If it was mere obedience God wanted, He could buy that by promising blessings. In human history a lot of obedience has been bought in a lot of areas. But Yahweh is after righteousness, and that cannot be bought. Righteousness comes out of a free spirit, a willingness, where you consent to it. And you consent to it because of the rightness of the right, not because of what you are going to get in return for doing right.

Here, then, is God's dilemma. He has all the power He needs to do anything, but what He wants is something that force cannot produce. In the same way, He has all the resources necessary to buy us if He wanted to buy us. But He is not going to buy us, because if He buys us He is not going to have what His heart yearns for: fellowship with beings who share His character. On this issue of buying, you can find a tension in the biblical text, and there are scholars who will be happy to show those supposed contradictions to you. But I think the "contradictions" are in the text because they are in the heart of God. On the one hand, He wants us to be righteous, and at the same time, since that's what we were made for, there are obvious rewards that come from being righteous. So why should we be righteous? For the rewards, of course! But no, for if we slip into that way of thinking, we have become unrighteous! The rewards are by-products, not the ends. God wants to reward us for doing right, but He is not going to bribe us.[189]

of God's work and to say that the faith of Yahwism goes beyond that, beyond the courtroom metaphor.

[189] [Editor's note] An excellent illustration of this point is to be found in

So, you get that kind of problem in the heart of God. What does He do with His creation? And how does He redeem it? After the episode in the Garden, He found that the thoughts and imaginations of men's hearts, the text says, twice, were evil and evil only (Gen. 6:5; 8:21). Now, how does He start over again? It is significant that He starts with an act of judgment and a saving act, and the two come in association with each other. On the one hand, there is the Flood, and on the other, there is the ark. So He makes a new start in saving His creation. But that new start is with a family. Here you can use that word that is so significant later on: *remnant*. He starts with a family and with a promise, a promise not to destroy the world with a flood again.

The same pattern can be found at Babel, where you get an act of judgment on man's arrogance and his effort to build a world of security without God, and a saving act in the encounter with Abraham. Once more He begins with a man and a family and a promise. And in this promise there is that universal note where the arms of God are stretched out to the whole of His creation: "And all the nations of the earth will be blessed through you" (Gen. 12:3). This particular aspect of the promise is repeated twice more to Abraham.[190] It is significant where it occurs. The first time is in Genesis 12, the second time in connection with the judgment on Sodom and Gomorrah, and the third after the offering of Isaac.

In the second instance (Gen. 18), Yahweh is about to act in judgment. But Abraham needs to know that Yahweh's desire is not to destroy, but to save. If there is any basis whatsoever for mercy, He will gladly extend it. Why does Abraham need to know that? Because it is God's purpose that through Abraham all the nations of the earth will have the opportunity of blessing. It is a chapter of judgment, but at the same time

---

Malachi 3. God calls on His people to stop robbing Him, and when they indignantly ask how they are robbing Him, he tells them it is when they withhold their tithes. In the context of the book, it is clear that they should tithe as an act of love to their Covenant Lord, who has been unfailingly faithful to them. It is the "right" thing to do. But God goes on and says that if they do tithe they will be blessed. Too much preaching has fastened on this secondary point to make it appear that the reason to give to God is so as to get blessed, which is exactly the opposite of what Malachi is saying in the context of the book.

[190] (18:18; 22:18). At least one aspect of the threefold promise—land, progeny, blessing to the nations—is repeated to Abraham seven times by God (12:1-3; 13:14-17; 15:18; 17:2; 18:10, 14-18; 22:15-18).

it is a chapter of salvation. Because Abraham will be faithful and teach his sons and walk before them, the promise is going to be kept to him and the ends of the earth are considered in it. It is also in that chapter that the name of Isaac, "He laughs," appears. As I said above, it may well be that what is being spoken about here is divine joy, because a way is set for the redemption of the world.

The third time this aspect of the promise occurs in Abraham's life is after the sacrifice of Isaac (Gen. 22:18). This child, who had been identified with the hope of the world, had been offered by Abraham and God said, "I don't want him. I'm not in the business of destroying humanity, no matter how great their sin. I'm looking for a way to redeem them." Because Abraham had trusted, believed, and obeyed, there was indeed hope for the world.

The next time this particular promise appears is again in the life of Isaac, but now when he is a grown man. The text (Gen. 26:1-5) does not elaborate on the situation, but simply says, "There was a famine." Apparently Isaac was thinking of going down to Egypt to escape it, because God said, "Don't go to Egypt. I will take care of you. I am not going to let you be destroyed, because I am not in the business of destroying. I am in the business of saving. And the promise I made to your father I am renewing with you: All the nations of the earth are going to be blessed through you." Do you notice the human involvement in that?

In chapter 28 the promise is made to the next generation so that we have three generations of promise. The promise of blessing now comes to Jacob. He is at Bethel. He is fleeing from his brother's wrath; he is alone; he is apprehensive; he does not know what the future is. And when God gives him a wonderful vision, he becomes a preeminent example of a sinner who wants to bargain with God. So he says, "What do I have to do to get you to protect me and take me as I go? I will tithe, I will give you a tenth." For Jacob, being who he was, I assume that was a significant step. I think it is the first reference to tithing in Scripture. Jacob said, "I will give that if you will keep your promise." And God said, "I will keep my promise, because what we have in mind is more than you, Jacob. What we have in mind is the ends of the earth."

So God is at work on the human level in history, with persons like you and me, moving to redeem the world. Then Abraham's family goes to Egypt for four hundred years. Can you imagine how much can be lost in four hundred years? But whatever may have been lost, there was still a memory from the past. It appears in the way Yahweh identifies Himself to Moses in Exodus 3. Moses had turned aside to take a closer look at this bush that burned but was not consumed. And God said to him, "Don't come any closer. Take off your sandals, for the place where you are standing is holy ground." Then God identified Himself. He said, "I am the God of your father, the God of Abraham, the God of Isaac, and the God of Jacob." At this Moses covered his face because he was afraid to look at God.

What is Yahweh saying when He introduces Himself in that way? He is saying to Moses, "Moses, we are not just dealing with how to get Israel out of Egyptian bondage. We are not just dealing with how to get this generation out of its enslavement in that country. If you remember my promises to your fathers, you know that what happens to Israel has implications for the ends of the earth. And it began back there with your ancestor." The evidence that Moses knew who Abraham and Isaac and Jacob were, and knew the worldwide implications of that introduction, is found in his fear to look on God. This was not some local desert spirit; this was the God who had plans for the whole earth.

The importance of this connection between Yahweh, as He named Himself, and the God of the Fathers runs throughout this passage. It establishes two things. One of them is of history. What is taking place is not something that is done in isolation from what has been before. It is a step in the process of what God wants to do. And the second thing is the concept of election. These people are not just any people. They are the promised descendants of Abraham, Isaac, and Jacob. Thus, they are God's people. Notice Exodus 3:7: "I have seen the misery of my people." When Yahweh identifies Israel, these slave people in Egypt, as "my people," there are centuries of history behind that as well as the divine election.

In verse 13 when Moses says to God, "Suppose I go to the Israelites and say to them, 'The God of your fathers has sent me,'" he is assuming that they will not have to be reminded of their history. They may have forgotten much in those four hundred years, but they had not forgotten that God had revealed Himself to their fathers. In verse 14 Yahweh gives him the Name and tells him in verses 15-18:

Say to the Israelites, "[Yahweh], the God of your fathers—the God of Abraham, the God of Isaac and the God of Jacob—has sent me to you." This is my name forever, the name by which I am to be remembered from generation to generation.

"Go, assemble the elders of Israel and say to them, '[Yahweh], the God of your fathers—the God of Abraham, Isaac and Jacob—appeared to me and said: I have watched over you and have seen what has been done to you in Egypt. And I have promised to bring you up out of your misery in Egypt into the land of the Canaanites. . . .' The elders of Israel will listen to you. Then you and the elders are to go to the king of Egypt and say to him, '[Yahweh], the God of the Hebrews, has met with us.'"

Four times in verses 13-18 (counting "God of the Hebrews") these paired concepts, God's involvement in the historical process and election, appear.

That, in a sense, is looking back. But what is the purpose of the Exodus? It was not simply to relieve the suffering of the Hebrews, as important as that was. God had something greater in mind, something that had been part of the promise from the beginning. That purpose is found in Exodus 19 when the people have reached the foot of Sinai. There God begins to unveil His covenant and He says He wants them to be His people, "a kingdom of priests and a holy nation" (19:6). What does that mean? In a sense, just as Abraham stood between God and the world in his day, and Moses stands between God and Israel in his day, now Israel is to stand between God and the nations. Priests are not priests for themselves, primarily. Priests are priests to serve other people and to stand as the intermediaries between them and the God that they worship. So Israel is to be a kingdom of priests, and what the family of Aaron and the Levites are to Israel, Israel is to be to the whole world.

Forty years later, Moses is talking to Israel for the last time and in Deuteronomy 9:5 he says,

"It is not because of your righteousness or your

integrity that you are going to take possession of [the Canaanites'] land; but on account of the wickedness of these nations, the Lord your God will drive them out before you, to accomplish what he swore to your fathers, to Abraham, Isaac and Jacob."

Let me tell you how I understand that statement. I would not argue that it is the only possible way to understand it, but I think it is one possible way. For many years I interpreted that as meaning that Israel was the best He could find. Although they were not models themselves (He goes on to tell them, "You are a stiff-necked people."), still I thought maybe He chose them because they were not as bad as the others. But then I realized that the statement could be turned around to mean, "I can start with you, and I am starting with you because of the great need of the others." So He is not speaking about the wickedness of the nations merely as a pretext for their destruction. He is speaking about their wickedness because He is putting together a plan to save the world. So when we find some of these references where judgment is linked with promise, we should remember that in the midst of that judgment, God's ultimate purpose is redemptive. He says He did it to fulfill the promises made to the fathers. I suggest to you that the promise mentioned there does not only refer to the promise of the land. Again, we have that historical reference and the election reference. It is because of the unrighteousness of the rest of the world, that so badly needs redemption, that He says, "I will use you, though you are a stiff-necked people."

So Israel was conscious that it was chosen, that it was elect. And in its best moments, it knew that that election was not for itself. God had something bigger in mind. He had the world in mind. Now, there is no question that at times the Hebrews did not understand. They sometimes were so concerned about themselves that the universalistic element is either not there, or it is only implicitly there, in their thinking. But before we start throwing too many rocks at them, we ought to consider what percentage of the budget of a typical church in America goes to reaching the world. So the fact that something is not actively practiced at certain times is not an accurate barometer of the heart of God and the purpose of the gospel and the thrust of the gospel.

Surely there were times when this understanding was at a very low ebb. The period of the judges was such a time. In one sense it was a survival period. It was like what you find in many moments of Christian history, when the difference between the church and what you find in the New Testament is as radical as the difference between the Pentateuch and what you find in the book of Judges. But we do know that it did survive, for when David appeared, it rang out crystal clear again. You see that very clearly in 2 Samuel 7 with its introduction of the Davidic covenant. Walter Brueggemann says about this passage,

> I judge this oracle with its unconditional promise to David to be the most crucial theological statement in the Old Testament. This ideological utterance is the tap-root of the messianic idea in ancient Israel. This enduring promise that God has made to David has placed messianism at the heart of both Judaism and Christianity. It has made these communities to be communities of hope.[191]

Ultimately he is saying that this promise to David is the taproot of what caused the temple to send down to John the Baptist and ask, "Are you the one we are looking for?" So, it is a significant passage.

> Go and tell my servant David, "This is what [Yahweh] says, Are you the one to build me a house to dwell in? I have not dwelt in a house from the day I brought the Israelites up out of Egypt to this day. I have been moving from place to place with a tent as my dwelling. . . . Now then, tell my servant David, "This is what [Yahweh of Heaven's Hosts] says: I took you from the pasture and from following the flock to be ruler over my people Israel. I have been with you wherever you have gone, and I have cut off all your enemies from before you. Now I will make your name great, like the names of the greatest men of the earth. And I will provide a place for my people Israel and will plant them so that they can have

---

[191] Walter Brueggemann, *First and Second Samuel*, Interpretation Commentary (Louisville: John Knox Press, 1990).

a home of their own and no longer be disturbed. . . . I will also give you rest from all your enemies. [Yahweh] declares to you that [Yahweh] himself will establish a house for you: When your days are over and you rest with your fathers, I will raise up your offspring to succeed you, who will come from your own body, and I will establish his kingdom. He is the one who will build a house for my Name, and I will establish the throne of his kingdom forever. I will be his father, and he will be my son. When he does wrong I will punish him with the rod of men, with floggings inflicted by men. But my [*hesed*] will never be taken away from him, as I took it away from Saul, whom I removed from before you. Your house and your kingdom will endure forever before me; your throne will be established forever.'"

Nathan reported to David all the words of this entire revelation. Then King David went in and sat before the Lord, and he said: "Who am I, [Lord Yahweh], and what is my family that you have brought me this far? And as if this were not enough in your sight, O [Lord Yahweh], you have also spoken about the future of the house of your servant. Is this your usual way of dealing with man, O [Lord Yahweh]? What more can David say to you? For you know your servant, O [Lord Yahweh]. For the sake of your word and according to your will, you have done this great thing and made it known to your servant" (2 Sam. 7:5-21).

"For the sake of your word," has Genesis 12:3 implicit within it. "For the sake of your word and according to your will." There are centuries of God's dealing with Israel behind that statement.

"How great you are, O [Lord Yahweh]! There is no one like you, and there is no God but you, as we have heard with our own ears. And who is like your people Israel— the one nation on earth that God went out to redeem as a people for himself, to make a name for himself. . . .

> You have established your people Israel as your own
> forever, and you, O [Yahweh], have become their God.
>   "And now, [Yahweh God], keep forever the
> promise [literally "word"][192] you have made concerning
> your servant and his house" (2 Sam. 7:22-25).

When David becomes king of Israel, Nathan the prophet gives Yahweh's word to him. It concerns him and his kingdom. Israel may be a petty kingdom, away from the world center of power, but what is happening here is not petty or marginal business. Nathan reminds David that this event is part of a bigger story. It is the next big step in the story after the call of Abraham, the Exodus, the Sinai covenant, and the Conquest—God is going to make David's name great. He is going to establish his kingdom *forever*. Now, the universal note is taking on an eternal dimension.

But the eternal dimension is not with Israel as a whole but with a part of Israel—David's house. Some commentaries make quite a point that this is an unconditional promise. The Sinai covenant, at least in the beginning, was centered around an "if." But when God speaks to David, the "if" is gone. Let me tell you my reaction. You have a different thing here from what you have in Exodus where He is saying, "You are to be a kingdom of priests, and you are to stand between God, the true God, and a world that needs Him, between the One who is the light and a world that is in darkness." But now He is saying that it is through this royal house of David that the Redeemer will come. That is not conditional. When you get to the Gospels and when Christ came, they said, "We don't know a great deal about the Messiah, but we know that He will come from the house of David."

Note that Yahweh is to be known to the world by His identification with a specific group of human beings, a historical entity. He called Abraham, who was a person; Israel, who was a people; David, who was a king; and David's house, which was a kingdom. And so we understand that God apparently moves from a part to the whole and moves from within history and within time and space to save His world.

---

[192] The *NIV* translation of *word* (*dabar*) as "promise" is correct. Because if Yahweh says something, it is certain.

He apparently needs a foothold and a witness, and that foothold is in a human spirit—the human spirit. So it was in Israel, and today there is a sense in which the body of Christ is the new Israel as we understand from the New Testament.

Now, one wonders how widely that promise to Abraham was known through the different generations of the Old Testament. And the Old Testament does not satisfy our curiosity on that. This is the reason I have gone back and reviewed the history, because periodically the promise surfaces again, and when it does, there are people who recognize it, saying, "Wait a minute. He is speaking to our history, and He is speaking to the purpose of our existence." That story never perished, and each new step that was taken presumed or assumed the steps that had been taken before.

Lecture 25

· · · · · · · · · ·

The Necessity of a Mediator

Let me remind you of the ground we covered in the previous lecture. When one takes the Old Testament from the beginning, God's purpose is redemptive; God is never first a judge. Furthermore, salvation is not going to come from the throne. It originates there but it won't be accomplished there. It is in time and space that redemption takes place. And redemption is not going to be done without us. Yet, although it is not going to be done without us, there is no salvation in any of us. All salvation is in Him and comes from beyond, but it takes place in the here and now and not without human involvement. So we raised the question: Are these the roots of the Old Testament promise of the God/man, the one in whom these two are combined? I believe all of this points very clearly to the fact that Old Testament religion, Yahwism, is a religion not only focused on Yahweh but on a mediator as well.

That concept of the mediator comes to something of a point in

2 Samuel 7 with the covenant God makes with the house of David. In Abraham you have a man and a family, and in Moses you have a man and a nation, and now you have a man and an eternal royal house.

It is very clear in Acts and Galatians that the New Testament believers saw the fulfillment of all of that in Christ. Let me remind you of some of that data. In Acts 3, Peter is taking advantage of the uproar created by the healing of the crippled beggar to preach Christ.

> For Moses said, "The Lord your God will raise up for you a prophet like me [Moses] from among your people; you must listen to everything he tells you. Anyone who does not listen to him will be completely cut off from among his people." Indeed, all the prophets from Samuel on, as many as have spoken, have foretold these days. And you are heirs of the prophets and of the covenant God made with your fathers. He said to Abraham, "Through your offspring all peoples on earth will be blessed" (Acts 3:22-25).

So Peter takes a quotation right out of Genesis to explain that the mission of Christ is nothing other than the fulfillment of the promise to Abraham. What God started in Abraham has culminated in Calvary and the Resurrection and the Ascension and now in the outpouring of Pentecost. Peter goes on to say, "When God raised up his servant, he sent him first to you to bless you by turning each of you from your wicked ways" (Acts 3:26). I would like to draw attention to "sent him first to you." I think what that means is that Christ's ministry can only be complete when the blessing of His salvation is made available to the ends of the earth. God started in Israel because that is the medium through which God has seen fit to redeem the human race. We wonder if Peter received this insight as a direct inspiration from the Holy Spirit or whether Jesus had talked about these things with His disciples at some time. In any case, you can see the way this vision of being a blessing to the nations is a continuing theme that runs through into the New Testament.

Turn now to Galatians 3, either Paul's first or second preserved letter.[193] Paul, formerly Saul, of Tarsus, now Paul the apostle, has received word that some of his Galatian converts have turned away from the faith of Abraham to more of a faith in the Law of Moses, if you will let me express it that way. Instead of trusting in Yahweh through Christ they are now coming to depend on Judaistic legalism. So he says in verse 6:

> Consider Abraham. "He believed God, and it was credited to him as righteousness." Understand, then, that those who believe are children of Abraham. The Scripture foresaw that God would justify the Gentiles by faith, and announced the gospel in advance to Abraham: "All nations will be blessed through you" (Galatians 3:6-8).

It is significant that he said "those who believe" and not "those who are circumcised." He is identifying the essence of Abraham's relationship as lying in neither the ethnic nor the legal character of his relationship, but in the personal relationship of trusting submission. This relationship is open to all, and Paul understands that to be the goal of God's self-revelation to Abraham.

Some years ago archaeologists in Jerusalem found a stone with an inscription on it, and the inscription supports something said in Josephus, I believe. On the outer edges of the court of Herod's temple was a barrier beyond which a Gentile could not pass. The inscription on the stone goes something like this: "Any Gentile who passes beyond this point will be responsible for his own death." I wonder if that was one of the reasons that Jesus cleaned out the temple. I also wonder if when Jesus spoke the words recorded in John 3:16 ("whosoever believes . . ."), He was giving His conclusion to the temple cleansing story (reported in John 2). In any case, notice the two passages of the Old Testament Jesus quoted while He was cleansing the temple. One is from Jeremiah's famous temple sermon recorded in Jeremiah 7:11 where he asks, "Has this house, which bears my Name, become a den of robbers to you?" But Jesus also quoted from Isaiah 56:7, "My house will be called a house of prayer for all nations." That passage from Isaiah is looking forward to

---

[193] First Thessalonians might have preceded Galatians, but that is not certain.

the day when the Gentiles are going to throng the courts of the temple in Jerusalem, praising Yahweh.

So there is a tension running right through the doctrine of election. God's election is for us. But God's election for the world. That is the point Paul belabors.

> The Scripture foresaw [when Israel did not] that God would justify the Gentiles by faith, and announced the gospel in advance to Abraham: "All nations will be blessed through you." So those who have faith are blessed along with Abraham, the man of faith (Gal. 3:8-9).

So it is clear how the New Testament understood the continuity of the promise to Abraham flowing through the son of David to the whole world.

But we might still ask with some scholars whether that is perhaps a misappropriation of the Old Testament message, or if not a misappropriation, at least a creative reappropriation. Did the Old Testament see this mediator in terms like these, and did it understand that this son of David would be the fulfillment of the Abrahamic promise? Turn with me to Psalm 72, which is a royal psalm. It is clearly about the king, the one who sits on the throne of David. Look at verse 17, "May his name endure forever; may it continue as long as the sun. All nations will be blessed through him and they will call him blessed." That is pretty clear, is it not? The promise given to Abraham is now being applied to the king who sits on David's throne. But who is this man? I think that if you will look closely at the psalm, you will see that it is describing someone utterly unlike any of David's merely human sons. The psalm begins:

> Endow the king with your justice, O God,
> the royal son with your righteousness.

Notice immediately what is being said. The king is not the source of justice. And the king is not the source of righteousness. So the people are praying for their king that he will receive justice and righteousness from the source of those things, who is Yahweh. Let me belabor the obvious; this is in marked contrast to much of the Middle East where the kings were looked upon as divine or else in a very unique relationship with the deity. But in Israel there was always this insistence on the distinction between God and king. I think one of the reasons was to keep the kingship in its proper perspective. The tendency was for power to become concentrated in the king's hands and for the king to think that he was more important than he was. And so the prayer is, let him know that he stands between Yahweh and us, and that what we need is not him. What we need is what Yahweh has, but we need what Yahweh has to come through him.

Ultimately, that is going to require a king who will lay down his life for his people, like the King of Isaiah 53. Read on in Psalm 72:

> He will judge your people in righteousness,
> your afflicted ones with justice.
> The mountains will bring prosperity to the people,
> the hills the fruit of righteousness.
> He will defend the afflicted among the people,
> and save the children of the needy;
> he will crush the oppressor (72:2-4).

That section offers what we might call the first accolade. This is a King who does not rule for the advantage of the mighty. Judging the people in righteousness means that He is to give justice to the afflicted. He is to defend the afflicted. He is to save the children of the needy, and He is to crush the oppressor. For whom does the King live and operate? The prayer is for Him to fulfill His function of being concerned about the neediest, the weakest, the least. Their welfare is His business.

This theme appears again in verse 12. It is like a musical motif that keeps recurring in a symphony.

> He will deliver the needy who cry out,
> the afflicted who have no one to help.
> He will take pity on the weak and the needy,
> and save the needy from death.
> He will rescue them from oppression and violence,
> for precious is their blood in his sight
> (72:12-14).

This was a public prayer; it was the cry of the people of Israel about their king. It was a prayer that he would be the guarantor of justice and of righteousness in Israel.

There are a couple of other features of the psalm worth noticing. Although this is a prayer focused on a rather small, circumscribed kingdom from the world's point of view, there are universal implications here. If the king judges people in righteousness, and guarantees justice to the afflicted, then the mountains will bring prosperity to the people and the hills, the fruit of righteousness (v. 3). If there is a righteous king on the throne, nature will join in by being supportive and productive. You will recall similar imagery in Isaiah 35, where when people return to God from their barren self-exaltation, all nature "will rejoice and blossom." You begin to get the picture that when righteousness prevails, nature responds to it. Now, does the king have any power over nature? Is he responsible for that? Oh no. Yahweh is the Lord of nature, and it is because you have found a king who is pleasing to Yahweh, who is representing Yahweh between Yahweh's throne and the earth. When you get him, then Yahweh acts and nature responds to his good pleasure.

Notice also the temporal dimensions of this kingship.

> He will endure as long as the sun,
>> as long as the moon, through all generations.
> He will be like rain falling on a mown field,
>> like showers watering the earth.
> In his days the righteous will flourish;
>> prosperity will abound till the moon is no more
>> (72:5-7).

How is it that in 900 or 800 B.C. singers are saying of a petty king of a small kingdom in the Middle East that his kingdom will last forever, as long as the sun and as long as the moon?

Notice also the extent of this man's kingdom. You will notice he says,

> He will rule from sea to sea
>> and from the River [Euphrates] to the ends of
>> the earth.

The desert tribes will bow before him
    and his enemies will lick the dust.
The kings of Tarshish and of distant shores
    will bring tribute to him;
The kings of Sheba and Seba
    will present him gifts.
All kings will bow down to him
    and all nations will serve him
    (72:8-11).

This is clearly a worldwide reign. How would someone from Tarshish, the far western end of the Mediterranean, know anything about this king in Jerusalem? Nevertheless, the psalmist is saying that the kings of Tarshish and other distant shores will bring treasure to this small kingdom, to Jerusalem. The kings of Sheba and Seba, from Arabia to Ethiopia, will bring presents. All kings will bow down to him and all nations will serve him. Why?

For he will deliver the needy who cry out,
    the afflicted who have no one to help.
He will take pity on the weak and the needy
    and save the needy from death.
He will rescue them from oppression and violence,
    for precious is their blood his sight
    (72:12-14).

The conclusion is what the old orators called a "preoration"—a ringing, driving windup to the whole address.

Long may he live!
    May gold from Sheba be given him.
May people ever pray for him
    and bless him all day long.
Let grain abound throughout the land;
    on the top of the hills may it sway.
Let its root flourish like Lebanon;
    let it thrive like the grass of the field.
May his name endure forever;

> may it continue as long as the sun.
> All nations will be blessed through him,
>   and they will call him blessed.
> Praise be to [Yahweh], the God of Israel,
>   who alone does marvelous deeds.
> Praise be to his glorious name forever;
>   may the whole earth be filled with his glory
>   (72:15-19).

Think for a moment about Micah 5:2, the prophecy about Bethlehem. I used to think that passage was primarily talking about the place where Jesus was going to be born. But that is not so. It is talking about Bethlehem as the center out of which the Davidic throne came. It is a completely different context from the way many of us have read the passage. In other words, it is not talking about the barn where a baby would be born. Rather, it is talking about the kingly nature of the One who would come from there. This is what von Rad has to say about Psalm 72.

> The man whom the royal psalms envisage as designated by God to be king of the whole world (Pss. II, LXXII), the anointed who redeems all victims of oppression and violence, and in whose sight the very poorest is precious (Ps. LXXII. 14), is a man who carries little conviction in the world of power politics. We do not know how contemporary Israel got round this contradiction; possibly, she was not greatly troubled by it. But this does stress the fact that a petty Judean king was given in God's name a claim to world wide dominion and a saving office which he could not possibly fulfill. After his death, this mandate had to be handed on to his successor, along with the question, "Are you he who is to come, or shall we look for another?"[194]

What a fascinating quotation. Now, how do you respond to that?

---

[194] von Rad, *Old Testament Theology*, vol. 2, 374-75.

Tradition (in the superscription) tells us that this psalm was attributed to Solomon and prayed about him. Many of the royal psalms were addressed to the king who was sitting on the throne. My point here is that if deliverance of the race is going to occur, it is going to take place at the human level, and humans are going to be involved. Somehow, this deliverance is going to be realized through a human son of David. I no longer believe that it is a single text in the Old Testament or a collection of isolated texts that predict Him. Rather, there is this whole thrust in the Old Testament from that day of Abraham up to the very hour that Peter said, "This is it!" As a result, the steady orientation of the Israelites' thinking was toward the future. So when a Davidic king failed, the Judeans did not say, "We had better give up on this," but they kept saying, "One of these days, the kind of king we are looking for is going to come."

In this area of kingship we come once again to the continuity/ discontinuity issue. Certainly extravagant things were said about rulers all over the ancient world. Beyond that you can find instances in non-Israelite literature where the king was supposed to uphold justice and care for the disadvantaged. That is the continuity side. But what about the discontinuity? Look at Psalm 101, which is attributed to David.

> I will sing of your love and justice;
> > to you, O [Yahweh], I will sing praise.
> I will be careful to lead a blameless life—
> > when will you come to me?
> I will walk in my house with blameless heart.
> > I will set before my eyes no vile thing.
> The deeds of faithless men I hate;
> > they will not cling to me.
> Men of perverse heart shall be far from me;
> > I will have nothing to do with evil.
> Whoever slanders his neighbor in secret,
> > him will I put to silence;
> whoever has haughty eyes and a proud heart,
> > him will I not endure.
> My eyes will be on the faithful in the land,
> > that they may dwell with me.
> He whose walk is blameless

will minister to me.
No one who practices deceit
    will dwell in my house;
no one who speaks falsely
    will stand in my presence.
Every morning I will put to silence
    all the wicked in the land;
I will cut off every evildoer
    from the city of the Lord
    (Psalm 101:1-8).

Translate all this into the modern corridors of power, and I think you can see how radical these words are. "Whoever slanders his neighbor . . ."? Can you imagine that in the royal court, in the White House, in Congress? You see, slander is a violation of one of the Ten Commandments. So in Yahwism it is a major transgression. And here is a king who is going to hold to that kind of standard for truth in His court. We do not have here merely lip service to some external standard of justice. Furthermore, notice that the "I" in all of that is the one who says, "I will sing of your love and of your justice. To you, O Yahweh, I will sing praise. But this is what I am going to do. . . ." Some way or other, the king in Israel was looked upon as a mediator. He was a mediatory in the sense that he was to see that patterns of righteousness and of truth and of integrity, of compassion and mercy and human love for one another, these patterns that had come from Yahweh, were translated into reality within the kingdom. I think you will be hard-pressed to find anything like this elsewhere among the kings of the Ancient Near East.

I think this is why von Rad says that there was something here that made each successive royal failure point to the future; someone was going to have to come sooner or later who would be, both in His person and in His administration, the means whereby the ancient promise to Abraham could be fulfilled. Thus, there was an institutional demand for Christ, and when He came He was called the Son of David. I think that you have a mindset developing in the society, in the social institutions, both politically and religiously and in the prophets, that we need to solve the problems we have in order to fulfill the promise that was given to Abraham.

Now, who would be the perfect ruler, and what would He be like? The Old Testament offers many snapshots in order to create a composite picture for them so they can conceive of who the perfect ruler and the perfect mediator would be. For instance, there is Moses. How would you describe him as the leader of Israel? What is his primary characteristic? Was he a priest? A political figure? A figure of power? The thing that impresses me the most is that he was a mediator, and more particularly, an intercessor.

But what does it mean to intercede? In modern usage, it tends to mean, "to speak on behalf of." For a long time I thought of intercession primarily as speech and intercessory prayer as simply a verbalization of your requests on behalf of someone else. But when you look at the origins of the word and then look at the implications of the word in the Old Testament, I think you will find out that there is more going on than merely speaking on behalf of someone else. The Latin for *intercession* means "to stand between," and that is exactly what we find the Old Testament intercessors doing. So when I talk about intercession in this lecture and the next one, do not limit your thinking to verbalization of prayers. Maybe we need another term, something like "intermediation," to begin to convey what is really going on.

Now intercession did not begin with Moses. In an earlier lecture we talked about Abraham's part in the Sodom and Gomorrah episode in Genesis 18. There Yahweh stands before Abraham to see if he will intercede for the righteous who might be found in the doomed cities of Sodom and Gomorrah. Intercession is not our attempt to persuade God to do something He would rather not do. Instead, God is looking for someone who will intercede. It is Yahweh Himself who wants to initiate the intercession. Why is that? Why is intercession important? I wish I could answer that question more fully than I can. It is not that we add something to the work of salvation; salvation is in God and God alone. But there is something in Him that causes Him to invite us to enter into that process, and that entering in seems vital to the completion of the process.

When we turn to Moses, we see something of the same thing. There on Mt. Sinai during the golden calf incident, Yahweh virtually invites Moses to intercede when He says, "Leave me alone so that my anger may burn against them" (Ex. 32:10). Leave me alone? What is

Yahweh saying? He is saying that all that needs to happen to prevent His just anger from having its appropriate effect on these covenant breakers is for Moses to step in and intercede for them. Here again we are not talking about cultic atonement, but about deeply intimate personal relations with the Almighty. Whatever the theological issues that this text might raise, it takes on a very relevant texture and tone for the pastor who finds himself dealing with a congregation that is recalcitrant and stubborn. Will we leave Yahweh alone?

That incident continues into Exodus 34, where God is renewing the covenant with the people in a unilateral way. There after the breathtaking revelation of the character of Yahweh, who is full of *hesed*, gracious and compassionate, but upon whose grace no one should think they can impose (vv. 6-7), Moses bows to the ground at once and worships, "O [Yahweh], if I have found favor in your eyes . . . , then let [Yahweh] go with us. Although this is a stiff-necked people, forgive our wickedness and our sin, and take us as your inheritance" (v. 9). Moses is standing between Yahweh and His holiness and a people and their sin.

Look at some of the instances in the book of Numbers where Moses plays the part of the intercessor. In chapter 12 you have one of those dark moments in Israel's existence, and a dark moment in Moses' existence, when his sister and his brother turn against him. There is dissension on the "church staff," and Miriam and Aaron want to straighten out "the senior pastor." Miriam and Aaron began to talk against Moses because of his Cushite wife. They said he had married into the wrong ethnic group, and his wife was a problem in the congregation. But that was a pretext; their real problem was professional jealousy: "'Has [Yahweh] spoken only through Moses?' they asked. 'Hasn't he also spoken through us?' And [Yahweh] heard this"(12:2). Here was an opportunity for Moses to engage in a bit of self-righteousness. They had not only challenged his authority, but his very position. But that is not what he did nor how he reacted. Look at the next verses:

> (Now Moses was a very humble man, more humble than anyone else on the face of the earth.) At once [Yahweh] said to Moses, Aaron and Miriam, "Come out of the Tent of Meeting, all three of you." So the three of them came out. Then [Yahweh] came down in

a pillar of cloud; he stood at the entrance of the Tent and summoned Aaron and Miriam. When both of them stepped forward, he said, "Listen to my words: 'When a prophet of [Yahweh] is among you, I reveal myself to him in visions, I speak to him in dreams. But this is not true of my servant Moses; he is faithful in all my house. With him I speak face to face, clearly and not in riddles; he sees the form of [Yahweh]. Why then were you not afraid to speak against my servant Moses?'" The anger of [Yahweh] burned against them, and he left them. When the cloud lifted from above the Tent, there stood Miriam—leprous like snow. Aaron turned toward her and saw that she had leprosy; and he said to Moses, "Please, my lord, do not hold against us the sin we have so foolishly committed. Do not let her be like a stillborn infant coming from its mother's womb with its flesh half eaten away." So Moses cried out to [Yahweh], "O God, please heal her!" (Numbers 12:3-13).

There are mysteries here that I cannot explain, but whatever else is being said, one of the things being conveyed to us is this: When you find someone who cares more about another person's well-being than his own face, name, reputation, or position, that other person has possibilities that are not there without someone like that.

Then turn to Numbers 14. Here is the greatest tragedy in the Pentateuch after Genesis 3. After all the careful preparations, after all the solemn oaths of the covenant, after God's gracious restoration after the golden calf episode, when Israel comes to the point of radically trusting God and entering the Promised Land, they refuse.

That night all the people of the community raised their voices and wept aloud. All the Israelites grumbled against Moses and Aaron, and the whole assembly said to them, "If only we had died in Egypt! Or in this desert! Why is the Lord bringing us to this land only to let us fall by the sword? Our wives and children will be taken as plunder. Wouldn't it be better for us to go back to Egypt?" And they said to each other, "We should choose a leader and go back to Egypt." Then Moses and Aaron fell facedown in front of the whole Israelite assembly gathered there. Joshua son of Nun and Caleb son of Jephunneh, who were among those who had explored the land, tore their clothes and said to the entire Israelite assembly, "The land we passed through and explored is exceedingly good. If [Yahweh] is pleased with us, he will lead us into that land, a land flowing with milk and honey, and will give it to us. Only do not rebel against [Yahweh]. And do not be afraid of the people of the land, because we will swallow them up. Their protection is gone, but [Yahweh] is with us. Do not be afraid of them." But the whole assembly talked about stoning them (14:1-10a).

Clearly there is nothing more to be done with this group of people but to destroy them. But what about the promise, will that go too?

Then the glory of the Lord appeared at the Tent of Meeting to all the Israelites. [Yahweh] said to Moses, "How long will these people treat me with contempt? How long will they refuse to believe in me, in spite of all the miraculous signs I have performed among them? I will strike them down with a plague and destroy them. But I will make you into a nation greater and stronger than they" (14:10b-12).

Here is the same offer that Yahweh made to Moses on Mt. Sinai in Exodus 32. Here is an opportunity for Moses to get some of his own back; these ungrateful people, these "children of Israel," will be wiped out and in the future the people of the promise will be called "the children of Moses." But once again, Moses comes through like gold. He responds,

"Then the Egyptians will hear about it! By your power you brought these people up from among them. And they will tell the inhabitants of this land about it. They have already heard that you, O [Yahweh], are with these people. . . . If you put these people to death all at one time, the nations who have heard this report about you will say, '[Yahweh] was not able to bring these people into the land he promised them on oath; so he slaughtered them in the desert.' . . . In accordance with your great [*hesed*], forgive the sin of these people just as you have pardoned them from the time they left Egypt until now (14:13-19).

Moses refused the invitation to aggrandize himself and instead asked Yahweh to forgive these people just as Yahweh had been doing ever since he brought them out of Egypt.[195] Here is an individual who stood between God and a people who did not want him to stand between them. The person interceding is the one who had been rejected by the people for whom he was interceding.

We can look at chapter 16, Korah's rebellion, or at chapter 21 where the people are again grumbling and impatient. If you go through Numbers, you will notice that one of the prime roles of Moses was as a mediator in the sense of an intercessor who stands between Yahweh in His wrath and a people in their sin. Again and again the thing that saves them is that intercession. Now, I think what is being developed is the concept of a Messiah, which will be spelled out ultimately in Isaiah 53. It will be a different concept of kingship than can be found anyplace else in the world. He will be a king, but it will be a different kind of king.

---

[195] The word *forgive* is the Hebrew word *salah*. The word *pardon* is the word *nasa'* "to bear." "*Bear* them just as you have *borne* them from the time they left Egypt until now."

Lecture 26

. . . .

The Relation of Intercession to Sacrifice and Atonement

In the previous lecture I said that the idea of the ideal leader being an intermediary prepares us for the picture of the Messiah given in Isaiah 53. But before we go there, we must think about the way intercession relates to the matters of sacrifice and cult and to consider the ways intercession produces a very significant alteration in the understanding of the efficacy of cultic activity. In that connection, let me remind you that from beginning to end Eichrodt is concerned to differentiate between Yahwism, the religion of Israel, the religion of the Old Testament, and the religions of the peoples around Israel. He never gets away from that. In Yahwism everything is changed by the personal character of Yahweh. This is where we began: Yahweh is the most determinative factor, and the reality of His nature and character changes everything. The mechanistic, as Eichrodt expresses it, the automatic, the magical are gone. When he makes a statement like that, I think of it in this way: Everything impersonal is put to one side because Yahweh is a Person, and at the center of everything is a personal relationship. Before the end of the lecture I hope to show you the significance of that reality as it relates to intercession and cult.

When we think about sacrifice and atonement in Israel the legitimacy of all sacrificial actions is established by Yahweh Himself. Thus it is not the sacrificial system in itself that interests us; it is the fact that this system is the one that *He* gave, and since He did, we want to know why He gave it and what His purposes were in doing so; we do not think of the sacrificial system apart from Him. The whole cultic institution of atonement is seen as the gracious creation of the covenant God, so that the cult is not just something inherited from a world around Israel. The cultic practices of Israel may have many similarities with the cult of the world around them, but the cult of Israel is one that has, as it were, Yahweh's imprimatur on it; it is His special gift to them. God Himself gives His people the possibility of having their sins expiated, and of assuring themselves of that fact, through the cult and its sacrificial system, through these signs of His mercy. So these cultic actions have no separate existence in themselves; they are signs from Him pointing to His free *hesed* that we need to get to.

Thus the whole sacrificial system in the Old Testament is basically symbolic. The blood of a bull or goat could never take away your sin or mine. But do not despise symbolism. We live by symbolism, because it translates the abstract into the concrete. We live by symbolism because that is the way we get in touch with reality. But if the sacrificial system was only symbolic, why such stress on it? Why could the constant sacrificing of the blood of animals not really deliver us from the effects of our sin? I cannot give an exhaustive answer to the question, but certainly a basic purpose of the whole sacrificial system was pedagogical. There were some things about spiritual reality that had to be taught in a concrete way. And one of the prime tools of pedagogy (too easily forgotten today) is precise repetition. One of these spiritual realities has to do with the nature of sin and forgiveness. If an offense has taken place, something has to be done to make things right. We cannot just walk away and forget it. Something has to be done. Something objective has to take place because I have offended you. Something objective needs to take place, because I have offended God. The constant repetition of the sacrifices tended to drive that point home. When we come to the New Testament, we see how this teaching function was designed to point to Christ. "The soul who sins is the one who will die" (Ezek. 18:4). If the heart of your religious expression was a sacrificial system, you would know that sin was relatively important. It was right there at the center, and it was not going to go away merely because I wanted it to.

But alongside that element of objectivity, something outside of me and my wishes, there is the element of the personal, the subjective. And this is where the Old Testament understanding of cult and sacrifice stands out as something different from its surroundings. Reconciliation is not something wrung out of God against His will by some application of magic. The sacrificial system only has effect because Yahweh wills to offer reconciliation out of His own heart. That means that if we are to receive that reconciliation, there have to be corresponding personal overtures from us. There has to be something from within us that says we recognize what we have done and want to be reconciled.

This is why the sacrifices are to be accompanied by some other things. They are to be accompanied by confession of sin and prayer. Thus, contrition and repentance are important elements; you could almost say that they are *the* important elements. Perfect performance of certain externals is not the primary point because we are not dealing with the concept of *en opera operato*, which we discussed above, but we are dealing with an interpersonal relationship. So, contrition and repentance are the important elements. To be sure, correct performance of the outward acts may be an important indicator of our heart condition, but in the absence of a genuine desire to follow, serve, and please God, perfect performance accomplishes nothing but divine disgust.

Now, the unique character of this sacrificial system is seen in that the sacrifices were limited in their effectiveness to sins of what Eichrodt calls "inadvertence." You find in the Pentateuch the prepositional phrase, *bishgagah*. The "b" on the beginning is the preposition "in" and the noun is *sh'gagah*, which probably means "an error, a mistake" (*NIV*, "unintentional wrong," cf. Lev. 4:1; Num. 15:26).

Sins that were committed in blatant contempt for the will of

Yahweh could not be atoned for by the regular system of sacrifice.[196]
That system was created for those whose intent was to remain in intimate covenant relation with Yahweh, but who might, because of human
ignorance, do something that was offensive to His perfection. God said
in effect, "I will make a way so that, despite my perfection and your
human shortcomings, we can live together." Clearly, there was forgiveness for sins that were committed intentionally, as David understood and
experienced; but also as he understood, that forgiveness was not to be
found through mere routine performance of certain cultic forms (see
Ps. 51:16-17).

The reason that "sin with a high hand . . . cannot be expiated by
sacrifice"[197] is because the subjective precondition for forgiveness, that
is, a genuine desire for good relations with God, is missing. The "impeni-
tent contempt" that is its foundation shows that there is no real desire on
the part of the sinner for any such relation. He or she might like to escape the consequences of sin, but that is all. In the end, as Eichrodt says,
"Reconciliation remains the gift of God's independent majesty,"[198] and
without a genuine concern for such reconciliation as expressed in confession and repentance, there is no reason for God to extend it. There is
no mechanical operation to work for us. All is determined by what is in
the heart and mind of Yahweh in relation to us.[199]

The connection between the inward attitude and the outward
expression finds an interesting illustration in the book of Job. God tells
Job's friends that because of their sin in accusing Job falsely, they need
to offer sacrifices. But there is nothing automatically effective in the sacrifices. They are effective because Job will pray for them. I find that a
fascinating implication of a man's relationship to God. It also throws an
interesting light on the fact that all salvation is in God alone. But here
He says, in essence, "Your sacrifices will be accepted because Job will
pray for you" (Job 42:8). In some way or another Job gets involved in

---

[196] The Hebrew refers to these as "sins with a high hand" (cf. Num. 15:30), i.e.,
with a fist raised defiantly.

[197] Eichrodt, *Thelology,* vol. 1, 160.

[198] Ibid.

[199] Eichrodt (ibid. 161-62, n. 6) discusses the possibility that the Bible implies a
third category of sin between the "sin of inadvertence" and "sin with a high hand."
These would be sins where the person knows well enough what he is doing (see Lev.
5:20ff; 19:20-22), but still is not doing it in open contempt of God and His Torah.

Yahweh's forgiveness of his friends.

After Moses, Samuel is one of the best representatives of intercession in the Old Testament (cf. Jeremiah 15:1). One of the places
where that is seen most clearly is in 1 Samuel 7. The people were grieved
over the oppression of the Philistines, and Samuel called them to abandon their idols and return to wholehearted commitment to God. He said
(v. 5) that he would "intercede" for them. The people fasted and confessed their sins (v. 6). "Then Samuel took a suckling lamb and offered
it up as a whole burnt offering to [Yahweh]. He cried out to [Yahweh]
on Israel's behalf, and [Yahweh] answered him" (v. 9). Here again, the
personal character of the relationship of the sinner to Yahweh is central.
Here also is the role of intercession. This is where one person, here
Samuel, cares enough about another or about others to stand between
Yahweh and the person who is in trouble with Yahweh, and as he stands
he pleads with Yahweh for the one who is in trouble with Yahweh. I
am intrigued with Eichrodt's language here. He speaks of "the atoning
efficacy of intercession."[200] And he says that is one more expression of
the way "the idea of cultic atonement was constantly being limited and
interpreted in terms of a purely personal intercourse of the faithful with
their God."[201]

Another instance of intercession is found in Samuel's life in 1
Samuel 12. The people had demanded a king. On God's instruction Samuel had bowed to their demand, but he was not happy about it. He did
not feel it was right. But now they have their king, and Samuel is retiring
from public life. We pick up his farewell message in verse 16:

> "Now then, stand still and see this great thing the Lord
> is about to do before your eyes! Is it not the wheat
> harvest now? I will call upon [Yahweh] to send thunder
> and rain. And you will realize what an evil thing you
> did in the eyes of the Lord when you asked for a king."
> Then Samuel called upon the Lord, and that same day
> [Yahweh] sent thunder and rain. So all the people stood
> in awe of [Yahweh] and of Samuel. The people all
> said to Samuel, "Pray to [Yahweh] your God for your

---

[200] Ibid., 167.
[201] Ibid.

> servants so that we will not die, for we have added to
> all our other sins the evil of asking for a king." "Do not
> be afraid," Samuel replied. "You have done all this evil;
> yet do not turn away from [Yahweh] but serve [Yahweh]
> with all your heart. Do not turn away after useless idols.
> ... As for me, far be it from me that I should sin against
> [Yahweh] by failing to pray for you. And I will teach you
> the way that is good and right" (1 Sam. 12:16-23).

What is happening is that a role, a ministry of intercession, is
developing. The people are beginning to realize that it is possible for
someone to stand between them and God in His holiness with the result
that their situation can be different because of it. These are very important passages in the development of the theology of the Old Testament
that leads to our understanding of Christ when He came.

Another example of intercession is found in 1 Samuel 14. In
the context of the defeat of the Philistines, Saul had placed a curse on
anyone who stopped to eat before the defeat was complete. His son
Jonathan, who was leading the charge, did not know of the curse and
refreshed himself during the battle with some honey from a bee-tree.
Now, we do not know how, but it became clear that the curse had been
broken. Saul, who was a very religious man, intended to fulfill the curse
no matter what. So when the lot fell on Jonathan, Saul was going to carry
out the death sentence. He had made a vow and he was going to fulfill
it.

> But the men said to Saul, "Should Jonathan die—he
> who has brought about this great deliverance in Israel?
> Never! As surely as [Yahweh] lives, not a hair of his
> head will fall to the ground, for he did this today with
> God's help" (1 Sam. 14:45).

So the men in the army stood between Jonathan and Saul. It is in
a different context than of a leader interceding, but it still illustrates the
role of an intercessor as he stands between God and His people.

The final example from Samuel's life that I want to focus on is
found in 1 Samuel 15, where the Lord rejects Saul. Samuel is speaking to
Saul:

"Although you were once small in your own eyes, did you not become the head of the tribes of Israel?[202] [Yahweh] anointed you king over Israel. And he sent you on a mission saying, 'Go, and completely destroy those wicked people, the Amalekites; make war on them until you have wiped them out.' Why did you not obey [Yahweh]? Why did you pounce on the plunder and do evil in the eyes of [Yahweh]?" (1 Sam. 15:17-19).

Saul tries to put the best construction on what he did, but Samuel will have none of it and announces that Yahweh has now rejected Saul from being king. Saul replies,

"I have sinned. I have violated [Yahweh's] command and your instructions. I was afraid of the people and so I gave in to them. Now I beg you, forgive my sin and come back with me, so that I may worship [Yahweh]" (15:24-25).

Initially, Samuel refuses, but in the end he relents and goes back with Saul to lead the people in worship. The implication is that although the kingdom is lost, Samuel is standing between Saul and Yahweh for the sake of Saul's own soul.

I have pulled out these illustrations so that we begin to get the concept of an intercessor, an intervener, a mediator, who stands between the sinner and God. But even with the stature of men like this, Moses and Samuel, there is nothing automatic, or to use Eichrodt's term, mechanistic, about what takes place in these incidents. Not even a Moses or a Samuel can do something that will force Yahweh to be reconciled. But it is almost as though, and I am not sure this is the best language to express what I am trying to say here, God's circumstances change when one person cares, existentially and deeply, about another. In some sense, the intercession releases the reconciliation that Yahweh has already made available in Himself. That is my way of saying that there is nothing mechanical here. It is a real interaction between a God whose ultimate desire

---

[202] The Hebrew would more naturally read, "Although you are small in your own eyes, are you not the head. . . ." See *NRSV, ESV, NLT,* etc.

is to save, not judge, and the intercessory contribution of the intercessor who on occasion seems to add something that alters God's circumstances (that is my language), that frees God's hands to work in another way. Though He is supreme, omnipotent, He chooses not to work in human circumstances without mortals like you and me. The person who is intimate with God is actually invited to remonstrate with Yahweh.[203]

What is the new element added by the intercessor? To me that is one of the most interesting questions in theology, whether Old Testament or New Testament. I do not believe you can deal with the New Testament teaching on prayer and intercession without looking into all of this Old Testament material, because the Bible's witness is one in this sort of thing. What is the new element added by the intercessor? Here there is a paragraph in Eichrodt by which I found myself deeply impressed. He says:

> In the process [of intercession] the rights of [the intercessor's] own life disappear so completely from his field of vision that any hardship and mortification he may personally experience are forgotten, indeed, his own existence is offered for the redemption of the one threatened by the wrath of God.[204]

Moses, seeing the judgment on Israel, is not thinking about Moses. He is saying, "My people, my people." Turn to Romans 9 where Paul is saying, "I could be a curse for my people Israel if they could be saved." Now, that is similar to what Eichrodt is saying. You will remember in one of those stories Moses said, "Strike my name out first if you are going to take them out."

> Thus, when the ancient Israelite narrators make Abraham strive with God for the life of the righteous, or

---

[203] This has tremendous significance for all those who find themselves in Christian service. We are not called simply to "assault" people with a revealed message. We are called to bear their burdens for them to the One who can lift all burdens, including the burden of sin. We are called to stand in between their sins and the holiness of Yahweh.

[204] Eichrodt, *Theology*, vol. 2, 450.

when they see Moses stake his own life for the election of his people, or they portray Samuel as a loyal advocate of the erring, despite the ingratitude which he has experienced, they are showing us *intercession as a complete turning of Man to God, a becoming one with the will of God to the point of self-sacrifice* [author's italics], and therefore, as something to which God ascribes atoning value sufficient for the removal of guilt.[205]

Now, we are walking a narrow line here because we must maintain the biblical thrust. There is no salvation in you and me. And there is no salvation in Moses or Samuel. But there is something that happens when a Moses appears and says, "Strike me out first," then Yahweh's saving power is able to work in a different way. And when I say "able," I find myself asking if I am putting conditions on the power of God. It is very fascinating to me that in the first half of the Sodom and Gomorrah story, Yahweh says, "Is anything too hard for me?" and in the rest of the story He is looking for a way to save Sodom and Gomorrah. One way to solve that problem is to hypothesize two different authors. But another way is to say the problem is not in the text but in the heart of God in whom love and justice meet, who is reaching out to save a lost world.

Eichrodt apparently feels the problem is in the heart of God. On the other hand, Eichrodt says such intercessory atonement is not a work with its own intrinsic value. It derives its meaning and its effective power from the fact that it is at bottom a reflection of God's will in a human soul. This is the reason why in the New Testament, prayer of this kind is ascribed to the operation of the Holy Spirit. Hence, God Himself can summon people to intercession and promise to hear it.

Now, if I understand what Eichrodt is saying, what is happening inside the heart of Moses when he says, "Take my name out first," is not something that originated in the goodness and nobility of Moses' heart. But it appeared in his heart as a result of the ministry of the Spirit of God there. In the same way, God permits—no, He seeks—some of us to stand between Himself and a world that is under judgment.

Now, I think that fits with the fact that when Yawheh called

---

[205] Ibid.

Israel at Mt. Sinai, He said to Moses, "You are to be my people and you are to be a kingdom of priests." And so, the role of the church, the role of the believer, and of the body of believers, the chosen ones, is to be intercessors, those who stand between. And the key to that is to come to the place where the other person's well-being is more important than your own.

I believe there are certain persons who reach a point of intimacy with Christ, and who are so passionately committed to Him, that when they see the way, for them there is a sense in which they have no option. They have already made that commitment. And so, their lives are to be laid down. I have come to the place where I am convinced that any great ministry of God normally rises and falls in a single heart, so that when in that central heart things are right, it is possible for things to happen in the hearts that are around.[206]

Have you noticed that sometimes the reality of something can be affirmed by its negation? For instance, how important are Moses and Samuel as intercessors in the Old Testament's thinking? In Jeremiah 15, in the opening verse, we read, "Then [Yahweh] said to me: 'Even if Moses and Samuel were to stand before me, my heart would not go out to these people. Send them away from my presence! Let them go!'" That is a negative witness to intercession, is it not? Jeremiah need not intercede for these people because nothing can change what is coming. But nevertheless, the way God says it to Jeremiah is an incredible witness to the power of intercession because He is saying, "There have been those occasions and there have been those people because of whose intercession the fate of other people was different."

In Amos 7 we see both sides of intercession. God gives Amos a vision of a plague of locusts destroying Israel. But Amos takes pity on Israel and asks Yahweh to relent, and He does. Then Amos sees a vision of a wildfire sweeping across Israel, and he responds in the same way and again Yahweh relents. But then there is a third vision. Here Israel is a city

---

[206] When I was in the pastorate, it seemed to me that when I as a pastor began backsliding in my heart, my congregation started coming apart. On the other hand, when in my own heart I was sensitive and obedient and trying to bear with Christ His burden for my people, there was a sort of pulling together in the congregation. Some people might call that magic, and others might call it my imagination. I believe it is grace and I believe it is *hesed*.

wall that is leaning, and a plumb line is put alongside it. This time Amos does not intercede. The clear implication is that the wall has reached the point of no return. It is going to fall, and nothing can save it. This underlines the point that Eichrodt makes repeatedly that reconciliation and salvation are free, independent gifts from God, and that intercession does not force God to do anything. Amos is enough in touch with the heart of God that he knows when intercession has become futile. This brings us back to our question: What is the extra element that is added when the intercessor steps in? Why does that make a difference? Why is the third party significant in this relationship? This is where Eichrodt's comments that I quoted above are so penetrating. One of the things I appreciate about him is that he clearly understands that the ultimate end of the Old Testament is to be found in the New Testament. He does not overdo that because he is trying to be fair—historically and critically—to the biblical text and to the development of Old Testament faith. He is not guilty of reading the New Testament back into the Old Testament. But occasionally you get those passages in Eichrodt where you can feel he has gone through the process so thoroughly that he is now free to shed New Testament light on what is taking place there in the Old Testament. This passage that we have been considering is one of those.

"The very existence of the intercessor is offered for the redemption of the one threatened by God's wrath. . . . [Thus we see] intercession as a complete turning of a person to . . . God to the point of self-sacrifice." As I read those lines I have a whole group of sayings from the lips of Jesus echoing in my mind. When a person plays the intercessory role, evidently a third element has been added to the Yahweh/sinner relationship; and when that third element is added, possibilities are now present that were not there before.

What is the power of that third element? Do you and I become co-saviors with God? Is there something salvific in you and me if we perform that kind of role? Eichrodt is very careful in his language here, because he knows very well that the foundational concept in the Old Testament understanding of salvation is that anything saving originates in, comes from, and is the very work of, Yahweh Himself. He alone is the Savior and there is nothing saving in you or in me. Thus salvation originates in Yahweh, not in any of His creatures. So Eichrodt says,

[Intercession] derives its meaning and its effective power from the fact that it is at bottom a reflection of God's
will in a human soul—which is the reason why, in the
New Testament, prayer of this kind is ascribed to the
operation of the Holy Spirit. [207]

That is, it is the Holy Spirit who brings someone like you or me
to the place where someone else's well-being is more important than our
own.

One of the things I find myself thinking as I read this is that
it is remarkably close to the essence of Wesleyan theology. So, it is only
the Holy Spirit who can bring a person in his self-centeredness to where
he cares more about someone else's well-being than he does his own.
Eichrodt is saying that the efficacy of intercession is dependent on an
identification of the personhood of the intercessor with the will of God
in a surrender of one's self in concern for another. This assumes that
the will of Yahweh is to save everyone. Even in those cases like Jeremiah
or Amos, where intercession is either explicitly or implicitly forbidden,
there is no question but that salvation is God's ultimate intent. If there
is anyone lost, it will not be because Yahweh wants anyone lost. It does
not matter how wicked, how evil, a person is, Yahweh's purpose is to save
every sinner without exception.

But how is that will to be achieved? "The atoning efficacy of
intercession was wholly a function of the intercessor's living intercourse
with God in personal self-surrender."[208] So the intercessor is a person
who gives up his own interests, loses himself or herself; loses his personhood or her personhood in concern for the other person. Now, I think
you can sense what Eichrodt is building toward. And it is a beautiful
movement to me. To use my language, this occurs when the well-being
of another becomes more important to me than my own well-being.
Now, how can a person as self-centered as I am ever get that way? That's
the reason it is all of God, and all of grace. Only God can break my self-
interest to that extent.

Now, we have talked about sacrifice and the Old Testament

[207] Ibid.
[208] Ibid., 451.

sacrificial system, seeing that its purpose was for atonement. And we have talked about intermediation or intercession, showing how it is ultimately to be understood as self-sacrifice. Then I have tried to show how intercession, that self-sacrifice, underlines the truth that the sacrificial system depended entirely on the personal element. Sacrifice in itself, apart from this, is not enough. It calls for the intermediary.

LECTURE 27–ATONEMENT AND THE DIVINE INTERCESSOR   393

Lecture 27

· · · · · · · · · ·

Atonement and the Divine Intercessor

We come now to the place where atonement and intercession meet in the Old Testament. That is, of course, in Isaiah 52:13–53:12. I want to begin by looking at it from an angle most of us Christians are unaware of. We have raised the issue several times of how it is that many of the Jews were unprepared for Jesus, the Messiah, when He came. And I have said to you that they, and we, tend to make God conform to our expectations. Here is a fascinating example of that in the handling of Isaiah 53.

When the Judeans came back from exile, one of the things they brought with them from Babylon was a familiarity with the Aramaic language. The Assyrians had begun to promote Aramaic as the common language in their empire during the 700s B.C., and the Babylonians had continued that practice. It would be interesting to know how the decision to use Aramaic for this purpose was first made, but we do not know. In any case, Aramaic continued to grow in popularity until, by the time of Christ, it seems to have become the everyday language of Palestine. The handful of direct quotations from Jesus in the Gospels (like *talitha koum*, "little girl, get up," Mark 5:41) show that Jesus spoke Aramaic.

The fact that Aramaic was increasingly replacing Hebrew as the street language caused a problem in the synagogue, for the scriptures were in Hebrew, which fewer and fewer people understood very well.[209] As a result, a special role developed for an interpreter or a translator called a *meturgaman* (Aramaic for "translator"). So in the synagogue one person, the appointed person, would stand and read out of the sacred scriptures in Hebrew, while the *meturgaman* stood alongside and gave a running translation. At first it was all done orally, and it appears that an oral tradition developed as to how to translate each section. Finally, some-time after Christ, these oral traditions were put into print. These printed versions, of which there are several different ones, are called the *Targums* (Aramaic "translations"). The Targums are not strictly translations as we think of translations; that is, they are more interpretive than a word-for-word rendering. The degree of interpretive freedom is different in other sections of the Hebrew Bible. For instance, if you check the Targum of the Pentateuch, you will find that it is a much more literal rendering than in either the Prophets or the Writings. Evidently that is because they held the Law in such high esteem that they were very careful to translate more literally there. Below is a translation of the Hebrew of Isaiah 52:13 through Isaiah 53:12 alongside the Targum of the same passage. You will see that they had no difficulty being interpretive in Isaiah.

---

[209] Two portions of the Old Testament are in Aramaic: Ezra 4:8-68; 7:12-26 and Daniel 2:4–7:28.

Hebrew Bible	Targum
52:13See my servant will act wisely; he will be raised and lifted up and highly exalted. 14Just as there were many who were appalled at him— his appearance was so disfigured beyond that of any man, and his form marred beyond human likeness15—so will he sprinkle many nations, and kings will shut their mouths because of him. For what they were not told they will see. And what they have not heard, they will understand.	52:13Behold, my servant, the anointed one [the Messiah], shall prosper. He shall be exalted and increase and be very strong. 14As the house of Israel hoped [or waited] for him many days, for his appearance was wretched among the nations, and his countenance beyond that of the sons of men. 15So shall he scatter many nations. Kings shall be silent because of him. They shall set their hands upon their mouths. For the things which they had not heard have they perceived.
53:1Who has believed our message and to whom has the arm of the Lord been revealed? 2He grew up before him like a tender shoot and like a root out of dry ground. He had no beauty or majesty to attract us to him. Nothing in his appearance that we should desire him.	53:1Who hath believed these our tidings and to whom hath the power of the mighty arm of the Lord been so revealed? 2And the righteous shall grow up before him even as budding shoots. And as a tree that sendeth forth its roots by streams of water, so shall the holy generations increase in the land that was in need of him. His appearance shall not be that of a common man, nor the fear of him that of an ordinary man. But his countenance shall be a holy countenance so that all who see him shall regard him earnestly.

Hebrew Bible	**Targum**
³He was despised and rejected by men. A man of sorrows and familiar with suffering. Like one from whom men hide their faces. He was despised and we esteemed him not.	³Then shall the glory of all the kingdoms be despised and come to an end. They shall be infirm and sick, even as a man of sorrows and as one destined for sicknesses. And as when the presence of the Shekina was withdrawn from us, they shall be despised and of no account. ⁴Then he shall
⁴Surely he took up our infirmities and carried our sorrows. Yet we considered him stricken by God, smitten by him and afflicted.	pray on behalf of our transgressions and our iniquities shall be pardoned for his sake. Though we were accounted smitten, stricken from before the Lord and afflicted. ⁵But he shall build the sanctu-
⁵But he was pierced for our transgressions. He was crushed for our iniquities. The punishment that brought us peace was upon him, and by his wounds we are healed.	ary that was polluted because of our transgressions, and given up because of our iniquities. And by his teaching shall his peace be multiplied upon us and by our devotion to his word, our transgressions shall be forgiven us.
⁶We all like sheep have gone astray. Each of us has turned to his own way and the Lord has laid on him the iniquity of us all.	⁶All we like sheep have been scattered. We had wandered off, each on his own way. But it was the Lord's good pleasure to forgive the transgressions of us all for his sake. For he made intercession for the transgressors.

Hebrew Bible	**Targum**
[7]He was oppressed and afflicted, yet he did not open his mouth. He was led like a lamb to the slaughter, and as a sheep before her shearers is silent, so he did not open his mouth.	[7]He was praying and he was answered. And before he opened his mouth, he was accepted. The mighty ones of the people shall he deliver up like a lamb to the slaughter and as a ewe that before her shearers is dumb, and there shall be none before him opening his mouth or speaking a word.
[8]By oppression and judgment he was taken away and who can speak of his descendants for he was cut off from the land of the living. For the transgression of my people he was stricken.	[8]Out of chastisements and out of punishment shall he bring our exiles near. And the wondrous things that shall be wrought for us in his days, who shall be able to recount? For he shall take away the dominion of the peoples from the land of Israel and the sins which my people sinned shall he transfer unto them. [9]And he shall deliver the wicked unto Hell, and those that are rich in possessions which they have obtained by violence unto the death of destruction, so that those who commit sin may not be established, nor speak deceits with their mouth.
[9]He was assigned a grave with the wicked and with the rich in his death, though he had done no violence, nor was any deceit in his mouth.	

Hebrew Bible	Targum
[10]Yet it was the Lord's will to crush him and cause him to suffer, and though the Lord makes his life a guilt offering, he will see his offspring and prolong his days, and the will of the Lord will prosper in his hand.	[10]And it was the Lord's good pleasure to refine and to purify the remnant of his people in order to cleanse their soul from sin. They shall look upon the kingdom of their anointed one. They shall multiply sons and daughters. They shall prolong days. And they that perform the law of the Lord shall prosper in his good pleasure. [11]From the subjection of the people shall he deliver their soul. They shall look upon the punishment of them that hate them. They shall be satisfied with the spoil of their king. By his wisdom shall he justify the just in order to subject many to the law. And for their transgression shall he make intercession. [12]Then will I divide unto him the spoil of many peoples and the riches of strong cities. He shall divide the booty because he delivered his soul unto death and subjected the rebellious to the law. And he shall make intercession for many transgressions and the rebellious shall be forgiven for his sake.
[11]After the suffering of his soul he will see the light of life and be satisfied. By his knowledge my righteous servant will justify many and he will bear their iniquities.	
[12]Therefore I will give him a portion among the great and he will divide the spoils with the strong because he poured out his life unto death and was numbered with the transgressors.	

The Targum changes the impact of the passage rather dramatically, does it not? Let me point out a few of what are to me the key points. Notice that in 52:13 the Targum has no hesitancy in identifying this material as being about the Messiah. To be sure, they were very uncomfortable with what the Hebrew says about the Messiah ("Surely it couldn't mean that!"), but they had no question who the passage was referring to (unlike many modern commentators).

Now look at the first verse of chapter 53. I think it is very significant that they identified the character of the arm as one of power and as one of might. Why would they do that? Well, if you look at uses of "arm" in the preceding chapters, 49 through 52, it is clearly talking about the power of God to deliver His people from their sin. What good is a weak arm? So clearly, from a human perspective this text cannot mean what it appears to. You see, we decide how God is supposed to act. Every people group decides how God is supposed to act, and the hardest problem that God has with us, I think, is to disabuse us of our wrong notions of who He is and what He is like. So here they are describing the way they think He must be. If He is going to win, and they are sure He will, He can only do so by power and by might.

While verse 2 might be interpreted in a couple of different ways, verse 3 is not ambiguous at all:

> Then shall the glory of all the kingdoms be despised and
> come to an end. They shall be infirm and sick, even as a
> man of sorrows and as one destined for sicknesses and
> as when the presence of the Shekinah was withdrawn
> from us. They shall be despised and of no account.

A complete reversal has taken place. It is the Messiah's enemies who are going to be like what the Hebrew text says the Suffering Servant will be.

Then look at verse 4:

> He shall pray on behalf of our transgressions and our
> iniquities shall be pardoned for his sake. Though we are
> accounted smitten, stricken from before the Lord and
> afflicted.

Notice that forgiveness comes through the Messiah's intercessory prayer, not His substitutionary suffering. Obviously, there is basis in Scripture for the importance of intercessory prayer, as we discussed about Moses in the previous lectures. But is that all the Messiah would, or could, do for His people? The same point is made again in the final verse, verse 12. Look at it and its final conclusion:

> I will divide unto him the spoil of many peoples and the riches of strong cities. He shall divide the booty because he delivered his soul unto death and subjected the rebellious to the law. And he shall make intercession for many transgressions and the rebellious shall be forgiven for his sake.

Once again, forgiveness comes through intercession instead of through personal self-sacrifice. They are doing what we oftentimes do, and that is to see in the Scripture what they have decided ahead of time it can say. Some of our preaching is like that; we come to the text to reinforce what we already believe instead of opening ourselves to the Word of God so that we really hear what is there.

The Jews of 26 or 27 A.D. were not surprised at Jesus in the sense that they were not expecting a Messiah. Clearly they were. The history of the times tells us of many people who were able to attract a following by claiming to be the Messiah. You will remember that in the first chapter of John (1:19-21), the temple had to send a delegation down to the Jordan to ask John the Baptist, "Are you the one we are looking for?" Obviously the reason for that was that there was enough discussion among the common people about the possibility of John's being the Messiah that the temple officials said, "We should check this out."

Similarly the Samaritan woman said, "We know that a Messiah will come" (John 4:25). Even among the Samaritans there was this kind of hope. Then there are those beautiful lines in Luke from Simeon and Anna. When the infant Jesus was brought into the temple for circumcision, Simeon lifted his voice and blessed God. The text tells us that he was there in the temple, waiting for "the consolation of Israel" (Luke 2:25). What was *the consolation of Israel*? It was the Messiah. He was looking ahead, looking for the messianic age, looking for the intervention of

God in history on their behalf. Anna was also in the temple at that time. The text says that she spoke to all who were there, all "who were looking forward to the redemption of Israel" (Luke 2:38). There is something amazing about the fact that these Jews kept looking forward confidently, no matter what happened to them politically or otherwise. That belief in the Messiah, and that belief in the kingdom age, was so endemic to their existence and to their identity, that nothing could shake it.

Yet, when Jesus appeared they missed Him. Why did they miss Him? I think the reason is that He did not perform the way they expected Him to perform.[210] And here in their handling of Isaiah 53 you get a glimpse of how they expected Him to perform. Never mind what the text actually says, this is how a Messiah acts, and if someone acts in some other way, a way of self-denial, humiliation, and loss, well, that person is definitely not the Messiah. How can a person like that deliver us from the oppressive power of Rome? And Rome is our most serious problem, right?

Now, you will notice in this Targum the role of the Law. In reading it, notice carefully, it is as they relate to the Law, as they obey the Law and as they have the Messiah pray for them (intercede for them), they find forgiveness. But what is the basis for the efficacy of any intercession? It is that something has taken place in the heart of God, something symbolized in the sacrificial system.

So how do atonement and intercession, or maybe better "intermediation" come together? Here I want to share with you something that has become something very significant to me in my own personal life in terms of prayer and in terms of my understanding of the Atonement of Christ.

You will remember that I said I have found five passages in Isaiah, Jeremiah, and Ezekiel where God says, "I looked for a person and could not find one. If I could have found one person, my circumstances would have been different." It is interesting when the Sovereign God has circumstances. Look at these passages with me. The first is in Ezekiel 22:30, which you know is the passage where God lists each group of people in the society and tells about their sinfulness. When He comes down to the end in verse 30, He says, "I looked for someone to stand in

10

the gap and to make up the hedge so that the judgment would not have to come, but I could not find one."

The other passage outside of Isaiah is Jeremiah 5:1 where He says, "If you can find but one person who deals honestly and seeks the truth, I will forgive this city." So you see God looking for someone to make it possible for Him to do His redemptive work.

The third and fourth passages are in Isaiah 50:2 and 63:5. But the occurrence that is most significant to me is Isaiah 59:16. This chapter is incredible. He is speaking about the moral and spiritual darkness, the sin, of the city of Jerusalem after the return from exile, and the desire of God to help. The chapter begins with a verse that has been widely quoted: "Surely the arm of the Lord is not too short to save, nor his ear too dull to hear." So there is nothing wrong with God in terms of His redemptive power, His capacity to save, and there is nothing wrong with His ear (or His heart either, by implication), for He is ready to hear their prayers. He is ready and wants to help. But how do you get His help and the need of Israel together?

Verse 2 begins one of the saddest passages in all the Old Testament: "But your iniquities have separated you from your God; your sins have hidden his face from you, so that he will not hear." Remember the Targum of Isaiah 53:3 where it says of the enemies of Israel, "Their fate will be like ours when the Shekinah [glory] had departed." These were people who knew what it was to have the face of the Lord gone from their lives.

And what were those *iniquities* and *sins*? Look at verse 3 and following:

> For your hands are stained with blood,
>   your fingers with guilt.
> Your lips have spoken lies,
>   and your tongue mutters wicked things.
> No one calls for justice;
>   no one pleads his case with integrity . . .
> So justice is far from us,
>   and righteousness does not reach us.
> We look for light,
>   but all is darkness;

We look for brightness,
>   but we walk in deep shadows.
Like blind persons we grope along a wall,
>   feeling our way like [persons] without eyes.
At midday we stumble as if it were twilight;
>   among the strong we are like the dead . . .
We look for justice, but we find none;
>   for deliverance, but it is far away.
For our offenses are many in your site,
>   and our sins testify against us . . .
Justice is driven back,
>   and righteousness stands at a distance;
truth has stumbled in the streets,
>   honesty cannot enter.
Truth is nowhere to be found,
>   and whoever shuns evil becomes a prey
>   (Isa. 59:3-15a).

Then, in the middle of verse 15, "[Yahweh] looked and was displeased that there was no justice. He saw that there was no one, he was appalled that there was no one to intervene" [some translations, "intercede"]. Now, Yahweh is appalled that there is no one who stands between. In the previous lecture we were talking about that thrust through the Old Testament of the demand for a mediator. We saw how Abraham stood between Yahweh and the world; Moses stood between Yahweh and Israel; Samuel stood between Yahweh and Saul. So you get this mediatorial role that is developed all through the Old Testament, and I think without any doubt, it is laying the basis for what we think of in terms of Christ.

So, God looks for one who can play that intervening, that mediatorial role, and He finds none. So He says, "When I could not find one, my own arm worked salvation for me and my own righteousness sustained me." Now, when I was working through those five passages, I thought, Can it really be that one person can change God's circumstances? And if one person can, what is the kind of person that God needs to do that? He wants to save a world, and He is looking for a person. When I got to that point I checked out this passage in Isaiah 59 in the Hebrew, just to see what that word was for "intercessor." The Hebrew word is *mapgia*. The root of this is a Hebrew word *paga* which means "to meet, to encounter." The form here in Isaiah is a causative participle, which yields the meaning of "someone who causes to meet." So Yahweh is saying, "I looked for somebody who could cause to meet. There is nothing wrong with my heart. There is nothing wrong with my power. I am ready. I am looking for someone who can cause my redemption to meet the persistent sin of the world. Now, where can I find somebody like that? When I couldn't find one, my own arm brought me salvation."

This causative form of the verb only occurs six times in the Old Testament. It occurs once in Job, twice in Jeremiah, and three times in Isaiah. Those three occurrences in Isaiah are this one in chapter 59, and twice in chapter 53. One of those in chapter 53 is in verse 6, and the other is in verse 12. The occurrence in Isaiah 53:6 is the one that I found most illuminating. The verse says, "We all, like sheep, have gone astray, each of us has turned to his own way; and [Yahweh] has laid on him the iniquity of us all." Now, I checked through every translation of that verse I could find, and it is translated that way consistently. But let me tell you what the literal Hebrew is for that last sentence in the verse. It says, "Yahweh has caused to meet in him the iniquity of us all." For me, "to cause to meet in him" gives a totally different picture than "to lay on him." When I think about "laid on him," I see a judgment in a courtroom. The legal obligation of one person is "laid" on another person. But the word *iniquity* used here is the strongest word in the Old Testament for the evil that is within us, the wrong that is within us, the depths and the great extent of our wrongness before God. So the picture here is of all our wrongness coming into this Mediator in whom is all of the goodness of God and meeting that goodness there.

All of this prepares us for some understanding of this incredible passage, the high point of the Old Testament on these points: Isaiah 52:13 to 53:12. Think how massively deprived we would be in explaining Jesus Christ if we did not have these 15 verses. They have facilitated and enabled the body of Christ, the church, to understand what was to take place centuries later at Calvary.

The Servant in Isaiah 53 makes Himself an offering for sin. At least He permits that. Yahweh makes him a guilt offering.[211] The term used there is used in the Pentateuch and in the Old Testament for exactly that: a guilt offering. It is interesting the way language is used in the Old Testament. The word *'asham* can be used for the act a person commits that brings the guilt on him. But the word also comes to be used for the guilt that comes upon the person who commits the evil act. It is also used for the punishment the guilty person receives for committing the guilt-pro-ducing act. So as you read the Old Testament you have to sense the full possibilities for meaning in those terms.[212] The same range of meanings applies to *hattat* in connection with sin. It can refer to the sin, the sinner, and the sin offering.[213]

So the *'asham* can be the punishment the guilt demands. And that punishment can either fall upon the guilty one or upon someone who stands in the guilty person's stead. Now, this term is found in Isaiah 53:10 where it is the innocent Servant who receives the punishment that the sin deserves, and in receiving that punishment becomes the sacrificial offering to remove it.

Eichrodt says that here we see the combination of the two elements we were talking about: the sacrifice, which is for atonement, and the intermediation. It's not just a sacrifice alone. It is a sacrifice with the personal element of intercession. It is done by the free will of the person who, by becoming the sacrifice or the interceder, makes a way of atonement. So through this act of intercession (notice the word *intercession*

---

[211] [Editor's note] The Hebrew text of Isaiah 53:10 says, "If *you* make his being a guilt offering." The most natural understanding of this would be that "you" refers to the hearer. However, given the strong Augustinian influence on most Protestant theology, with its insistence that we humans can do nothing in the work of salvation, most modern translations alter the text (without any textual grounds). The *NIV*, as here, reads "and though the Lord makes his life a guilt offering." The *NKJV* reads, "when You make his soul an offering for sin," although God is not referred to in the second person elsewhere in the passage. *ESV* reads, "when his soul makes an offering for sin." *NLT* has "when his life is made an offering for sin." Only *NRSV* is courageous enough to let the text stand as it is. It is interesting when theology "trumps" the text. One is reminded of the Targum: "Oh no, the text can't mean that. Our theology won't allow it."

[212] All forms of the root occur about 105 times in the Old Testament. Of these, about half refer to the guilt offering.

[213] It can even be used to refer to removing sin from something. So to "sin" the altar is rather like "dusting" the table. We are not putting dust on the table, we are taking it off.

in Isaiah 53:6, 12) the way of salvation is open for Israel and for a world.[214]

Eichrodt says:

> This feature [intercession involving surrender of one's own right to life] is now intensified by the acceptance of a whole lifetime of nothing but contempt and mis-understanding, even to the point of dying the death of one branded by God as an evil-doer, and therefore in total incognito—a fate which utterly eliminates any trace of self-seeking or self-exaltation. Because, however, this means the attainment of complete identification with the divine will, such intercession becomes powerful to atone for many, and results in the accomplishment of that "blessed exchange" of *musar* and *shalom*, punishment and salvation, by which the sinners become righteous.[215]

Let's look at what Eichrodt calls a "blessed exchange" of punishment and salvation. The one who does not need salvation receives the punishment. And the one who does not deserve salvation, but deserves punishment, receives salvation. So the atoning efficacy of sacrifice and intercession are completed in Eichrodt's "blessed exchange."

Now I want to return to our discussion of Yahweh's looking for someone. I said the best illustration of it is to be found in Isaiah 59. If you remember, the chapter begins with a statement of God's readiness to save. But then it moves to a lengthy description of the iniquities that separate the people from God's saving intent. There is a great chasm between the sinful people and the saving God. So God says, "I looked for a person to stand in between, for someone who could bridge the gap. I looked for an intermediary." But he says, "I was appalled that I could not find one." So He said, "When I could not find one, my own arm brought

---

[214] It is apparent that those who created the Targum did not make this connection between self-sacrifice and intercession. They were clearly seeking to avoid that idea of denying oneself for another to the point of self-sacrifice. For them intercession was limited to the act of praying for another.

[215] Eichrodt, *Theology*, vol. 2, 452.

Me salvation." And again, you may remember that I pointed out that in chapters 40 through 55 "the arm of the Lord" refers to God's mighty power to save. But Isaiah 53:1 tells us that that arm, when it was revealed, did not look at all like what this world calls power. It is the power of self-sacrifice. The power of one to sacrifice himself. It is a far greater biblical illustration of power to see one sacrifice himself for another than it is to see one impose his way on another. The world only understands power in terms of imposition. But what we are talking about here, it seems to me, is the exact reverse. In God there is enough power so that He can let us impose our way, our evil way, upon Him.

God says, "I looked and I couldn't find one. Abraham doesn't fit this bill. Moses doesn't fit this bill. Samuel doesn't fit this bill. David doesn't fit this bill. Where am I going to find one? When I couldn't find one, I became one." And why did the Trinity become one of us? *So that we could become one of them.* Oh, not so that we could become Deity—of course not—but so we could become part of that divine fellowship.

I want to turn now to a consideration of a passage out of Torrance's book *The Mediation of Christ.* It is one of the most perceptive approaches to this subject that I know of, and I do not believe that Torrance could have ever thought these thoughts without the Old Testament. He says:

> Since in Jesus Christ God himself has come into our human being and united our human nature to his own, then atoning reconciliation takes place within the personal being of the Mediator.[216]

Now, I understand that differently from the way I understood it ten or fifteen years ago when I read it for the first time. I do so because of the interpretation of Isaiah 53:6 I presented earlier: "Yahweh has caused to meet in him the iniquity of us all." This also reminds us of Eichrodt's expression, "blessed exchange." An exchange has not taken place externally to Christ. It is an exchange that takes place internally, in Christ. So Torrance says that in Jesus Christ the mediation takes place

---

[216] This quotation and the succeeding ones are taken from Thomas F. Torrance, *The Mediation of Christ,* rev. ed. (Colorado Springs: Helmers & Howard, 1992), 62-64.

within the personal being of the Mediator.

> In Jesus Christ the Creator Word and the Son of God incarnate, his Person and his Work are one. [Intercession is not just something he did for us, it is what Jesus Christ is.] What he does is not something separate from his personal Being and what he is in his own incarnate Person *is* [author's italics] the mighty Act of God's love for our salvation. Christ and his Gospel belong ontologically and inseparably together [i.e., his being and his message become one], for that is what he is, he who brings, actualizes and embodies the Gospel of reconciliation between God and man and man and God in his own Person. In him the Incarnation and Atonement are one and inseparable, for atoning reconciliation falls within the incarnate constitution of his Person as Mediator, and it is on that ground and from that source that atoning reconciliation embraces all mankind and is freely available to every person.

> [Note this sentence.] I believe it is important for us to ask ourselves today whether we tend to regard atonement for sin as some external [note the word *external*] transaction between God and man, worked out by Jesus, or whether we think of it as having taken place within the Being of the Mediator.

Now, I would like to link that with the meaning of intercession as I have developed it in these lectures. Intercession is not something you say; it is not even something you do; it is what happens in the most internal part of your being.

That will disclose to us whether we have ultimately taken the line of the Arians or the Liberals, or whether we have taken the line of the Nicene Creed and the great Greek Patristic theology, to which the whole church is so deeply indebted for bringing to light and expressing the inner structural connections of the faith once delivered to the saints.

Now, what is interesting is, Torrance is an Edinburgh scholar and a Scottish Presbyterian who stands in about as strong a line of Reformed thought as there can be. But the line of thought he is following here does not come from Augustine, who is the spiritual father of Reformed theology; it comes from the Eastern fathers.

> If in Jesus Christ the Son of God became incarnate within our fallen, guilt-laden humanity, then in becoming incarnate he not only took what is ours to make it his, but thereby *really* [author's italics] took upon himself our sin and guilt, our violence and wickedness, so that through his own atoning self-sacrifice and self-consecration, he might do away with our evil and heal and sanctify our human nature from within and thus present us to the Father as those who are redeemed and consecrated in and through himself. He did all that precisely as Mediator, who brought God and man together in himself, thereby actualizing reconciliation and recreating our humanity within the holiness and perfection of his own sinless human life, crucified for our sins and raised again for our justification.

I would like to urge you to digest every line of this section of Torrance's book [*The Unity of Christ's Person and Work*, pages 61-67]. This is a man who has spent his life working on the Atonement, and I think it is the best expression of it that can be found in a twentieth-century theologian.

Before we conclude the lecture, I want to call your attention to one more passage. He is talking about what happened in Christ, about Eichrodt's "blessed exchange," when Christ in His holiness met us in our evil, and took our evil and gave back to us His holiness. He says,

> The Greek Fathers used to speak of that experience as *theopoiesis* or *theosis* [*theo* is "God" and *poiesis*" is "making," so "making God-like"] which really does not mean "divinization" as is so often supposed, but refers to the utterly staggering act of God in which he gives *himself* [author's italics] to us and *adopts* [author's italics] us into the communion of his divine life and love through

Jesus Christ, and in his one Spirit, yet in such a way that we are not made divine but are preserved in our humanity. That is what constitutes the sustaining inner cohesion of our cognitive union with Christ through faith and the very substance of our personal and corporate union with Christ through the Word and the Sacraments, for in Christ our human relations with God, far from being allowed to remain on a merely external basis, are embraced within the Trinitarian relations of God's own Being as Father, Son and Holy Spirit [that is, in an intimacy greater than what was in the Garden in the beginning].

Lecture 28

·········

Wisdom Literature: Order in the Tangle of Life

In the next two lectures I want to look at what is designated as Wisdom Literature in the Old Testament. Eichrodt treats this topic only very minimally, and critics have judged this to be a weakness in his work. It has sometimes been suggested that his choice of the theme of covenant necessarily limits him on the subject because the wisdom literature makes so little of covenant. Whether that is true or not, he does not, so I want to fill in that gap for you in some small way.

In the Old Testament the category of Wisdom Literature includes Job, Proverbs, Ecclesiastes, and various psalms. This literature looks at life from the viewpoint of experience. It is looking for the verities of life, as we will discuss more fully in a few moments. Wisdom Literature is well-known in the Ancient Near East, with the oldest examples coming from Egypt in the second millennium B.C. It is divided into two categories: optimistic and pessimistic. Optimistic Wisdom Literature is confident that experience will show you some fundamental truths of life and that, if you conform to those, you will be successful and prosperous. In the Bible, Proverbs is an example of that type of literature. But while experience does show that there are some fundamental truths, it also shows, if we are honest, some very puzzling variances from those truths: The wise do not always succeed; the diligent do not always prosper; the upright are not always blessed. What are we to make of that data? This is the subject of pessimistic wisdom. In the Old Testament, Job and Ecclesiastes are examples of this type.

I want to begin by looking at wisdom thinking, and then we will move to a consideration of Wisdom Literature itself. Thus far in these lectures we have majored on what we might call "the big issues," the central, or the foundational, matters of Old Testament theology. It is crucial that you recognize those and understand them. For instance, there is the covenant. The longer I live with Eichrodt and the more I read of other Old Testament theologies, the more I have felt that he was getting to the heart of things when he took this as his central theme.

Then of course there is the whole subject of monotheism, that there is only one God behind all of creation and all of existence, and that that God is Yahweh. So we focused on the fundamental characteristics of Yahwism. For instance, Yahweh is the Holy One. And central to Yahweh's holiness is His moral, ethical character that keeps coming through, whether you are in the Psalms, or the History, or the Torah or the Prophets. But also central to Yahweh's holiness is His *hesed* and the expression of that *hesed*, His commitment to save. So while His moral and ethical character would call for judgment, His overriding concern is how to save.

That concern for salvation of real human beings is what underlies the Old Testament interest in history, the insistence that Yahweh is the Lord of history. Ultimately that understanding of time and space and of their importance is shaped by the succession of promises to bless and the fulfillment of those promises. And that gives Old Testament religion its distinctive future orientation. Israel, when at its best, is looking forward; it looks back but in order to look forward in hope. And that future orientation is what lays the groundwork for the New Testament.

So history becomes almost a sacred subject in the Old Testament, and Christianity is influenced by that.

This idea of promise and fulfillment in history leads us to what I call the "progress of dogma" in the Old Testament. This is the idea that there is a growing understanding of the faith as we move along. That has certainly been true in the history of the Christian church, and I think something very similar happened in the Old Testament. I got an illustration of this in regard to the Christian faith when I was a student at Princeton sitting in a class with Emile Cailliet, a philosopher. He was giving some lectures on holiness in the Reformed tradition, and I wondered what a good Reformed philosopher would have to say on that subject. As you might expect, he dealt with Luther and Calvin and their predecessors, and then with the development of the Reformation. But after he had done that, he said that if you want to find the classically stated Reformed doctrine on holiness, you do not look to the Reformers. Their concern was how to be justified; how a person could be accepted before God, be justified before God. But the human mind does not learn two lessons at the same time. The lesson that needed to be learned in the Reformation was justification. So, he said, if you want to find the classical statement of the Reformed doctrine of holiness, you cannot look at Luther or Calvin. Rather, you must look to John Wesley, and when the Methodist movement calcified, to the Salvation Army and its doctrinal statement on entire sanctification. There is the classical statement of the Reformed doctrine of holiness.

Now, what he was saying was that in one period the church will learn one thing, and you trust that when the church moves into the next generation it maintains what it has learned and then expands its understanding of the Gospel and expands its intellectual frontiers. I think there is clear evidence of that taking place in the Old Testament, and I am going to refer to that later in this lecture.

Now, as we developed those major themes, we did not look at matters that might qualify them, or even, some might say, contradict them. That was intentional because if we had spent too much time with the qualifications we might miss the major thrust. But there are those elements that are present in the text. As God was inspiring it; the Old Testament was a living document. It is not one-dimensional, but multi-dimensional, and sometimes you can only really understand something in its depths if it is expressed in other terms. As a result, you can find what we might call crosscurrents in the text, currents that move, as it were, against each other so that you will have to think awhile before you can get the streams consonant with each other. To my mind, this is what Wisdom Literature does. We have the central truths as given to us by revelation, it seems to say. Now let's test those truths out in the light of experience. Let's lay revelation on one side for the moment and see whether experience will bear them out, or modify them or even contradict them in some way. In this sense, I am grateful for this literature, because it says to us that we are not called just to blindly accept, but to examine and test the great elements of faith in the most rigorous ways.

For an introduction to wisdom thinking, I want to refer you to the treatment in von Rad's *Old Testament Theology*. This is one area where I think von Rad does a better job than Eichrodt.[217] Von Rad says that while Israel's Wisdom Literature is not philosophy in the Greek sense, it does have as its goal, like philosophy, the discovery of the fundamental principles of reality. The main difference is that wisdom's primary appeal is not to abstract logic, but to experience. Reason plays its part, but you might say that wisdom is really an appeal to practical reason.[218]

What the Wisdom Literature wants to know is whether it is possible to discover something of an order in the tangle of life. "Tangle" is the operative word, for although Yahweh made the world and He is good and is the God who orders all things, somehow things have gotten tangled up. So the wisdom writers are asking whether it is possible to wrest some order from the chaos of life. Furthermore, von Rad believes that the search was for principles that were generally and universally valid, ones that could be discovered, and applied, anywhere.

Now, this interest, he says, expresses itself in the study of riddles and paradoxes. Let me talk about paradox for a moment. Paradoxes are apparent contradictions, such as "a gentle tongue breaks bones." We do not think of gentleness as having the power to break, but when we think about it we understand the point being made. Another proverb says,

---

[217] I, 408-59. Von Rad's material on wisdom was later expanded and revised and appeared as *Wisdom in Israel*, tr. James D. Martin (Nashville: Abingdon, 1972).
[218] W. F. Albright coined the term *empirico-logical* to describe this kind of practical reasoning.

"The one who is satisfied tramples honey underfoot, while the hungry one, to him the bitter is sweet." Or there is, "He who loves his son chastises him."[219] The wisdom writers were intrigued by such proverbs. They sensed that somehow behind the paradoxical there was "hidden order, and that that hidden order would rob chaos of the last word in human existence."[220] Now, that is a very significant passage from my point of view. They believed that somewhere in this tangle and somewhere in this seeming chaos and paradox, there was a hidden order that would ultimately rob chaos of the final victory.

The wisdom writer's purpose was to understand. But more than that it was to be able to pilot himself and those who listened to him through the confusion of life. Von Rad says, "There are two completely different forms of the apperception of truth for mankind. One is systematic (philosophical and theological) and one is empirical and gnomic."[221] The Greek world at the end of the first millennium B.C. is a good illustration of the first of these. Israel's wisdom is an excellent example of the second. Von Rad says,

> Empirical and gnomic wisdom starts from the unyield-
> ing presupposition that there is a hidden order in things
> and events—only it has to be discerned in them, with
> great patience and at the cost of all kinds of painful
> experience. And this order is kindly and righteous.[222]

Now, that last is an item of faith. You cannot see it. When the righteous are getting what the unrighteous deserve and the unrighteous are getting what the righteous deserve, you do not see that. But you still believe it. He goes on to say,

---

[219] I will never forget when our son looked up at me after a spanking and said, "You must hate me." And I said, "No, I paddled you because I love you." So later he said to his sister who was a year and a half older than he, "Sister, Daddy is confused."

[220] von Rad, *Theology*, vol. 1, 420.

[221] Ibid., 421. "Gnomic" refers to a clever saying, an aphorism, that contains within it a bit of truth stated in such a way as to brighten up the moment of understanding.

[222] Ibid.

But characteristically, it is not understood systemati-
cally—and therefore not in such a way as to reduce the
variety experienced and perceived to a general principle
of order, and least of all by a search for a formula which
might be spacious enough to comprehend the infinitely
varied world of phenomena.[223]

He is contrasting this approach with the Greek philosophical
one. The Greek philosophers were looking for that abstract formula that
would explain everything. The Wisdom writers were more interested in
concrete phenomena, but they still were convinced of that underlying
order.

Thus you will find proverbs, back to back, that are contradictory. I remember when I first began noticing some of these. Proverbs
26:4 says, "Do not answer a fool according to his folly, or you be like
him yourself." And Proverbs 26:5 says, "Answer the fool according to his
folly, or he will be wise in his own eyes." So you have one proverb that
says do not, and the very next says do.

That is reflective of much of the Wisdom Literature. Life has
its antinomies. Wisdom recognizes this and feels there is no need to try
to resolve them all, because there is truth in both expressions, depending
on different circumstances. Sometimes we can be so intent on making
everything fit together that we force the data to fit our grid. The attitude
of wisdom is one of learning, not of knowing. The assumption is that
the one who is learning is capable of enlargement. So the wise man is
learning as much as the student he is teaching. They are examining the
data together and trying to take cognizance of it all. Thus wisdom can
never have the absoluteness of Law. That is so because the Law comes
from Sinai and Yahweh, and what is learned here comes from life "under
the sun."[224] It is obvious that the perspective here is not that of revelation. It is not a viewing of life from above, from the standpoint given to
Moses on Sinai. It is man under the sun, looking at life from below, from
the midst of its anomalies and relativities. But there is a mindset behind it
that makes it draw comparisons (e.g., between a boastful man and clouds

---

[223] Ibid., 421f.
[224] See the discussion of this phrase below in the study of Ecclesiastes.

and winds without rain). But these comparisons, says von Rad, are not merely "for the purpose of illustration; is not the implication rather the existence of a relationship of correspondence between two phenomena lying upon totally different planes?"[225] That is a profound statement. Take the time to think about it. The empty clouds are not just an illustration of the emptiness of the boaster's boasts. Rather, there is a correspondence between the two that exists on a deeper plane of reality.[226]

What he is talking about is the doctrine of creation. Wisdom Literature is seeking for truth that emerges from a study of creation, as opposed to truth that is only available through revelation. If truth through creation is limited, it is still truth. He goes on to say,

> Thus the point of these maxims is a comparison of totally different realms of order. . . . Wisdom's constituent is this incisive will for the rational clarification and ordering of the world in which man finds himself, the will to recognize and pin down the orders in both the events of human life and natural phenomena.[227]

Let me illustrate this point with Psalm 89. For a long time I just overlooked it. And then, when I saw what was really there I thought, "I'm sorry He put that into the Old Testament." But as I have lived with it for a while, I find myself very glad it is here. That does not mean that I have answers for all the questions it raises. But I am glad that it is included, precisely because it seems to put contradictory questions side by side. In other words, the positive is not maintained only because it does not admit the contradictions. No, the positive is maintained in the full understanding of some of the tough questions.

The superscription makes it clear that this is a Wisdom psalm. It is attributed to Ethan the Ezrahite, who is probably the wise man identified in 1 Kings 4:31. While we have no certain date, I suspect that it is a later psalm in Israel's history. That is because the situation described

---

[225] von Rad, *Theology*, vol. 1., 424.

[226] One of the reasons I appreciate von Rad on these points is that he often states things that I have dimly perceived but was never quite able to articulate. But then he takes me further into thoughts I had never thought before.

[227] Ibid., 425.

in the latter half looks like the one just before or during the Exile (586–539 B.C.). As to its composition, there are two possibilities: that two psalms, one earlier and one later, have been combined into one; or that it is a single composition, which the internal evidence would argue must be fairly late. But I think the interpretation will be the same in either case.

It begins very beautifully:

> I will sing of [Yahweh's] great [*hesed*] forever;
>> with my mouth I will make your faithfulness ['*emunah*] known through all generations.
> I will declare that your [*hesed*] stands firm forever,
>> that you established your '*emunah* in heaven itself.

Now, I have worked with the Psalms long enough that I pay more attention to the first verses than I do to some of the later ones because oftentimes in those first verses you get the basic thrust of what the psalmist is saying. As I said in regard to some other psalms we have looked at, many times you will get the psalmist's conclusion in the first verses. And so now he is saying, "I have something I want to sing about. I want to sing about Yahweh's *hesed*, his covenant love, and with my mouth I want to make known Yahweh's faithfulness, the fact that He is true to His people and His word, through all generations." So he begins on the solid foundation of Yahweh's undeserved loyalty and utter reliability.

Now he turns to a second subject. He reports what Yahweh has said:

> You said, "I have made a covenant with my chosen one,
>> I have sworn to David my servant,
> 'I will establish your line forever
>> and make your throne firm through all generations'"
> (vv. 3-4).

So now you have this Yahweh, whose *hesed* and faithfulness he is singing about, making a covenant with David, and He is saying, "Your throne will be permanent and enduring, an eternal throne."

The next section goes back to Yahweh's faithfulness.

The heavens praise your wonders, O [Yahweh],
>your faithfulness too, in the assembly of the holy ones.
For who in the skies above can compare with [Yahweh]?
>Who is like [Yahweh] among the heavenly beings?
In the counsel of the holy ones God is greatly feared;
>he is more awesome than all who surround him.
O [Yahweh], God Almighty, who is like you?
>You are mighty, O [Yahweh], and your faithfulness surrounds you (vv. 5-8).

So the theme of this first part is very clear. It is on the loving faithfulness of Yahweh. He keeps His covenant.

Next the psalmist turns to Yahweh's power and His control over nature and over history.

You rule over the surging sea;
>when its waves mount up, you still them.
You crushed Rahab[228] like one of the slain;
>with your strong arm you scattered your enemies.
The heavens are yours, and yours also the earth;
>you founded the world and all that is in it.
You created the north and the south;
>Tabor and Hermon[229] sing for joy at your name.
Your arm is endued with power;
>your hand is strong, your right hand exalted
>(vv. 9-13).

There is nothing wrong with the power and sovereignty of Yahweh.

---

[228] In the origin myths of the Ancient Near East, "Rahab" is one of the names given to the pre-existing chaos monster from which all things have emerged. The gods were thought to have fought against this monster to produce the present world. But when this name is used in the Old Testament, it is most commonly associated with the Exodus, when God is bringing His people into existence. So the biblical writers are using this name merely as a figure of speech to express how Yahweh has overcome His enemies in history and scatters them with His strong arm.

[229] These are two mountains. Tabor (the traditional site of the Transfiguration) is in the Jezreel Valley south of Mt. Hermon, also known as Mt. Lebanon, which stands at the northern end of the Huleh Valley, north of the Sea of Galilee.

In verses 14 through 18 the psalmist speaks of what it means for people to have a God like this who is righteousness itself and who intends to establish righteousness, who is justice itself and who intends to establish justice. Those are the foundations of His sovereignty, and they rest on His love and faithfulness.

> Righteousness and justice are the foundation of your throne;
>> love and faithfulness go before you.
> Blessed are those who have learned to acclaim you,
>> who walk in the light of your presence, O [Yahweh]
> They rejoice in your name all day long;
>> they exult in your righteousness.
> For you are their glory and strength,
>> and by your favor you exalt our horn.
> Indeed, our shield belongs to [Yahweh],
>> our king to the Holy One of Israel
>> (vv. 14-18).

You notice what he is talking about. He is talking about the kind of God Yahweh is, how He is a covenant God and has established that covenant through David.

In verses 19-37 we have a recapitulation of the covenant with David, and he concludes with these words:

> I will maintain my love to him forever,
>> and my covenant with him will never fail.
> I will establish his line forever,
>> his throne as long as the heavens endure.
> "If his sons forsake my law
>> and do not follow my statutes,
> if they violate my decrees
>> and fail to keep my commands,
> I will punish their sin with the rod,
>> their iniquity with flogging;
> but I will not take my [hesed] from him,
>> nor will I ever betray my faithfulness.
> I will not violate my covenant
>> or alter what my lips have uttered.

> Once for all, I have sworn by my holiness—
>> and I will not lie to David—
> That his line will continue forever
>> and his throne endure before me like the sun;
> it will be established forever like the moon,
>> the faithful witness in the sky"
>> (vv. 28-37).

Now I notice that the sun has not gone out yet, and neither has the moon. These are very sweeping, universalistic promises.

But now look at what follows. The subject changes; and what a dramatic change.

> But you have rejected, you have spurned,
>> you have been very angry with your anointed one.
> You have renounced your covenant with your servant
>> and you have defiled his crown in the dust.
> You have broken through all his walls
>> and reduced his strongholds to ruins.
> All who pass by have plundered him;
>> he has become the scorn of his neighbors
>> (vv. 38-41).

I wonder if this was written in the days of Zedekiah and the last days of the kingdom of Judah when Judah was a pawn between the different powers, Babylon and Egypt, even to the point of being plundered by Edom (see the book of Obadiah). He continues,

> You have exalted the right hand of his foes;
>> you have made all his enemies rejoice.
> You have turned back the edge of his sword
>> and have not supported him in battle.
> You have put an end to his splendor
>> and cast his throne to the ground.
> You have cut short the days of his youth;
>> you have covered him with a mantle of shame
>> (vv. 42-45).

Notice that the word *Yahweh* never occurs in that section, nor does the word *God.* Maybe he is a little afraid to use those names, because he is talking back to God. He is saying, "You have made the promises, but the realities don't fit." But that is not the end of the psalm. There is more:

> How long, O [Yahweh]? Will you hide yourself forever?
>   How long will your wrath burn like fire?
> Remember how fleeting is my life.
>   For what futility you have created all men!
> What man can live and not see death,
>   or save himself from the power of the grave?
> [O Sovereign], where is your former great [*hesed*],
>   which in your faithfulness you swore to David?

Notice those two words; "*hesed*" and "faithfulness" sound very nice, but where are they?

> Remember, [O Sovereign], how your servant has been mocked,
>   how I bear in my heart the taunts of all the nations,
> the taunts with which your enemies have mocked, O [Yahweh],
>   with which they have mocked every step of
>   your anointed one (vv. 46-51).

The final verse, "Praise be to [Yahweh] forever. Amen and Amen" (52), seems out of place after the bleakness of what just precedes it. Perhaps it is not intended to be taken with the psalm itself but has been inserted as the closing of the third book of the Psalms, something that is characteristic of the closing of each book (see 41:13; 72:18-20; 106:48). Personally, I would rather have it that way than as a pious attempt to say, "With all the problems we've got everything is all right. Let's just praise the Lord anyway."

So what you have in the psalm is a reflection on the "disconnect" between the glorious past with its wonderful promises and a present that does not seem to fit with that at all. The psalmist is saying, "Reality doesn't fit the promises that have been given to us."[230] The language,

---

[230] The point would be the same whether we think that two poems have been

"How long," reminds us of the psalms of lament in which some of the same kinds of concerns are raised, although usually on a more personal level. The psalmists say, "We don't question who you are and what you have done in the past. But why aren't you doing that now? And when are you going to start doing it again?"

So here we have one of those "crosscurrents" I was talking about earlier. Yes, God is a God of *hesed* and *'emunah*, love and faithfulness. But if that is true, why do we not see it all the time and everywhere?

As I said above, the more I have lived with this psalm, the more grateful I have become for it. It says to us that it is all right to ask questions, when things do not seem to fit in our faith. But it also says that present distress need not diminish the reality of our faith. The psalmist did not question that God really is the God of *hesed* and *'emunah*, steadfast love and faithfulness. It was just the question that those did not seem to be present in the circumstances. By the same token, genuine faith does not require us to deny our pain and uncertainty. This is so very clear in a passage like Lamentations 3. Its opening verses are very bleak.

> [God] has driven me away and made me walk
> > in darkness rather than light;
> indeed, he has turned his hand against me
> > again and again, all day long (vv. 2-3).

It continues in that vein through the succeeding verses. So verses 15 and 16 say:

> He has filled me with bitter herbs,
> > And sated me with gall.
> He has broken my teeth with gravel;
> > he has trampled me in the dust.

So that is the reality of life, and there is no denying it. But then look at verses 21-23:

> Yet this I call to mind

---

put together or whether we think it is a single composition. In its present form this psalm is highlighting the disjunction between God's purported faithfulness and a situation that on the surface calls that faithfulness into question.

and therefore have hope:
Because of [Yahweh's] great love [*ḥesed*] we are not
    consumed,
        for his compassions never fail.
They are new every morning;
        great is your faithfulness [*'emunah*].

This is what Old Testament Wisdom Literature is dealing with; that is, without denying anything of what we know is true, let us look life squarely in the eye and see how the faith comes out.

Lecture 29

· · · · · · · · · ·

Ecclesiastes

We concluded the last lecture with the quotation from Lamentations 3:21-23. Yes, God is a God of *hesed* and *'emunah*, love and faithfulness. But if that is true, why do we not see it all the time and everywhere? That is basically the issue in the book of Ecclesiastes, the subject of this lecture. But the book carries the point to an extreme, so that it almost seems to deny that there is a God of love and faithfulness at all. For that reason, some people would say Ecclesiastes is the most unorthodox book in the Bible; others would go further still and say that it is just heresy and should not have been included. Certainly a case can be made that this is the most pessimistic and cynical book in the Bible. R. B. Y. Scott, an Old Testament professor and scholar, says the author is a rationalist, an agnostic, a skeptic, a pessimist, and a fatalist.[231] So what *is* this book doing in the Canon?

Let me review the argument of Ecclesiastes and how it develops.

---

[231] R. B. Y. Scott, *The Way of Wisdom in the Old Testament* (New York: Macmillan, 1971), 170-71.

The title of the book is *Qohelet*, which is a Hebrew participle that seems to refer to someone who gathers a congregation. Thus, in the past the author has sometimes been called "the Preacher." However, the content of the book is not really very sermonic, so it is more common today to refer to the author as "the Teacher."

In the book the Teacher is looking at the world around him and reporting his conclusions. The so-called "Prologue" in 1:1-11 summarizes his conclusions about the world. He says in a nutshell, "Meaningless, meaningless, everything is meaningless." You are probably more familiar with the King James language, "Vanity of vanities. All is vanity." The Hebrew term is, *hebel hebel*, which can be translated pretty literally as "empty air of empty air." That construction is one Hebrew way of expressing the superlative, so that what you have is, "The emptiest of empty air." He says, "What does a man gain from all his labor at which he toils under the sun?" [As you read Ecclesiastes, notice that "labor" and "toil" are significant concepts.] He is speaking from the human perspective.

> What does man gain from all his labor
>> at which he toils under the sun?
> Generations come and generations go
>> but the earth remains forever.
> The sun rises and the sun sets,
>> and hurries back to where it rises.
> The wind blows to the south
>> and turns and blows to the north;
> round and round it goes,
>> ever turning on its course.
> All streams flow into the sea,
>> yet the sea is never full.
> To the place streams come from,
>> there they return again.
> All things are wearisome;
>> more than one can say.
> The eye never has enough of seeing,
>> nor the ear its fill of hearing.
> What has been will be again,
>> what has been done will be done again;

there is nothing new under the sun.
>Is there anything of which one can say,
>"Look! This is something new"?
It was here already, long ago;
>it was here before our time.
There is no remembrance of men of old,
>and even those who are yet to come will not be
>remembered by those who follow
>(Eccl. 1:3-11).

So, do not get excited when you get an invitation to be in *Who's Who in America*. Just wait, and the day will come when nobody will know that you were ever there. You will notice that the Teacher's emphasis as he looks at life is cyclical. Wherever you are today, if you wait long enough, you will be at the other end of the spectrum. And if you continue to wait, you will be back where you started. Life on this earth is essentially cyclical. Now in the light of Eichrodt and our previous studies, that sounds more like pagan literature than it does biblical literature, does it not? And from here on in the book, you get that point of view developed.

So the Teacher, looking at life as what is apparently both a ceaseless and a meaningless cycle, says, "Where can I find something to make sense out of this?" There are two passages later that give us a clue to what he is looking for. Look at verse 25 of chapter 7. He is testing things by wisdom and he says, "I turned my mind to understand, to investigate and to search out wisdom and the scheme of things." Note that expression: "the scheme of things." Then look at the first verse of chapter 8: "Who is like the wise man? Who knows the explanation of things?" So, you see, he wants to find out, "How do I make sense out of my existence? And how can I make sense out of the world of which I am a part?" He is an existentialist[232] and he would like to find, if he could,

---

[232] [Editor's note] Existentialism is a European philosophy from the second third of the twentieth century. It was a reaction against the determinism of naturalism and posited that everything that happened was a matter of chance, so there is no meaning in anything that happens. Therefore, the truly courageous thing is to commit suicide. But since most of us lack that much courage, if we wish to truly "exist" (and not just "live," like a cow), we must each choose to inject our lives with meaning. This act of free choice in the face of meaninglessness will invest our lives

some significance in life.

After the prologue where he discusses the cyclical character of life, he says that he tried pleasure. But when he was sated with pleasure, he found that it did not help. So he tried work and undertook great projects. But when he finished those, that did not help either. So then he tried possessions, to get rich and own things. But that did not do it. So then he tried wisdom. But there were intellectual problems wisdom could not solve.

So after he has tried pleasure, work, possessions, and wisdom, he comes to a conclusion:

> So I hated life, because the work that was done under the sun was grievous to me. All of it is meaningless, a chasing after the wind. I hated all the things I had toiled for under the sun, because I must leave them to the one who comes after me. . . . For a man may do his work with wisdom, knowledge and skill, and then he must leave all he owns to someone who has not worked for it. This too is meaningless and a great misfortune. What does a man get for all the toil and anxious striving with which he labors under the sun? All his days his work is pain and grief; even at night his mind does not rest. This too is meaningless (2:17-23).

When you go on through 2:24-26, you come to the well-known passage in 3:1-8, where he again affirms the cyclical nature of life, and seems to affirm a basically stoic way of thinking. "This is the way things are, and you just might as well get used to it. Take life for what it is and don't break your back trying to make something out if it that you can't."

> There is a time for everything,
>   and a season for every activity under heaven:
> a time to be born and a time to die,
>   a time to plant and a time to uproot, [etc.] (3:1-2).

---

with the dignity of genuinely authentic existence. The existentialist understanding of reality is what underlies what is called "postmodernism."

From this point on through the remainder of the book the Teacher reports his investigations in more detail (chapters 3–6) and then he gives some maxims coming out of his experience (chapters 7–11). He speaks of times and seasons. He speaks of man and of beast. He speaks of oppression and death. He speaks of toil and vanity. He speaks of companionship, suggesting that maybe in friendship there is an answer to the question of the scheme of things and the meaning of life. He speaks of kings as if maybe we could find a clue if we understood the role of kings. He speaks of religion, of religious care. He speaks of political officials, those who are leaders in our society. He speaks of money and of moderation, as if being moderate might do it. He speaks of wisdom. He speaks of retribution and in the same breath turns and speaks of inequities: sometimes it looks like you get what you deserve in life, but then you turn around and there is someone who did not get what he deserved, and worse, someone who got what he did *not* deserve. He speaks of life and death and of good and evil. And then he goes back to talk again about wisdom and a word of value about it.

Finally, we come to the conclusion, which looks to have been written by someone else.

> Not only was the Teacher wise, but also he imparted knowledge to the people. He pondered and searched out and set in order many proverbs. The Teacher searched to find just the right words, and what he wrote was upright and true. The words of the wise are like goads, their collected sayings like firmly embedded nails —given by one Shepherd. Be warned, my son, of anything in addition to them. [Then the favorite text of the student] Of making many books there is no end, and much study wearies the body (12:9-12).

But then there is still a further word which is, I think, the real conclusion of the book:

> Now all has been heard; here is the conclusion of the matter: Fear God and keep his commandments, for this is the whole duty of man. For God will bring every deed

into judgment, including every hidden thing, whether it is good or evil (12:13-14).

Now these are the things that are present in Ecclesiastes, and they are very interesting. But it is equally interesting to look at some of the things that are absent. Let me mention some of them. There is no reference to the covenant anywhere in it. The word *Israel* occurs once. There is no reference to election, which corresponds to the fact that there is only one reference to Israel. There is no specific reference to the Law or the prophets, and there is no great interest in history because everything he sees is cyclical. There is no real interest in the future, and especially not in Israel's future. Although the word *Elohim* occurs forty times, the name "Yahweh" never occurs once. So, it seems almost as if there is no distinctly Israelite flavor to the book. It is almost as if the piece could have been written by anybody in the world in any culture.

But as I have thought about these things and read and reread the book, there is an interesting phrase that occurs again and again. Look at the first chapter, verse 3: "What does man gain from all his labor at which he toils under the sun?" Then look at verse 9 in the same chapter: "What has been will be again, what has been done will be done again; there is nothing new under the sun." Do you see that phrase *under the sun?* If you will check a concordance you will find that it occurs no less than twenty-nine times in Ecclesiastes. When you add the variation "under the heavens" we have thirty-one occurrences in twelve chapters. So what is very clear is that the perspective here is a man who is looking at his world strictly from this world's point of view. So he is limiting his search for the meaning of things, the scheme of things, the explanation of things, as he says in 7:25, and again in 8:1, to this world. And what is the outcome? He says, "When I had searched it all, I found it to be the emptiest puff of air, vanity of vanities, meaningless meaninglessness." What he is saying, and this is very profound, is that this world is not self-explanatory; if you limit your search for the meaning of existence to what is under the sun, you are not going to find anything, or at least, not much.

So he is speaking as a man separate from revelation. And what he finds is dramatically different from what the Law and the prophets tell us about the meaning of life. Nine times he says, "I'll tell you what I found. I found a chasing after the wind." He is saying that without the light of special revelation, God's word from beyond the sun, life *does* seem to be an endless round, going nowhere. Did you notice, there is not a reference to life after death. It is written as though John 14 and 1 Corinthians 15 were never to be written. It speaks as if injustice is as common as justice. Life is futile and there is no way you can make a case to prove anything different.

But he cannot completely avoid the effects of revelation in the life of Israel. He has no wish to deny the existence of God, something that a resolute commitment to chance seems to lead to. As I said, he refers to God, *'elohim,* forty times. God reigns in this world and it is what it is because of Him. There is no discussion of the demonic in this. The devil does not get any credit for any of the negatives, unlike the religious literature around Israel, where that is a common theme. So the God who is and who reigns is to be respected. At six strategic points, he refers to the fear of God.[233] As you know by now "the fear of God" is a way of living where you take into account that there is an all-powerful God who expects you to give an accounting for how you used His resources in your life.[234] In that light you will notice that the Teacher distinguishes between the sinner and the righteous person, and between the one who pleases God and the evil person.

There is a further feature of the book that is very positive. As he goes through his disillusionment, he stops periodically and makes a statement about where he is. One example appears in verse 24 of chapter 2: "A man can do nothing better than to eat and drink and find satisfaction in his work." In other words, he is not ready to commit suicide. But neither does he say, "Eat, drink, and be merry for tomorrow I die." He says, "It is good for a man to eat and to drink and to find satisfaction in his work." Now, you will find a tension in the book in his use of the words *toil, labor,* and *work.* In many cases he will say that work is just weariness and futility, because you do not really gain anything lasting. But then there will be a passage like that one in 2:24. There is another in verse 22 of chapter 3. Like the previous one it occurs at the close of a section. "So I saw that there is nothing better for a man than to enjoy his work, because this is his lot. For who can bring him to see what will

---

[233] 3:14 (two times); 5:7; 8:12; 8:13; 12:13.
[234] Eichrodt's treatment of the fear of God is frankly beautiful (*Theology,* vol. 2, 268-77). It should not be overlooked.

happen after him?" Similar statements are found in 5:18 and 8:15. A more lengthy one is found in 9:7-10:

> Go, eat your food with gladness, and drink your wine with a joyful heart, for it is now that God favors what you do. Always be clothed in white, and always anoint your head with oil. Enjoy life with your wife, whom you love, all the days of this meaningless life that God has given you under the sun—all your meaningless days. For this is your lot in life and in your toilsome labor under the sun. Whatever your hand finds to do, do it with all your might, for in the grave, where you are going, there is neither working nor planning nor knowledge nor wisdom.

So, despite all his unanswered questions, he still believes that there is something in life to be treasured and enjoyed. Strikingly, it is centered around the family relationships [see the following lecture]. He concludes that this must be so because the transcendent Creator made things that way. But what frustrates him is that human intelligence is not enough to figure out exactly what God is doing. Verses 11-15 of chapter three are very memorable in that regard:

> He has made everything beautiful in its time. He has also set eternity in the hearts of men; yet they cannot fathom what God has done from beginning to end. I know that there is nothing better for men than to be happy and do good while they live. That everyone may eat and drink, and find satisfaction in all his toil—this is the gift of God. I know that everything God does will endure forever; nothing can be added to it and nothing taken from it. God does it so that men will revere him. Whatever is has already been, and what will be has been before; and God will call the past to account.

So I see Ecclesiastes as making two contributions to the Canon of Scripture. The first is this: Even when life seems meaningless and futile, do not either deny the reality of those feelings or give up in despair.

The Israelites' faith did not blind them in a way that prevented them from seeing the evil or the unanswered questions—their faith did not express itself superficially. They found nothing in their faith to demand that they deny reality. Sometimes we use religion as an escapism. But you do not find that in Ecclesiastes.

But it is also significant that as he builds a case for skepticism and unbelief, he never draws what appears to be the logical conclusion from the data he produces. And I think the reason is that he is a Hebrew; he is the heir of revelation. And there are some things that have been given to him that he is not going to repudiate. One of them is, he is a monotheist. There is only one God. And he would rather live with the consequences of the intellectual problems with that belief than he would to go back to the nature worship out of which his people were drawn. So there is still good reason to be a reliable and trustworthy person who finds satisfaction in work and family, and who lives an upright life keeping the commands of God. This is a good word, because faith is truly faith only when we continue to believe while we are in the darkness. If we only believe when everything makes sense and all our efforts are rewarded, I question whether that is faith at all.

The second contribution of Ecclesiastes is to underline the inadequacy of so-called "natural revelation" by itself.[235] If you rule out "special revelation" the very best you can possibly end up with is the point of view found here. While, as I just said, this is better than nothing, still, it is not enough. Ecclesiastes gives remarkable support to the claims of the rest of Scripture that its understandings of the meaning of life can only be explained on the grounds it gives: direct revelation from the One who is beyond the sun.

So what shall we say about Wisdom Literature, especially Ecclesiastes? What we see here, I believe, is one of the stages in revelation. We see such different stages very clearly between the Old and the New Testament. For instance, the Teacher knew nothing about life after death as we get it in John 14 or 1 Corinthians 15, or some of the other passages in the New Testament. So we know there are stages between the Old Covenant and the New. But I am convinced there are stages within the Old Covenant. The initial stage was the battle for transcendence

---

[235] This is a point the Karl Barth is famous for emphasizing.

and monotheism. It had to be established against all the world of pagan thought that there was one God alone who is not to be identified with this world. So you move through the revelation to Abraham and then to Moses, and ultimately as Israel moves along, that battle is won—there is one God and one alone. Of course, it was not a straight-line progression. There were great advances and almost equally great setbacks. But the major thrust is there.

But once you have won that battle, that there is only one God, there is a sense in which I think God lets Israel stop and think about the implications of that understanding. "Well, if that's true, then there are a lot of data that don't fit." So they needed to examine all that data to get ready for the next stage in God's revelation. I think that Ecclesiastes represents that kind of thing, where a man is an heir to revelation and says, "I am grateful for that, but I'm working down here at the brick factory and there are a lot of things down here that aren't very easy to explain." Or maybe he is a politician in Washington, and he says, "How do you put that monotheistic understanding together with all these things that don't seem to fit in with it?" And the Scripture says, "Go to it. Raise all the questions you can raise. Ask them all. But as you ask them, don't ditch what has been given to you." If you do that, then there is the possibility of further truth opening up and further understanding.

I have been with some men during my life who would preach and talk as if they never had a battle, never had a problem, never had an intellectual question. I think they were afraid that if they admitted to me that they had ever had a serious intellectual question, that might encourage my doubts. But I want to say that some of the people who have influenced me the most, who have been most helpful to me, are those who said something like this: "God came to me in a glorious way and I could not doubt it. I knew that I had met Him. I knew that He existed. I knew He had laid His hand on my life. But then He led me into a dead-end street, an absolutely dead-end street, where nothing seemed to fit the promise that I felt was there when He came to me." That did not encourage my doubts, but rather gave me hope that if they could continue to believe in that kind of a situation, then I could too. And I think that is what you are getting in the Wisdom Literature and especially the pessimistic Wisdom Literature.

Look with me at Psalm 126. I did not pay much attention to it for years because of the way it begins. It says, "When [Yahweh] brought back the captives to Zion . . ." And I thought, *I'm never going to be in military or political captivity, so it doesn't relate to me, it's all theoretical and of no real significance to me.* So I just skipped over it until one day I decided to work my way through it in the Hebrew. The first thing I saw was that the word translated "captives" (*shibat*) is from the root meaning "to turn." So the sentence says, "When Yahweh turned the turnings (circumstances) of Zion . . ."[236] Everything had been going straight and suddenly everything turned wrong. But then Yahweh came and turned it back right again. He says, when that happened,

> We were like men who dreamed.
> Our mouths were filled with laughter,
>> Our tongues with songs of joy.
> Then it was said among the nations [the *goyim*,
>> the Gentiles, the neighbors],
> [Yahweh] has done great things for them (vv. 1b-2).

It is impressive when your pagan neighbors talk about how good God has been to you. That is testimony; that is witness. Not with the lips, but with your life.[237] That is what we find in the life of Israel when they came out of Egypt. God did something for them so significant that the people all around them knew that Israel's God was on a completely

---

[236] [Editor's note] This is the only occurrence of this word in the Old Testament. Since the LXX reads "captivity" (*aichmalosia*) it seems probable that this is a mistake and that the original was *shebit*, "captivity," and not *shibat.*

[237] Let me illustrate that with a story from the life of an evangelist, John Church. He was driving down the peninsula on the east side of the Chesapeake Bay to take the ferry across to Portsmouth and Norfolk. He said the last ferry was at six o'clock, so he was driving as hard as he could to get there. It was during the Second World War, and he had stopped and picked up a GI. He said, "We were riding along and I was pushing it. But suddenly an inner voice said, 'Stop.'" And it kept saying it strong enough that he finally pulled off on the berm. And he said, "Just as I got the car stopped, the front left tire blew out. So I just took the key out of the ignition, went back, opened the trunk, got the jack, and started jacking up the front end. I had it half jacked up before that GI moved. When he finally got out he came around and stared at me and said, 'Mister, did you know that tire was going to blow out?' I said, 'No.' 'Well,' he said, 'Why did you stop?' I said, 'The Lord told me.' The soldier just stood there and shook his head and said, 'Man, I'm not a Christian but there's nothing in the world I wouldn't give for your connections.'"

different level than any other so-called god. You will remember that that
is what Rahab the prostitute said to the spies in Jericho: "When we heard
of it, our hearts melted and everyone's courage failed because of you,
for the Lord your God is God in heaven above and in the earth below"
(Josh. 2:11). So the psalmist concludes this thought by saying,

> [Yahweh] has done great things for us,
>   and we are filled with joy (v. 3).

But in verse 4 the thought changes pretty radically. That was
the past and this is the present, and we are in trouble again. Our circumstances[238] need turning again. The great promises of the prophets
regarding the circumstances that would exist after the return did not
seem to be coming true. Jerusalem was not the center of the world; there
was no Davidic messiah on the throne; there was not even a throne!
They were not prosperous and influential. So the psalmist says there is
no laughter and rejoicing now; we are like the dry and dusty Negev in
the southern part of Israel. There is little rainfall in the Negev and the
watercourses are normally empty, eroded gullies. But from time to time
there are cloudbursts in the hills to the north, and suddenly on a bril-
liantly sunny day the watercourses are full of rushing water. The psalmist
is saying that Israel needs something as dramatic and as life-giving and,
for all practical purposes, as inexplicable as that to happen to them.[239]
    Then we read,

> Those who sow in tears
>   will reap with songs of joy.
> He who goes out weeping

---

[238] [Editor's note] Here the Hebrew consonantal text has the word as *shebit*
"captivity" (see note 235 above), but the Masoretes vocalized it as "fortunes,
circumstances" (*shebut*). It looks as though the poet was engaging in wordplay with
shub, "return" or "restore," and *shebit* and *shebut*, but that the similar sounding
words got mixed up with each other in transmission.

[239] Some years ago I read a newspaper account of people drowning in the
Sahara. We think of the Sahara as drifting sand, but a lot of it is baked-hard crust. So
when the occasional rainstorm comes, the water hits the ground but is not absorbed.
Instead, it all goes pouring to the lowest spot. In this case a group of people were
camping in a depression, and when the unexpected rain came there was enough
water so that seven or eight people drowned—in the Sahara Desert.

> carrying seed to sow,
> will return with songs of joy,
> carrying sheaves with him (vv. 5-6).

Now, I have heard, "Those who sow in tears will reap with songs of joy" applied to prayer. The idea is that if you pray sincerely enough, weeping, that the weeping will make your prayer more effective. However, I do not think that is what is being talked about at all. I think you and I ought to be sincere in prayer, but the key to interpreting this psalm is in the linkage between *sow* and *tears*. When you sow, your interest is tomorrow, not today. And the probabilities are that when you sow, your interest is in somebody beyond yourself. But when my circumstances go wrong, I do not want to think about the future; I want to forget all about it. The last thing I am interested in is spending what energy I have left thinking about something way down the road and preparing for it. Despair makes you captive to the moment. But the psalmist says, when despair comes, don't let it capture you; keep thinking about tomorrow and planning. He does not say to stop weeping; but he does say not to let the weeping prevent you from sowing in faith for the future.

Verse 6 confirms this interpretation, because of the Hebrew sentence structure.[240] It begins with an emphatic statement: "He surely goes forth," which is followed by a construction stressing the manner of carrying, namely weepingly. Then the next line begins with that same emphatic construction: "He will surely come in." The one who determinedly goes out and sows for the future, though weeping, will assuredly come in with good results. Keep putting one foot in front of the other in the best faith you can muster. Do not ditch anything you know, but keep going. And one day you will certainly come in, bringing your "sheaves" with you, and your future will be what you have dreamed about.

Now, this kind of thing is latent within much of the so-called pessimistic Wisdom Literature, most famously Job and Ecclesiastes. We do not know all, or sometimes, any, of the answers; but we do know some things about God and about reality, enough so that we have something for which to go on. So there have been times when I have found

---

[240] Infinitive absolute plus finite verb of the same root = emphasis: "going he goes" = "he certainly goes"; infinitive absolute plus finite verb of a different root = manner: "weeping he is carrying" = "he is carrying weepingly."

myself on what I thought was a dead-end street, saying, "I'm grateful these passages are in here for they have given me a guide as to what I ought to do." And if you will, then that God whom you refuse to deny now will one day honor and reward you.

Lecture 30

· · · · · · · · · ·

The Song of Songs

In this lecture I want to think with you about the Song of Songs (Song of Solomon, *NIV*). It is clearly a piece of poetry about human love, love between a man and a woman. You will find very little in it to mark it as specifically Hebrew except the language it is written in. Like Ecclesiastes, there is something universal about it. Anyone in any culture who has ever experienced human love can say, "I understand this and it speaks for me." There is no effort at theology in the text. You have to work hard to find even an appearance of the name of God. It is one book that we know had its canonical status questioned by Jewish leaders at Jamnia toward the end of the first Christian century. At the same time, there have perhaps been more commentaries written on this book than any other single book of the Old Testament. So let me say some things about the Song of Songs and the way it has been interpreted down through history.

It is fascinating to me the way scholars have not been able to stay away from the Song of Songs; but they either dismiss it, or when they deal with it there is always the feeling that they are overstating their case.

In the first century of the Christian era, we get an insight into Jewish thought concerning the book. Rabbi Akiba pronounced a curse on those who would use it in secular circumstances in celebration of human love. But then he turned around and said, "The world itself was not worth the day on which this book was given to Israel." So, you sense something of the uneasiness over it, but at the same time his incredible respect for it.

The earliest Christian commentary on the Song of Songs comes to us from Origen (circa 185–251). He said that it obviously was a wedding song, and he thought it was in honor of Solomon's marriage to an Egyptian princess. But he found himself asking the question why it was in the Scripture, and he said he felt that it was obviously there only because it could be interpreted allegorically. So it is in the Canon, he said, because it is not really talking about human love but about the Divine Being's love for us. So he supplied a theological justification for its presence in the Canon.

But Origen had a clear precedent for approaching the book in that way. It was interpreted allegorically by Jewish scholars from at least the beginning of the Christian era. The Jewish Midrash explains the book in terms of the beloved as Israel: the lover as Yahweh, and the place is Sinai. Moses is the one sent to make arrangements with the bride for Yahweh. When you come to Augustine, you will find that he just simply changes the identity of the loved one and says that it is the church and that it is a picture of Christ and the church.

One of the commentators who intrigues me most is Bernard of Clairvaux who lived in the twelfth century A.D. He wrote 86 different sermons on the Song of Songs, using some seventeen thousand words. But when he died, he had not gotten past the first verse of the third chapter! Since he was only sixty-one when he died it is interesting to speculate how much farther he might have gotten in another ten years or so. The church can never quite give up pondering this interesting bit of literature.

Although not all commentators in the history of the church have thought the book should be understood allegorically, most have. Theodore of Mopsuestia in the fourth century said that it should be taken literally. But a century after that, his views were condemned by the church as unfit for human ears. And from then on through the Middle Ages the predominant view was that it should be interpreted allegorically.

Its presence in the Canon was justified by insisting that it was not talking about human love, the kind of love that a man and woman can have for each other, but that it was talking about the kind of love that God has for me and that I am supposed to have for Him.

When the Enlightenment came with its insistence that all things must bow to reason, allegorical interpretation of any parts of the Bible tended to be dismissed. As a result, there has been a resurgence of the literal interpretation of Song of Songs in the modern period. But even in many of these more literal approaches the book is often looked upon as a celebration of the Creator who made us male and female, and who put within each one of us our profound interest in the other. It seems that there is something within us that wants to say that when you have pure, beautiful love, there is more to it than biology. Yes, the biological and physical are there. We do not deny that. But there is something more here.

Oftentimes, Song of Songs is classified as Wisdom Literature. That is partly because of the placement of the book in the *Septuagint*, following Ecclesiastes and preceding Isaiah.[241] It is difficult to find some of the typical wisdom themes in the book, but it shares at least a couple of characteristics with that literature. One of these is its radically this-worldly orientation. There is no obvious reference to revelation or to theology derived from revelation.

A second characteristic of wisdom that is closely related to the first point is the special interest in nature and the world of creation. There are more references to the flora and fauna of Israel in the Song of Songs than any other portion of the Old Testament. In those eight chapters, there are twenty-one varieties of plant life mentioned, much to the dismay of the Hebrew student who has to translate it. The problem is that many of the names occur just once in the Bible, and the occurrence in Song of Songs is that once. There are also fifteen species of animals mentioned in the Song of Songs.[242] So, if Ecclesiastes is man under the

---

[241] In the Hebrew canon it appears in the third section, the Writings, and is grouped with Ruth, Ecclesiastes, Lamentations, and Esther, with each of the five being associated with one of the festivals.

[242] When Elsie and I were courting, one of the things we used to do was take hikes. I found myself interested in nature during those days in a way I never had been before, and never was again. So in the Song of Songs there is this quickened fascination with the world around us. There is something about love that when it

sun, looking at the negative character of a fallen world and trying to decide what to do; the Song of Songs gives us a writer who is excited about
some of the beauty, the wonder, and the mystery of this world of which
we are a part, and particularly in the relationship between the sexes.

There is another aspect in which this book may be seen as part
of the wisdom tradition, and I find this helpful. Recall von Rad's comment that the wisdom writers looked for comparisons and correspondences between things on different planes. Let me raise the question
about how it is that an eternal world can communicate with a temporal
world, or how a temporal world can communicate with the eternal? How
can a created world communicate with an uncreated world, or how can
the Creator communicate with His creation?

When we ask those kinds of questions, we are driven back to
Genesis 1 with its statement that we are made in the image of God. And
in that concept of image, we come back to that ability to compare and
of some kind of correspondence. So there is enough correspondence
between human and Divine that communication is possible. It is not easy
given our darkness and our fallenness, but nevertheless it is possible.

Thinking about these questions I found myself drawn to the
problem faced by Christ, the incarnate Son of God.[243] How did Jesus
communicate eternal truth to earthbound people? We talked about this
in an earlier lecture, and I refer you there for the full discussion. But I
said there that in a study of the gospel of John, I discovered that Jesus
was able to find correspondences in this world to make the connections.
So he could talk about the wind and the Spirit, or about water and eternal
life. As I looked more closely at Jesus' use of figures of speech, I discovered that there were almost no similes, but many metaphors. A simile is a
figure of speech where one thing is compared to another. The relationship is expressed with a comparative term such as "like." So we may say,
"My love is like . . . a red, red rose," or, "He is happy as a lark."

But a metaphor is different. Here one thing is identified with another. In a metaphor there is no comparison. Here we say, "This *is* that."

---

strikes us, everything takes on new sanctity and meaning.
[243] The very concept of the Incarnation has within it the implication of some
kind of correspondence. There is enough compatibility between God and us, despite
His transcendence, that the second person in the blessed Trinity could become one
of us.

So when Jesus spoke about Herod, he said, "Go tell that old fox . . ." He did not say, "Herod is like a fox, go tell him." I think you can see in that example that the metaphor is much more powerful than the simile. Another example might be, "My heart is a heavy stone."

A textbook on English style will tell you that figures of speech are used for three reasons. One is to produce clarity: "The bird sits atilt like a blossom among the leaves." The second reason for using figures of speech is to give force to language: "a gush of violets." That is much more forceful than "a lot of violets." If you have ever seen a field of bluebonnets in Texas, you will understand exactly what the person using that figure is trying to convey. But the third reason for using a figure of speech is the one that fascinates me the most. It is to suggest unity. An apt figure of speech stirs us to the depths of our being. Why? Because it subtly suggests that there is a fundamental oneness in things. It helps us to unify our world. The rose in the garden unfolding its petals to the sun and the morning light spreading out its cloud petals over the earth are both manifestations of a single source of beauty. So a powerful figure of speech is able to have its effect because it is a revelation of an underlying truth. This is what von Rad was talking about when he said that wisdom is looking at creation and trying to find in the correspondences evidence of that order that lies behind everything.

Roland Frye, former Felix E. Schelling professor of English Literature at the University of Pennsylvania, writing in *Speaking the Christian God*, says this about simile and metaphor:

> In that simile compares and metaphor names or identifies, simile differs from metaphor in that it merely states resemblance, while metaphor boldly transfers the representation. While the simile gently states that one thing resembles another, the metaphor boldly and warmly declares that one thing is the other.[244]

Now, if I am going to be a witness for Christ, that ought to be significant to me. If I am going to preach the Gospel, preaching is only

[244] Roland M. Frye, *Language for God and Feminist Language: Problems and Principles* (Princeton: Center of Theological Inquiry, 1988); also found in *Speaking the Christian God*, ed. Alvin F. Kimel, Jr. (Grand Rapids: Eerdmans, 1992), 37.

pertinent when you touch some point that you have in common with the people who are listening to you. So what are the metaphors, the transfers of identity, that Jesus uses?

The first one is, of course, the family. Go through the gospel of John and listen to Jesus talk about God the Father, of whom He is the Son. Do you realize what that means? Adam and Eve did not have the first family. I lived for decades not relating the doctrine of the Trinity to the human family. But the reality is, biblically, the family is not an institution that is originally rooted in human society. The family is an institution that is originally rooted in the nature of Deity. As I said earlier, that explains why the U.S. government does not know how to define a family. The government does not have the frame of reference out of which the family came. So this teaches us that we are put together in our basic relationships the way the basic nature of Deity is put together. That does something for the significance of the family.

But the second metaphor is marriage. At a minimum it is very clear that the Creation story ends with a marriage, and so does human history as described in the book of Revelation. The first is the kind of marriage that my wife and I have, and the other is the kind that Christ has with His church. In the Gospels we are told that the kind Elsie and I have will end or at least will be changed when one of us dies.[245] But the kind of marriage that Christ has with His church is eternal. So in the final pages of the book of Revelation, the Christ is presented as the Bridegroom, and the church is presented as the Bride. And the climax of human history is the marriage supper of the Lamb.

Now, I think that means, as I understand it, that if one metaphor, one likeness, one correspondence—the family—is rooted in the nature of Deity, this other social institution that we speak of as marriage, human sexuality and the biology of that, is more than biology. The personhood that is essential to it is rooted in the sovereign, eternal purposes of God. If God created us so that ultimately everybody could be His son or daughter—a child of the Father—and if He created us so that everybody ultimately could be part of the bride of the Son, then human sexuality gets very interesting. Suddenly, it is not at all surprising to me that the Song of Songs is in the middle of the Old Testament.

---

[245] [Editor's note] Elsie Kinlaw died in 2003.

Now you recognize that I am interpreting the Song of Songs in the light of the New Testament; but I want to say again that the division between Old Testament theology and New Testament theology is ultimately an artificial one. We need the New Testament to help us understand the richness and the greatness of the Old Testament.

As I just said, and also said earlier, there is a great deal of evidence in the New Testament supporting this "nuptial" theology, and that helps us understand the Song of Songs. Is the book about human love? Absolutely! But is that all it is about? Absolutely not! Why is this collection of love poetry in the Bible? Because someone sneaked it in when the canonization committee was looking the other way? No. It is in the Bible because there is a profound correspondence between human love and the meaning of life. It is there because human love is a metaphor for the way God wants to relate to His creatures. It is there because something of ultimate significance is going on in human love. It is not an allegory for divine love, but it partakes of and corresponds to the divine love.

There is no question but that when we think about God and about redemption, we think metaphorically. A common term in our day is "paradigms," that is, patterns. I have come to believe that there are four very important paradigms in biblical theology. One of these paradigms is the political one: the king and his kingdom; the ruler and his subjects. And you will remember how many times Jesus used the phrase "the kingdom of heaven," in Matthew, Mark, and Luke. The only places where that phrase occurs in John are in connection with Nicodemus (chap. 3). Nicodemus was a teacher of Israel; he was supposed to know all about the kingdom. So the political paradigm is a legitimate one. God is the Sovereign, the King of kings. In 1 Corinthians 15, we are told about a day when every knee will bow and every tongue will confess, and Christ will render up the kingdom to the Father from whence it came. So, you have that paradigm that runs all through Scripture.

Then there is a second paradigm that is very important biblically, and that is the juridical one, the court scene. This is an important theme in the Prophets, where Yahweh has a case against Israel and against the sinner. The basic concept in this paradigm is not power but right. There is the Law of God, and there is sin against that Law. The question is whether we can be made right with God. So we are thinking about justification. How can we be justified before the Judge who sits on the bench?

And the good news is that there is a way, a way provided by the Judge Himself.

But there is something within us that is never content to leave our relationship with God in merely legal or political terms. Something within us wants a closer relationship than a subject has with his king, or an acquitted defendant with the judge. At five o'clock the judge goes home. When the case is over, the judge goes his way and you go yours. But there is something within us that wants a deeper intimacy. And so we have the third metaphor, the family metaphor, the family paradigm. Here we are not talking about being a subject or an acquitted criminal; we are talking about a very real personal relationship in which we can look up at God who is the King and who is the Judge and say, "Father." It is a very different relationship when you come to the place where you call him "Father" as well as God, King, and Judge. Here the emphasis is upon new birth, and upon adoption, belonging. Who is there among us who has ever been genuinely born again who does not find something within leaping up in great joy at this thought?

But as wonderful as that is, there is something inside of us that yearns for a yet deeper and more intimate relationship than that. This is the fourth paradigm of marriage, the groom and the bride. As I think is clear to you by now, I am convinced that there is much more biblical support for this paradigm than many of us in American evangelicalism have tended to recognize. I do not want to diminish the glory of the Reformation in any way. Thank God for everything that He was able to do through Luther and Calvin. But when we use that juridical paradigm, we have not exhausted our relationship to God. There is something within us that yearns for that more intimate and more personal relationship. We long for a relationship in which we are not only connected but where we give ourselves to Him. That self-giving is the essence of the relationship as it is the essence of the marriage relationship in which two people give themselves to each other, without reserve, totally and unconditionally.

Now, sometimes there is a tendency to speak dismissively about that kind of experience as "mysticism." But if you read the literature of the Christian church, you will find a yearning for oneness with God. And if you read the apostle Paul, you will find a significant biblical base for that concept of oneness with Him. There is also a good basis for it in our own tradition. One of Wesley's young preachers was named Tommy

Walsh. He was twenty-eight when he died. Let me read you just two or three passages from his journal:

> I sensibly felt the Lord impressing his image on my soul.
> O perfect Love! It is all in all in religion. I want it above
> everything, even this fullness of God in Christ.
>> O, shed it in my heart abroad,
>> Fullness of love, of heaven, of God!
> The Lord gives me to drink of his love, as out of a river.
> All things work together for my good. May everyone
> that is godly praise him for this, and trust in his name
> forever.[246]

Now, you notice the cry for love. It is a little different from what you find in the political paradigm, or the juridical one. And it is something even more intimate than what you have in the family paradigm.

"O what a mystery is the love of Christ! How sweet a banquet! How delicious a wine!" Does that make you think of the Song of Songs? Remember the second verse of the first chapter: "Let him kiss me with the kisses of his mouth, for your love is better than wine." He goes on:

> Lord, thou hast ravished me with thy love! Death is now
> sweet to me; and eternity affords me a most blessed
> and glorious hope. Oh, what has God done for me!
> Holy Lord, accept of my heartiest praise, and the most
> perfect love that I at present can give. I feel the life
> which never shall end. Both my body and soul were
> affected with the great power of God resting upon me
> this day. My whole nature bowed before the present
> Deity; and his high praises were in my mouth. He said
> unto my soul, 'Thou art made whole.' I replied, 'Lord,
> I believe.'[247]

This young man was only twenty-eight years old, but you sense

---

[246] *Wesley's Veterans,* 6 vols., ed. John Telford (Salem, Ohio: Schmul Publishers), vol. 5, 164.
[247] Ibid., 166.

the depth of intimate relationship there. It is this kind of experience that produced "Love divine, all loves excelling. Joy of heaven to earth come down. . . . " And it is a part of our heritage.

Now here is the conclusion of the journal, written by the editor.

> It was, however, not until a short time before his complete and his eternal deliverance that his Lord appeared to his help; and by making Himself known as Jesus, his well-known Saviour, entirely eased the anguish of his oppressed soul. The beams of his brightness dispersed the clouds; and the smiles of his countenance more than compensated for all his night of sorrow. He spoke and said unto him, "The winter is passed, arise my love, and come away!" [That is, of course, from Song of Songs 2:11 and 13.]
>
> The manner of his deliverance was as follows: A few friends being at prayer with him, on Sunday evening, as soon as they concluded he desired to be left alone, in order, as he said, 'to meditate a little.' They withdrew; and he remained deeply recollected for some time: just then, God dropping into his soul, no doubt, some lively foretaste of the joys to come, and spreading the day of eternity through the regions of his inward man, he at length burst out in transport, and pronounced in a dying voice indeed, but with the joy of angels, 'He is come! He is come! My beloved is mine, and I am his! His forever!' And uttering these words he sweetly breathed out his soul into the arms of his Beloved on the 8th day of April, 1759 and in the twenty-eighth year of his age.[248]

Now, there is a wealth of literature in the history of the church expressing that kind of intimacy, that kind of personal love relationship, between believers and their God. The basis for that understanding is

---

[248] Ibid., 189-90.

found in the Old Testament and it is hard to avoid appealing to the Song of Songs for language to express it even though the text itself has no theological thrust obvious within it. But the one who gave it to us, or the tradition that gave it to us, the body of believers that gave it to us, is the body of believers that felt that they were the elect Bride of Yahweh. This is where I want to appeal again to this idea of correspondences: without saying that the book is really only talking about our love relationship for God, it is still possible to say that when we talk about human love, that love is so profoundly affecting, and so profoundly significant because it corresponds to the love that defines the Creator of the universe.

Now, this whole matter is of more significance for you than it ever was for me. And that is because of the way the theological landscape has changed since 1960. The barriers that existed when I was in seminary have all come down. I think I mentioned to you hearing Hans Küng in 1961. It was at Boston College and there were about one thousand Jesuit priests there listening to him. He said things that I never dreamed I would hear from a Roman Catholic theologian in my lifetime; he sounded like Martin Luther to me.[249] And as you know, that was only the beginning. With Vatican II immense changes have come into the relationship of Roman Catholicism.

The political climate has contributed to the change as well. Now you have fundamentalist Baptists and Roman Catholics together outside of abortion clinics, making their protests together, arm in arm, brothers and sisters in Christ, something that earlier was not even in the realm of imagination.

But not only is there the dialogue with the Roman Church, there is the beginning of dialogue with the Eastern Orthodox Church, something that is inevitably going to increase. And that is going to have a great impact on Western Christianity. For there is a tradition in the Eastern Church that is radically different from either the Reformed theology of Protestantism or from Roman Catholicism. So there are many of us who are just now beginning to get a little understanding of orthodoxy and its

---

[249] [Editor's note] In the 1964 presidential race, the Goldwater campaign used the slogan, "In your heart, you know he's right." A Jesuit friend of mine told me that a card had become very popular among Jesuits in 1965 and 1966. On the front was a picture of Martin Luther nailing his ninety-five theses to the door of the Wittenberg cathedral. Inside was the message: "In your heart you know he was right."

basic faith. And what you are going to find in that dialogue is that in the East the courtroom paradigm is not the most common one. In that tradition much more is made of the other paradigms, especially the family and the marriage ones. Those paradigms are much more a part of their thinking than is the political or the juridical. That leads to more of an emphasis upon sanctification and personal holiness than there has commonly been found in the Reformed tradition.

So, I think all of that will be a part of life and future discussions. And one of the marvelous things is that when we dialogue with those who come from another tradition, it is amazing what we see about our own that we missed before, both of good and, may I say, ill. The two-and-a-half years I spent at Princeton were priceless for me. They did not make a Calvinist out of me, but they saved me from great amounts of Arminian heresy. For when you only talk among yourselves you inevitably overstate your case. Could I repeat that? This is my observation. When we only talk to those who agree with us, we inevitably overstate our case. So we need a dialogue with those who differ from us so we will be forced to make our case cleanly and clearly, saying what is inherently logical and consistent with our position rather than a safe overstatement. So I say all of this hoping that what I have said about the marital paradigm in the context of the Song of Songs will be of service in theological dialogues in the future.

Lecture 31

· · · · · · · · · ·

Biblical Studies at the Beginning of the Twenty-First Century

In this final lecture I want to discuss the state of biblical studies at the end of the twentieth century and the beginning of the twenty-first. And I want to begin by talking about a movement called "canonical criticism." This movement, primarily associated with two American scholars, Jack Sanders and Brevard Childs, seeks to understand the Bible in the light of its final canonical form. It assumes all the other forms of criticism, such as the documentary hypothesis, form criticism, redaction criticism, and the like, but then says, "Yes, those all tell us how the Bible developed (according to the critics' understanding) into its final form; but what does that final form tell us about how the believing community wanted us to understand what the Bible is saying?" In this lecture I am going to focus on Childs and his thinking because I believe his views on the subject are the most helpful.

I want to use two quotations from Childs as starting points. They are both taken from his *Old Testament Theology in a Canonical Context.* Here is the first:

> Up to this point I have argued that to reflect on the Old Testament theologically in the context of the Christian canon establishes a perspective from which the enterprise is engaged. It rules out a stance which distances itself from Christian faith and tries merely to describe the development of Israel's faith in God or to picture different concepts of an ancient deity.[250]

I want to emphasize his use of the word *perspective*. He is looking for a viewpoint from which to understand the text. In the quotation he identifies three such perspectives. One of them looks at the development of Israel's faith in God as sort of a historical thing of interest, something out there, objective to us. The second perspective sees the history of Israel as a picture of a people with successively different concepts of an ancient Deity. This would be what we have called the comparative religions approach. But he is arguing for another point of view. Rather than distancing itself from the Christian faith in God, as the other two do, this perspective would look at the text from within the Christian faith.

Now, what he is saying is that a great deal of the biblical study during the last three hundred years has been done by people who had no particular commitment to the church, as evidenced by their own personal lives and oftentimes by their own personal witness. They saw themselves as objective scholars who could stand apart from any faith perspective and thus really see the data for what it was. This approach has so dominated the scene that many scholars from within the church have felt that they too had to look at biblical studies as if from outside the Christian faith.

But Childs says,

But then does not this canonical context [where we

---

now accept the depositum as it were of the Hebrew and the Christian tradition] imply that a reflection on the Old Testament faith in God be immediately related to Christian faith in Jesus Christ? The very fact that the Christian canon treasures a portion of the scripture in which the name of Jesus is not mentioned offers an initial warrant for seeking another theological option. The implication of the Old Testament canon, both on a formal and material level, is that the Christian life is still lived between promise and fulfillment, not as a unilinear *heilsgeschichtliche* pattern, but as a description of the essential eschatalogical dimension of divine redemption. To reflect on God's revelation in the Old Testament is not a pre-Christian stage which has been rendered inoperative by the full revelation in Jesus Christ. Rather, it belongs to the nature of the Christian faith that the perception of God through the witness of the old covenant remains a constitutive stance for Christian theology. The struggle to perceive God in the testimony of the Hebrew scriptures is not an historical anachronism, but a consciously Christian understanding of the continuing, authoritative function of the Old Testament for the church. Although the ultimate task of biblical theology is to hear the witness of both testaments, such an enterprise does not call into question the legitimacy, even necessity, of serious theological reflection on the old covenant in its own right as scripture of the church.[251]

What he is saying is that the Old Testament is Scripture for you and me. And that when we come to it, it is legitimate, and this is the way he wants to come. He wants to come to it as a person who is a part of the body of Christ, and sees the Old Testament as part of that body of literature that is normative for him and that is authoritative. The Old Testament is not a pre-Christian stage that can be dispensed with. It is an

---

[251] Ibid., 30.

indispensable part of Scripture as a whole.

Now, there is something implicit here. As I have already said, he would not deny the work of the so-called "objective" scholars on the development of the Bible. In his understanding, all those findings and opinions have to be taken into account. But when it comes to "the rule of faith" for the Christian, he says, "It is the biblical canon that is the basis of our faith. And it is the canonical scriptures that are our authority." So he believes that scholarship that works from a "non-faith" point of view must be taken account of, but in so doing he does not want to sacrifice the unity of Scripture, nor the authority of Scripture.

Childs is not the only one concerned about this issue. In 1990 there appeared a book titled *Biblical Interpretation in Crisis: The Ratzinger Conference on Bible and Church.*[252] It grew out of a conference in New York City where a group of American scholars invited Cardinal Ratzinger, the theological counselor to the pope, to give the Erasmus Lecture at St. Peter's Lutheran Church.[253] They drew together twenty-five biblical studies scholars, attempting to be somewhat representative (while most of the participants were from universities and seminaries of the "main line" of biblical criticism, there were two participants who had association with evangelicalism).

In his lecture Ratzinger called modern "scientific" biblical criticism to its own self-criticism. He focused on Rudolf Bultmann and Martin Dibelius, two of the leading European form critics. He said that although many of the details of their work have been superseded, the agenda for biblical criticism that they established still prevails. Then in a very careful analysis of their work he makes it clear that their approach is not adequate to do justice to the Scripture as the Word of God. They are too much captive to the philosophic presuppostions of modernity. He says of Bultmann, "He is certain that it cannot be the way it is depicted in the Bible, and he looks for methods to prove the way it really had to be."[254]

In his conclusion the cardinal called for a new synthesis. I would summarize his conclusions in this way: For its first sixteen hundred years

---

[252] Richard J. Neuhaus, ed., *Biblical Interpretation in Crisis: The Ratzinger Conference on Bible and Church* (Grand Rapids: Eerdmans, 1989).
[253] Cardinal Ratzinger has since been elected pope.
[254] Ibid., 16.

the church had a hermeneutic, a method for exegeting the Scripture, a faith stance in approaching the Scripture, that gave to the church a sense of unity and a coherent witness to the world. But with the coming of the Renaissance and the Enlightenment, a second methodology developed. We might call the first methodology "A", and we might call the second one that has existed for the last four hundred years "B". Now, everyone using method "B" dismissed everyone using method "A" for sixteen hundred years as "pre-critical." This is to say that those people had an inadequate understanding of reality, and that those of us in "B" know better. But in fact, he said, it is not at all clear that "B" is a better methodology. It is as captive to its own times as the "A" folks were to theirs. Now obviously we cannot go back, but maybe the day has come to look for a new methodology, a "C" methodology, that will combine the best of both, seeking to be more self-critical of its presuppositions and its limitations.[255]

I found one of his comments about what this new synthesis must involve very refreshing:

> The exegete should not approach the text with a ready-made philosophy, nor in accordance with the dictates of a so-called modern or "scientific" worldview, which determines in advance what may or may not be. He may not exclude a priori that (almighty) God could speak in human words in the world. He may not exclude that God himself could enter into and work in human history, however improbable such a thing might at first appear.[256]

There are people other than Cardinal Ratzinger who concur with his concern. One of the papers that was read in the conference was by George Lindbeck, professor at Yale. I want to read for you a passage from Lindbeck. He talks about the sense of faith that has been lost in the modern church, and the need for its recovery.

> Yet there is no room for complacency. To return to our

---

[255] Ibid., 17-23, see also 107-08.
[256] Ibid., 19.

starting point, the sources of nourishment and support just mentioned [liturgy, preaching, catechesis, personal reading, and the general culture] are growing weaker. Even the Roman Catholic scriptural renewal anticipated as a result of the liturgical reforms of Vatican II and its emphasis on preaching and Bible study seem moribund on the popular level. My experience is that the Roman Catholic undergraduates who take religion courses in the University at which I teach, are now less scripturally literate than 20-odd years ago when they had been drilled on pre-Vatican II catechisms [which many in the West said were really pre-critical and represented outdated exegesis]. The Bible is increasingly a closed book even for those Protestants and Catholics who make an effort to know it better. To the degree that instruction is guided by historical criticism, as it is for most educated laity, the lesson is that interpretation is a technical enterprise which requires prolonged specialized training. If their biblical interest survives this kind of discouragement, educated lay people, (indeed, the clergy also) turn by preference to popularized commentaries by those presumed competent to read the text, the professional exegetes and theologians. In those circles where the text itself is widely and assiduously studied—conservative Protestant, charismatic, base communities, and groups interested in spirituality, the reading is often so remote from the classic hermeneutics, so divisive and/or individualistic, that the kind of historical reconstructions which stay within the Christian mainstream seem preferable. It is now the scholarly rather than the hierarchical clerical elite which holds the Bible captive and makes it inaccessible to ordinary people.[257]

Now, that is an amazingly accurate and perceptive statement, and it is wonderful to have it come out of the mouth of George Lindbeck.

---

[257] Ibid., 89-90.

It is good to see biblical scholars now coming to grips with reality in our context. What Lindbeck is saying is that whereas in the Middle Ages only the church could interpret Scripture, now what we are saying is that only the academy, only those who are technically trained in higher criticism of the Bible, are competent to interpret the Word of God.

That takes me back to a passage in Childs. He is responding to James Barr and others who argue that the Old Testament is really not revelation and has no particular interest in such a concept.

> Actually, the use of the term *revelation* in respect of the Bible entails a far greater threat than that envisioned by any of its recent critics. It is constitutive of human sinfulness to turn the witness to God through the scriptures into a manageable object,[258] and thus fail to reckon with revelation as a means of encountering the living God on his own terms.
>
> The theological issue is not resolved by positing a sharp contrast between pre-critical and modern critical interpretation. Both Barth and Bultmann tried to teach us that lesson in the 1920s. The threat of domesticating the Word is equally present on both the right and left of the spectrum. If the canonical approach is conceived of as a closed system by which to handle biblical revelation, it is also doomed to failure and should rightly be rejected. However, if it can serve as a means for taking seriously the human form of the witness to divine revelation, which God continues to bring alive through each new generation through his Spirit, it may serve as a useful tool for grappling with the real issues at stake in the theological enterprise.[259]

Now, I might not come out at the same point as Brevard Childs

---

[258] In other words, we would like to "de-fang" the Bible so it will not bite us. I think of the history of Israel in that regard. Every time there was a spiritual advance, the next stage was regression. Advance—regression. There is something in the heart of humans that keeps turning against God and trying to reduce Him to our terms.

[259] Childs, *Old Testament Theology*, 26.

does as to how to answer the problem, but rejoice in the fact that he recognizes the problem.[260]

When I read that I thought of a friend of mine who is a Ph.D. candidate in biblical studies with whom I was in a renewal conference recently. And at the end of the renewal conference, he sat down with another friend of mine and said, "I can't tell you what these last three days have meant to me. They have given me back my Bible." Now, this is a fellow who is getting ready to do Ph.D. comprehensives in Scripture. He has spent the preceding three years doing nothing but studying the Scripture. He went on, "I have changed my stance. Instead of being a critic of the Scripture, I have come again to submit myself to the Word of God. And I feel free, and I feel human again."

Now, I am not wanting to castigate scholarship. I am not in-terested in that. But we dare not come to the place where we let the Scripture become something we control instead of the Word of God being something that controls us. All unwittingly, the text has become an end in itself for us to study, master and control, instead of a means for encounter with God. One of the things that I appreciate about Childs

---

[260] [Editor's note] As welcome as Childs' proposals are, they still leave unaddressed the problem that all the heirs of Karl Barth have. That problem is the level of continuity between "the human witness" and the "divine revelation." The Bible maintains, both implicitly and explicitly, that the theological content and the reporting of the historical means by which that content came to us are inseparable. The validity of the one cannot be separated from the other. Thus classical higher criticism, having reached the conclusion that certainly the Old Testament, and probably the New Testament, was of very dubious historical worth, tended to reduce the biblical theology to humanistic platitudes. Barth recognized that this was to deprive the church of its lifeblood. So he attempted to separate the inspired revelatory content from the fallible historical witness. But that left him and all his successors with the logical fault inherent in that separation. One of the issues was, what was the means of revelation, if not as the text reports it. W. F. Albright and several of his influential students argued that it must have lain in great historical events *like* those reported in the Bible. Ironically, it was Childs himself who was one of the chief participants in destroying that idea. If we agree that the witness is faulty, and indeed that it is the only access we have to those supposed "historical events," then who is to say what took place, or indeed, if *anything* took place? But that has only worsened the problem, as Barr has famously pointed out. If our only access to "revelation" is through a fictional narrative that is the product of successive rewritings and, indeed, reconceptualizations by different communities with different, and often, competing agendas, it may be best just to discard the term "revelation" all together.

is that he has pointed out that if we think the pre-critical world before the Renaissance and before the Enlightenment was time-conditioned, was conditioned by its times to think in certain ways, so is the twentieth-century biblical scholar. The scholar of today can be as conditioned by his context as the fifteenth-century biblical theologian was by his. That brings me back to my earlier anecdote about Thomas Oden, to whom a Jewish scholar said, "Tom, you will never be a wise man because when you pick up the text you have already decided what it can say to you and what it can't." That is what you call "domestication." He said, "You've already decided, so you can't hear. And because you can't hear you will never be a wise man."

Let me tell you something that came to me out of my experience at Brandeis University. We were reading Hebrew, and so I was referring constantly to my *Brown-Driver-Briggs Hebrew Lexicon*. And one of the things that I appreciated about that lexicon was that in every entry they would give equivalents in other languages, like Arabic, or Assyrian, or Coptic—it might give you equivalents in twelve languages. The reason for that was that biblical studies grew up in that context where you knew the Bible was a part of a larger world, and you knew that if you were going to understand it you had to know that larger world. So the biblical scholar knew the various language groups of the various literatures around Israel and was able to do comparative work.

But when I was working in the Assyrian literature, I turned to the *Chicago Assyrian Dictionary*. It is an amazing, multi-volume work that covers all the dialects of Assyrian and Babylonian in an exhaustive fashion. But as I was using it, something dawned on me: the *Chicago Assyrian Dictionary* does not have a linguistic equivalent anywhere in it. It is written as if everything that was ever written in the ancient world was written in Assyrian or Babylonian, and there was nothing to be learned by reference to any of the other disciplines. So I began to question why. And slowly I began to find out.

All Ancient Near Eastern studies, Egyptian, or Babylonian, or whatever, began in the same way. Scholars got into those fields because of the way they illuminated the Bible. But slowly those scholars lost their interest in the Bible and began to specialize narrowly in just one field. So, what happened was, Egyptology developed as a discipline without any reference to biblical studies, while biblical studies was trying to draw from these others.

But in this process, something interesting happened. The Ancient Near Eastern scholars developed an entirely different attitude toward their texts than the biblical scholars did. Kenneth Kitchen, an Egyptologist, highlighted this in his book *Ancient Orient and Old Testament*.[261] Biblical scholars have come to take a skeptical attitude toward their text. You assume that it is false until it is proven true. Ancient Near Eastern scholars assume that their text is reliable until it is proven false. Kitchen enunciates four principles that Ancient Near Eastern scholars use that illuminate how conditioned by their context biblical scholars have become:

1. *The primary importance of facts over subjective theories or speculative opinions.* We do not have one piece of factual evidence supporting the existence of a "J" Document or "E" Document, yet that theory is still taught as fact in many places.

2. *The attitude toward the source material is a positive one.* When you have a manuscript in front of you, you assume its reliability unless you have objective evidence to the contrary. Notice the emphasis upon objective? So we have a single psalm, Psalm 89. The first half has one mood in it and the second half has another; you can say that perhaps it is a work by two different people. But we have no objective evidence for that, so why not say that it is possible that a single author has a conflict in his own mind and that the text is one not two?

3. *The inconclusive nature of negative evidence. Silence is no proof of anything.* Lack of reference to Abraham outside the Bible is no indication that Abraham never lived. Yet many biblical scholars will not believe anything the Bible says unless there is irrefutable evidence from outside the text.

4. *A proper approach to apparent discrepancies.* When you come to an apparent discrepancy in a text, you start with the assumption that it can be reconciled, and only if it cannot be reconciled, do you recognize it as a discrepancy. But biblical scholars are often determined to find discrepancies where none obviously present themselves.

---

[261] Kenneth Kitchen, *Ancient Orient and Old Testament* (Chicago: InterVarsity Press, 1966). The discussion of the four principles may be found on pp. 28-34.

And so I became conscious that twentieth-century biblical studies has had its own agendas, and that those agendas have affected our conclusions to the point where Ratzinger's suggestion that we may need to find a new approach to biblical interpretation sounds very appealing. If academic biblical studies so "domesticate" the Bible that its power to confront us with the living God is destroyed, something irretrievable is lost.

Let me illustrate that as I close. Last July in Medellin, Colómbia. as a guest of some missionaries there, one of whom was Jeannine Brabon. She teaches Hebrew in the Inter-American Seminary in Medellin, but over the last three or four years she has been heavily involved in prison work. When she asked me if I would be interested in going with her to visit the major prison there, I replied that I would be very interested. So, we went into one of the maximum security prisons in the country where there were a lot of Pablo Escobar's men. She and a Colómbian chaplain had been ministering there for a few years. Before they started there were thirty to sixty murders a month inside the prison, but in the last three years before I visited there had been a movement of the Spirit so that when I was there no murders had been committed in the prison for months. A Medellin newspaper ran a full-page story about the change that had taken place in this prison.

When we got inside we went to a chapel where they were getting ready for their chapel service. It was clean. The walls were white. The prisoners, after they began to get converted, said, "This place is a dump. Couldn't we clean it up?" So they got permission from the authorities to clean it up. The prisoners said to the authorities, "If you will give us paint we will paint it." So they painted the walls, and on every wall is a Scripture verse.

As the service started, a young man came up to Jeannine. She turned to me and said, "He would like to give you his witness." He looked like a college kid to me, but he was twenty-eight. So we went into a side room, which was a classroom with desks in it. They have a Bible institute in that prison. This young man is one of the professors. And we sat down almost nose to nose, so I could hear him over the noise in the place, and he told me his story. At age four he was on the streets; he never knew who his father was. He became a policeman. Escobar put a bounty on the head of every policeman in Colómbia and I think more than one hundred policemen were killed, so they became defensive and began to strike back. So he said, "I found myself involved in murder. And evil possessed me. Then I got to the place where, if I had not killed somebody that day, I had trouble going to sleep. I killed a man one day in the presence of his dearly beloved just to watch the horror in her face while I killed him. One night I killed five men. I had nowhere to go and so I got drunk. And while I was drunk I got involved in a shootout and was injured, and they threw me in prison." He has a twenty-nine year prison sentence.

He said, "I had never heard the Gospel. But when I got into prison I began to hear it. Still I knew it could not be for me, because what self-respecting God would ever have anything to do with a person like me? They gave me a New Testament. I was curious so I started reading. But I knew it had nothing to do with me, because no good God would ever relate to me. It was that way until I got to the seventh, eighth, and ninth chapters of the book of Acts. When I read the seventh chapter, to my shock I read about the murder of a good man, Stephen, and the person who was orchestrating it was a fellow named Saul of Tarsus. When I got to the ninth chapter, and Saul of Tarsus was saved, I was deeply shocked. All I had wanted to do was to kill all the bad people in the world. But this man had wanted to kill all the good people. If God could save a man who wanted to kill all the good people, surely there was hope for a man who wanted to kill all the evil people." At that point his face began to light up. Do you remember how the text says that Stephen's face glowed? I think I have seen that.

He said, "And He redeemed me. He has taken the hatred out of my heart and the despair. And He has put love and hope there. I have tried to contact the families of some of the people I have killed. I would like to ask them all to forgive me. I have the matchless privilege of teaching the Word of God. I am right where I belong; I'm doing exactly what I want to do. I could not be happier." And I thought, how interesting that Ph.D. studies in Old Testament and New Testament cannot seem to produce that passion, or that kind of an encounter with the living God. Now, I think they ought to, and I think they can. And that is what our business should be.

Name and Subject Index

E

H

Sanders, Jack 451
Sara 139, 140
Satan 60, 290, 291, 335, 336, 337, 343, 345
Saul 178, 272, 280, 323, 324, 334, 359,
    384, 385, 403
Saul of Tarsus 365, 462
Scapegoat 250, 255
Schools of the prophets 325
Scott, R.B.Y
  The Way of Wisdom 425
Seba 369
Segub 46
Self-centeredness 390
Self-sacrifice 391, 400, 407, 409
Separation of church and state 325
Septuagint 64, 65, 66, 69, 161, 172, 173,
    230, 231, 232, 233, 441
Sermon on the Mount 58
Sexual behavior 113
Sexuality 244, 245, 339
Sheba 152, 369
Shebe 369
Shechem 45, 105
Sheen, Fulton J., Archbishop
  *Communism and the Conscience of the
    West* 72
Shekina 396
Shelah 63
Shem 111
Shen 242
Shepherd's Festival 276
Shiloh 45, 272, 273
Shuah 152
Siba 369
Simeon 400
Simile 442, 443
Sin 15, 19, 61, 105, 113, 131, 135, 175,
    176, 178, 181, 200, 201, 208, 215,
    222, 251, 254, 255, 256, 257, 259,
    262, 269, 286, 289, 307, 318, 348,
    354, 374, 375, 377, 381, 382, 383,
    384, 385, 386, 397, 398, 399, 402,
    403, 404, 405, 408, 409, 420, 445
acknowledgment of 257
agent of 335
and imputation 288
an understanding of 255
as blinding and as a separtation from God
  221
a separation from 221
as misbehavior with God 113
a taking away of 263
burdern of 386
cleansing from all 133, 249

confession of 252, 257, 259, 381
consequences of 256
covering of 254, 255, 256, 288
death as a result of 381
effects of 380
expiation of 380, 382
forgiveness of 254, 286, 290, 294, 374,
  377
grievous 142
guilt of 257
introduction of distance 261
law of 215
nature of 380
of blatant contempt 381
of inadvertence 381, 382
of the fathers 102, 224
offering 404, 405
original 112
redemption from 293
remission of 31
removal of 405
result of 251
sinking into 290
taking away of 380
turning from 310
ultimate/immediate causes 345
with a high hand 382
Sinai 86, 102, 105, 139, 175, 202, 229, 269,
    273, 276, 322, 356, 360, 416, 440
Sinai Covenant 229
Social concern 36
Socrates 110, 282, 284, 285, 296
Sodom and Gomorrah 142, 143, 162, 353,
    373, 387
Solomon 43, 44, 45, 132, 152, 177, 223,
    242, 266, 267, 272, 281, 326, 339,
    371, 440
Son of God 54, 294, 408, 442
  as Lamb 107
Son of Mary 54
Sovereignty 100, 134, 217, 218, 348, 350
Spirit
  walking in the 133
Spirit-filled life 61
St. Augustine 254, 348, 405, 409, 440
Stephen 116, 199, 462
Sumeria 73
  gods of: Anu 79
  hymns of 301
Sumerians 174
Superstition 334
Swedish Baptist 330
Syncretism 51
Systematic theology 88, 197, 199, 263

Widow 26, 29, 36, 37, 113
Wilberforce, William 38
Williams, Charles
  The Descent of the Dove 349
Wisdom 14, 18, 134, 398, 411, 412, 414,
      415, 416, 417, 424, 427, 428, 429,
      432, 433, 441, 442, 443
  empirical and gnomic 415
Wisdom literature 14, 18, 411, 412, 414,
      424, 433, 434, 441
  and order 416
  and paradox 416
  and truth 417
  chaos and order 414, 415
  chaos and paradox 415
  experience and reason 414
  optimism of 417
  order and contradiction 417
  pessimistic 412, 434, 437
Word
  as burden 315
  as operative reality 311, 414
  as operative reality (hypostasis) 300
  as primary authority 330
World salvation 361, 364, 390
  and human involvement 348, 361, 363,
      371, 373
  and sovereignty 348
  from within history 349
Worship 15, 42, 46, 47, 126, 148, 179, 187,
      198, 199, 218, 227, 231, 238, 253,
      263, 273, 300, 320, 322, 385, 433
  acts of 263
  and historical emphasis 199
  and mutilation 48
  and sacrifice 261
  as deep-seated awe (fearful) 16
  attitude of 156
  exclusiveness of 223
  forms of 263
  heart of 154
  idolatrous 174
  individual 236
  not a separation of theology 13
  of Baal 50, 311
  of Canaanite gods 63
  of God 179, 200, 240, 356
  of images 222
  of pagan gods 102, 104, 119, 224, 320
  of the forces of Nature 50
  of the Holy 218
  of the king 320
  of the sun, moon, heavens, and earth 51
  of Yahweh 49, 101, 385

pagan 103, 339
public 93
system of 196
Writings 394, 441

Y

Yahwism 101, 245, 334, 341, 363, 372,
      379, 412
faith of 352

Z

Zechariah 133
Zedekiah 314, 421
Zephaniah 314
Zimran 152
Zion 14, 26, 29, 167, 261, 435

Greek Index

Hebrew Index

Hebrew Index (continued)

Scripture Index

Scripture Index

Scripture Index

Scripture Index

Scripture Index

Scripture Index

Scripture Index

Scripture Index

LaVergne, TN USA
17 August 2010

193509LV00001B/1/P